Scientists
&
Inventors

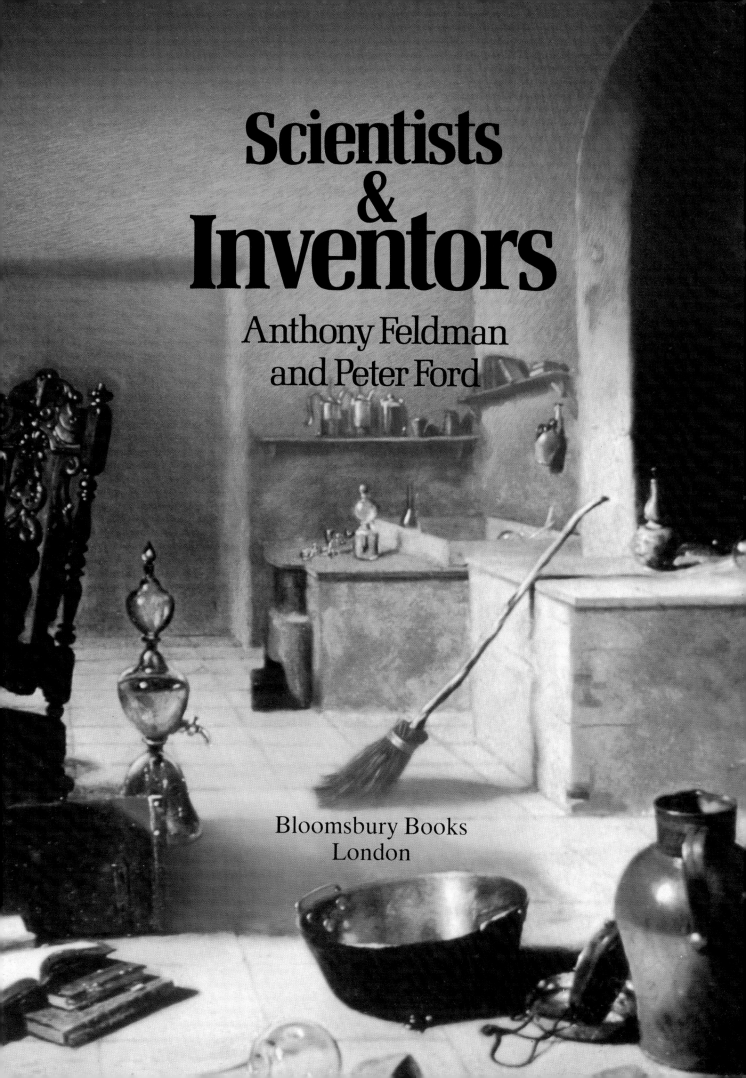

Scientists
& Inventors

Anthony Feldman
and Peter Ford

Bloomsbury Books
LONDON

Editorial Coordinator: John Mason
Art Editor: Grahame Dudley
Designer: Adrian Williams
Editor: Krystyna Krzyzak
Research: Marian Pullen
Frances Vargo, Sarah Waters
Update photo researcher: Gloria Dennert

ISBN 1 870630 23 8
© J.G. Ferguson Publishing Company U.S.A.

This edition published 1989 by
Bloomsbury Books an imprint of
Godfrey Cave Associates Limited
42 Bloomsbury Street, London WC1B 3QJ
Printed in Hong Kong by Regent Publishing Services Ltd.

INTRODUCTION

Mankind's scientific and technological progress, from the invention of movable type to the discovery of penicillin, is full of amazing contributions made by single individuals. This book is a history of such breakthrough discoveries and inventions. It tells the stories of over 150 inventors and scientists, from Empedocles to Christiaan Barnard, from Galileo to Einstein, from Gutenberg to Pasteur, from the Wright brothers to the Curie family. Some, like Thomas Edison, turned out many inventions and worked in well-equipped laboratories; others, like James Watt, concentrated on one field and had limited resources for experiment. Each is described on a double-page spread with illustrations and diagrams to explain his or her contribution to the material progress of mankind. Set out in chronological order, the result is a fascinating account of human progress, told through the lives and achievements of the outstanding men and women whose imagination and ingenuity brought us into the technological age of today. A complete index to the scientists and inventors whose achievements are described in the book may be found on page 318.

Empedocles
c490-430 BC

Turning to natural philosophy only after an early interest in politics, Empedocles' most important work was his theory of the four elements. This theory was one of the earliest to recognize that the universe is made from more than one basic substance. Empedocles also realized that there are forces which act on matter to create changes in it, and developed this concept into a rudimentary theory of the evolution of life.

Empedocles grew up in the small Sicilian village of what is now Agrigento. While still a young man he was actively involved in local politics and acquired a reputation as a fierce opponent of tyranny and corruption. By middle-age, Empedocles' interest in politics began to wane and he concentrated increasingly on philosophical studies. Throughout his life he was widely acclaimed as an important statesman, philosopher, teacher, and poet.

He was especially interested in constructing a world picture, a philosophical view of how the universe itself was made. He was attracted by the arguments of the earlier philosophers Thrales, Anaximander, and Heraclitus, who had attempted to identify a single basic substance from which all matter was made. Empedocles instead identified four such substances or elements: fire, air, water, and earth. All matter, he said, was composed of various combinations and arrangements of these natural elements.

Empedocles believed in two mystical forces that acted on the elements and caused them to mingle, separate, and recombine. According to

him, the force that tended to draw the elements together was Love, the force driving them apart, Strife. These two forces were responsible for the creation and evolution of the cosmos. At the beginning of time, he held, Love dominated all things and matter existed as a harmonious intermingling of the elements. The creation itself began when Strife entered into conflict with Love and the elements were flung apart in disorder. After thousands of years of chaos, stability returned with the elements in partial or complete states of combination. Empedocles pointed to rivers and volcanoes as examples of imperfect combinations of water and fire with earth.

Empedocles extended his notions of Love and Strife into one of the earliest theories of the evolution of life. He believed that in its earliest stages, life was an indistinguishable mixture of species and sexes. Strife forced organisms apart to form the different varieties of plants and animals. A continuing interplay between the forces of Love and Strife caused plants and animals gradually to change their shape until they evolved into the species known at the time Empedocles formulated his theory.

This interest in the evolution of life led Empedocles to speculate on the nature of human physiology. He held that blood represented the most perfect intermingling of the four natural elements and that the heart was the center of the blood-vessel system. He therefore believed that the heart was the seat of life itself.

Below left: portrait of Empedocles, a detail from a fresco in Orvieto Cathedral, Italy, painted by Luca Signorelli.

Below right: the Greek Temple of Peace in Acragas (now modern Agrigento). Acragas was Empedocles' home town in Sicily, at that time a Greek colony, and noted as a center of the arts.

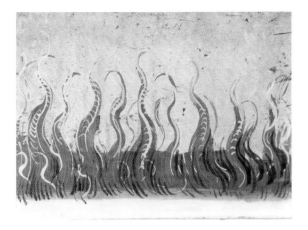

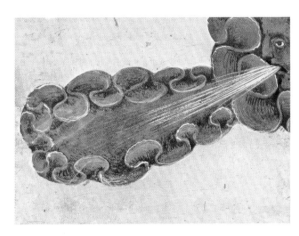

Above: Empedocles' view of the universe. The four elements were linked together by four qualities, each element possessing two of these. Fire was hot and dry with heat predominating. Air was hot and moist with moisture predominating. Water was moist and cold with cold predominating. Earth was cold and dry with dryness predominating. The interplay of the elements created matter.

Above: there was a practical side to Empedocles' work. This coin of Selinus was struck to celebrate his attempt to eradicate a malaria epidemic by draining the local swamps.

Empedocles' concept of the four elements had the most influence on later thinkers. Almost a century later, Aristotle adopted and extended Empedocles' ideas. Aristotle believed that the four elements were the basic ingredients only of earthly substances, and that the heavens were composed of a fifth element which he called "ether." He argued that each of the four earthly elements had its own regular position and that all motion was an effort to reach that place. Earth lay at the lowest level, water above it, air above water, and fire at the highest level. Aristotle claimed that this order explained why an object consisting mainly of the element earth, such as a rock, fell downward if released in the air. Bubbles of air, on the other hand, rose through water, and fire flickered upward.

Despite the mystical basis of Empedocles' ideas of the natural elements and the forces that control them, his theory, improved and extended by Aristotle, remained the cornerstone of chemical science for nearly 2000 years. When modern chemistry began to replace superstition and mythology with verifiable scientific concepts, Empedocles' theory of the four elements was quickly swept away. In its place a new theory emerged according to which more than 90 chemical elements react and intermingle in ways governed by the complex principles of mathematics, physics, and chemistry to form the material universe we know today.

7

Democritus
c460 - c370 BC

Possessed of a rational mind untouched by the superstitions of his time, Democritus' greatest work was a theory which has become a cornerstone of modern science – the atomic theory of matter. He suggested that all substance in the universe was made up of particles so minute that nothing smaller could be conceived. These particles were the absolute limit of smallness in nature and therefore could not be broken down further. The word "atom," later used to describe these tiny particles, comes from a Greek word meaning "indivisible."

example, that the atoms of rock and earth were rough and jagged so that they held firmly together to make tough stable materials. Atoms of water were by contrast rounded and smooth so that water always flowed and assumed the shape of its container rather than having a definite shape of its own.

Democritus took his ideas further. Atoms, he explained, could neither be destroyed nor created but could be rearranged in different combinations. So although matter could not be created or destroyed, it could change its form. Today we recognize these ideas as the first rudimentary statement of the law of conservation of mass and energy, one of the most fundamental in modern science.

Democritus was a rationalist. He rejected the view held by many of his contemporaries that nature was controlled by the actions of gods, demons, and spirits. On the contrary, he held that there existed a number of fundamental natural laws governing the phenomena of the

Below right: Democritus believed that the structure of matter was governed by the shape of its atoms. Modern science holds a similar view. This crystal, highly magnified, is jagged because it is made up of roughly-shaped particles.

Born in Abdera in eastern Greece, Democritus had always felt a great hunger for knowledge. His early life was spent in travel, visiting the great cities and centers of learning in Egypt and the Middle East. It must have been during this period that Democritus developed his startlingly modern view of the universe. He regarded atoms as unchangeable and indestructible, and as the only content of the universe besides the very space in which they existed. He argued that some atoms differed from each other physically and that these differences explained the variety of kinds of matter in the universe. He suggested, for

Right: Democritus' theory expressed pictorially. Matter consists of mixtures of atoms; the white hand (top left) contains some black, as shown in the enlargement (top right). In the bottom left-hand picture the black and white dots are mixed; in the bottom right-hand one all the black and white dots are grouped together, forming a hand.

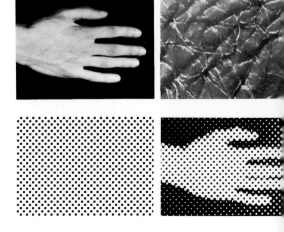

Philosophy

Left: according to Democritus, one kind of basic indivisible particle, the atom, makes up all things. The variety in the world results from differences in the shape, arrangement, and position of atoms. The diagram shows how he conceived the same element making up different kinds of substance.

Below: Democritus was a leader of the rationalists – philosophers who rejected empricism and accepted only intuitive reasoning as a basis for reaching the truth. He was noted as much for his epigrams as his scientific ideas, and was known as the laughing philosopher.

universe. Democritus saw no justification for a "shaping force" to be at work in nature and saw the creation itself as a blind chance, a combination of the effects of natural laws to form the arrangements of atoms we know as the universe.

Although Democritus developed many ideas upon which modern science depends, he certainly did not reach his conclusions by modern techniques. In his time, the science of experiment and observation was unknown and philosophical doctrines grew only in the mind. The unique gifts Democritus displayed were therefore intuitive rather than analytical, and largely incapable of scientific proof. Unhappily for Democritus, his great contemporary Socrates scathingly rejected his view of nature. Socrates had such immense influence and standing that Democritus was widely regarded with scorn and even contempt. It was not until centuries after his death that modern chemists and physicists confirmed the accuracy of his remarkable reasoning and intuition.

Hippocrates
c460-377 BC

The Greek physician Hippocrates was the first to free medicine from its traditional link with magic and religion, and at the same time established the foundations of medical diagnosis based on experience and observation. He has since classical times been universally regarded as "the father of medicine."

What is known about Hippocrates' life is sparse and based mainly on word of mouth. He is said to have been born on the island of Cos, the son of a physician, and to have taught in the medical school there, though he also traveled widely and lectured throughout mainland Greece as well as in Asia Minor.

The body of work known as the *Hippocratic Collection*, a series of practical and descriptive treatises on most aspects of medical treatment and research, probably made up the reference library of the medical school on Cos. The work of many hands has been detected in it, but there seems to be no doubt that it embodies Hippocrates' own writings. It clearly demonstrates his historical existence as the founder of a philosophical tradition in medicine which has retained

Below left: portrait of Hppocrates, taken from a 14th-century Greek manuscript. Very little is known of his life.

Below right: treatment of a dislocated elbow by manipulation, as laid down by Hippocrates. Hippocrates' treatise on dislocations was used by physicians right up to the mid-19th century.

its influence down to the present day. Some of the individual volumes in the collection were still being used as textbooks in medical schools in the 19th century, notably the *Aphorisms*. The first saying in this book is the one that runs: "Life is short, and art long; opportunity fleeting; experiment dangerous, and judgment difficult." This was, in fact, part of the advice to physicians to exercise care when treating a fever.

Hippocrates always emphasized the importance of the body's own ability to heal, saying, "Our natures are the physicians of our diseases." He believed that every disease had a natural cause, and he was the first to scorn the notion that epilepsy, the "sacred disease," was an infliction from the gods. By systematic observation, and by his insistence on recording failures as well as successes in treatment, Hippocrates established standards of objectivity. His idea that physicians must study patients in their whole environment has a surprisingly up-to-date ring.

After Hippocrates, progress in medical know-

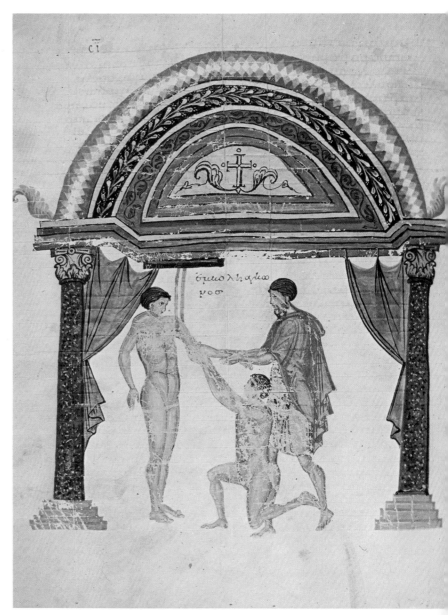

ledge came through the biological research of Aristotle, and even during the height of the Roman Empire it remained largely a Greek preserve. Celsus, Roman writer of the famous textbook *De Medicina*, that appeared in about AD 30, based his work for the most part on Greek medicine. Galen, a Greek physician who flourished in Rome and who laid the foundations for experimental physiology, accepted the Hippocratic method of medical practice and Empedocles' theory of the four bodily humors.

Above: the Hippocratic Oath.

Below: Greek family offering a bull to Asclepius and Hygieia, goddess of health. According to Greek mythology, Asclepius was taught the art of healing by his father Apollo. His cult gave rise to the Asclepiadae, a sect devoted to medicine, to which Hippocrates belonged.

Galen's influence in turn extended throughout the Middle Ages and into the Renaissance period.

However, Galen had never during his career dissected a human body, and his widely accepted teachings on anatomy were based on animal studies. Human anatomy was only established as a science in the mid-16th century by the Renaissance physician Andreas Vesalius. After dissecting many cadavers he published a series of books known collectively as the *Fabrica*. This revolutionized medical teaching and made accurate surgery possible.

The Hippocratic Oath, which has provided a blueprint for medical ethics for more than 2000 years, was probably named after Hippocrates rather than formulated by him. It may, however, be regarded as an authentic legacy of Hippocrates' principles. It first lays down the obligation of a doctor to his teacher and his teacher's family. Then it outlines his standards of behavior in serving the patient's interests:

"Whatsoever house I enter, there will I go for the benefit of the sick, refraining from all wrongdoing and corruption, and especially from any act of seduction, of male or female, of bond or free. Whatsoever things I see or hear concerning the life of men, in my attendance on the sick or even apart therefrom, which ought not to be noised abroad, I will keep silence thereon, counting such things to be as sacred texts."

The oath provides a framework for ethical practice rather than a rigid rule. As such, it has allowed flexibility of interpretation in a way that has helped it retain its validity.

Aristotle
384-322 BC

The importance of Aristotle to Western civilization cannot be overestimated. In writing on every then-known field of human knowledge, he laid the foundations for modern scientific study and systematization of knowledge.

Aristotle was born in Stagira in northeastern Greece, the son of a well-known physician. At the age of 17 he went to the Academy in Athens. There he came under the intellectual influence of the philosopher Plato, who in turn carried on from Socrates. Aristotle remained in Athens for 20 years, perfecting his understanding of the Socratic method. This explored the nature of reality by using dialogue to raise questions, pose answers, and confront contradictions and paradox, thus taking the inquirer ever closer to objective truth. On Plato's death, Aristotle left the Academy and traveled for 12 years.

During this period he helped to establish a center in Assus to spread the influence of Greek thought in Asia Minor. He also studied natural history and marine biology for two years on Lesbos. Then, in about 343 BC, he was invited by Phillip II of Macedon to go to Pella as tutor to his 13-year-old son, the future Alexander the

Below: Phillip II of Macedon had a great respect for the Athenian civilization. For him the natural choice of tutor for his son Alexander (later Alexander the Great) was Aristotle, at the time the Athenian Academy's most distinguished philosopher. Generally Aristotle preferred to teach his pupils while walking about, giving rise to the word "peripatetic."

Great. Aristotle remained in Pella for three years. When he finally returned to Athens at nearly 50 years of age, he worked to establish the Lyceum as a rival to the Academy.

The emphasis of his work at the Lyceum differed from that of the Academy in that it represented a switch from pure philosophy and mathematics to biology and history. Over 12 years Aristotle organized it as a center for the broadest scientific investigation. In 323 BC, following the death of his former pupil Alexander the Great, Aristotle retired from Athens in the face of anti-Macedonian disturbances, and the next year died in exile on his estate in Chalcis.

Of all Aristotle's writings, 47 texts survive, although even these were probably put together from notes of lectures by editors after his death. They include several volumes on logic and such collections of treatises as *Physics*, *Metaphysics*, *Rhetoric*, *Politics*, and a fragment of *Poetics*. With some modifications, they follow the Socratic dialectical method.

There was for Aristotle a total cohesion between philosophy and politics, logic and scientific method. The practical influence of his thought on scientific investigation has therefore

Philosophy

	Man	
	Mammals	
	Whales	
	Reptiles and Fish	
	Octopuses and Squids	
	Insects	
	Mollusl s	
Jellyfish	Zoophytes *(corals, sea anemones, etc)*	Ascidians *(sea squirts)*
		Sponges
	Higher Plants	
	Lower Plants	
	Inanimate Matter	

Above right: Aristotle's *Ladder of Nature*. A keen biologist, he sought to classify nature in the same way that he tried to classify statements. Although he visualized a progression between classes of animals, culminating in man, he did not propose any theory of evolution; nor did he claim that the classes were related in any way.

been highly complex. In effect, he founded logic, physics, biology, and the humanities as formal disciplines. He based his system on classification, using resemblances and differences to define categories. By gathering facts about phenomena in an orderly and systematic way, he also became the first encyclopedist.

Aristotle, in his extension of Empedocles' theories, saw everything in nature as occupying its proper station. The world was as it had always been: a constant within which the cycles of creation and decay took place. Physics for him meant the way everything grew and tended to behave. The answer to the questions of why stones fell to the ground, why fish swam in water, why some men were born slaves, was the same: "Because it is their nature."

His method was most successful in his studies of natural history and the classification and anatomy of animals. Everything in nature, he thought, sought to attain the highest degree of perfection of which it was capable. Each species had its fixed place in the scale of being, and since nothing changed and everything had its position in that scale, animate was above inanimate matter, mankind was above the animals, and God, the "unmoved mover" of the universe, was above mankind.

Even in politics the fixed scale was equally applicable for Aristotle. He remained a believer in government by an enlightened oligarchy. As for ordinary people, they were to follow a policy of moderation if they wished to preserve their happiness. So long as everyone avoided the extremes, all would remain well in the body politic of the city-state.

Aristotle's works were lost after the fall of Rome and were not reintroduced into Europe until the 12th century. Then his influence became overriding for hundreds of years. The irony was that in the end, it was the use of his own methods which undermined and discredited practically every assertion he had made on the structure and working of the cosmos. Even so, the progressive rejection of Aristotelian doctrines was in effect a justification of his methods. Ultimately it was Aristotle's emphasis on observation and classification, and on initiating research to that end, that was his central and lasting contribution to science.

Above: a 13th-century sculpture of Aristotle on the Royal Doorway of Chartres Cathedral, France. Aristotle's works were reintroduced into the West in the late 12th century and developed to form a basis for Christian metaphysics and theology, most notably by the Italian saint and scholar, Thomas Aquinas.

Archimedes
c287-212 BC

A mathematician first, an inventor second, Archimedes was probably the greatest scientist of the ancient world. His formulation of the law of buoyancy, known today as Archimedes' Principle, and his work on the lever and the pulley were important contributions to basic scientific discoveries.

Born in Syracuse, the Greek colony on the island of Sicily, Archimedes lived and worked there all his life except for a few years of study in Alexandria. He made his best-known discovery on buoyancy as the result of his friendship with Hieron II, ruler of Syracuse, who often turned to the mathematician for advice and guidance. On one such occasion Hieron had bought a gold crown from a local goldsmith. Hieron doubted the goldsmith's honesty and wanted to be sure the crown was made from pure gold. He asked Archimedes to check the gold content without damaging the crown in any way. Archimedes spent several days considering the problem, but could not seem to solve it. Then one afternoon as he stepped into a full bathtub, he was suddenly aware of a wash of bathwater overflowing the sides. On thinking about this, Archimedes realized that the amount of water displaced from the bath was equal to the volume of his own body entering it. This was the answer to his dilemma. If he immersed Hieron's crown in water and measured the volume displaced, he would know the volume of the crown. To determine whether

Below: a fresco from a villa at Pompeii showing a slave raising water by treading an Archimedean screw. This instrument was a hollow helical tube wound round a cylinder. It was partly immersed in water and, when turned, the water moved up the helix.

it contained any metal other than gold, he had simply to compare the total weight of the crown with the weight of that given amount of gold. Legend says that Archimedes was so excited by his discovery that he ran naked from his bathroom into the streets of Syracuse crying "Eureka!" (meaning "I have discovered it!") That cry has echoed down the centuries so that even today it is used to announce a sudden inspired discovery.

The genius of Archimedes was the undoing of the goldsmith. The crown he claimed as gold contained a sizeable amount of base metal, and Hieron put the man to death.

Later Archimedes extended his famous principle to show that a body in water received an upward force, called an "upthrust," equivalent to the weight of water it displaced. This explains why heavy objects can float. For example, a modern ship built of steel can float because it displaces a large volume of water, while a single bar of the metal will sink in an instant.

Archimedes' more abstract discoveries were confined largely to geometry. He had always enjoyed the intellectual challenge of pure mathematics and had benefited in Alexandria by studying under a man who was himself a pupil of Euclid. Archimedes' only surviving published works are his mathematical treatises. In *Measurement of the Circle* he worked out the ratio of the

length of a circle's circumference to its radius, usually denoted by the Greek letter "pi," to a degree of accuracy never before achieved. He did this by a technique that foreshadowed the discovery of differential calculus by Isaac Newton nearly 2000 years later.

Throughout his life, Archimedes balanced his more abstract philosophical studies with a keen interest in mechanics. His fascination with mechanisms led him to explore the principle of the lever. He showed how a lever, pivoted about a fulcrum, could lift a heavy weight with a relatively gentle force applied to the end of the lever's arm. Archimedes, in his usual excited way, once exclaimed to his friends: "Give me a place to stand and a lever long enough and I will lift the world!"

Archimedes' final years were spent in the defense of Syracuse from invading Roman armies. For three years the Romans laid siege to the town. Time and again their attacks were beaten back by strange and terrible "war machines" designed by Archimedes. Stories are told of huge lenses that concentrated the sun's rays on the Roman battle fleet, scorching the troops and setting ships ablaze. On another occasion cranes are said to have been used to lift and overturn the enemy ships. The invention of the catapult during that period is credited to him as well.

In spite of all, Syracuse fell in 212 BC and the city was sacked. Although the Roman commander Marcellus had given orders that Archimedes was to be brought to him and treated with

Above: a model of the Archimedean screw. An ivory ball passes down the lower tube and is scooped by the bottom of the hollow helical copper tube as it rotates. The ball moves up and when it reaches the top, drops back into the lower tube.

Above: Archimedes refuses to obey the soldier's instructions to accompany him to Marcellus and is stabbed to death.

Left: Archimedes applied his mechanical discoveries to the building of practical machines. During the siege of Syracuse he designed many machines to help defend the city.

honor and kindness, fate would have it otherwise. A Roman soldier came upon the old man as he was deep in the contemplation of a mathematical problem. The soldier, perhaps remembering Archimedes' part in the defense of Syracuse, insisted on taking him to Marcellus immediately. Archimedes, thinking only of his problem, impatiently waved the soldier away saying "Go, do not disturb me!" They were his last words. In blind fury the soldier drew his sword and struck Archimedes dead.

Johannes Gutenberg

c 1400 - 1468

Printing from movable type is an invention that changed the world, yet little is known of its German inventor, Johann Gutenberg. It is not even certain which of the first printed books in the western world were by his hand, although the famous 42-line Bible, produced around 1455, was undoubtedly his work. His method of mechanical reproduction of printed matter was so viable that no important change was made for some 500 years.

What Gutenberg did was to develop a mold of an individual letter, an alloy that melted at low temperature and solidified without distortion, and a press that borrowed features from those used in wine making, paper making, and book-

binding. He also adapted an oil-based ink from the paint mediums known to early Flemish artists. His invention enabled the printer to make words of the individual letter molds, range them in even lines, and lock many lines together into a form. Paper was then pressed down on the inked form to produce thousands of copies of one page. The type could be separated and stored for re-use. This system owed nothing to the printing methods developed earlier in China and Korea, which had none of Gutenberg's special features and which in any case he could not have known about. It is also more adaptable than the system credited to Laurens Janszoon Coster, a Dutch church official who is said by some to have invented movable type about 20 years earlier.

Gutenberg was born in Mainz around 1400. He was of an aristocratic family named Gensfleisch, but was most often called after his mother's family name of Gutenberg. The only records concerning his life are those showing his association with the goldsmiths' guild, of which he was reputedly a skilled member, and those relating to financial transactions, which indicate ill-fortune in money matters. In fact, it was during a lawsuit ending in 1444 that his invention began to come to light. That was in Strasbourg, to which Gutenberg had been exiled in 1430 after troubles between his guild and the rulers of Mainz.

Gutenberg had taken two partners who knew he was working on a secret enterprise, and who wanted to be included in order to get a return on their loans. They signed a five-year contract stipulating that their heirs be entitled to repayment from Gutenberg, though the business remained his alone. On the death of one of the partners, the heirs tried to get a partnership and took the case to court. Gutenberg won, but testimony at the trial revealed that he was working on an invention relating to printing.

The next that was known of Gutenberg after the trial was four years later when, back in Mainz, he won backing from the wealthy financier Johann Fust. At first Fust merely accepted Gutenberg's printing tools and equipment as securities for a loan, but later he became a partner. Problems arose when Fust began to push for a quicker return on his investment by commercialization, while Gutenberg – like many creative geniuses – wanted to strive for perfection. Finally in 1455 Fust sued Gutenberg, won his suit, and took

Below: before 1455, when Johannes Gutenberg produced the first European book printed with movable type in a frame, books were rare, precious possessions that only the rich could afford. Scribes worked for months producing a single book. Although early printing was slow and clumsy by modern standards, as this 16th-century "printing of books" shows, printers could nevertheless produce as many copies of a book in a day as a scribe could in a year. The result was a drop in the price of books, and the world of thought and learning was opened up to a vast new public.

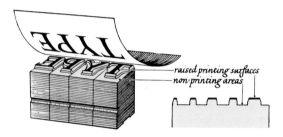

TYPE
raised printing surfaces
non-printing areas

Left: a page from Johannes Gutenberg's first book, the 42-line Bible, printed in 1455. The text, St Jerome's Latin version of the Scriptures, was apparently put through the press quickly to yield a rapid profit. The illuminations were then added by hand.

Right: Gutenberg's process is a type of printing called letterpress or relief. The ink is applied to the raised surface of the type (set in reverse) and the image is then transferred to the paper.

Toward the end of his life Gutenberg enjoyed some measure of security through the patronage of the ruler of Mainz, who made him a member of the royal court and gave him a yearly allowance of grain, cloth, and wine. Gutenberg died in 1468 and was buried in the Franciscan church in his birthplace.

Gutenberg lived to see his invention spreading rapidly throughout Europe, though the commercial success went to others. By his death at least eight major cities or towns had printing establishments, and in the next few decades the revolutionary technique reached as far north as Stockholm, as far east as Cracow, and west to Lisbon. William Caxton learned the technique in Bruges and then took it to London, where it flourished to an unusual degree.

everything away from the luckless inventor.

Fust and his son-in-law Peter Schöffer, once Gutenberg's most talented student, went into the printing business together. On August 14, 1457 they published the Psalter (a book of hymns), the first book in Europe to bear the names of the printers. However, the exceptional quality of the decorations led many experts to believe that Gutenberg did this part of the book.

Below: printing office of William Caxton who printed the first book in English, *The Game and the Playe of the Chesse*, in 1476. Caxton (right) is seen showing proofs to King Edward IV.

Printing by movable type was to the 15th century what mass-production technology has been to the 19th and 20th centuries: it enabled one person to do the work of many. A printer could make in one day what it took a scribe one year to produce. Printing was the first mass-production industry – and its product led to mass communication as a key to modern civilization.

Leonardo da Vinci
1452-1519

Of all the intellectuals of the Renaissance period, Leonardo da Vinci probably came closest to its ideal of the Universal Man. He was as much at home in the worlds of science and natural phenomena as he was in the worlds of art and philosophy. However, while his status as one of the greatest figures in art history is beyond question, his role in the field of science is far more controversial. He possessed one of the most inventive and ingenious minds ever, but his practical influence on the progress of science and technology was minimal.

Anyone who studies Leonardo's notebooks today feels an instant flash of recognition as they come across sketches and carefully annotated drawings that relate directly to technological advances of the present century. During his lifetime, however, Leonardo made no attempt to publish his findings or inventions, and at his

death his numerous papers were left to a favorite pupil. In time these papers were dispersed and lost sight of in private libraries and collections. As a result they remained generally unknown for several centuries, and Leonardo's obvious technological genius is of prophetic rather than practical value. It had little effect on the subsequent progress of science.

To take one simple example: in the Codex Madrid I in the National Library of Madrid, there is a whole page of chain drives with sprocket

Below left: Leonardo depicted as Plato in Raphael's *The School of Athens.*

Center: design for an "automative wagon with two driving axles," in effect a motorcar.

Below right: Leonardo rarely tested out his designs in practice. This model of a car driven by springs, built much later according to his specifications, actually functioned as an automobile.

wheels. Such a device could have been produced in Leonardo's day but no chain drive of this type was developed before 1770. Leonardo's solution to this specific problem lay buried in the Madrid manuscripts until they were rediscovered in 1967. Many of Leonardo's notebooks are rich in similar examples.

Leonardo was born in Vinci in Italy, the illegitimate son of a peasant girl and a Florentine notary. He served his apprenticeship as a painter in Verrocchio's studio in Florence, and it is said that Verrocchio abandoned painting after seeing the angel his young assistant painted in the left-hand corner of his *Baptism.* Leonardo's career as a painter was illustrious despite the fact that the number of projects he actually completed was relatively small. Sometimes his work suffered from his urge to experiment with techniques. When he was commissioned to paint the fresco of *The Last Supper* for the church of Saint Maria della Grazie in Milan, for example, he decided to attempt it with oil on plaster. The result was disastrous. The work already showed serious deterioration in his own lifetime, and has had to be restored and repaired many times over.

The anatomical drawings of human and ani-

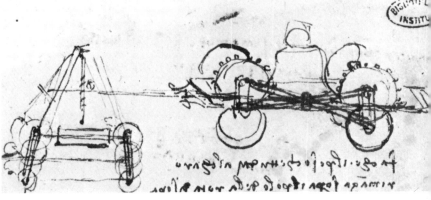

Engineering

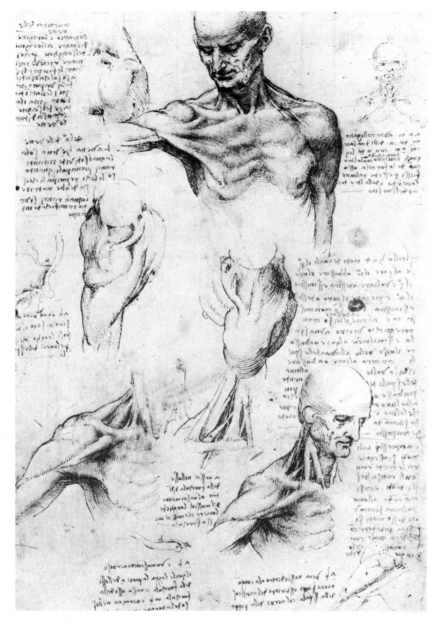

invasion, he returned to Florence where he worked as a military engineer for Cesare Borgia. In 1507 he accepted the patronage of King Francis I and went to live in the castle of Cloux near Amboise, which was a gift from the French king. There he lived out his closing years, devoting them almost exclusively to scientific inquiry.

Many of Leonardo's mechanical devices would not have worked. Others would have remained impractical until a power source such as the steam engine became available. It is the sweep of his imaginative ideas that is amazing: a mechanical structure that would give winged flight, an ironclad vehicle for use in battle, a grenade-shaped and finned mortar missile that would explode on impact, a vessel to travel under water. These are but a few of his projects.

Toward the end of his life Leonardo became convinced that great floods would eventually sweep humanity with all its vanities and evils into oblivion. This was the source of inspiration for his extraordinary series of drawings called *Deluges*, studies of currents and vast masses of water in violent motion.

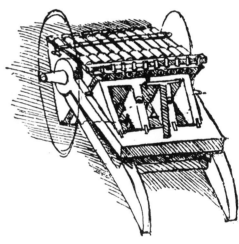

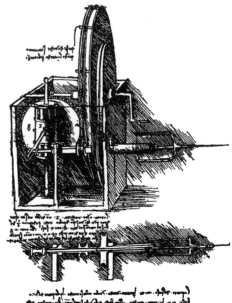

mals that Leonardo produced throughout his life were often more accurate and always incomparably finer than anything done by his medical contemporaries. Like his inventions, they reflect his quest for knowledge for its own sake. His details of the structure of muscles and blood vessels and of the heart and brain in section represent an amazing talent for observation. It has even been suggested that the famous enigmatic smile on the face of the *Mona Lisa* is a consequence of Leonardo's attempt to indicate the underlying muscular structure of facial expression. With anatomical study so restricted in his day, it is not surprising that his drawings contain some inaccuracies. For instance, the drawing of the act of coition in cross-section shows the non-existent tubes that according to Hippocratic theory carried the "thickest part" of the semen, containing the animal or human soul, from the base of the spine.

Leonardo was in service to the Duke of Milan from 1483 to 1499. When the city fell to a French

Above left: anatomical study of the shoulder, demonstrating Leonardo's remarkable powers of observation. Many of his paintings were as much attempts to convey his anatomical discoveries as they were works of art.

Above right: Leonardo's design for a multiple-barrel gun.

Right: spinning wheel sketched by Leonardo. The mechanism includes a flyer for twisting the yarn that automatically moves across the bobbin as the yarn is wound on. Such a device is not seen in any early spinning wheel and was invented again independently in the 18th century.

Copernicus
1473-1543

Polish cleric Nicolaus Copernicus is often described as the father of modern astronomy. He formulated the theory that the sun is the center of the solar system and that the planets revolve in circular orbits around it. Copernicus' idea contradicted the traditional belief, laid down by the Greek philosopher Ptolemy, that had dominated astronomy for over 1300 years. Ptolemy had established the school of thought holding that the earth was the center about which the heavens turned. It was a view that had a powerful religious appeal. By challenging it Copernicus was defying not only his fellow scientists but the entire religious establishment of his time.

Copernicus was born in Torún on the Vistula

Below right: Copernicus' room in Frauenberg, where he was a canon. Copernicus was educated by the church but was to overthrow one of its fundamental teachings. He replaced the view proposed by the Greek astronomer Ptolemy that the earth is the center of the universe with his own heliocentric theory. Fear of offending Christian orthodoxy made Copernicus delay his announcement.

river in what is now Poland, and following his father's death was brought up by a wealthy and aristocratic uncle. The benefits of financial security and a fine education meant that Copernicus was able to study as much as he wanted. He mastered theology and mathematics, and studied medicine for a time. However, he was most attracted by the science of astronomy.

He had not studied astronomy long before he began to doubt Ptolemy's theory of the heavens. In his efforts to justify his assumption that the earth was the center of the universe, Ptolemy had been forced to propose some vastly elaborate and complex orbits. One of the main contradictions that Ptolemy had tried to explain was the fact that at certain times of the year some planets

seemed to be motionless in the sky for a few days, then actually to move backward. This puzzling behavior was shared by all the planets except two, Mercury and Venus. Even these behaved strangely, appearing to have orbits strictly limited to a region close to the sun and showing none of the inconsistencies of the other planets. Ptolemy's explanations turned modern scientific method on its head. Instead of working from known observable facts to devise a theory to explain them, he had struggled to fit the facts to his preconceived idea of the earth's position in the universe.

Copernicus found it hard to believe that nature could be as complex as Ptolemy's ideas implied. He turned to the most up-to-date tables of planetary positions available and tried to find a simple hypothesis that would explain them. He discovered that he had to ignore Ptolemy's theory altogether. Instead he assumed that the sun was at the center of the solar system with the planets orbiting around it. On this basis he was able to formulate an accurate and far simpler theory.

On working out his theory in full mathematical detail, Copernicus found he could predict planet-

ary positions to a far greater accuracy than had been possible under the old system. In addition, the behavior of Venus and Mercury were easily explained. Under the Copernican system, Venus and Mercury as viewed from earth never moved outside a region close to the sun because their orbits always lay closer to the sun than to the earth's orbit. Conversely, because the other planets moved in orbits that were always farther from the sun, the earth periodically "overtook" them and caused them to appear to move backward across the sky.

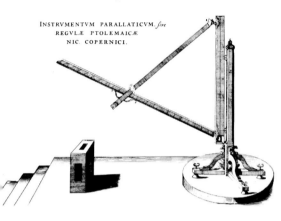

Copernicus expounded his theory in a book which he called *De Revolutionibus Orbium Caelestium* (*Concerning the Revolutions of the Heavenly Spheres*) but decided against publishing it for fear of religious reprisals. However, word of Copernicus' theory spread to many of Europe's scholars and aroused great interest and speculation. In 1543 Copernicus, by then an old and ailing man, was persuaded by his friends to publish his book. Before it was sent to the publisher, Copernicus took the wise precaution of adding a flattering dedication to Pope Paul III. Unfortunately, the publisher was still worried about the reception the book would have and, in an effort to protect himself, added a preface without Copernicus' knowledge. In it he stated that the Copernican theory was not advanced as a description of actual facts but as a novel and convenient device for the more accurate calculation of planetary positions. This unauthorized preface, which many scholars believed to be written by Copernicus, undermined the impact of the book and damaged the astronomer's reputation. Worse, Copernicus was then critically ill following a stroke, and could do little to defend himself. He died only hours after seeing the first copy of his book.

Despite the offending preface, the seeds of the destruction of Ptolemy's theory were sown. Copernicus' work created for the first time for astronomy a rational framework upon which succeeding generations could build. It helped to sweep away traditional superstitions, clearing the path for the development of modern scientific method. Subsequent discoveries by astronomers such as Johannes Kepler and Christian Huygens stem directly from Copernicus' work.

Right: the Copernican sun-centered universe (top) in contrast with the Church's view (bottom) in which the planets, including the sun, orbit around the earth.

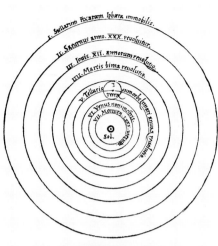

Left: the triquetrum, an instrument used by Copernicus to measure the altitude of heavenly bodies.

Below: A colored engraving of Copernicus' sun-centered universe from Andreas Cellarius' *Atlas*, published in the 17th century. Proceeding outward from the sun are the orbits and astrological signs of Mercury, Venus, Earth, Mars, Jupiter, and Saturn. Uranus, Neptune, and Pluto were still to be discovered. It took about a century for Copernicus' discovery to be widely accepted. When it was it revolutionized astronomy.

Paracelsus

1493-1541

Paracelsus' style of grandiose speech gave rise to the word "bombast," derived from his surname Bombastus. Capable of fierce invective, he once told a group of professors with whom he was in conflict: "You are not worthy for a dog to lift his hind leg against you." He never lost his relish for treading on the toes of the academic establishment, or for attacking by ridicule much that was dubious, worthless, or positively harmful in the orthodox medicine of his day. When he took up a teaching post in Basle, Switzerland, he scandalized the authorities by publicly burning the works of the renowned Greek physician Galen. He made matters worse by opening his lectures to everyone and teaching in the vernacular of German instead of Latin. Students flocked to him from the ends of Europe, but he never stayed in one place for long. He made enemies wherever

Paracelsus was the Renaissance physician and alchemist who established the use of chemicals in the treatment of illness. He was largely responsible for the advance of practical medicine during the early 16th century, and the essentially rationalist approach of modern medicine can be traced back directly to his influence.

Below: illustration from Paracelsus' work *Prognosticatio*, emphasizing the necessity of man's humility to God. He considered theology an essential part of medicine because a doctor should also treat the soul.

FAMOSO·DOCTOR   PARESELSVS.

Paracelsus' real name was Philippus Theophrastus Bombastus von Hohenheim. He was born in a village near Zurich, Switzerland, the son of a physician and chemist. He had his early education at the town school in Augsburg, Austria, which specialized in training overseers and analysts for the local mines. At the age of 14 he began to travel, visiting most of the leading universities in Europe in the hope of finding teachers whose views he could respect. Being extremely unconventional and outspoken, he soon offended most teachers and others in authority with his skeptical and strongly expressed opinions.

Nonetheless Paracelsus took his baccalaureate in medicine in Vienna in 1510 and his doctorate in Ferrara, Italy in 1516. At about that time he adopted the name Paracelsus, meaning "above Celsus," to show his contempt for the ancient Roman physician who was so admired in the 16th century.

Travels took Paracelsus as far west as Ireland, as far east as Constantinople, present-day Istanbul, and into Russia where he was briefly captured by Tatars. He served as an army surgeon in various local wars. He constantly sought to add to his knowledge of medical treatment and, as he put it, to discover "the latent forces of nature."

Right: an illustration for a medical work by Paracelsus which shows the physician treating one of his patients. Paracelsus said that since man contains all the elements, and needs them for the curing of his illnesses, a good physician must understand all the physical sciences as well as alchemy. Among Paracelsus' medical achievements were his anticipation of homeopathic medicine – like curing like – and chemotherapy, the use of chemicals to treat diseases. Although Paracelsus incurred the emnity of many doctors and apothecaries, through his rudeness as much as his revolutionary treatments, he was extremely considerate to his patients and by all accounts very popular.

Der ander Theil

Der grossen Wundtartz-
ney deß weitberühmpten / bewerten / vnnd
erfahrnen / Theophrasti Paracelsi von Hohenheim /
der Leib vnd Wundartzney Doctors / Von der offnen
Schäden vrsprung vnd heylung. Auß rechtem grundt vnd
bewerten stücken treüwlich an
Tag geben.

Mit Röm. Keif. Maiestet Freyheit nicht
nachzudrucken.

he went, and those in Basle hounded him out of the city.

Like Hippocrates, Paracelsus believed in the treatment of the whole person and in nature's own healing tendencies. He anticipated homeopathic medicine in his statement that, in small doses, what "makes a man ill also cures him." He is said to have devised an effective treatment for the plague by making a pill of dough and a minute speck of the patient's excreta. In spite of his scientific approach to medicine, he saw magic, or "mental power," as an element in the healing process. No less an authority than the 20th-century Swiss psychologist Carl Jung has acknowledged him as a pioneer of "an empirical psychological healing science."

This imaginative and egotistical man was a brilliant diagnostician. "Resolute imagination can accomplish all things," he said. While he scorned the assumptions of astrology, he searched in alchemy for fundamental truths: "Magic is a great hidden wisdom – reason is a great open folly," he declared. He bridged the divide be-

Above: a painting of Paracelsus lecturing on the *Elixir Vitae*, the elixir of life. In addition to prolonging life, this magical substance was supposed to be able to transmute base metals into gold, and was hence synonymous with the philosopher's stone. Paracelsus' lectures were very popular with students but he infuriated his colleagues and critics by his insistence on teaching in German rather than Latin, as befitted a scholar. When short of a word Paracelsus would often invent one, usually without defining it, which has made much of his work incomprehensible. Some, such as "zinc" and "alcohol," have passed into popular usage.

tween the old alchemy and the new science; it was his interest in alchemy that led to certain of his basic insights in the area of chemotherapy.

Paracelsus was the first to suggest that diseases of the chest in miners were caused by the inhalation of metallic "vapors" rather than by malicious spirits. Nor had anyone before him connected the lack of minerals in drinking water with the incidence of goiter in certain districts. His description of syphilis was a pioneering treatise which first suggested the treatment of it with mercury compounds.

The Great Surgery Book, published in 1536, represented one of the peaks of his reputation and led to his being cultivated by nobles and princes. Nevertheless he continued to move from city to city and from country to country till the end of his life. He died in an inn in Salzburg, Austria, where he had gone to take up an appointment in the service of Duke Ernst of Bavaria. Some said he was poisoned, others that he died of injuries sustained from rolling down a hill when drunk.

Georgius Agricola

1494-1555

The German physician and scholar Georgius Agricola was the first scientific writer to make a systematic study of mining and minerals. He was the first to treat minerals as objects belonging exclusively to the natural world, and by so doing earned the title of "father of mineralogy."

Agricola was born as Georg Bauer in Glachau in eastern Germany, later taking the latinized form of his name (*agricola* is the Latin and *bauer* the German for farmer). Knowledge of his family background is vague, but he was known to have studied philosophy and classical languages at Leipzig University and to have become a school-teacher. In 1523 he went to Italy to add medical studies to his qualifications. While in Venice he worked on the important Aldine Press edition of the Greek physician Galen's writings, and met the great humanist philosopher Erasmus.

Returning home, Agricola took up an appointment as town physician in Joachimsthal. This town lay in the center of what came to be the most important metal mining and smelting district in Europe. Agricola began to spend more and more time visiting the mines, hoping to find minerals that might be useful to medicine. In the end, however, he became increasingly interested in the processes of mining and metallurgy, and the classification of rocks and ores. It seems likely that he also acquired a financial interest in some of the more profitable mines.

He evidently made a point of talking to the miners themselves, and grew indignant on their behalf over the accidents they suffered because of the low standards of safety, and the illnesses and premature senility caused by their work. Like

his contemporary, Paracelsus, Agricola saw clearly that these were "industrial diseases," though they were not as yet called that. He wrote a detailed description of the skin lesions with which salt miners were often inflicted.

More than any scientist before him, Agricola rejected earlier authorities as well as magical and philosophical links to science, and based his work on direct observation and field study. With Erasmus' encouragement, he wrote a series of books and treatises on several aspects of mining and mineral ores. The most important of these was *De Natura Fossilium* (*On the Nature of Fossils*) which has been described as the first textbook on mineralogy, the word fossil then applying to any object dug up from the ground. He described the role of erosion in forming the shapes of mountains and deduced correctly that veins of mineral ore in rocks had an origin in silt deposits. He worked out a classification of crystals based on their geometric shapes and advocated the use of magnetic needles in surveying for metal ores. He very probably coined the word "petroleum" from *petra*, meaning rock, and *oleum*, meaning oil.

Even though Agricola was a Catholic, the Protestant duke of Saxony appointed him to be mayor of Chemnitz in 1546. The duke also sent

Right: an illustration of the smelting of ores, taken from *De Re Metallica*, Agricola's most important work. (A) and (B) are furnaces into which the ores are fed and in which they are smelted. The molten metal runs out of the tapholes (C) into the forehearths (D) and is extracted at the forehearths' tapholes (E). (F) is the dipping pot. A smelter (G) is carrying a wicker basket of charcoal to the furnace. The other smelter is breaking up the slag which has solidified at the taphole of the furnace with a hooked bar (H). The molten metal is then poured into molds. (I) is a heap of charcoal, quantities of which are measured up in a wicker box on the barrow (K). This type of furnace system was very efficient in that it could smelt large quantities of metal for continuous periods of up to three days. Copper, lead, silver, and gold could be extracted from very poor ores without the use of expensive fluxes, and the extraction rate was very high.

him on a delicate diplomatic mission to the Holy Roman Emperor. Aside from these two forays into politics, Agricola managed to keep clear of partisan involvements even though the religious wars of the 16th century were by then gaining momentum. A result of these wars was to dis-

perse German engineers and miners to other countries. Many went to England, where their skills found a ready market and helped to lay the basis for their adoptive country's industrial future.

All Agricola's lifelong scholarship moved toward its culmination in the production of his greatest work, *De Re Metallica* (*On Metals*) though it was still unpublished at the time of his death. The first edition, in Latin, came out a year later, and the first German edition came out in 1557, illustrated with the superb woodcuts of Hans Manuel. The book was swiftly recognized as a text of high scientific stature. It went through many editions, remaining the standard text for 200 years.

De Re Metallica is a comprehensive treatise on every aspect of metallurgy and mining. It summarizes all that was known on the subject from classical times onward and describes the techniques of mine engineering and surveying as well as of ore processing. It even covers the law of land ownership insofar as this bears on mining, the patterns of employment and labor manage-

Above left: a German silver mine c.1500.

Above right: composite picture from *De Re Metallica* of three types of bellows used to ventilate mine shafts. A–F: bellows operated by workman. G–M: a horse trod on the steps covering a wooden wheel; cams attached to the axle compressed the bellows. N–R: two-wheeled system with a horse driving an upright wheel which in turn drove a horizontal one attached to the bellows.

Right: before the use of bellows, mine shafts were ventilated by the constant shaking of linen cloths. This method dates back to Roman times.

ment, and the economics involved. In writing his book, Agricola established mineralogy as a scientific discipline. He also fulfilled the prophecy made about him some years before by Erasmus, who had said that he would one day "stand at the head of the princes of scholarship."

Gerardus Mercator

1512-1594

The Flemish cartographer Gerardus Mercator devised the Mercator projection as a solution to the problem of how to project a two-dimensional representation of the curve of the earth's surface on a flat in a way that was free from distortion. The Mercator projection was the most influential development in the history of cartography.

Mercator was born in Rupelmonde, Flanders as Gerhard Kremer, though he used the latinized form of his name throughout his working life (*mercator* is the Latin and *kremer* the Flemish for shopkeeper). In 1532 he took his master's degree in humanities and philosophy at the University of Louvaine, then went to work with the mathematician and astronomer Gemma Frisius in constructing scientific instruments, globes, and maps.

Within a few years Mercator built up a reputation as a superlative cartographer and instrument maker, also showing clear signs of becoming one of the foremost geographers of the 16th century. In 1537 he printed a celebrated map of Palestine, and the next year published his first world map on a double cardiform projection. A map of Flanders followed in 1540.

An interruption in Mercator's career occurred in 1544 when his Protestant inclination led to his being arrested under suspicion of heresy. After he had been in prison seven months, the university authorities secured his release and he was able to go on with his research unhindered. In 1552, however, he moved his workshop to Duisburg in the Duchy of Cleve, where a more liberal

religious atmosphere prevailed. He taught mathematics in the grammar school and geography in the university, and worked on his projects under the patronage of Duke Wilhelm of Cleve. In 1590 he suffered the first in a series of strokes that led to his death four years later.

The map of the world that first used the Mercator projection was published in 18 sheets in 1569. It was prompted by the demand for more reliable map and chart making created by the

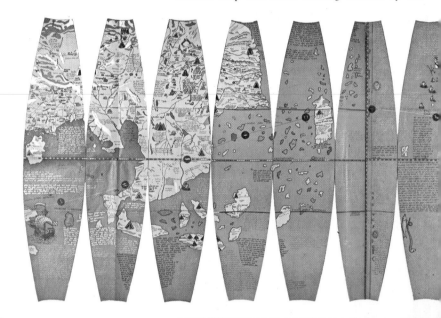

Above: an example of early cartography. These lens-shaped flat sections called gores can be pasted onto a sphere to make a geographical globe. They were first used by the German Martin Waldseemüller in 1507 and are still used today for the mass production of globes.

Right: the map of Africa from Mercator's *Atlas sive Cosmographicae Meditationes de Fabrica Mundi et Fabricati Figura.*

epic voyages of exploration that had begun in the 15th century. The new technique projected a world map as if from a cylinder so that it filled a rectangle on which the lines of latitude and longitude ran straight and parallel. This enabled navigation to be charted in straight lines on a far more accurate basis than had been possible before. Ship's masters of Mercator's time were slow to appreciate the advantages, however, and it was not until the next great age of exploration in the 18th century that this projection came into its own.

In the same year that he published his world map, Mercator embarked on his most ambitious project. This was to produce a comprehensive account of the world from the creation, illustrated with maps. He called it his *Atlas*, taking the name of the mythical Greek giant who supported the world on his shoulders as his symbol. This incidentally established the word "atlas" to describe any published collection of maps. Mercator's project began with a chronology published in 1569. An edition of Ptolemy's maps with commentary and corrections followed in 1578, and sets of maps of Europe, the Balkans, and Greece in 1585 and 1589. After his death his son Rumold completed the project, and other hands later revised and supplemented the original editions.

Mercator's achievement was made possible by a combination of intellect and craftsmanship. Although his maps contained inaccuracies and some imaginative assumptions where factual knowledge ran out, they took full account of the best scientific knowledge available, and combined it with mathematical precision and supreme workmanship. For two centuries, geographers and explorers owed him a debt beyond paying. Today, Mercator's maps, with their handsome italic script and sense of graphic design, have become increasingly valued as objects of beauty.

Below: the oldest globe of the world still surviving, made by pasting the gores around a sphere. It was produced by Martin Behaim of Nuremberg in about 1492. It does not, of course, include the Americas, but it does show Japan lying beyond the Atlantic.

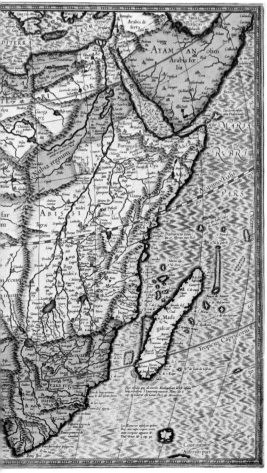

Right: the title page from Mercator's *Atlas sive Cosmographicae Meditationes de Fabrica Mundi et Fabricati Figura*, published by his heirs in 1595, the year after his death. It was the first time the word "Atlas," taken from the figure in Greek mythology who was tricked into carrying the Earth on his shoulders, was used to describe a collection of maps.

ATLAS SIVE COSMOGRAPHICÆ MEDITATIONES DE FABRICA MVNDI ET FABRICATI FIGVRA.
1637

Hans Lippershey
c1570-1619

Hans Lippershey, a German-born spectacle maker who lived in the Netherlands, is by tradition called the inventor of the telescope. In exercising his craft as an optician, Lippershey had great skill in grinding lenses, and his workshop was naturally full of the samples of his trade. According to one often-told story, a child playing in his shop one day lined up one lens with another in the shop window and, on looking through the two, noticed that distant objects came closer. Whether or not that was his inspiration, in 1608 Lippershey submitted for sale to the government of the Netherlands an invention which consisted of a tube with one fixed lens and an eye lens that could be adjusted for focus. This he called his *kijker* (a viewer). Its potential military use was obvious and, after he had made a few modifications and produced a binocular version, the government paid him 900 florins for the device.

Lippershey's invention was the first known example of a practical refracting telescope. Nonetheless, it is doubtful whether his claim to have been its inventor could ever be substantiated. James Metius, another Dutchman, put forward a rival claim that was supported by no less a personage than the 17th-century French philosopher René Descartes. In any case, the Netherlands government turned down Lippershey's request for a 30-year patent on the grounds that "many other persons had a knowledge of the invention."

The science of optics and the principle of using lenses to magnify objects had been known since classical times. According to Sir Richard Burton, the Arabian scholar and explorer, the telescope had been known to Islamic scientists before the Middle Ages. In the 13th century, Roger Bacon, the English monk, scholar, and scientist, wrote prophetically in a passage which described the possible combinations of lenses and concave mirrors: "thus from an incredible distance we may read the smallest letters . . . the sun, moon, and stars may be made to descend hither in appearance." Leonard Digges, an English mathematician, had referred in 1571 to the "miraculous effects of perspective glasses" in his *Geometrical Practice*.

The truth probably is that the telescope was evolving in fact and theory for the best part of 300 years, awaiting improvements in the manufacture of lenses for final perfection.

In part the significance of Lippershey's device is that it made practical use of an effect that might well have been regarded as little more than a lens grinder's parlor trick. More important, the telescope advanced the work of Galileo, who learned about it through the French scientist Jacques Bovedere. Seeing its potential for advancing the science of astronomy, Bovedere passed on an account of the telescope to Galileo. He in turn reconstructed one according to his own calculations, and put the "optic tube" to creative use in his study of the heavens.

Below left: portrait of Hans Lippershey, the man who invented the refracting telescope.

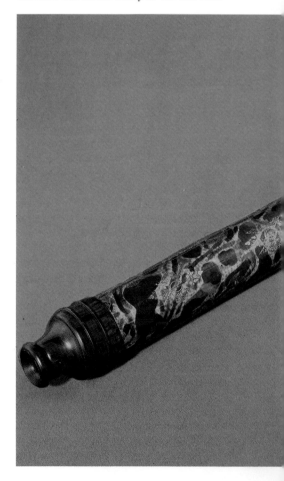

Right: a terrestrial telescope, made by Christopher Cocks, a noted London optic-glass grinder. Hans Lippershey developed the telescopic principle into a practical instrument and provided the impetus for other lens specialists to manufacture and improve upon the telescope, especially once its potential as a tool in astronomy was realized. This particular model, made in 1673, has five draw tubes. The object glass is nearly 3 feet in focal length, with an aperture of ⅛th of an inch. The three-lens eyepiece gives a magnification of about 14 with a field of view of 1 foot, 6 inches.

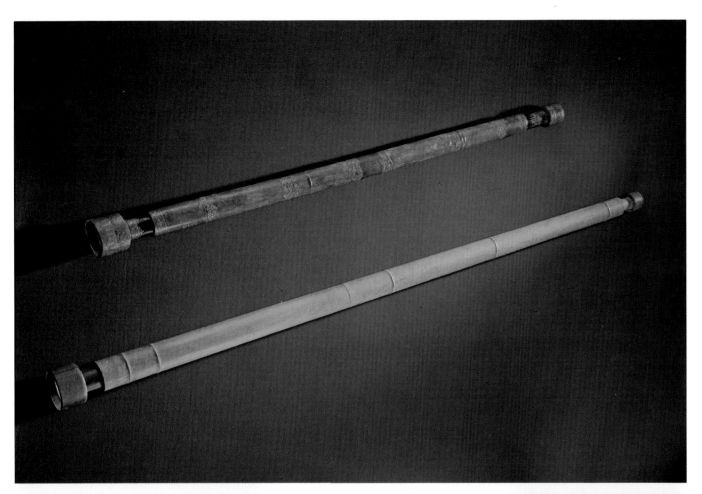

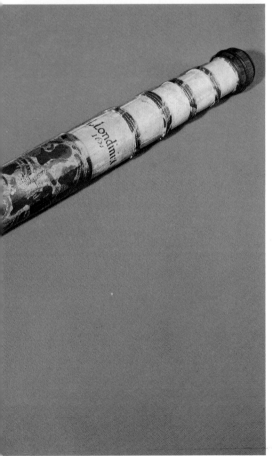

Above: Galileo's telescopes based on Lippershey's invention of the "optic tube," Galileo constructed one himself and was one of the first astronomers to use the telescope for observing the skies.

Right: a plate from Camille Flammarion's *Histoire du Ciel* (1872) illustrating Lippershey's discovery of the telescopic effect of two lenses. According to legend a child playing outside his lens shop noticed that the lenses made distant objects appear closer. This was supposed to have given Lippershey the idea for his invention.

Galileo
1564-1642

Galileo, who was equally gifted as a mathematician, physicist, and astronomer, was the first scientist to rely on observation and experiment for much of his research, and his advocacy of this approach helped to found modern scientific method. Among his major discoveries were the principle of the pendulum and the law on the behavior of falling bodies. He also refined the telescope into an instrument suitable for studying the heavens, by which means he amassed powerful evidence to show that the sun was the center of the solar system rather than the earth as then believed.

The son of a talented musician, Galileo was born in Pisa and educated at a monastery near Florence. His parents wanted him to become a doctor and in 1581 he entered the University of Pisa to study medicine. He made his first scientific discovery in the same year. While at a service in Pisa Cathedral, his attention was caught by the swaying of the chandeliers in the air currents and drafts above his head. Struck by their steady rhythm and wishing to study such a sway, he designed a simple pendulum in order to investigate the regularity of its swing. Using his own pulse beats to measure the swing, he found that the time each swing took was independent of the length of the arc described by the pendulum. He suggested that pendulums might therefore be used to regulate the measurement of time, an idea that was later applied in the first accurate mechanical clock.

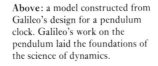

Galileo's passion for mathematics and physics soon outstripped his interest in medicine and he decided to pursue a scientific career. His early work gained him enough recognition to secure a post at the University of Pisa. While there he formulated the law of falling bodies, which says that all bodies fall at the same rate whatever

Right: copy of Galileo's design for an escapement or pendulum clock.

Below right: Galileo's *Dialogo*, published in 1632, takes the form of a discussion between disciples of Aristotle, Ptolemy, and Copernicus, whose portraits appear in the frontispiece.

Above: a model constructed from Galileo's design for a pendulum clock. Galileo's work on the pendulum laid the foundations of the science of dynamics.

their weight, provided they do not encounter air resistance. Stories are told how Galileo caused consternation among the citizens of Pisa by dropping cannon balls of different weights from the famous Leaning Tower. Proving his conjection, the balls were all seen and heard to strike the ground simultaneously.

In 1592 Galileo took an appointment at the University of Padua to escape the political difficulties he faced in Pisa, teaching mathematics and astronomy. On learning about the recently invented telescope, he designed and built a vastly improved one for his use in studying the heavens. With it he discovered that the moon has mountains, that some planets have moons orbiting them, and that the sun occasionally has spots which move across its surface. Galileo's remarkable work established the telescope's central role in observational astronomy.

Galileo was more than a great scientist. He could also lecture and write brilliantly, and the impact of his ideas on European scholarship owed much to his ability to communicate them clearly and persuasively. In the 1620s he published one of his most outstanding papers outlining the basic ideas of what is today known as modern scientific method. He proposed that the results of experiments should form the basis of mathematical formulations of new theories, and that these theories should themselves be tested by further experiment. He argued that the tradition of treating mathematics and science as separate disciplines should be discarded. "The book of nature," he said, "is written in the characters of mathematics."

Conflict with the Church overshadowed Galileo's last years. His astronomical observations had convinced him that the earth moved around the sun. This outraged theologians who preferred the traditional view of the earth as the center of the solar system. In 1633 Galileo was brought to Rome, charged with heresy. Found guilty, he was ordered on pain of death to recant his views. An old and ailing man, Galileo gave in. But it is said that as he rose from his knees following the re-

cantation, he muttered, "and yet it moves!," referring to the earth. Galileo knew that not even a body as powerful as the Church could stifle the truth for long.

Banished to his estates near Florence, Galileo spent the last years of his life in correspondence with other scientists and scholars. When he died, he was mourned by scholars throughout Europe – but the Church in a final shallow gesture refused to allow his burial on consecrated ground.

Right: one of Galileo's views of the moon. He obtained it with the use of a crude telescope and it is surprising that he was able to show the details of the surface as well as he did.

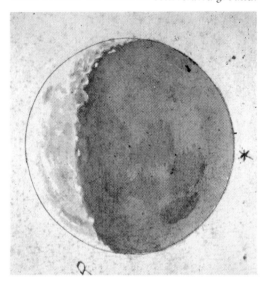

Below: an anonymous painting of Galileo's trial. Galileo's insistence that the sun, not the earth, was the center of the universe, outraged the Church. He outlined his views on the heliocentric universe in the *Dialogo* which he published in defiance of Pope Paul V. As a result he was summoned by the Inquisition and brought to trial in 1633 accused of heresy. He was found guilty and forced to recant his theories on pain of death.

Johannes Kepler

1571-1630

By his outstanding contributions to astronomy and optics, Johannes Kepler triumphed over a life troubled by illness and continual financial worries. He worked out basic laws governing the motion of the planets, establishing the Copernican theory of the solar system beyond doubt and laying the foundations of astronomical science. He also founded modern optics by giving the earliest accurate account of the way in which the human eye works. Although doing so much to destroy old superstitions, Kepler was by nature a mystic, and his passion for the occult frequently hampered his more rational scientific work.

Born in Weil der Stadt, Germany, Kepler was plagued by childhood illness that left him weak-sighted and partially crippled. His intellectual talents were unaffected by his physical disabilities, however, and his remarkable gift for mathematics enabled him to secure a teaching post at the University of Graz in Austria. He remained at Graz until 1597 when local religious troubles forced him to leave. For several years he worked

Below right: the apparent movements of the planets against the starry background over a long period. These movements cannot be reconciled with the idea of uniform motion of planets around the sun in circular orbits. Basing his work on Tycho Brahe's observations of Mars, Kepler resolved the anomaly by proposing that the orbit of a planet around the sun is an ellipse. The temporary east-to-west movement of a planet, known as retrograding, is due to the combined movements of the planet itself and the earth's motion.

time trying to fit the data to various occult ideas. After repeated failures he turned to a more rational theory. In 1543 Nicolaus Copernicus had proposed that the sun and not the earth was the center of the solar system. Kepler realized that it fitted the data better than any other although it was still a highly controversial theory. Not only was he able to verify Copernicus' basic heliocentric idea but he actually refined the theory and used it to formulate three important laws of planetary motion.

The first of Kepler's laws states that planets do not move in circular orbits as Copernicus had believed, but in ellipses. Unlike a circle, an ellipse has foci rather than a center. The law shows that for every planet's orbit the sun occupies one of the foci of the ellipse described. Kepler's second law states that the closer a planet is to the sun, the faster it moves in its orbit. His third law describes a simple relationship linking the time a planet takes to complete an orbit around the sun with its average distance from the sun during the orbit.

Kepler was quick to realize that the sun was exerting a strong influence on planetary motions and he suggested that a magnetic force of some kind acted between the sun and the planets. However, he could not explain either the nature or likely origin of the force and it was left to Isaac Newton, nearly 50 years later, to formulate the universal law of gravitation and to show that Kepler's laws were a natural consequence of the force of gravity.

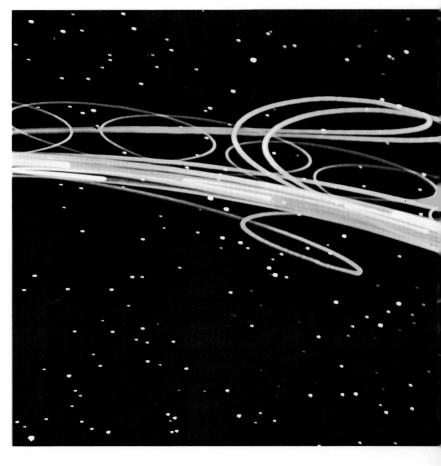

as an assistant to the celebrated astronomer Tycho Brahe whose detailed observations of planetary positions provided a basis for much of Kepler's important work.

Kepler had the insight to recognize that the observations provided the possibility of constructing a major new chart describing the heavens. He hoped he would be able to prove many current astrological beliefs and spent some

Astronomy

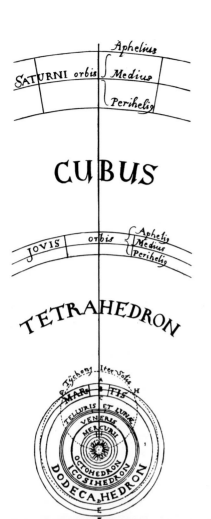

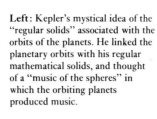

CUBUS

TETRAHEDRON

Left: Kepler's mystical idea of the "regular solids" associated with the orbits of the planets. He linked the planetary orbits with his regular mathematical solids, and thought of a "music of the spheres" in which the orbiting planets produced music.

Right: Kepler's observatory at Prague, Czechoslovakia, where much of his research was done.

Below: the apparent movements of the individual planets.

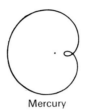

Mercury

Venus

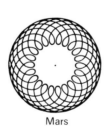

Mars

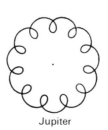

Jupiter

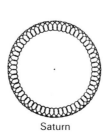

Saturn

Through his interest in astronomy, Kepler became fascinated by the way in which telescopes worked and from this began speculating about the nature of human vision. His analysis of vision provided the foundation of all future advances in the understanding of the function and structure of the eye, and helped to establish optics as a recognized science. He correctly identified the pupil as a diaphragm through which light rays enter the eye and described the way in which they are refracted.

He suggested that people with blurred vision had an optical defect which meant that rays were focused either in front of or just behind their retina. The accuracy of Kepler's remarkable deductions did not stop with an account of the human eye. He went on to explain how telescopes worked by refracting light and bringing an enlarged image to focus in the eyepiece. His work provided the theoretical basis for subsequent improvements in telescope design and for the development of opthalmic optics as a recognized branch of medicine.

Kepler had to make astrological predictions in order to earn a livelihood for himself and his family. He had many patrons, but most were slow to pay and time and again he had to go on tiring journeys to plead for his fees. During one such journey his health finally broke down and he died before he could be brought home.

33

Jan Adriaasz Leeghwater

1575-1650

Jan Leeghwater was the engineer who succeeded in draining the vast Beemster lake in the Netherlands in the early 17th century. It was one of the most extensive projects that had ever been undertaken in hydraulic engineering, and it added 17,000 acres of cultivable soil to the country's agricultural economy.

Land is of particular importance to the Dutch, a relatively small nation whose countryside consists largely of land reclaimed from the low marshlands of the western European seaboard. For several centuries there has been a constant need to defend the reclaimed areas, called polders, from such forces as sea, lakes, or swamps, which constantly try to reassert themselves. Since the Netherlands is one of the most intensively cultivated countries in the world, there has been a continuing demand for new land to be tamed and won – in Leeghwater's time as now.

The ambitious and expensive project to drain the Beemster lake came about when a group of directors of the Dutch East India Company sought ways in which they could use the wealth that the company's enterprises in the Far East had produced. The contract was put out for bids, and several candidates came forward before it was given to Leeghwater on April 10, 1608. The contract stipulated that the ring dyke be completed by November 1, 1609.

Twenty-six water mills were placed at intervals to start the pumping operation for a dyke of the necessary 25 miles in length. The contractors finished work only a short time past the deadline,

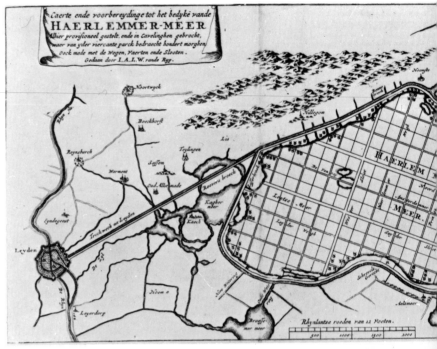

Right: Dutch polderland. The Dutch have quite literally built up their country by reclaiming some 3000 square miles of previously submerged land, an engineering feat initiated by Leeghwater, and continued to this day. The principle of creating agricultural polderland from the sea has not changed much since Leeghwater's days. Dykes are erected and pumping stations are installed to drain off the water. When the water has been pumped out the muddy surface of the polder is sown with reeds to enable the rest of the water to evaporate and to prevent weeds from clogging up the land. Water channels are also dug to improve drainage. The reeds are then destroyed, an open-field drainage system (later replaced by pipe drains) is laid, and the first crop can be sown.

but within a month a violent winter storm breached the dyke and destroyed half of it. Work began again immediately, and in three years the Beemster polder was ready for cultivation.

The Amsterdam merchants who had put up the money took the credit for this triumph of engineering, and it is said that the low-born Leeghwater had to wait at table in order to be present at the banquet in celebration of the successful project. The scheme's profitability was

Left: Leeghwater's plans for draining the Haarlemmer Lake. The project was unsuccessful. The watermills at the time were incapable of coping with the high levels of water and the draining of the lake had to wait until the steam-pumping engines of the 19th century.

beyond all expectations. Within a short period the proceeds from crops grown in the fertile soil of the new polder had more than covered the costs of the engineering work.

Leeghwater, born of a poor peasant family in the northern village of De Rijp, had been trained to be a carpenter. The pursuit of knowledge seems to have been a natural feature of his character, and he was almost entirely self-taught in the skills he acquired in mechanics, engineering, and linguistics. In 1605 he astonished a group of spectators, which included members of the royal household, by staying under water for three quarters of an hour, using a form of diving bell that he invented and patented. He later became a mill builder and architect.

After his great feat of draining the Beemster lake, Leeghwater's services were in constant demand. He saw to the draining and reclamation of 30 more lakes and swamps, and was invited to Bordeaux to advise on the draining of the swamp outside that town. He helped bring about the downfall of the fortress city of s'-Hertogenbosch, thought to be unassailable because of the marshes surrounding it. Leeghwater diverted two rivers and started water mills working to drain the marshes, and within four months the city was taken. A commemorative coin was struck in the engineer's honor.

Leeghwater was a person of many interests. He designed and built furniture, drew sketches, and made sculptures in wood, stone, ivory, and metal. He also constructed bridges and church towers, among them the Westerkerk and the Zuiderkerk in Amsterdam, both of which he equipped with bells. His contemporaries described him as a man of strong intellect and energy who said little but achieved a great deal.

In spite of accomplishing much, Leeghwater

Above: a Dutch watermill. This type is called a "hollow-post mill," the body, which carries the sails, being mounted on a post. An upright shaft passes through the post and drives a scoop wheel which lifts water up from a lower to a higher level.

never realized his ultimate ambition. This was to drain the constantly growing Haarlemmer lake, a task which he calculated would require no less than 160 water mills. The project also remained too daunting for all successors until the engineering techniques and steam pumping stations of the 19th century made it possible. Before that day Leeghwater had brought the traditional Dutch polder drainage system to new levels of sophistication, and in so doing earned a place among the foremost engineers of history.

William Harvey

1578-1657

His discovery of the circulation of the blood and his concept of the heart as a pump have made physician and physiologist William Harvey one of the key figures in medical science. His book *De Motu Cordis (On the Motion of the Heart)* revolutionized physiology, and is one of the most important medical texts ever written.

Harvey was born in Folkestone, England, where his father was a well-known businessman. The eldest in a family of nine children, he was educated at an exclusive boy's school in Canterbury and later at Cambridge University, where he studied medicine. In about 1600 he went to Padua, Italy for two years to continue his medical training in the city's famous Medical School under the tutelage of Fabricius, the Italian anatomist and founder of the science of embryology. When Harvey returned to England, he started medical practice in London.

His career as a fashionable doctor was a story of success, and he built up a distinguished clientele. In 1609 he began his long association with

St Bartholomew's Hospital, and in 1618 was made physician extraordinary to King James I. He was later personal physician to King Charles I. Harvey's scientific ambitions, however, overshadowed any he may have had on the social side. Possessing one of the most formidable intellects of his day, he followed the tradition of strict observational inquiry that was founded by the Greek philosopher Aristotle.

Right: the circulation of the blood according to Galen, the 2nd century Greek physician whose medical teachings were accepted unquestioningly for about 15 centuries after his death. According to Galen three types of blood ebbed and flowed through the body in two separate trees – the veins carrying purple blood and the arteries carrying scarlet blood. The liver made the blood from food received from the intestines and charged it with "natural spirit." Part passed through the right ventricle into veins; part went through the left ventricle, absorbing "vital spirit" and passed into arteries which originated in the lungs. Some of this blood reached the brain, absorbed "animal spirit" and was carried into the nerves, believed to be hollow. Galen rejected the idea that the veins and arteries terminated in the heart. He considered the heart not as a pump but an organ to warm the blood. The heartbeat and pulse were due to the alternating expansion and collapse of the body as vital spirit was released and absorbed. Unfortunately, although Galen was a great physician in his time he did not take the trouble to study human beings but transposed anatomical details of animals onto the human body. And, despite his dictum that "the experimental path is long and arduous but leads to the truth," he frequently disregarded his own observations if they did not tie up with preconceived ideas. As there were few physicians of comparable stature until medieval times Galen's theories prevailed.

At that time, it was still thought that the blood originated in the heart and somehow managed to ebb and flow through the veins and arteries in the manner proposed by Galen in the 2nd century AD. Fabricius, Harvey's former teacher, had discovered the valves in the large veins, but had failed to understand their function. Harvey approached the problem without preconceptions, devising a series of experiments in which he tied up the blood vessels of living animals.

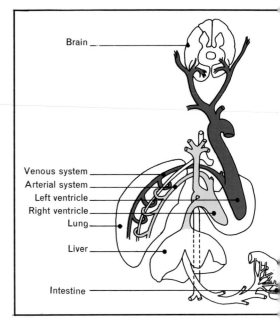

- Brain
- Venous system
- Arterial system
- Left ventricle
- Right ventricle
- Lung
- Liver
- Intestine

From these tests he established, first, that blood flows away from the heart through the arteries and, second, that it flows back into the heart through the veins. He discovered that the valves in the larger veins directed the return flow of blood toward the heart, and that the valves of the heart kept the flow of blood going in one direction only – to the lungs from the right side and to the limbs from the left.

Harvey also applied practical hydraulic calculations to the volume of blood flow, incidentally becoming the first scientist to use mathematical techniques in biology. His calculations showed that the blood had to circulate continuously, and he concluded that the heart acted as a pump to keep it circulating. "So the heart is the beginning of life," Harvey wrote, ". . . and this familiar household-god doth his duty to the whole body, by nourishing, cherishing, and vegetating, being the foundation of life and the author of all."

When Harvey published his discovery in *De Motu Cordis* in 1628, a storm of abuse and argument broke over his head. He was in conflict with established medical thought based on centuries of authority. Although he ignored the controversy as much as he could by refusing to answer adversaries, he suffered professionally. "I have heard him say," wrote his friend the antiquary John Aubrey in *Brief Lives*, ". . . that he fell mightily in his practice, and that it was be-

Medicine

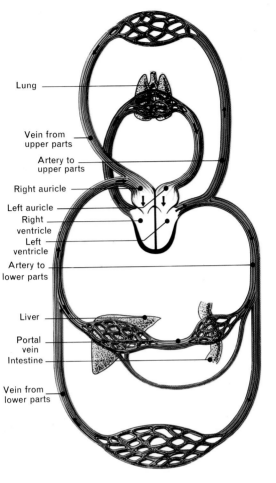

Lung

Vein from upper parts

Artery to upper parts

Right auricle

Left auricle

Right ventricle

Left ventricle

Artery to lower parts

Liver

Portal vein

Intestine

Vein from lower parts

Left: simplified diagram of Harvey's discovery that the same blood circulates throughout the body carrying oxygen and food. Blood flows from the heart through the arteries (red) to all parts of the body and returns through the veins (blue) to the heart. It then passes from the heart to the lungs and back again into the heart. Harvey guessed that there must be capillary blood vessels connecting the smallest veins to the smallest arteries.

Below left: this series of drawings shows how Harvey proved that blood circulates around the body in the same direction. By constricting the arm above the elbow the veins stand out and the valves are seen as swellings. Fingertip pressure applied to the vein causes that portion of the vein up to the next valve to be drained of blood.

Bottom right: 17th-century anatomy lecture. Harvey was appointed lecturer at the Royal College of Physicians in 1615.

lieved by the vulgar that he was crack-brained. . . . Many wrote against him." By contrast, Aubrey says that 30 years later Harvey's discovery was received in the world's universities "with much ado at last."

There was only one gap in Harvey's theory. It was the question of how the blood that left the heart by way of the arteries got into the veins to make the return journey. Harvey guessed that minute blood vessels must be present to provide the connection, but he was not able to prove it. In 1661, within four years of Harvey's death, the Italian biologist Marcello Malpighi detected these tiny vessels in the lung tissues of a frog, and the last piece of the jigsaw puzzle fell into place.

Other work that Harvey undertook involved charting the development of the chick embryo in the egg, which in 1651 led to a major book on reproduction in animals. However, it lacked the originality of thought that marked Harvey's previous work, and it is unfortunate that the bulk of his earlier research papers was destroyed by the parliamentary troops during the English Civil War.

During his last years, Harvey largely withdrew from active life, partly as a result of his being afflicted with gout and gallstones. He died of a stroke and was buried in a family vault at Hempstead Church in Essex. His personal library, which he gave to the College of Physicians, was lost in the Great Fire of London in 1666, but by then his fame as a scientist was secure in history.

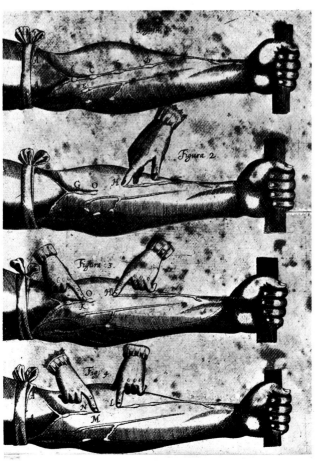

Evangelista Torricelli

1608-1647

The Italian physicist and mathematician Evangelista Torricelli invented the mercury barometer, long known as the torricellian tube. This instrument was not invented for any specific purpose, but was the by-product of an experiment mounted to test the truth of the Aristotelian doctrine that "nature abhors a vacuum."

Torricelli was born in Faenza, Italy, and gained his initial scientific inspiration from Galileo's writings. These led him to write *Concerning Movement* (1641). When this work was brought to Galileo's attention, he offered Torricelli a post as his secretary and assistant. Torricelli accepted, and became involved in Galileo's last scientific quest which concerned the Aristotelian assertion that no vacuum could exist in nature.

Doubts about the truth of this statement were raised by reports of miners working suction pumps to prevent flooding in mines. These pumps depended upon the vacuum principle to draw up the water. The miners found that it was not possible to lift water higher than 33 feet above its natural level, and that this limit was a constant – no matter what the size or power of the pump used. Perhaps, thought Galileo, there was some kind of limit to how much nature disliked a vacuum. It seems likely that, during this period with Galileo, Torricelli began to wonder what would happen if the same phenomenon was tested with a heavier and denser liquid such as mercury, which is 13.5 times denser than water.

Only three months after Torricelli arrived in Galileo's laboratory, the great scientist died with-out having tested his ideas on vacuums. In 1644, two years after Galileo's death, Torricelli carried out an experiment designed to prove or disprove Aristotle's statement. He filled a 4-foot-long glass tube with mercury, sealed it at one end, and inverted it in a dish of mercury. Some of the mercury flowed out of the tube, but in the space that remained a vacuum was created. This proved Aristotle right in the sense that vacuums must be created because there are no natural ones. But it also led to even more important discoveries.

Continuing the experiment over a period of time, Torricelli found that the height of the column of mercury in the glass tube was subject to fluctuations. He correctly concluded that this fluctuation was the result of variations in the pressure (the force exerted on a surface over a certain unit area) exerted by the atmosphere, and that it was therefore the atmospheric pressure that supported the column of mercury in the tube. On this basis he began the first accurate measurement of the pressure or weight of air, which scientists before him had always regarded as weightless. At the same time he had accident-

Below: Diorama (reconstruction with lighting effects) in the Science Museum, London, of Torricelli's famous experiment to test whether or not a vacuum could be created. He is seen inverting a tube of mercury, sealed at one end, into a dish of the same.

ally devised the first rudimentary version of the instrument, now called a barometer, for measuring atmospheric pressure.

Torricelli's main interest lay in the areas of pure mathematics and the motions of fluids and projectiles. His geometric theories contributed to the development of integral calculus. He also evolved Torricelli's theorem, an equation to calculate the rate at which a liquid will flow out of a tank under gravity through an opening a given distance below the liquid's surface.

The mercury barometer has gone through many refinements since Torricelli's simple experiment to create a vacuum. In the mid-17th century, the French scientist Blaise Pascal built mercury barometers to compare the atmospheric pressures in Paris and at the top of the Puy-de-Dôme mountain. The 17th-century German engineer and physicist Otto von Guericke made a barometer with a float that moved the arms of a small figure, so pointing the way for its use in meteorological forecasting. This instrument is nowadays a barograph. Today the mercury barometer is still the most sensitive instrument available for measuring atmospheric pressure.

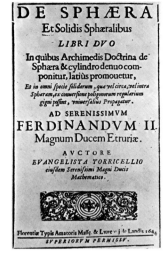

Above: the title page of Toricelli's book *De Sphaera* (1644).

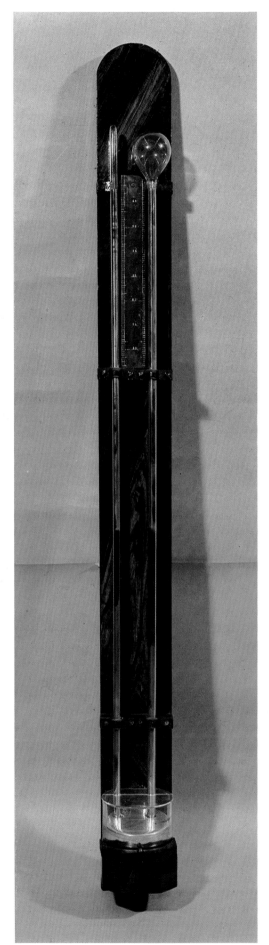

Above: barometers have come a long way since Torricelli inverted a tube of mercury. The top picture shows an open-scale barograph which records the changes in atmospheric pressure on a revolving cylinder by means of a stylus. The bottom picture is of an aneroid barometer which dispenses with the use of mercury. Instead, the air pressure acts on an elastic lid stretched over a container from which most of the air has been evacuated.

Right: a copy of Toricelli's original mercury barometer.

Robert Boyle
1627-1691

Both as a physicist and a chemist, Robert Boyle was a firm believer in the importance of experimental method in science. During his lifetime he was one of the leaders of a group of British scientists following the new experimental approach first advocated by the astronomer Galileo in the early 17th century. Using strict, common sense methods, Boyle made major discoveries about the physical characteristics of gases. These have been used ever since by scientists and engineers to investigate the behavior of gases under pressure. He went on to show how his discoveries suggested a rudimentary atomic theory of matter.

The 14th child of the Earl of Cork, Boyle was born in the family castle in Lismore, Ireland. Although an aristocrat by birth, Boyle was not so by inclination. Instead of a life of idle richness, he dedicated himself to his two great

passions of experimental science and Christianity. As a child, he traveled widely in Europe and spent several months in Italy. There, at the age of 11, he studied and was profoundly influenced by the writings of Galileo. In fact, they led Boyle to the rigorous experimental method that characterized all his work.

In the 1640s Boyle helped to found an association of scholars in Britain dedicated to furthering experimental science. Originally named The Invisible College, it received a Royal Charter in 1663 and was renamed the Royal Society. Its motto, "Nothing merely by authority," was suggested by Boyle and epitomizes a fundamental

Right: The Royal Society, of which Boyle was a founder member. The Royal Society was originally called the "invisible college," a group of men dedicated to the ideals of free discussion and experiment. Apart from scientists, its members included notable figures in other fields, such as the architect Sir Christopher Wren, and the diarist Samuel Pepys. The College received its Royal Charter in 1663 when it was renamed the Royal Society, and in 1680 Boyle was offered its presidency – an offer he refused. The Royal Society is still one of the important and influential scientific bodies in the world. It has moved three times since its foundation and is now housed in Carlton House Terrace, London.

Right: a reconstruction of the Boyle-Hooke vacuum pump, the design of which was based on vacuum apparatus at that time in use on the European continent. Boyle's pump was able to produce an almost complete vacuum. Apparatus could be placed in the globe-like receiver, which had a stopper that could be made airtight by means of cement. When the globe was evacuated, flames were extinguished and any animal placed inside perished.

commitment to experiment as the basis of scientific discovery.

Around 1659 Boyle became interested in the investigations being carried out in Europe on the nature of vacuum. He designed and constructed a new kind of air pump, using it to create a near vacuum so that he could study the phenomenon for himself. With the creation of a virtual vacuum, Boyle was able to prove Galileo's assertion that in the absence of air resistance, bodies

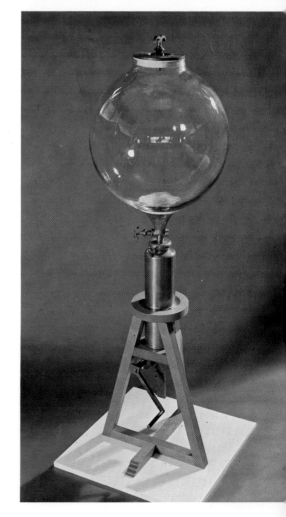

of different weights nonetheless fall at the same rate. He also discovered that sound is dependent on air for its transmission, and that even the loudest noise is barely transmitted in a near vacuum.

Boyle's experiments culminated in 1662 in the discovery of the now famous law which bears his name. This law describes a simple but important inverse relationship between the volume of a gas and its pressure. Boyle found that if a certain quantity of a gas was kept at a constant temperature and the pressure was doubled, its volume was halved. If the pressure was increased threefold, the volume was reduced to a third. Boyle's Law is still widely used today to calculate the way in which the pressure and volume of gases vary. Boyle took his discovery further. He concluded that since air could be compressed, it must be made up of tiny particles. Developing this idea, he rejected the belief that all matter consisted of combinations of the four elements – earth, air, fire, and water. He proposed instead that matter consisted of "primary particles" that could collect together to form "corpuscles." The first statement of an atomic theory since ancient times, Boyle's idea of primary particles forming corpuscles anticipated the modern chemist's view of atoms forming bonds with each other to produce molecules.

Right: Boyle's experiment to demonstrate the greatest height to which water could be raised by pumping. He used a long tin tube plated with iron as it was not possible to have that length of glass tubing constructed. By standing on a roof 30 feet above the reservoir of water and sucking up the water with a pump, Boyle showed that because of atmospheric pressure there was a maximum height beyond which water could not be drawn up.

Below: Boyle's illustration of his vaccum pump and other equipment he used for the formulation of his gas laws. The two-legged tubes, center right, are the pieces of apparatus he used to show that the pressure and volume of a gas are inversely related.

Boyle always kept up his charitable and religious works as well as his scientific efforts, but in later years turned increasingly to furthering his Christian ideals. In 1680 he was offered the presidency of the Royal Society but declined on obscure religious grounds. On his death he left money for a series of scholarly lectures dedicated to "proving the Christian Religion against notorious Infidels." These Boyle lectures still continue today, and despite history's view of Boyle as one of the greatest of British scientists, they remain true to Boyle's religious intentions.

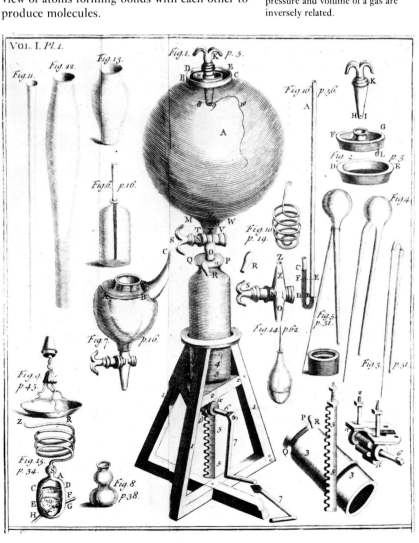

Christiaan Huygens
1629-1695

Astronomer, physicist, and mathematician, Christiaan Huygens made many major contributions to science. As an astronomer his main achievement was the construction of the first high-resolution telescope with which he made important discoveries among the planets and the stars. In physics he worked out a theory to describe the way force acts on a body moving in a circle. Using the theory, he designed a special kind of pendulum by which he made the first accurate clock. His mathematical abilities enabled him to formulate a way of representing light as a kind of wave, an idea that dominated science for 250 years and is still vital to our understanding of light.

Huygens was born in The Hague, Netherlands, and grew up in a wealthy and comfortable home where learning was a natural part of life. His father, a distinguished poet and diplomat, counted some of the most respected scholars in Europe among his friends. The young Huygens was especially influenced by René Descartes, a frequent visitor to the household, and his conversations with Descartes established his firm belief that science would some day explain all natural phenomena. His dedication to this idea remained unwavering throughout his life and in-

fluenced all his scientific work. A mechanistic view of nature particularly appealed to Huygens because of his own aptitude for practical skills, an aptitude that played an important part in many of his achievements.

Always attracted by observational astronomy, Huygens revolutionized the subject by discovering, in 1655, a new method for grinding lenses for telescopes. Using the technique, he constructed a telescope of extremely high resolving power. This enabled him to observe the heavens in hitherto unseen detail, and almost at once he discovered that Saturn was surrounded by a system of rings with at least one moon orbiting the planet. He was also the first to observe surface markings on Mars. Huygens' discoveries were not confined to the solar system, however. He also discovered the huge nebula in the constellation of Orion.

Huygens' practical mind prompted him to seek ways in which to express his scientific observations as quantities. In the course of his astronomical research, for example, he invented a special micrometer to measure angular separations between heavenly bodies. It was in the reckoning of time that he made his most remarkable breakthrough in measurement, inventing

Below: Huygens' aerial telescope. The telescopes of Huygens' time had very poor definition because of the quality of the lens. Magnification was improved by building longer tubes, but beyond a certain point these became unmanageable. Huygens used two short tubes, one at the objective, and one at the eyepiece. He also perfected a method of grinding lens to produce high definition. With this improved instrument he was able to see Saturn's disk.

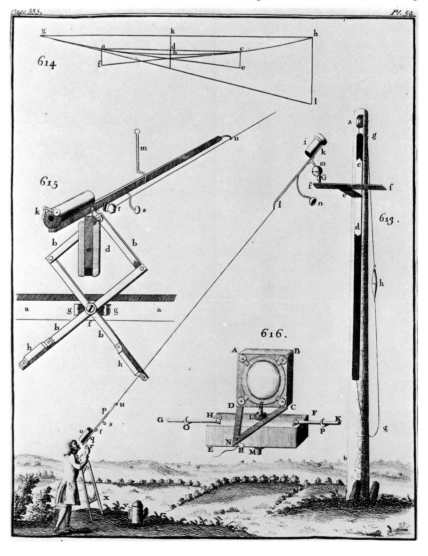

the first accurate mechanical clock. At the time, Huygens was looking for a way of putting to use a theory he had just worked out explaining the way in which forces act on a body moving in a circle. He applied it to the motion of a pendulum, the bob of which usually describes an arc of a circle. By modifying the arm of the pendulum,

Above: the house where Huygens lived as a small boy.

Above right: Dutch bracket clock designed to utilize Huygens' modifications of the pendulum.

Below: Huygens' drawings of Saturn and its rings.

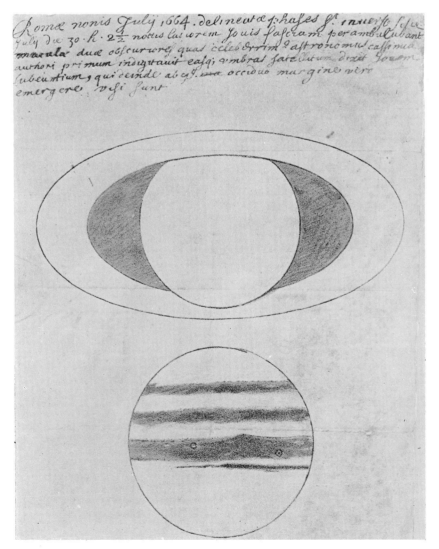

he discovered that it could be made to swing in a rhythm of exactly equal time intervals. The potential of such precise regularity in measuring time was immediately clear to Huygens and he designed a means of keeping the pendulum swinging while linking its movement to a clock. His invention heralded the age of the chronometer, providing science with the first accurate means of measuring time.

Troubled throughout his life by recurrent sickness, Huygens' last major contribution to science came shortly before a bout of illness that destroyed his health. By contrast with his previous work, his final achievement was of a more abstract and theoretical nature. Although an admirer of the ideas of the British physicist and mathematician Isaac Newton, he was doubtful about Newton's view that light consisted of a flux of innumerable luminous particles. Huygens worked out an alternative theory that showed how light could be thought of as a wave which pulsated longitudinally in the overall direction of its motion. In fact, although in later years it was shown that light in fact pulsates in a wave perpendicular to its overall motion, Huygens' work established the basic concept of light as a wave. It also provided the mathematical foundations of a theory that is still valid and still applied in physics today.

Antonie van Leeuwenhoek

1632-1723

Though not a trained scientist, Antonie van Leeuwenhoek was the first person to study protozoa and bacteria, and his work laid the foundations for the sciences of microbiology and bacteriology. He came to his scientific studies through his interest in lens grinding, by means of which he developed a microscope of high efficiency.

Leeuwenhoek was born in Delft, Netherlands, where he learned the drapery trade and owned his own shop for a time. In 1660 he was appointed city chamberlain, and the financial security of this position enabled him to devote himself more to his outside interests.

The microscope that Leeuwenhoek developed owed little to the compound microscope then widely available in Europe. The compound type, which has two or more lenses arranged in sequence to produce an enlarged image, was probably invented by the Dutch spectacle maker Zacharias Janssen in about 1590. Because of the difficulty of making sufficiently pure glass at that time, however, microscope lenses distorted the image. They also created fringes of color around the edges of the objects being observed.

To get around these problems, Leeuwenhoek concentrated on producing single lenses of high quality and short focal length, which he mounted singly between a pair of thin brass plates. So great was his skill that some of the lenses he made were as small as a pinhead. During the course of his lifetime he is known to have ground more than 400 lenses whose powers of magnification varied between 50 and 300 times. His method of lighting his minute samples under the microscope has remained something of a mystery. It was the one secret he was determined not to reveal, and he succeeded in taking it with him to the grave.

Leeuwenhoek has been criticized for a lack of formal scientific method in pursuing and recording his research. Nevertheless, his observations and deductions were accurate to a remarkable degree. He was working at a time when the theory of spontaneous generation (the origin of living things from nonliving matter) was a generally accepted scientific belief. It was thought, for example, that maggots were bred out of corrupt meat, that fleas were generated by sand or dust, and that weevils came from wheat stored in granaries. Leeuwenhoek showed for the first time that all these creatures reproduced themselves, being hatched from eggs fertilized by the male and laid by the female in the manner of other insects. He also discovered that aphids reproduce by parthenogenesis (without male fertilization of eggs), and further destroyed the theory of spontaneous generation by showing that eels did not spring out of dew or shellfish out of tidal mud.

His most far-reaching observations were in the areas of protozoology and bacteriology. On studying rainwater samples, he observed tiny organisms that he called "animalcules" (small animals). He concluded that these animalcules could be "carried over by the wind, along with bits of dust floating in the air." Leeuwenhoek later took samples from the human mouth and

Below: Leeuwenhoek's drawings of the parts of the adult flea. Also shown, in the top left hand corner, are the larval and pupal stages. Leeuwenhoek was a highly accomplished draughtsman and made extremely detailed and accurate drawings of his observations through the microscope.

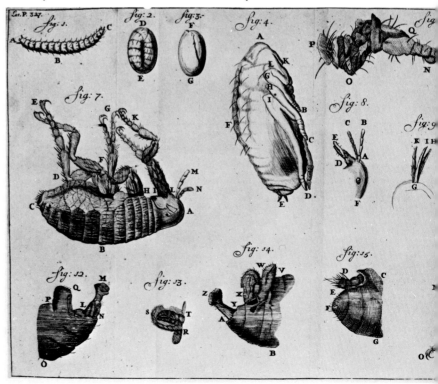

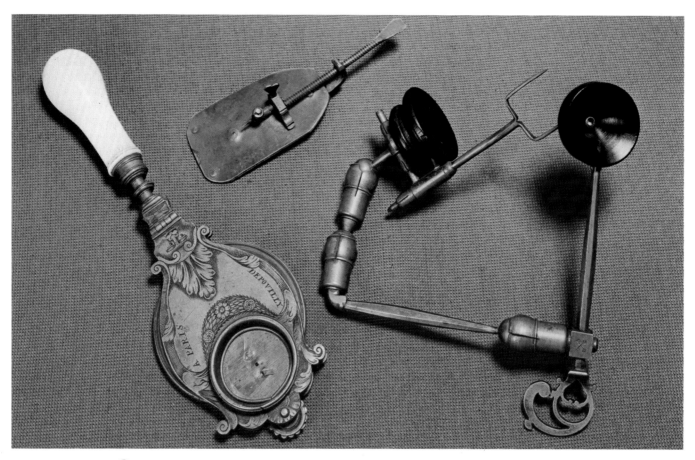

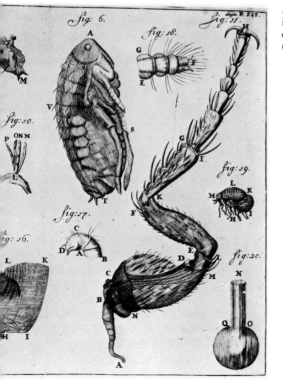

Above: some early microscopes, including a copy of Leeuwenhoek's original model which could magnify up to 270 times.

gut, and found similar animalcules there, including bacteria responsible for disease, though he did not see the link. The earliest representation of bacteria appears in a drawing by him which was published in the Royal Society's *Philosophical Transactions* in London in 1683.

The first accurate descriptions of red blood cells and of the spermatozoa of men, dogs, and insects are contained in the correspondence between Leeuwenhoek and the Royal Society from 1673 until his death. Most of his discoveries were made known to the scientific world through these informal letters, and 14 volumes of them were eventually published. He was elected a Fellow of the Royal Society in 1680, and in his will he bequeathed to the society a sample of his lenses.

The nature of his discoveries seemed sensational to his contemporaries, and if they were slow to accept that he had discredited the idea of spontaneous generation, his fame was quick to spread internationally. Many of the highly placed or famous visited him in Delft, among them Peter the Great of Russia on his diplomatic and fact-finding mission to western Europe in 1697.

Leeuwenhoek continued to work with his lenses almost to the end of his long life. His sense of enthusiasm and spirit of inquiry never seem to have left him, and it helped him open a window onto a previously unknown aspect of creation. This fulfilled his goal of showing the complexity of all creatures, even the humble flea that was "minute and despised."

Sir Isaac Newton

1642-1727

Universally recognized as one of the greatest scientists in history, Isaac Newton's remarkable achievements laid the foundations of modern science. His three laws of motion and his theory of gravitation are cornerstones of present-day physics. In the field of optics, Newton's speculations on the nature of light and his discovery that "white" light consists of a spectrum of colors, play an important part in modern optical science. In mathematics, he worked out infinitesimal calculus, one of the most powerful of mathematical techniques.

Born in Woolsthorpe, England, and educated at Cambridge University, Newton received his bachelor's degree in 1665. Within months of his graduation, Cambridge was closed as plague swept through the country. Fortunately, Newton escaped the disease, having gone to live with his mother in Woolsthorpe. The next year there was the most creative of his life.

Newton's first major achievement was to work out the three laws of motion which now form the basis of all mechanical science. The first law tells us that an object at rest will remain at rest and a steadily moving object will remain in steady motion unless an outside force acts on it. The second law sets out the definition of the concept of force as something that produces an acceleration in a body. The third law states that for every action there is an equal and opposite reaction, a principle that today finds a practical application in rocket and jet engines.

Shortly after his formulation of these laws, a commonplace event inspired Newton to one of his most profound insights. While sitting in an orchard he noticed an apple fall from a tree, and he found himself wondering why the apple had fallen. Was it perhaps attracted to the earth by some hitherto unsuspected force? Following this line of thought, he theorized that the force – if it existed – might well affect all bodies, even the planets. Using his idea and employing the newly discovered laws of motion, Newton worked out a theory which shows that all bodies in the universe are attracted to each other by a force varying inversely with the distance between them. He named the new force "gravity" and went on to demonstrate that the motions of the planets were natural consequences of an underlying law of gravitation. At a stroke, Newton eliminated the need to attribute the movement of planets to the actions of angels and demons and established that the laws governing events

Right: Newton's first reflecting telescope, built in 1688. Light is collected by the main mirror and directed onto a small flat mirror, about one inch in diameter and tilted at an angle of 45°. This turns the light through a right angle and brings it to the side of the telescope tube, where the image is magnified by an eyepiece. Many reflecting telescopes today operate on the same principle.

on earth also apply to the motions of heavenly bodies.

Newton's discoveries in 1665 were not confined to mechanical science. His studies of optics revealed for the first time that ordinary white light could be split by a glass prism into colors, which could then be recombined back into white light by a second prism. His work on the color spectrum later encouraged him to search for an alternative to the common refracting telescope of the time. In Newton's day, the glass lenses used in telescopes invariably produced an image partially obscured by a spectrum of colors due to imperfections in the glass. Newton decided to use mirrors instead of lenses, and after careful experimentation devised a system of curved mirrors that formed magnified images of distant objects. Newton's invention of the first reflecting telescope provided astronomers with an invalu-

able alternative to existing refracting telescopes.

Newton revealed little about his work in his home village. In fact, it was not until 1687 that he published the laws of motion and the theory of gravitation. They appeared in *Philosophiae Naturalis Principia Mathematica* (*Mathematical Principles of Natural Science*), a book today regarded as one of the greatest works of science ever written. The mathematical exposition accompanying the theories and proofs indicates

Below: Woolsthorpe Manor, Newton's house in Lincolnshire where he retired when the Great Plague hit Cambridge. It is here that Newton is said to have watched an apple fall to the ground and realized that there was a force which compelled it to do so.

Newton's personal relationships with other people were fraught with arguments and unhappiness, and he had few close friends. Of a neurotic and vindictive nature, he had at least two nervous breakdowns. One, caused by the death of his mother, was followed by a self-imposed isolation lasting over six years. Despite his egotism, Newton was always ready to acknowledge his debt to the chain of scientific progress started by Galileo. He once wrote: "If I

that in order to formulate his ideas about gravitation, Newton had found it necessary to invent a powerful new mathematical technique now known as infinitesimal calculus. This kind of calculus was in itself an immense contribution to science, since without it much of the progress of the last three centuries would have been virtually impossible. It is a measure of Newton's genius that in the context of his work, this calculus was no more than a tool necessary for formulating new scientific principles.

Maintaining his interest in the science of light, Newton in 1704 published his second great work, *Optics*. It set out the results of his prism experiments, discussing the nature of color and possible theories explaining the bending of light. He also suggested that light consisted of flux of luminous particles, a concept which is still accepted in our modern ideas of the nature of light.

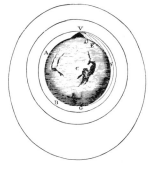

Above: Newton's diagram showing what happens to a projectile launched from a great height and at different speeds. The laws governing the speed of objects falling to the ground also determine the motion of the planets.

have seen further than other men, it is because I have stood on the shoulders of giants."

The greatness of Newton was recognized by his country, and by his fellow scientists at home and abroad in his own lifetime. Elected President of the Royal Society in 1703, he was reelected every year thereafter until his death. He was knighted in 1705. Shortly before he died, in a rare moment of personal insight, he summed up his life more eloquently than any biographer:

"I do not know what I may appear to the world but to myself I seem to have been merely a child playing on the seashore, diverting myself in now and then finding a pebble more smooth or a shell more beautiful than others, whilst before me the great ocean of Truth lay all undiscovered."

From a man acknowledged as one of the geniuses of physics, it was a true example of British understatement.

Thomas Newcomen

1663-1729

Thomas Newcomen, an English hardware store owner, was the first to build a steam engine that was practical both economically and in terms of its ability to perform a specific task. His accomplishment played a key role in developing the power source that drove the machines of the new industrial age for over a period of two centuries.

The theory of using steam as a power source can be traced back to the Greek scientist Hero of Alexandria, who some time during the 1st century AD described how the force of steam could open the temple doors. Hero also built a simple reactor turbine. This was a spherical device which, set on an axle above a boiler, whirled around rapidly when steam was expelled from two twisted nozzles. After Hero, no one had much success in harnessing steam power until 1698 when the English military engineer Thomas Savery patented his pump to raise water "by the impellant force of fire."

Savery built upon the research of the French physicist Denis Papin, who was the inventor of the pressure cooker and also the first man to

Below left: the Newcomen engine, consisting of a cylinder enclosing a piston which is attached to the right-hand side of the rocking crossbeam. At the other end of the beam is a pump rod connected to the plunger of a water pump. Steam entered the cylinder; when the weight of the pump mechanism raised the piston it was then cut off and cold water was injected into the cylinder, cooling the steam and creating a partial vacuum. The pressure of the atmosphere pushed the piston down and raised the pump plunger. Steam would then be readmitted to the cylinder, repeating the cycle.

envisage the possibility of drawing up water by condensing steam in an enclosed vessel above a suction pipe. Savery saw the possibility of using Papin's principle to pump water out of coal mines, which was an urgent problem in his day of increasingly extensive mining. The Savery pumping engine consisted of a boiler connected to a pair of vessels and a system of hand-operated cocks and automatic valves. It was capable of drawing water upward but had several short-comings that restricted its usefulness, one being the inability to lift a column of water any higher than 20 feet.

When Newcomen began to develop his engine, he did so because he had become interested in the possibility of using steam power to work the pumps that kept the tin mines in Cornwall from flooding. At the time, these pumps were operated by horses, and they represented a high cost factor in running the mines. Newcomen, like Savery, also turned to one of Papin's ideas: the notion for a piston device worked by the force of steam trapped in a cylinder. Papin did in fact produce a working model, but it did not seem at that stage to have proved effective enough for further development.

Newcomen began his experiments with the assistance of John Calley, a fellow tradesman and plumber, in his native town of Dartmouth. It took the two men 10 years to develop the world's first practical piston engine. The first one reported in use was constructed in Staffordshire in 1712. Because Savery's patent prevented Newcomen from taking out a patent of his own, he

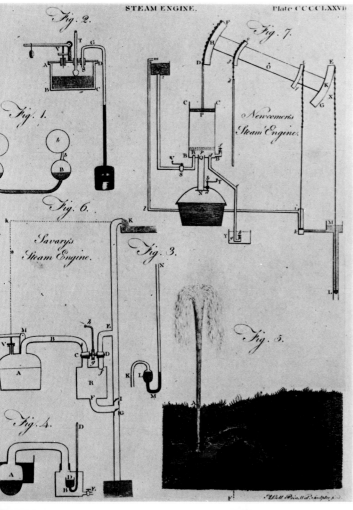

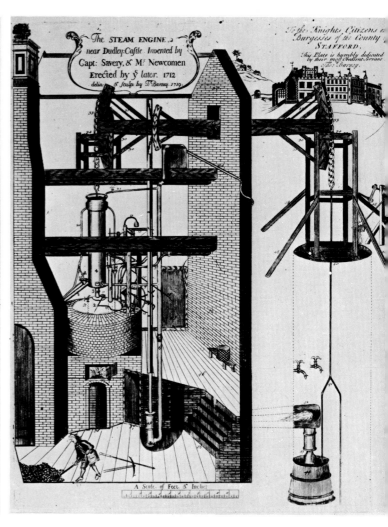

Above left: an engraving of the workings of the early steam engine, showing Savery's (left) and Newcomen's (right). Both engines used the principle of atmospheric pressure thrusting after the steam was condensed, rather than the force of expanding steam.

Above right: a Savery and Newcomen engine erected near Dudley Castle in 1782. Because their patents overlapped, the inventors went into business together manufacturing engines for use in mines.

Left: a painting of a coal mine, showing a Newcomen engine in use. Although Newcomen's engine was inefficient and wasteful of energy compared to later steam engines, it continued to be used in a modified form up to the 20th century.

entered into a partnership with the older man to manufacture and market the Newcomen mine engine.

The engine proved successful though the piston cycle had the disadvantage of wasting heat, and hence energy. Steam entered a vertical cylinder mounted above the boiler, pushing up the rod that rocked the heavy crossbeam. This in turn worked the pump. Water admitted into the cylinder then condensed the steam, so that a partial vacuum was created and the atmospheric pressure forced the piston down again as the water drained away.

This meant in effect that the cylinder had to be cooled all the way down and heated all the way up again in the course of each completed movement of the piston. Air and other vapors also tended to accumulate in the cylinder, sometimes bringing the engine to a standstill. Nonetheless, Newcomen engines were put to extensive use in Europe as well as throughout Britain. The incorporation of automatic valves gradually improved performance, and some Newcomen engines, with modifications, still survived as working machines into the early 20th century.

Newcomen's engine made a huge contribution to steam power. However, it was James Watt in the later part of the 18th century who ultimately opened it to wide application.

Abraham Darby

c1678-1717

A cornerstone of the Industrial Revolution was laid in Coalbrookdale, England, in 1709 when the iron manufacturer Abraham Darby perfected his technique for using coke to smelt iron ore. Until then, the process of smelting iron ore to produce cast or pig iron relied on charcoal to fire the furnaces. This placed a strict limit on the amount of iron that could be produced at any one firing because charcoal broke down quickly under the intense heat necessary for smelting. In addition, the forests of England were already seriously depleted by the demands of the iron trade for wood to make charcoal. From the beginning of the 17th century there were attempts to substitute coke, a product of coal, for charcoal in the production of pig iron. The presence of sulfur in coke, however, tended to make the iron too brittle for practical industrial use.

In 1708, when Abraham Darby set up the Bristol Iron Company in Coalbrookdale in the Severn valley, he chose his location carefully. The district was known to have supplies of coal with a relatively low sulfur content, as well as deposits of iron ore close at hand. The use of coke enabled Darby to build taller and hotter blast furnaces than had been possible before, and he soon began to turn out iron of a high quality. It was also competitive in price with the charcoal-fired product.

At first Darby's iron was used mainly to cast cooking utensils and iron fittings because the forge owners and blacksmiths regarded charcoal-smelted iron as the only kind suitable for their trade. A breakthrough occurred when Thomas Newcomen came to Darby to have the cylinders cast for his steam engine.

Through a combination of reticence and business acumen, the Darby family managed to keep its industrial secrets largely within its own sphere for three generations. When Abraham Darby II succeeded his father in the business, he continued to supply the cylinders for the Newcomen engine. The association of the Coalbrookdale factory with steam power continued to the end of the 18th century, when the plant built the first high-pressure boiler for Richard Trevithick.

Meanwhile the industrial uses to which iron could be put continued to expand. In 1779 Abraham Darby III, grandson of the founder,

Below left: a plaque erected at Ironbridge to commemorate Abraham Darby's building of the bridge. As Quakers Darby, his son, and grandson refused to have their portraits painted.

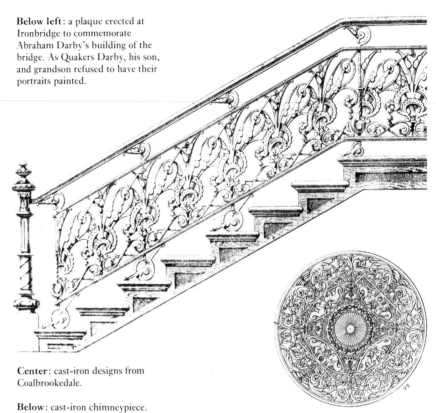

Center: cast-iron designs from Coalbrookedale.

Below: cast-iron chimneypiece.

THIS IRON BRIDGE WAS ERECTED IN 1779 AND WAS THEN THE FIRST CAST-IRON BRIDGE. IT WAS MADE AT COALBROOKDALE BY ABRAHAM DARBY TO THE DESIGNS OF THOMAS FARNOLLS PRITCHARD OF SHREWSBURY. IT WAS CLOSED TO VEHICULAR TRAFFIC IN 1934 AND IN THE SAME YEAR WAS SCHEDULED AS AN ANCIENT MONUMENT. THE PROPRIETORS OF THE IRON BRIDGE HANDED IT OVER TO THE SALOP COUNTY COUNCIL ON 12TH OCTOBER 1950.

and John Wilkinson built the world's first iron bridge. It spanned the gorge of the Severn river around the corner from Coalbrookdale where the river traffic came up from Bristol. The bridge's roadway was supported by an arch of five iron ribs, each of which had been cast in two halves. Although Darby and Wilkinson intended the bridge to be an advertisement for another use of iron it immediately became regarded as a great wonder, and today is one of Britain's national monuments.

The enterprise of the Darbys in Coalbrookdale made the whole area into what has been called the "cradle of the Industrial Revolution." Intense and more varied manufacturing industries, the building of more furnaces and kilns, the mining of iron ore and coal, and the digging of a network of canals, made it a leading center of industry. The stench of sulfur hanging over the entire valley and the noise were endless – one factory even took the name of Bedlam. In the course of time, however, the mines became worked out and many of the factories moved elsewhere. The canals, forges, and factories fell into disuse, decay, and silence.

Above: the Iron Bridge over the Severn River built by Abraham Darby II, near Coalbrookdale, Telford.

Right: the old Blast Furnace at Coalbrookdale, Telford, used by Abraham Darby I to produce his high-quality cast iron. It was taken over by Abraham Darby I on 1709 and adapted to use coke instead of charcoal. Water from a pool was led over a waterwheel which powered the bellows. The furnace was charged from above with alternate layers of coke and iron ore, with limestone added as a flux to remove the impurities. The air blast enabled the furnace to heat up to a temperature high enough for smelting.

Darby and Wilkinson's bridge, however, continued to carry traffic as late as the 1950s when the foundations became unsafe. After that it was fully restored, and today is the centerpiece of the open-air Ironbridge Gorge Museum, which preserves a great range of industrial relics in their original setting. In 1978 this museum was elected as European Museum of the Year by an international jury.

Benjamin Franklin

1706-1790

Benjamin Franklin's life is the classic story of a self-made man achieving wealth and fame through determination and intelligence. In addition to his many business ventures and his key role in the turbulent events of the American Revolution, Franklin maintained a constant interest in science. He made important contributions to an understanding of electricity, showing that lightning is caused by natural static electricity in the atmosphere. His inventions include the lightning conductor, a household stove used for heating and still manufactured today, and bifocal lenses for spectacles.

Born in Boston of a soap and candlemaker who believed in big families, Franklin was one of 17 children. He left school at 10 and became ap-

prenticed to a printer. Quickly mastering the trade, he soon became a successful publisher of almanacs, newspapers, and journals, some of which he wrote. He maintained a lively correspondence with scholars, politicians, and writers throughout the American colonies and Europe, rapidly becoming a well-known international figure. A man of great integrity and liberal ideals, he founded many charitable institutions. Looking upon politics as a means of improving social conditions, he soon became deeply involved as a politician, first in Philadelphia, Pennsylvania where he had moved, and then internationally. As an envoy to Britain he played an important role in the politics of the Revolution, spending

much time in Europe canvassing support for the American cause. This naturally did not endear him to the British, but he won admirers and friends everywhere else. In post-Revolutionary France especially he was received with acclaim as the embodiment of the ideals of liberty and equality in society.

His travels and correspondence brought Franklin into contact with some of the best scientific minds in Europe, and his own imagination was caught by the popular studies of electricity that had become fashionable in the 1740s. Although Franklin had never had any scientific training at all, he started experiments to investigate electrical phenomena with such skill and insight that he was soon recognized and respected as a scientist. In one of the earliest formulations of a theory to explain electricity, Franklin proposed that it was an "element diffused among and attracted by other matter." With remarkable foresight, he identified two kinds of electricity. One kind was possessed by a body "undercharged with electrical fire" and the other by a body "overcharged." Replacing Franklin's words "electrical fire" with the modern word "electrons," we have an accurate description of the present theory of positive and negative charge. Franklin went on to propose that when an "overcharged" body approached an "undercharged" one, an electrical spark leaped between them, equalizing the amount of "electrical fire" in the two bodies. Today we recognize this as the first accurate description of the mechanism by which

Below: an illustration from "*Maritime Observations*," one of the volumes of Franklin's *Complete Works*. This was a compendium of Franklin's large range of scientific interests, published posthumously in 1806. Franklin traveled widely and consequently spent much time at sea. During these periods he made a detailed study of sea currents, weather conditions, and the mechanics and behavior of vessels in water.

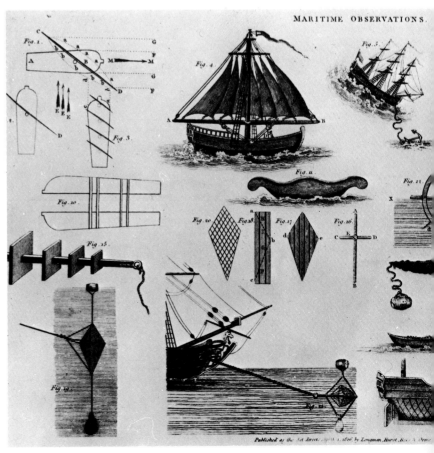

Electricity

THE BLESSINGS OF PEACE.

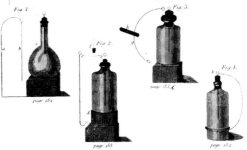

electrons pass between bodies of differing electrical potential, a process fundamental to electrical science.

Franklin's best-known discovery, that lightning is caused by discharges of static electricity in the atmosphere, was made by means of a spectacular and dangerous experiment. He fixed a

Above left: *The Blessings of Peace*, a contemporary cartoon showing England's sun setting to the right and United States starting to the left. Franklin, the figure marked "1" on the extreme left of the picture, was one of the founding fathers of the United States and helped draft the Constitution of the United States of America.

Above right: Franklin, experimenting with a metal key attached to a kite by a silk thread, discovers that lightning is caused by a discharge of static electricity.

Right: apparatus used for Franklin's experiments with static electricity or "electrical fire" as he called it.

metal key to a kite by a conducting thread of silk and flew it in a lightning storm. It showed that electrical sparks would leap from the metal. In effect Franklin was diverting some of the deadly electrical energy of the lightning through the key and into the earth – and he was lucky to escape with his life. In the months following publication of his findings, several scientists in Europe were electrocuted trying to repeat the experiment. The immediate practical result of Franklin's work was a design for the first lightning conductor. He suggested that pointed metal rods be placed on the roofs of houses and connected to the earth to divert lightning away from the structure of the houses, dissipating the energy harmlessly in the ground. An instant success, Franklin's lightning conductors are still widely used today.

In later years, despite his failing health, Franklin continued to maintain his interest in science and politics. It was only three years before his death that he helped to draft one of history's major documents, the Constitution of the United States of America. Franklin was mourned by his countrymen as a founding father of the nation and by Republican France as an outstanding scientist and statesman who symbolized the spirit of freedom and enlightenment.

Linnaeus
1707-1778

Linnaeus is the Latinized name of Carl Linné, the Swedish botanist and explorer who developed the method of classifying plants and animals still used in a modified form today. The system, known as "binomial nomenclature," gives to each plant or animal two names. The first indicates the *genus* or related group to which it belongs, while the second gives the *species* or its specific name within the genus. Thus the orange tree is *Citrus aurantium*, and the lemon tree is *Citrus limon*. Linnaeus himself recognized that the system was artificial and had its shortcomings, but it had one overriding virtue. It enabled students of botany and zoology to place plants and animals quickly and efficiently within a universally recognized category, at a time when scientific exploration throughout the world was at its height.

Linnaeus' father was a clergyman who kept a small botanical garden where the young Carolus earned the nickname of "the little botanist." At the University of Uppsala he studied medicine, but in 1730 he was appointed lecturer in botany. In 1732 he went on an expedition to Lappland for the Swedish Academy of Sciences. In 1735 he

Below left: a Wedgwood portrait medallion of Linnaeus.

Below right: Linnaeus' house in the grounds of the Old Botanical Gardens, Uppsala. The garden was built up by Linnaeus' father, an amateur gardener. One of its features was a raised circular bed designed to imitate a dining-room table, with flowers for dishes, and shrubs planted around it to represent the guests.

published his *Systema Naturae* and two years later *Genera Plantarum*. The first of these he showed to the Dutch naturalist Jan Frederik Gronovius who was so impressed that he had it published at his own expense. Linnaeus' *Species Plantarum*, published in 1753, is now regarded as the starting point for the systematic classification of flowering plants and ferns.

The binomial system of classification was not new, a Swiss botanist and anatomist having originally developed it in the 17th century. But it was Linnaeus who improved on the system and brought it into universal use at a time when such a system was badly needed. His basic approach to plants was to divide them into the flowering and nonflowering, subdividing the latter according to characteristics such as stamens and pistils. His whole system pays little attention to internal anatomy, which becomes particularly apparent when dealing with the animal kingdom where, for example, he placed an extraordinary variety of animals under the single group *Amphibia*.

In 1742 Linnaeus was appointed to a medical professorship at Uppsala, but a year later became professor of botany. The publication of *Species Plantarum* brought him international recognition. In 1755 the king of Spain invited him to settle there with a generous salary, but

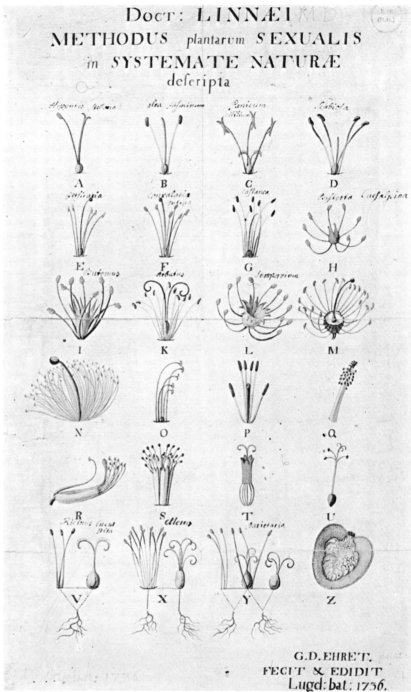

Above left: frontispiece of *Hortus Cliffortianus*, a description of the plants and herbarium of George Clifford, who was Linnaeus' patron and benefactor in Holland. The book was the first of its kind in that the plates illustrated the dissections of flowers and their mode of growth in addition to actual portraits. It marked the start of classical botanical illustrations.

Above right: Linnaeus' system of classifying plants.

Linnaeus refused. In 1761 he became known as Carl von Linné, a title of nobility.

Linnaeus had a cheerful and humorous nature which greatly appealed to his students. He used to take about 150 of them on Saturday expeditions into the Swedish countryside, and if anyone discovered a rare specimen, he announced it with a trumpet blast. After his death an English admirer, Sir J. E. Smith, bought up Linnaeus' complete collection of manuscripts, his herbarium, and his collections of insects and shells, and shipped them to London. The Swedish king was furious and sent a frigate to recover these treasures for Sweden. The English ship got away, however, and the complete collection is now preserved in the Linnean Society in London.

James Hargreaves

c1722-1778

James Hargreaves was the English weaver who started the move toward full mechanization of spinning by inventing the spinning jenny. It may have been so called from the word "gin," the local dialect for engine.

In Europe, the weighted distaff and the spindle were the basic tools used to spin wool into yarn from prehistoric times until the Middle Ages, when the spinning wheel was introduced from India. The spinning wheel took the process of making a yarn a stage further in mechanization, speeding it up and producing a more uniform thread. Until the 18th century and the advance of the Industrial Revolution, cloth was manufactured largely by means of what was known as the "putting out" system. A cloth merchant would provide raw wool, cotton, or flax to spinners and weavers. They would process it into bales of cloth and return it for marketing to the merchant, who would pay them at the current piecework rate. It was a cottage industry for the most part, and the system fed a traditional rural craft in the counties of Yorkshire and Lancashire in the north of England.

Hargreaves, who lived in the village of Stand-hill, Lancashire, was one of these cottage weavers who owned his own spinning wheel and loom. A period of employment in a local calico printing works may have added to his technical expertise. In any case, the idea for the spinning jenny reputedly came about in 1764. His daughter Jenny tipped over a spinning wheel by accident and the spindle continued to revolve. It made Hargreaves think that a whole line of spindles could be worked off one wheel.

He built his model of the jenny using eight spindles onto which the thread was spun from a corresponding set of rovings. All eight threads could then be spun by the muscle power of one person. Its limitation was that the thread it produced was coarse and lacked a certain degree of strength, making it suitable only for the filling or weft, the threads woven across the warp. Nevertheless, Hargreaves had produced his invention at the right time – in the formative days of the factory mill system. It came about 30 years after John Kay's flying shuttle, which speeded the loom operation by mechanizing the passing back and forth of the shuttle through the warp. Use of the shuttle in turn created an urgent demand for thread in cloth manufacture, and the jenny helped answer this need.

Hargreaves began to build his machines for more general sale, improving them to the point where each one could work up to 30 spindles. Before long he ran into trouble with the hand spinners, who detected a threat to their livelihood and independence. A group broke into his house in 1768 and smashed all the machines they found there. Hargreaves thereupon moved south to Nottingham, setting up in partnership with a businessman. They constructed a small mill which used jennies to spin hosiers' yarn. Un-

Above: the Spinning jenny, one of the machines that launched the Industrial Revolution and the modern industrial age. The strand of fiber in the jenny passed through a clasp to a spindle on which it was wound. The jenny stretched and twisted the fiber into a thread.

Right: Samuel Crompton's spinning mule in operation. This was an improved adaptation of Hargreaves' jenny, producing extremely fine yarn of a much higher tensile strength.

Above: the spinning of linen in an Irish cottage. Before the introduction of Hargreaves' jenny and Crompton's mule, spinning and weaving were rural cottage industries.

fortunately, Hargreaves delayed in applying for a patent for his spinning jenny, and did not get it patented until 1770. His resulting fortune was thus less than it might have been.

The spinning mule, invented in 1779 by Samuel Crompton, was an adaptation of Hargreaves' jenny. Crompton improved on it so that the machine he built produced yarn of a tensile quality matching that produced by hand spinning. The mule also applied some of the principles of the water frame developed by Richard Arkwright some 10 years earlier. One operator on the mule could spin up to 1000 threads.

Although there were 360 mills using Crompton's invention by 1812, he profited little. He had received only £60 because manufacturers neglected to honor guarantees given to him. A parliamentary grant of £5000 went some way toward compensating him, though he sank most of it in business ventures that failed. Crompton's position in history was secure, however. Along with Hargreaves and Arkwright, he was one of the three figures whose ingenuity made possible the vast cloth-making industry of northern England in the 19th century.

John Hunter

1728-1793

The British 18th-century surgeon John Hunter was the founder of experimental medicine in Britain, and the physician who elevated surgery to a professional status. Through his teaching he was responsible for the establishment of surgery as an accepted branch of medical study throughout Europe and North America.

John Hunter, the son of a Scottish gentleman and the youngest in a family of 10 children, seems to have received little formal education. He did, however, have a persistent curiosity about the natural world, spending a large amount of time out in the countryside. In 1748 he left his native Scotland and came on horseback to London to assist his brother William Hunter, already a well-known obstetrician and medical lecturer.

His job was to prepare dissected anatomical specimens for William's lectures and he soon began to show a remarkable, delicate skill with a scalpel. Within a year he was sufficiently expert to perform surgical operations himself and superintend William's pupils.

Medical teaching was not very well organized at the time and surgeons gained their experience through practice or apprenticeship. There was still a deep social division between the physician, usually a university graduate, and the surgeon, who was regarded as a craftsman.

John Hunter spent 11 years learning anatomy from his brother. He obtained his cadavers by striking bargains with the "resurrection men" who stole newly buried corpses for doctors and medical students to practice on. By 1754 he was assisting his brother in lecturing, and in 1758

became a teaching surgeon himself at St George's Hospital. He also performed original research during this period. His discoveries included the descent of the testes in the fetus during the eighth month of pregnancy, the functions of the lymph glands, and the structure and function of the placenta.

In 1760, Hunter entered the army as a surgeon. He joined a military expedition to Belle Isle, off the French west coast, and served in Portugal during the closing phases of the Seven Years War. His experience made him an expert in gunshot wounds, and he showed that amputations regarded as standard procedure could often be avoided if wounds were properly treated. As a result he produced his most important book, *A Treatise on the Blood, Inflammation, and Gunshot Wounds* (1794), which revolutionized the surgeon's attitude to his patient.

During his period abroad he began to collect specimens for what would ultimately become a unique museum of assorted anatomical, biological, and pathological specimens, comprising over 13,500 exhibits. After his return to London in 1763, he went into private practice and started his own anatomy school. In 1776 he was appointed physician extraordinary to King George III, and in 1790 surgeon general and

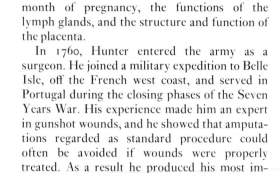

Below: *The Dissecting Room* by Thomas Rowlandson. This illustration shows John Hunter learning anatomy from his brother William, then an obstetrician and medical lecturer in London. William is the figure standing up above the rest, with John on his right-hand side.

Left: a portrait of John Hunter painted by Robert Home, his brother-in-law.

inspector general of hospitals. Meanwhile he pursued his passion for collecting by negotiating with various menageries, including the Tower of London, for the bodies of any animals that happened to die. It was said that as soon as he had accumulated enough money in surgeon's fees, he would go out to buy another specimen for his museum.

Hunter's passion for collection went to the extent of his pursuing the Irish giant Charles Byrne, later known as O'Brien, for his skeleton after death. O'Brien, in life about 8 feet tall, had requested that his body be sealed in a lead coffin and buried in the Thames estuary to outwit the surgeon. Nevertheless Hunter managed to bribe the undertaker to steal the corpse. According to one story, he had it taken to his house in his own carriage – naked, so that he could not be accused of stealing the graveclothes. The whole transaction cost him £500.

The scope of Hunter's researches and speculations was immensely wide. He was the first to suggest that blood is a living substance like other components of the body. He speculated that the embryo in its development may go through various phases resembling more primitive creatures. He pioneered the art of tissue grafting in a series of experiments which included transplanting a human tooth onto a cock's comb. He founded what is still the standard treatment for a

Below left: the leg spur of a fighting cock grafted on its head.

Below: surgery in the 18th century, before the introduction of anesthetics. This scene depicts an amputation operation at St Thomas' Hospital, London.

Below right: Hunter's signature from his letter to Edward Jenner, a former pupil of his and discoverer of vaccination.

torn tendon by experimenting on himself when he ruptured a tendon in his leg after dancing.

His powers of concentration were phenomenal, and a contemporary described him as "standing for hours, motionless as a statue, except that, with a pair of forceps in each hand, he was picking asunder the connecting fibres of some structure he was studying." His professional attitude was summed up by his own observation: "We should always make a material distinction between an operation which is to cure a person of a disease which will probably kill of itself. . . . and an operation which is performed to cure an inconvenience only, and the danger is not in the disease but the method of cure."

After his own death, John Hunter's collection was preserved intact, as he had wished, and eventually formed the basis of the Hunterian Museum in London, under the custodianship of the Royal College of Surgeons. Although a German bombing raid in 1941 inflicted serious damage, the collection has been painstakingly restored according to its founder's intentions, and the museum was reopened in 1963.

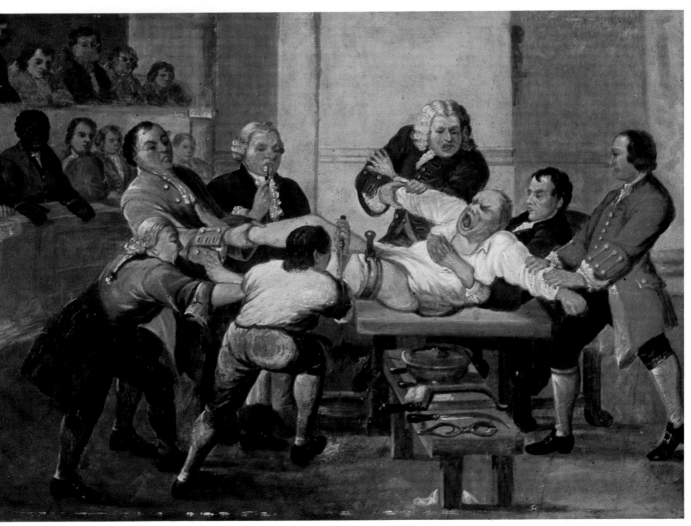

Henry Cavendish

1731-1810

Eccentric and absent-minded, Henry Cavendish was nonetheless one of the most outstanding British scientists since the time of Isaac Newton. A man of few words, Cavendish rarely had visitors. Few of his contemporaries suspected the true importance of his research and only later generations were able to appreciate his achievements from the notebooks and papers he had left. Cavendish's best-known discovery was the composition of water as a compound of hydrogen and oxygen. However, he also made major contributions to the understanding of electricity. In one of the most painstaking and delicate experiments in history he succeeded in directly measuring the force of gravitational attraction between two small bodies.

Cavendish was born in Nice, France, the son of an English lord. He studied science at Cambridge University but, with typical lack of concern for conventional formalities, left before taking his degree. A recluse throughout his life, Cavendish disliked the company of men and was terrified of women. His female servants were forbidden to cross his path and he communicated with them by handwritten notes. His sole pleasure in life was science and he devoted himself to research with an enthusiasm bordering on obsession. So single-minded and dedicated was he that in his electrical research he measured electric currents by giving himself shocks, gauging the amount of current by their severity. He cared nothing for public recognition, hardly bothering to report even the most important of his findings. He lived and worked alone, and when eventually his health failed, he even insisted on dying alone.

Cavendish's earliest research established many of the modern concepts now vital to the theory of electricity. He defined the nature of the electrical force of attraction or repulsion existing between two charged bodies, a force which plays a key role in electrostatics. He also introduced the concept of electrical potential, today popularly called voltage, and studied the way certain materials can store electrical charge. Anticipating one of the most fundamental laws of electricity, he showed that the amount of current flowing can vary between different conductors depending on the material from which they are made. Some years later, Cavendish's observations were formalized as Ohm's Law, a principle that relates current and voltage to a property of conductors known as electrical resistance.

For a great part of his life Cavendish studied gases, and was the first to recognize hydrogen as a gas separate from air. He investigated its properties, showing it to be the lightest of the known gases. He also discovered that oxygen and hydrogen when mixed burn explosively to produce small quantities of water. By this experiment he established that water, the most abundant compound on earth, consisted of oxy-

Below left: the only known portrait of the eccentric and reticent Henry Cavendish.

Below right: late 18th century burning glasses for igniting chemicals. The single lens belonged to Joseph Priestley, and the double lens to Cavendish.

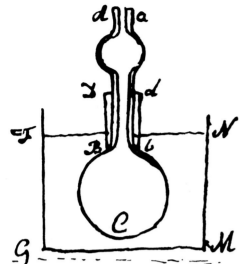

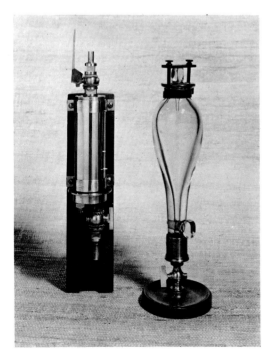

gen and hydrogen combined chemically.

Cavendish's most exacting research took place when he was nearly 70. His goal was to make the first direct measurement of the force of gravitational attraction between two small bodies. Because the force acting between bodies of comparatively small masses is itself very small, Cavendish had to devise an extremely sensitive and delicate experiment. He suspended a light metal rod by a fine wire attached to its center. At each end of the rod, he fixed a small lead ball. He then brought two large lead balls close to the smaller ones but on opposite sides of the rod. The gravitational attraction between the large and small balls had the effect of turning the rod; by measuring the resulting twist in the wire, Cavendish was able to work out the strength of the gravitational force. With this information and Newton's equation of the law of gravitation devised a century before it was possible to calculate the mass and density of the earth itself. Cavendish's results showed that the mass of the earth was around 6.5 million billion tons, a density about 5.5 times that of water. Remarkably, these figures are close to the best estimates made by modern scientific methods.

Above: Cavendish's notes on the electrical properties of heated glass. He found that the passage of electricity through the glass increased with rising temperature.

Left: Cavendish's spark eudiometers for measuring the composition of gases. The instrument on the left is made of brass and the one on the right of glass.

Right: Cavendish's experiments on "factitious" air – gases released from substances by the chemical action of acids or alkalis, or putrefaction. Fig. 1: collecting the gas. Fig. 2: transferring it to a storage vessel.

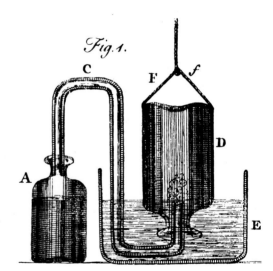

Fig.1.

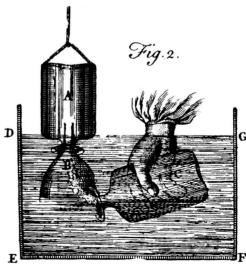

Fig.2.

Sir Richard Arkwright

1732-1792

Richard Arkwright was the inventor of the water frame, one of the most important innovations in the mechanization of yarn spinning. He virtually founded the power loom industry as well as the mass production factory system that hastened the Industrial Revolution.

Born in Preston, England, the youngest in a family of 13 children, Arkwright began his career traveling throughout the country as a barber and wigmaker. He perfected a method of dyeing human hair, buying the hair from servant girls whenever he could. It is said that he took an interest in spinning machinery when wigs started to go out of fashion.

The foundation for the mechanization of spinning and weaving had been laid several years before with John Kay's flying shuttle and James Hargreaves' spinning jenny. Arkwright wanted to take the process a stage further by dispensing with manual operation and applying an independent power source. After employing a clockmaker to help him with the technical details, he brought his ideas to fruition and took out his

first patent for a spinning frame in 1769.

Discouraged by riots against the new machinery in his native country of Lancashire, he joined with a consortium of businessmen to open factories in the city of Nottingham and in Cromford, Derbyshire. At first he tried to operate his frame by using horses as the power source, but he soon turned to water power. Thereafter known as the water frame, the machine's main innovation was the use of rollers to draw out the rovings, or loose threads, as they were fed onto the spindles. The water frame was the model for all later spinning machinery. It overcame the deficiences of Hargreaves' jenny in that it was able

to produce a yarn strong enough to use for the warp threads on a loom.

Arkwright was one of the earliest industrialists, pioneering the factory system on a large scale and helping to lay the basis for the irresistible advance of industrialization during the late 18th and early 19th centuries. In time, his factories had machines capable of carrying out each stage of thread manufacture from the carding and combing of the raw materials to the finished yarn.

In 1773, when coarse woolens were no longer in fashion, he started to produce calico, a plain white serviceable cotton cloth for which there was an immediate demand. By then raw cotton was available in bulk from the slave plantations of the West Indies and the American South. Within a few years, the weaving of cotton had become northern England's most important industry. By the 1840s, some 50 years after Arkwright's death, it was responsible for 40 percent of Britain's exports.

Arkwright has been strongly criticized for taking over and exploiting the ideas of others. The fact remains that he made the ideas work commercially and created the setting in which they could do so. His first patent of 1769 was followed by others, but they were all constantly in-

Below: Arkwright's spinning frame, the first spinning machine to use an independent power source. Arkwright eventually decided that water power was the most suitable means of running the machine and thereafter it became known as the water frame. The machine was one of the foundations of the modern textile industry.

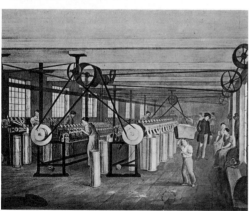

A cotton factory during the Industrial Revolution

Above: cleaning the fibers by passing them through a machine with revolving spikes, a process known as willowing.

Center left: bobbin and drawing frames.

Below left: printing the finished cloth.

fringed and contested. When he went to court to establish his rights, the judgment went against him and his patents were rescinded in 1785. By then, however, he was firmly established and wealthy enough for the decision to do his fortunes little damage.

While he was directly responsible for establishing the factory system that undermined and eventually destroyed the craft trade of the cottage spinners and weavers, Arkwright is usually regarded as an enlightened employer. At one time he had as many as 5000 employees in his factories, and he was conscious of the need to provide decent conditions of work and housing for them. In return he demanded the highest standards of efficiency and cleanliness in his establishments, and expected others to be as diligent as he was himself. Ever conscious of his lack of formal learning, he often worked long into the night to educate himself.

In 1785 Arkwright was the first to drive a cotton mill by means of the new steam engine perfected by James Watt. It was installed in his factory in Nottingham. In 1786 he was knighted and in the following year was appointed High Sheriff of Derbyshire. His wealth enabled him to build Willersley Castle as a home and to put up the money to rebuild Cromford church, where he was buried on his death.

Joseph Priestley
1733 - 1804

During his lifetime, Joseph Priestley was known as a religious dissident and political free thinker. Today his fame rests on his scientific achievements, in particular his research on gases and the discovery of oxygen.

Ironically, science was a subject in which Priestley received no formal education. His childhood in the small Yorkshire village of his birth was overshadowed by ill-health. Despite missing several years of formal schooling, however, he excelled as a student of languages, theology, logic, and political philosophy. He developed a fiercely independent turn of mind which, in later years, led him to challenge openly many established religious and political beliefs. He was

a radical, believing passionately in the freedom of the individual and the need to question orthodox conventions in society before conforming to them.

In 1766 Priestley met Benjamin Franklin, then an envoy to England from the American colonies and a respected scientist. It was a turning point in Priestley's life. An admirer of Franklin's political views, Priestley became increasingly interested by his scientific research. Soon he was hard at work on studies of electricity, and in the next year published a definitive history of electrical science which included a summary of its state and developments at the time, and possible future lines of research. The book established Priestley's reputation; but while scientists in

Europe and North America were admiring this work, Priestley's interests were already turning to chemistry and, in particular, the study of gases.

One of Priestley's earliest discoveries was of a gas we now call carbon dioxide. The discovery owed itself to the fact that Priestley was then living next door to a brewery. He had observed that during the fermentation of grain a gas of unusual properties was produced. He discovered that it was heavier than air and could put out flames, properties that later made the gas invaluable in the first fire extinguishers. He also noted that when dissolved in water, it produced a refreshing drink and he suggested that the "soda water" so produced could be used on sea voyages to envigorate jaded palates. Priestley could not anticipate that his discovery would one day form the basis of a worldwide soft-drink industry.

As Priestley's interest in gases grew, he invented effective and original new techniques for studying them. Previously chemists had isolated gases in glass tubes sealed by water. This only worked satisfactorily if the gas was insoluble in water. Priestley was the first to collect gases over mercury, which enabled him to identify water-

Below: a collection of Priestley's equipment, including his "fine burning glass" for concentrating the sun's rays on chemicals. Much of the equipment which Priestley invented is still used in chemical laboratories today.

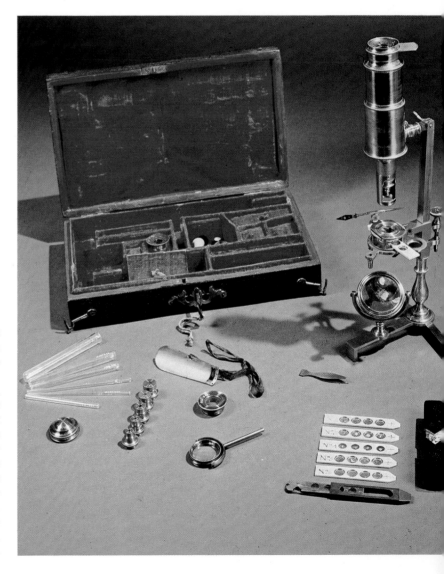

64

soluble gases such as ammonia and hydrogen chloride.

In 1774 Priestley made his most famous discovery, isolating the gas we know today as oxygen. It came through his use of mercury in his work, which led him to examine some of mercury's own properties. It had been known for some years that if mercury was heated it formed a tough, solid substance today called mercuric oxide. Priestley heated the oxide and found that metallic mercury was formed once again and, in

SEDITION, LEVELLING, and PLUNDERING;

Or, The PRETENDED FRIENDS of the People in Council.

Left: Priestley with Tom Paine, author of *The Rights of Man*. Priestley's radical beliefs made him very unpopular, as the title of this cartoon: *Sedition, Levelling and Plundering: Or the Pretended Friends of the People in Council*, shows.

Below: an engraving of Priestley's laboratory, showing his apparatus for experiments on gas. Priestley devised the pneumatic trough, the mercury trough, and gas jars to replace bladders for collecting gases.

addition, a gas with some startling properties was released. The contemporary theory of burning held that materials burned by releasing a substance called "phlogiston" into the air. Priestley called the new gas "dephlogisticated air" because it seemed able to draw out the phlogiston in a substance. In other words, materials burned readily in the gas. Even a splint of wood, barely glowing, would burst into flames in its presence. Priestley also studied some of the physiological effects of this newly discovered gas, finding that it had a pleasant and invigorating effect when inhaled. He even speculated that oxygen sniffing might one day become a popular vice in fashionable circles.

Priestley's scientific discoveries brought him international fame but his liberal politics and radical religious beliefs made him unpopular in the conservative English society of his day. On one occasion his home was burned down by a mob angered by his sympathies for the French and American revolutions. Finally he left England for the newly independent United States where he was warmly received and spent the last years of his life widely admired as a man of enlightenment.

James Watt
1736-1819

Of all the inventors whose genius made the Industrial Revolution possible, James Watt was among the foremost. He took the rudimentary engine of Thomas Newcomen and transformed it into a reliable and efficient power generator capable of meeting the needs of a whole range of industrial processes. In effect he made available to the Industrial Revolution the source of power that was essential to its technical progress.

Watt was born in Greenock on the Clyde river in Scotland, the son of a shipowner and shipbuilder. Because he was a delicate child, he was educated at home by his mother although later on

he attended the local school. It was in his father's workshops that he garnered his early technical knowledge. In 1755 he went to London to learn to be an instrument maker, and after about two years returned to Scotland to open an instrument-making and repair shop within the University of Glasgow.

In 1764 a client brought into Watt's repair shop a working model of one of the steam engines designed by Newcomen earlier in the century. Watt realized that its considerable wastage of energy would be reduced and its efficiency improved if a way could be found of avoiding the alternate heating and cooling of the piston cylinder. His solution to the problem was arrived at a year later: to attach to the cylinder a separate but connected chamber in which the condensation of the steam could take place.

He built his first demonstration model and patented it in 1769 as a "new method of lessening the consumption of steam and fuel in fire engines." His innovation in fact achieved a saving of 75 percent in fuel costs, and it attracted the attention of Matthew Boulton, a Birmingham engineer and industrialist. Boulton acquired an interest in Watt's patent in order to explore its application in his own factory.

Watt was well aware of his own shortcomings

Below right: diagram of Watt's patent rotative steam engine. The engine improved upon Newcomen's design by channeling the steam from the cylinder into a separate cold container – the condenser. This dispensed with the need for alternate heating and cooling of the engine, which meant that it was far more efficient. Watt's engine also used the expanding force of steam to push a piston up and down; movable rods linked the pistons to wheels and turned them around. Present-day steam engines stem directly from Watt's design.

as a businessman, being diffident in character and disliking the inevitable rough-and-tumble involved in any commercial venture. In 1775 he accepted a partnership with Boulton, whose Soho factory in Birmingham was already widely known for the quality of its metal products, from coins and buttons to Sheffield plate and silver. The additional business of manufacturing Watt's steam engines was soon under way and showed every sign of fast expansion. One engine was installed in Staffordshire as a colliery pump and another was set up to work the blast furnaces in the iron foundry of John Wilkinson in Shropshire. Wilkinson, who was the inventor of the iron barge, contributed one vital detail to the success of Watt's invention when he developed a boring machine able to drill cylinders to an unprecedented standard of accuracy.

Shortly after the Boulton and Watt partnership was set up, they took into their employment a young engineer named William Murdock. With Murdock's help they filled contracts to install pumping engines in the tin and copper mines of Cornwall, replacing many of the old Newcomen engines that had by then been in use for 50 years. Watt constantly worked at improvements and modifications of his engine. When Boulton foresaw industry's need for a piston shaft that would rotate rather than be confined to a straight up-and-down motion, Watt produced one. Next he developed the double-action piston in which steam is alternately fed into each end of the cylinder, increasing its working capacity and rendering obsolete the earlier model that relied on atmospheric pressure to return the piston to

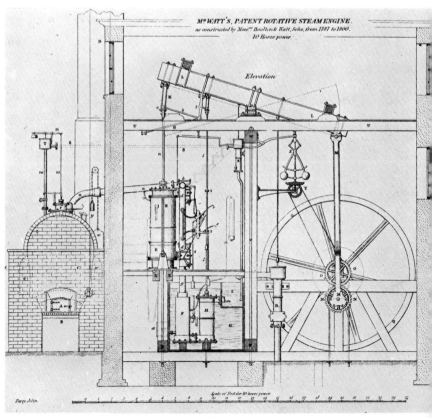

Mr WATT'S, PATENT ROTATIVE STEAM ENGINE,
as constructed by Mess.rs Boulton & Watt, Soho, from 1787 to 1800.
10 Horse power.

Elevation

Engineering

Above: Watt's garret workshop.

Left: the Boulton and Watt lap engine (1788). It drove the lapping machines in Boulton's factory.

its starting position. He also devised a centrifugal governor that automatically controlled the speed of the engine by regulating the steam flow, and invented a pressure gauge.

The versatility and efficiency of Watt's engines meant that they found a multitude of applications as the industrialization of Britain's economy gathered momentum. By the closing years of the 18th century, almost 500 engines had been built, making Watt a man of considerable personal wealth. Recognition came as well, and in 1785 he and Boulton were elected Fellows of the Royal Society. Five years later Watt retired from business but remained busy and active, receiving many honors, although his natural modesty led him to decline the offer of a baronetcy.

Watt seemed most content while exercising his inventive skills in his garret workshop. His other inventions included the office copying press, which used a special ink to record copies of correspondence and invoices in a ledger, and a device to reproduce sculptured busts. After his death a statue was erected in his honor in Westminster Abbey. His body was buried beside that of his former partner, Matthew Boulton, in Handsworth Church near Birmingham. The unit of electric power, the *watt*, was named as a tribute to him.

Sir Frederick William Herschel

1738-1822

Widely regarded as the greatest observer in the history of astronomy, William Herschel is best known today as the discoverer of the planet Uranus. In addition, however, he made the earliest systematic study of the stars, building up the first accurate picture of the shape of the galaxy and suggesting that distant nebulae were in fact other galaxies independent of our own.

In his childhood, Herschel was encouraged in his musical abilities by his father, an army musician, who arranged for him to join a military band in his hometown of Hanover, Germany, when he was 15. The youth hated the army, however, and with Germany and France at war and enemy troops already occupying Hanover, he decided to quit the service and make a new life. Leaving Germany for the peace of England, he found work as a musician first in Halifax and later in the resort town of Bath. Although an outstanding instrumentalist, music was never Herschel's greatest interest. Once established in his new home he turned again to astronomy, his favorite childhood hobby. In 1772 he was joined in Bath by his sister Caroline who shared his interest in astronomy and worked closely with him.

The only telescopes the Herschels could afford to rent were small and of such poor quality that they barely provided a clear image. The two decided to build their own telescope and Herschel worked out a design similar to that invented by Isaac Newton about a century before. Using mirrors, and lenses painstakingly ground in his spare time, Herschel gradually pieced together his first telescope and was ready to start serious work.

Right: Herschel's 7-foot telescope. This was a reflector type first used by Sir Isaac Newton in about 1688. It was so-called because the image was formed by reflection of light from a speculum (concave metal mirror) as opposed to a refractor telescope in which the image was produced by the refraction of light through a lens. Herschel initially used refractors, but their high cost and unwieldiness caused him to start constructing reflectors. The metal mirrors could be cast by an amateur, unlike the lens of the refractor which had to be bought ready-ground.

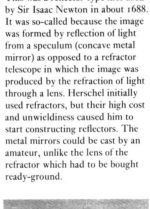

Above: Herschel's 40-foot telescope. It was made of a sheet-iron tube with a 4-foot speculum at the lower end. It was mounted in a wooden frame and could be directed toward any part of the sky by a system of pulleys. The cost of building it was financed by King George III.

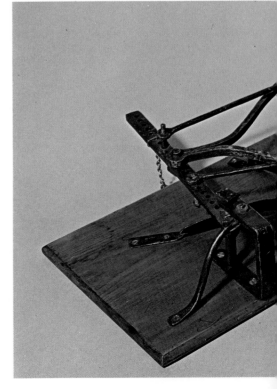

Astronomy

His plan was simple. He reasoned that the most likely way of making important discoveries was to systematically observe every heavenly body, noting interesting features and relative positions. In 1781 Herschel's dogged approach was rewarded by his discovery of the planet Uranus. At first Herschel thought the greenish disk moving steadily across the field of stars somewhere beyond the orbit of Saturn was merely a new comet. But after enough observations had been made,

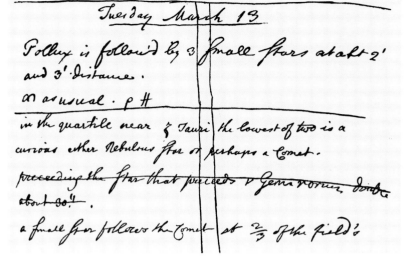

Above: Herschel's notes on the discovery of Uranus in March 1781. Herschel was undertaking a"survey of the sky" when he found an object which showed a disk, and therefore could not be a star. Initially he thought it to be a comet but realized later that its orbit was too circular.

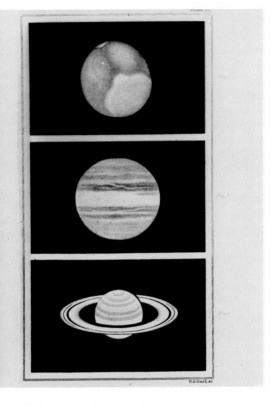

Above left: Herschel's drawings of Saturn (top) and Jupiter. The small circle in the bottom picture is Jupiter's third moon and the black dot is its shadow. His estimate of Saturn's rotation about its axis is about two minutes out from present estimates of 10 hours, 14 minutes.

Left: Herschel's polishing machine for polishing the speculums or mirrors of his telescopes. The mirrors were made from a mixture of metals including copper, silver, and tin. The casting was done in molds of earth baked with charcoal. The casts were then finished off with grooved brass tools. Herschel then polished the mirrors using metal bases covered with pitch. The process was not standardized as each mirror had to be made to the specific requirements of the individual telescope. Herschel acquired a reputation as a skilled instrument maker and established a successful business manufacturing telescopes for other astronomers.

Herschel realized that the orbit was too circular to belong to a comet. To his delight he concluded that he had in fact discovered a new planet, the first to be discovered since ancient times. Herschel tried to name it *Georgium Sidus* (*George's Star*) after King George III, the then reigning monarch, but astronomers insisted that the tradition of using mythological names be continued; Uranus was the name finally chosen.

The discovery of Uranus made Herschel famous throughout Europe. He was able to give up music and devote himself to a career in astronomy, which proved to be brilliant. His most important discoveries in the years that followed were based on observations of stars. For example, by inventing a technique for counting stars called "star gauging," he was able to calculate distributions of stars and from that work out a description of the galaxy's shape. He deduced that it was the shape of a double convex lens, like two plates clapped together by their rims. Although it is now known that the true shape is more complicated than this, Herschel's theory was a major step forward.

In sticking to his original plan of a systematic review of the heavens, Herschel and his sister spotted over 1500 new nebulae. These cloudlike bodies had long puzzled astronomers. Some appeared to be made up of stars; others were indistinct, like wisps of gas. In one of his most inspired suggestions, Herschel speculated that these mysterious objects might well be independent galaxies, far beyond the limits of our own Milky Way. Herschel's was the first intimation of the true immensity of the universe, and although his idea was not confirmed until more than a century later, it was enough to extend the borders of astronomy from interstellar into intergalactic space.

Herschel was knighted in 1816, a high state honor in a career already marked by virtually every scientific honor that could be bestowed. Through his son John, Herschel's name continued to be associated with major new astronomical discoveries of the next generation.

Montgolfier Brothers

Joseph-Michel 1740-1810
Jacques-Etienne 1745-1799

Man's centuries-long dream of taking to the air was fulfilled on November 21, 1783 when two passengers made the first free flight in the man-carrying hot-air balloon invented by the Montgolfier brothers.

Joseph and Jacques Montgolfier were paper manufacturers whose family business could be traced back to the time when a crusader ancestor was held in Damascus as a slave. On his release in 1386 he brought back the secret of paper making to France. As well as their interest in the business, the two brothers also took a lively and informed interest in scientific matters. Both were responsible for innovations in the paper-making process, and Joseph was familiar with the researches into gases that Joseph Priestley was currently undertaking in England. It was this, rather than the apocryphal story of Joseph seeing his wife's chemise rise in the hot air when put to dry before the fire, that was responsible for starting his interest in balloons.

Joseph was also aware of the discovery of hydrogen by Henry Cavendish in 1766, and of

the implication that a gas which is 14 times as light as air could be made to lift a load if trapped inside an airtight membrane. The production of hydrogen in any quantity was still a cumbersome business and it was difficult to find a suitable leak-proof material. The brothers therefore concentrated on the hot-air principle without knowing that the basis for this is that hot air decreases in density as it expands, and so in effect becomes lighter. They seem to have thought that gases in the smoke from a fire caused the balloon to rise, and hence that damp straw and other similar smoke-producing materials would make the best sort of fire for their purposes.

To begin with, they built small models of silk. As their models became larger, they experimented with layers of paper pasted on linen.

Their first public release of a balloon took place at Annonay on June 5, 1783, when, to the amazement of everyone who saw it, a globe 30 feet in diameter filled with hot air from a fire under its launching platform and rose majestically to about 6000 feet. It descended half a mile away after 10 minutes. When the news reached Paris, the Academy of Sciences at once invited the Montgolfiers to the capital to set up a demonstration. The next launching was arranged for

Below left: the two Montgolfier brothers, Jacques (left) and Joseph.

Right: the ascent of the Montgolfier brothers' balloon on November 21, 1783.

Below: the descent of the balloon. It caught fire, burst, and landed in the village of Gonesse. The alarmed inhabitants, thinking that it was the skin of a monstrous animal, attacked it with pitchforks and stones.

GENERAL ALARM of the INHABITANTS of GONESSE, occasioned by

September 19, to take place at Versailles in the presence of Louis XVI and Marie Antoinette.

It was thought that unimaginable dangers awaited anyone who ventured into the upper air, and the idea of traveling in a balloon was regarded as utter folly. The passengers on this spectacular occasion were to be a duck, a cock, and a sheep, and their balloon was royally decorated in blue and gold. It had a diameter of 41 feet, and reached an altitude of 1700 feet before it began to descend gently into the forest about two miles away. The animal passengers were unharmed, except that the sheep had kicked one of the cock's wings and damaged it slightly.

The way was now clear for a man to make the ascent, but the king insisted that any passengers should be criminals whose lives were expendable. Fortunately, the king's historian, a young scientist named Jean-Françoise Pilâtre de Rozier, was able to overcome the royal forebodings, and was the passenger in a test series of tethered ascents that preceded the first free flight by man. By now the fire was slung under the neck of the balloon in an iron basket, and could be controlled and replenished by the balloonists. The diameter had grown to almost 50 feet.

For the historic first flight, Pilâtre de Rozier was joined by the Marquis d'Arlandes, who left a memoir of his experience:

"Astonished, I cast a glance toward the river. I perceived the confluence of the Oise. And naming the principle bends of the river by the places nearest them, I cried, 'Passy, St Germain, St Denis, Sèvres.'

'If you look at the river in that fashion you will be likely to bathe in it soon,' cried Pilâtre de Rozier. 'Some fire, my dear friend, some fire!'"

In 25 minutes they traveled just over five miles, and the trip was one of the wonders of the age. Later, the hot-air balloon was improved, but the future of ballooning lay with the hydrogen balloon, invented and perfected in all its essentials by Jacques-Alexandre-César Charles in 1783. It was far easier to control its height above the ground with its use of ballast and a gas-release valve.

Charles was in fact only 10 days behind the Montgolfiers in making his first ascent on December 1 from the Tuileries. He completed a two-hour inaugural flight, and the history of the hydrogen balloon led forward over the following century to navigable balloons and airships. Hot-air balloons were revived as a sport in the 1960s, made practicable by easily transportable propane-gas cylinders.

Right: the future of ballooning lay with the hydrogen balloon, invented by Jacques Charles. His inaugral flight on December 1, 1783, covered 27 miles in two hours.

Below: an unsuccessful attempt at ballooning, Lille, March 26, 1785, by Jean-Pierre-Francois Blanchard and John Jeffries, a Boston physician. Blanchard and Jeffries were the first aeronauts to cross the English Channel and to carry international airmail.

ᴀLL of the AIR BALLOON of Mʳ MONTGOLFIER.

Antoine-Laurent Lavoisier

1743-1794

The French chemist Antoine-Laurent Lavoisier is known today as the father of modern chemistry. His strict approach to research helped to overthrow many of the old notions that had for centuries encumbered chemistry. During his brief lifetime, Lavoisier established among chemists the vital importance of accurate measurement, formulated an important new theory of combustion, and drew up the first rational system of chemical nomenclature.

Parisian-born Lavoisier achieved early public acclaim. When only 23 he was awarded a gold medal by the Academy for work on a new improved system of street lighting, and was subsequently elected one of their youngest ever members. Although he came from a wealthy home, Lavoisier needed to earn a living to support his all-important scientific research and in 1768 he took an administrative appointment in the Ferme générale, a private agency engaged by the French government to collect taxes. Lavoisier could not foresee the terrible consequences that would follow his association with this much-hated organization. Neither could he realize his mistake when he opposed the election to the Academy of Sciences of Jean-Paul Marat, a self-styled scientist who later was a leading figure of the French Revolution. In any event, Lavoisier was too absorbed in his scientific work to speculate about the future.

This scientist's research was always characterized by an insistence on careful measurement. He was convinced that accurate observation was the only reliable basis for scientific progress. The success of his approach resulted in his formulation of a new theory explaining the process of burning. For many years scientists had believed that all materials contained a mysterious substance called "phlogiston." The process of burning was thought to occur when a material was made to release some of its phlogiston. Lavoisier thought the idea was unsound and decided to test it. In characteristically systematic fashion he devised a series of experiments to investigate com-

Right: Lavoisier's calorimeter, a piece of equipment for measuring the amount of heat produced by combustion.

Below right: the great burning-lens constructed for the French Academy of Sciences, and used by Lavoisier for igniting chemicals. The large lens (A) was made of two pieces of the glass and the hollow interior filled with spirit of wine. The movable lens (B) further concentrated the rays of the sun on the substance to be ignited. The operator had to protect his eyes by wearing dark glasses.

bustion. By heating different materials in air and carefully weighing them before and after heating, he found that far from losing an ingredient, the materials often appeared to absorb something from the atmosphere. Lavoisier, having heard of the discovery in England of a gas that encouraged the process of burning, 'showed that the unknown quantity absorbed from the atmosphere during burning was in fact the newly identified gas. He called the gas "oxygen" and defined burning as the uniting of a substance with oxygen, a definition still used today. Lavoisier's results disposed of the idea of phlogiston and

provided chemists with the first tested and proven theory of burning.

Lavoisier was not only concerned about discovering underlying concepts in chemistry, but was also convinced of the need to create a technical language capable of expressing those concepts clearly and accurately. Unsatisfied with the fanciful names many chemical substances were given, he published a treatise called *Methods of Chemical Nomenclature* in 1787. In this book he laid down principles by which chemical compounds could be named by referring to the elements of which they were composed. Lavoisier's approach was so logical and straightforward that it was quickly accepted and remains the basis of naming chemicals to the present day.

In 1789 Lavoisier published his research on combustion and his ideas about scientific method in the first truly modern chemistry textbook, a work he modestly entitled *An Elementary Treatise on Chemistry*. It was his last major contribution to science. Within two years France was plunged into a bloody revolution, and Lavoisier's earlier association with the Ferme générale hung over his head like a death sentence. Throughout the country monarchist tax collectors were hunted down and killed, and eventually Lavoisier was also arrested by the revolutionary militia. The arresting officer silenced the pleas of Lavoisier's colleagues who insisted that his scientific achieve-

Left: apparatus used by Lavoisier to investigate combustion. He heated mercury in the retort for several days until its whole surface was covered with red particles. During this process the air in the bell jar diminished in volume. Lavoisier found that the air remaining in the bell jar could no longer support either life or combustion. He then heated the red powder which was converted back into mercury. Moreover, the powder gave off a gas equal in volume to that used up in heating the mercury. The gas, identical to the one discovered by Joseph Priestley, enabled substances to burn vigorously and could be inhaled. Lavoisier called it oxygen. As a result he formulated the oxidation theory which replaced the notion that burning involved the dissociation of a substance from phlogiston.

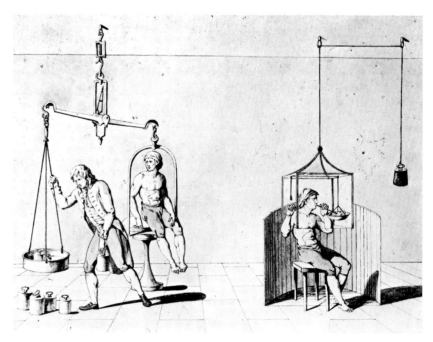

Above: heliogramme drawing of Lavoisier's experiments on respiration. He showed that the body takes in oxygen and converts it into "fixed air" in the lungs.

ments should excuse him with the pronouncement: "The Republic has no need of scientists."

In 1794 Lavoisier was brought before a tribunal. With Jean-Paul Marat as one of his judges, he stood no chance of acquittal. Still smarting from his humiliating rejection from the Academy of Sciences, Marat demanded Lavoisier's death. On the same afternoon of his trial, Lavoisier was guillotined and his body flung into an unmarked grave.

Count Alessandro Volta

1745-1827

The Italian physicist Alessandro Volta gained world-wide fame with important contributions to the studies of static and current electricity. He invented both a new technique for storing static electrical charge and the first device for generating electric current, today called an electric battery.

Volta was born in Como, Italy. While working as a physics teacher in the village high school he began his first serious research into electricity. Eighteenth-century science was dominated by research into electricity, a natural phenomenon of often dramatic and mysterious effects. In 1775 he invented the electrophorus, a device for storing electric charge. It soon superceded the Leyden jar as the most commonly used storage system of the time. The electrophorus consisted of a metal plate coated with a substance called ebonite, and a second metal plate with an insulated handle. Ebonite had been known for many years as a material that acquired a negative charge when rubbed with a dry cloth. Holding the metal plate by the insulated handle above the charged ebonite, Volta found that the negative charge in the ebonite attracted a positive charge in the lower surface of the plate, leaving a negative charge in its upper surface. Volta also found that this negative charge could be drained away by means of a metal wire connecting the upper surface of the plate to the earth, leaving an overall positive charge on the plate. By repeating the process, he built up large quantities of positive

charge. The electrophorus quickly became the standard means of storing charge and is today the basis of the condenser, the device used for storing electricity in electric circuits.

His invention of the electrophorus made Volta famous. In 1794 he made his best-known discovery, a device for producing a steady current known today as the electric battery. For some years, Volta had followed with interest the experiments of the Italian anatomist Luigi Galvani. Galvani had found that if two different metals were brought into contact in the presence of animal muscle, an electric current was generated. Galvani mistakenly believed that the current was a kind of "animal electricity" contained in the tissue and released by the touch of the metals. Volta believed it should be possible to generate the current without the tissue, and began a series of experiments to test his hypothesis.

By 1800 Volta had succeeded. He discovered that if two dissimilar metals were brought into contact in a salt solution, a current would be produced. This led to the first working battery, which used several bowls of a salt solution connected by a wire cord that dipped from one bowl into the next. One end of the cord was copper and the other zinc and when they made contact, a current was produced. Volta refined

Below: page from the letter sent by Volta to announce the invention of his new apparatus, the battery. Volta discovered that a current could be produced by a series of bowls of salt solution connected by wires with one end made of zinc and the other of copper. He then modified this to make a less cumbersome source of generating an electric current – the battery or voltaic pile – by using columns of dissimilar metal plates separated by cardboard disks.

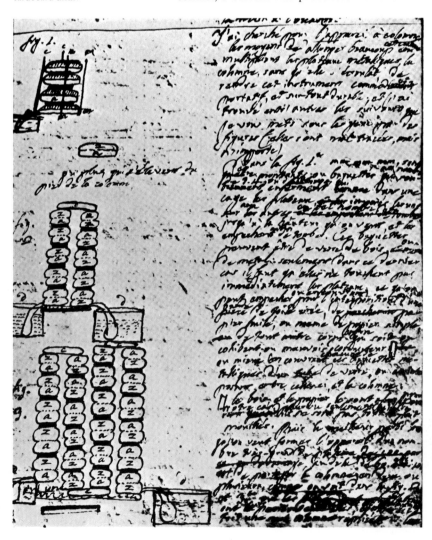

Electricity

Above: fresco showing Volta demonstrating his voltaic pile and electrophorus. Seated on the left is Napoleon, who rewarded Volta's work by presenting him with the Legion of Honor and making him a count.

Left: Volta's electrophorus.

Below: Volta's electrophorus could be used to store large quantities of positive charge. When placed on a negatively charged surface, the upper surface of the electrophorus plate acquired a negative charge, the lower surface a positive charge. The negative charge could then be drained away by a wire.

this somewhat unwieldy apparatus by using a series of small round plates of copper and zinc. A pair of dissimilar metal plates were kept apart by a cardboard disk soaked in salt water. Volta's columns of metal and cardboard disks later became known as "voltaic piles" and were, in fact, the first convenient source of electric current. They led directly to the discovery of the phenomenon of electrolysis and enabled rapid progress to be made in the study of the laws governing electricity.

Volta received innumerable awards for his work. Napoleon showed his esteem by making him a count and conferring the Legion of Honor on him. Perhaps Volta's most enduring reward was to have the unit of electrical potential, the *volt*, named after him, which made his name a household word in succeeding generations.

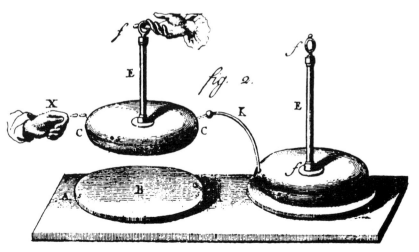

Joseph Bramah

1748-1814

One of the contributions to the health and well-being of millions of town and city dwellers was that of the cabinet-maker and engineer Joseph Bramah. It was he who invented the first practicable lavatory system to be extensively marketed – the "Bramah" water closet.

It is obvious today that the water closet, combined with efficient sewage systems to prevent the seepage of effluent into natural water supplies, is essential to health in urban communities – and indeed, to people everywhere. For centuries European townspeople accepted open drains and gutters choked with filth as inevitable features of their lives. The more prosperous citizens took care to live close to or over running water, or had cesspits built under their houses. These had to be emptied at regular intervals by the night-soil men.

The valve closet was originally invented in the 16th century by Sir John Harrington. Queen Elizabeth I had one of his closets installed at Richmond Palace, but the idea failed to catch on at that stage. Almost 200 years later, in 1775, Alexander Cumming, a London watchmaker, took out a patent for his own version of a water closet.

Cumming's valve closet worked with a handle which, when pulled upward, operated a flush of water from a cistern and simultaneously slid back the valve at the bottom of the basin so that its contents were washed into the waste pipe. A

syphon trap (or S-bend) then closed off the domestic pipe from the main sewer. Cumming's valve system was not satisfactory, as Joseph Bramah discovered when, as a young cabinet-maker, he had the job of installing the new valve closet in people's homes. In 1778 he patented his own model, which featured a vastly improved valve system that worked with a hinged flap.

The "Bramah" was the leader in the field of sanitary plumbing for the best part of a century, though it could not always keep out the foul gases that built up in poorly ventilated sewers and cesspits. Sewage engineering was not really taken seriously until the middle of the 19th century when the first virulent cholera epidemics swept through the growing cities of Europe and arrived in London in 1894, making the efficient rebuilding of sewers a social priority. During the second half of the 19th century the water closet then evolved into the "washdown" model as we know it today, where the bowl and S-bend are molded as a single unit.

While humanity was in debt to Joseph Bramah for having constructed and marketed his water closet, he also had other claims to fame. Outstanding among these was his invention of the

Below: Bramah's original patent lock, designed in 1787. It was inscribed: "This lock requires 479,001,600 keys to open under all its variations."

Engineering

"Bramah" lock, so strong and intricate that it was stated to be pick-proof. Bramah exhibited it in a store window with a notice offering 200 guineas to anyone who could pick it. The reward went unclaimed for 67 years. Then an American locksmith, in London for the Great Exhibition of 1851, won the challenge. Even so, his achievement took him 51 hours.

The only problem with the "Bramah" lock was that its intricacy made it slow to manufacture. Bramah therefore took into his workshop a young blacksmith named Henry Maudslay to help him build machines that would cut out the parts of the lock, ready-made and to precise standards. Maudslay's machines were the prototypes for the whole machine-tool industry as it developed in the 19th and 20th centuries. As an engineer of genius, he went on to invent the metal lathe and to earn himself the title of "father of the machine-tool industry." Bramah's workshop is often referred to as the cradle of the machine-tool industry.

Maudslay probably also played a crucial role in Bramah's invention of the hydraulic press, a highly important workshop machine that made it possible to magnify pressure smoothly and

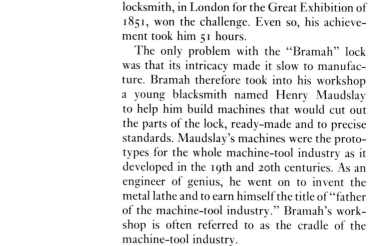

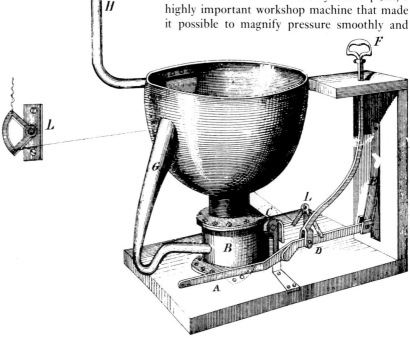

Above: Bramah's water closet of 1778. The handle (F) that released the contents of the soil pan was connected with a wire that opened the valve of the cistern above, releasing the flush of water.

steadily from comparatively slight impulses. Bramah's other inventions included a device for numbering banknotes and an instrument for planing wood. He originated a device for cutting quill feathers into lengths so that each feather could yield up to four segments, each of which could become a quill nib in its own right. The nibs could then be slipped into a specially designed holder, and it was a useful economy at a time when most quill feathers had to be imported. Bramah was probably also the first to see the possibility of using a propeller rather than a paddle wheel to drive a ship through water, though it took another 60 years before his notion became a reality with the building of the *Great Britain* by the British engineer and inventor Isambard Kingdom Brunel.

Edward Jenner

1749 - 1823

The English country doctor Edward Jenner earned his place among the undoubted benefactors of humanity by his important discovery of the principles of vaccination.

Jenner, the son of a village clergyman, was born at Berkeley, Gloucestershire. His father died when he was still very young, and he was apprenticed to a surgeon at the age of 13. As soon as he completed his apprenticeship he left for London, where he became a medical student of the famous surgeon John Hunter at St George's Hospital. Hunter's brusquely practical approach and his limitless curiosity for all biological phe-

nomena were profoundly stimulating influences on the young Jenner. Above all he took to heart Hunter's robust independence of the medical opinion of the period, and his advice not to waste time speculating, but to "try the experiment."

After two years in London, Jenner returned to Gloucestershire to start his career as a doctor, in which he was successful and highly regarded by his patients. He collected materials for Hunter's museum of biological specimens and made some original observations on aspects of natural history, including bird migration. He also wrote a classic essay on the cuckoo's nesting habits.

Before and during Jenner's time smallpox was one of the most serious health hazards in Europe.

Each successive epidemic claimed many victims. It was particularly dreaded because of the damage to the skin's surface by blisters that left permanent scarring. Those who survived the onslaught of the disease suffered disfigurement that might range from a scattering of pockmarks to an almost complete obliteration of the features.

Many centuries before, the Chinese discovered that it was possible to promote some immunity by blowing the powdered scabs that flaked off a

Above: *Cow-Pock – or the Wonderful Effects of the New Inoculation.* This cartoon was published in 1802 by the Anti-Vaccine Society as part of their campaign against Jenner. It depicts Jenner inoculating patients at the Smallpox and Inoculation Hospital, London. When first introduced in England, vaccination was widely condemned by many doctors and violently attacked in pamphlets and newspapers.

smallpox victim up the nostrils of someone who had not contracted the disease. The practice of inoculation against smallpox originated in Turkey and Greece in the 17th century during the Ottoman Empire. Serum from the blisters of sufferers was scratched with a needle into the skin of those who were healthy inducing, it was hoped, a mild attack of the disease. Lady Mary Wortley Montagu learned about the practice when she was wife of the English ambassador in Constantinople (now Istanbul), and brought it back to England. She had her own son successfully inoculated in 1721 as a demonstration. The method came to be widely used throughout Europe during the 18th century, though the risks of inducing a virulent or fatal strain of the disease remained high.

During his work in the Gloucestershire countryside, Jenner came across the old belief that dairymen and milkmaids who caught cowpox from the cattle they worked with would be safe from contracting smallpox. From his own observations he confirmed that this appeared to be true. He also recognized its implications in that the mild disease of cows might well confer

Right: statue of Edward Jenner vaccinating a child. He performed the first vaccination in May 1796. He took the lymph from a sore on the hand of a dairy maid who had contracted cowpox, and injected it into the arm of a healthy child. The vaccination caused a very mild illness, which lasted a few days only. The child then became immune to smallpox. Later Jenner found that he could inoculate an individual by using lymph taken from the pustule of a previous vaccination.

immunity against the fierce disease to which humans were vulnerable. For 20 years Jenner worked cautiously on experimenting with his idea, until, in 1796, he was confident enough to put it to an ultimate test. He inoculated James Phipps, an eight-year-old boy, with cowpox, and the boy duly showed the signs of the disease's mild rash. Two months later, Jenner inoculated him with smallpox. The boy showed no sign of the disease and was clearly immune.

Jenner named this method "vaccination," from the Latin word *vaccinia* for cowpox, and its use spread rapidly in a world where fear of smallpox was considerably stronger than the obstacles which many members of the medical establish-

Above: Jenner's work eventually won deserved recognition, and he received many honors and tributes. This 18-carat gold snuff box was presented to him when he was given the Freedom of the City of London "as a token . . . . of his skill and perseverance in the discovery of and bringing into general use the vaccine inoculation."

ment tried to place in Jenner's way. His initial paper to the Royal Society on the subject was turned down, and attempts were made to attack and discredit his work. One doctor went to the lengths of contaminating a batch of vaccine in a hospital with smallpox virus.

In promoting his discovery and his confidence in its effectiveness, Jenner worked tirelessly and without a thought for financial reward. As the death-rate from smallpox fell dramatically, so his personal fortunes suffered and his medical practice was neglected. During the 1800s he received many honors from around the world and the British parliament twice voted him considerable sums in compensation.

The role that microorganisms such as the smallpox virus played in causing disease by invading and multiplying in the body cells of the host was still far from being recognized in Jenner's day. Nevertheless his work was an important step toward an understanding of bacteriology. Its most practical long-term effect was eventually the virtual elimination of smallpox as a European and North American-based disease and also the containment and control of the disease in other parts of the world. It was one of the single most important breakthroughs in the history of medical science, and a triumph for objective scientific method in medical practice. Current immunization programs against the many crippling or fatal diseases stem from Jenner's pioneering discovery.

Nicolas Appert

c1750-1841

The art of preserving food in sealed containers was first made practicable by a French chef, Nicolas Appert, who has been called the "father of the modern canning industry."

From earliest times men have sought ways of preserving food to carry them through the winter months when the growing season is over and meat or game is hard to come by, and also through

times of famine and scarcity. Long sea voyages or extended military expeditions were other occasions where stores of reliably preserved food could be essential for survival. Among the preservation methods known to some of the earliest civilizations were fermentation and pickling in brine. The smoking and curing of meat and fish were other traditional methods. The pemmican used by the North American Indians, for example, was a cake of dried and pounded meat.

In 1795, during the wars and upheavals that followed in the wake of the French Revolution, the French government, or Directory, as it was known, offered a prize to anyone who could develop a new method of preserving food in such a way that the product was easily transportable. Nicolas Appert, a chef, confectioner, and distiller from the town of Châlons-sur-Marne, decided to concentrate his skills on the problem. There followed a period of experimentation that lasted for 14 years until, in 1810, he was ready to claim the prize of 12,000 francs. The next year, as a condition of the award, he published a description of his system as *The Art of Preserving*

Below: laboratory for cooking tinned foods (top); workshop for filling and rolling the cans (bottom). Appert's method of canning preserved food for several decades. He insisted on scrupulous cleanliness and only canned freshly picked products.

All Kinds of Animal and Vegetable Substances for Several Years (1811).

Appert's basic discovery was that decomposition could be prevented if food such as soups, stews, jams, and whole fruits were sealed inside glass bottles or jars so that all air was excluded. The jars with their contents had to be immersed in boiling water for several hours, stoppered with corks that were held in place with wire and then sealed with sealing wax. The success of his system was demonstrated by the fact that it worked, though no scientific explanation yet existed to account for why it should. The connection between microorganisms and putrefaction was not understood for another 50 years, when another Frenchman, the pioneer bacteriologist Louis Pasteur conducted his investigations into fermentation.

The prize money was used by Appert to set up

Food Preservation

the world's first bottling and canning factory which, as the House of Appert, continued in business until 1933. He went on to develop a method of extracting acid-free gelatin, and the prototype of the modern meat-stock cube, as well as to perfect a type of steam sterilizer. Meanwhile in England, also in 1810, a merchant named Peter Durand took out patents for preserving food in glass, pottery, and tinplate containers, so giving birth to the tin can. By 1813, Durand was under contract to supply canned meats to the Royal Navy. Appert started using tin-plate containers in his factory in 1815.

The "tin can" is, of course, a misnomer, because the cans are made of sheet steel, which is given a thin coating of tin. Methods of canning, health, and safety factors improved steadily throughout the 19th century. Canning was, to start with, a slow process because between four

Above: the harbor of Brest, France, where Appert's products were loaded. Appert formed connections with the maritime authorities there so that his conserves would be accepted by the French Navy.

Below right: canning today. The canned food is cooked in retorts similar to giant pressure cookers. By subjecting the cans to temperatures around 240°F for 10-30 minutes, the food is cooked and sterilized, and remains fresh and healthy. Once out of the retorts the cans go under a cold-water douche and then, via a conveyor belt, to a labeling machine.

and five hours of boiling were needed to ensure absolute sterility. In the 1860s this period was reduced when it was found that adding calcium chloride to the boiling water could raise its temperature through more than 28°F. This enabled canneries to increase their daily production rates from about 2500 to 20,000 cans. Early in the 20th century, the modern type of can was introduced and made the soldered-top kind used by Durand and Appert obsolete.

Canning was introduced into the United States in 1819, but it was slow to gain popularity until it received an impetus during the American Civil War. From 1895 it was placed on a mass-production basis, and the vast modern industry was well on the way to catering for a civilization that based a good deal of its life-style on prepackaged convenience foods. A particular advantage of canning is that the preserved food retains a high proportion of the vitamin content.

L'ART DE CONSERVER,

PENDANT PLUSIEURS ANNÉES,

TOUTES LES SUBSTANCES

ANIMALES ET VÉGÉTALES;

OUVRAGE soumis au Bureau consultatif des Arts et Manufactures, revêtu de son approbation, et publié sur l'invitation de S. Exc. le Ministre de l'Intérieur;

PAR APPERT,

Propriétaire à Massy (Seine-et-Oise), ancien Confiseur et Distillateur, Élève de la bouche de la maison ducale de Christian IV.

DEUXIÈME ÉDITION,

REVUE ET AUGMENTÉE DE PLUSIEURS OBSERVATIONS ET DE NOUVELLES EXPÉRIENCES.

A PARIS,

Chez PATRIS et Cⁱᵉ, IMPRIMEURS-LIBRAIRES, rue de la Colombe, n° 4, dans la Cité; Et au Dépôt des Préparations, rue Boucher, n° 8.

1811.

Above: title page of Appert's book on canning and preserving, published in 1811.

Joseph-Marie Jacquard
1752-1834

Joseph Jacquard, a French silk weaver, invented the loom that made automatic weaving practicable for the first time. Named the Jacquard loom after its inventor, it was the most important stage in the evolution of textile weaving by mass production methods.

Until Jacquard's machine came into use, the draw-loom had been the best improvement over the traditional horizontal frame loom. However, the draw-loom weaver had to have an assistant, known as a "draw boy," sit on top of the loom and work the cords.

By the end of the 17th century, France had become an international center for silk weaving and various improvements to the loom were introduced. Some thought was also being given to the problem of finding a fully mechanized way of feeding the pattern into the machine in order to avoid human error by the draw boy. One such device, consisting of a perforated roll of paper on a cylinder, is known to have been invented in the late 1720s, but it never found its way into general use. It did, however, furnish the idea on which Jacquard based his invention between 1790 and 1801.

Jacquard was born in Lyon, the son of a weaver. In 1790 he was given the task of overhauling and restoring a loom built 50 years before by Jacques de Vaucason. Vaucason stands among the earliest developers of auto-

Below left: portrait of Joseph-Marie Jacquard woven on a Jacquard loom.

Below right: a silk-weaving factory in Lyons, France, around 1830, using an early version of the Jacquard loom. The Jacquard loom initially encountered resistance from silk weavers but by the early 19th century it was being widely used in textile factories in France and elsewhere.

matic mechanical devices later put to use in modern industry. He began to take an interest in the mechanization of silk weaving when he became an inspector of silk manufacture, and built a power loom that was to be worked by water or animals. Automation was achieved by perforated cards that governed a system of hooks which linked with the warp threads. Vaucason's loom eventually ended up in a museum of 18th-century inventions that the inventor himself founded in Paris, and it was there that Jacquard was able to examine it.

The disruptions of the French Revolution, in which Jacquard fought on the Republican side, put a stop to his experiments for a while, but Jacquard returned to the problem as soon as he was free to do so. At the Paris Exhibition of 1801 he demonstrated a new improved type of silk draw-loom, and in 1805 he produced the Jacquard loom in its final form. It linked Vaucason's system of punched cards with sprung needles that lifted only those threads corresponding to the punched pattern on the card. In this way it was possible to weave patterns of remarkable com-

plexity in silk materials such as brocades and damasks for tablecloths and bedspreads.

The silk weavers, fearful of being put out of work by the Jacquard loom, attacked the inventor personally and burned his machines. The furore died down when the loom's efficiency spoke for itself. It was taken into the public domain by the government, and Jacquard was granted a royalty on each machine sold as well as a state pension.

The development of power looms had not proceeded well in England following the first patent for an unsatisfactory one in 1785. The introduction of the Jacquard loom in the 1820s gave the industry a great boost. It has been established that between 1813 and 1833 the number of operating power looms in Britain increased from 2400 to about 100,000.

The Jacquard loom was the basis for all the power looms used in modern textile manufacture. Its punched-card system was also adapted by Charles Babbage for the calculator he invented, so making it the forerunner of today's methods of computer programing.

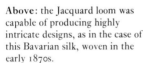

Above: the Jacquard loom was capable of producing highly intricate designs, as in the case of this Bavarian silk, woven in the early 1870s.

Right: a Jacquard loom in operation in a modern textile factory. Although it was originally designed for weaving silk, Jacquard's system of punched cardboard strips regulating the raising of the warp threads has been adapted to produce elaborate designs on virtually every type of fabric.

Sir Benjamin Thompson

1753 - 1814

Benjamin Thompson, who became Count Rumford on the basis of his work as a government official in Bavaria, formulated the first modern theory of heat. His investigations overturned the existing idea of heat as a kind of fluid contained by substances, showing it to be a form of motion instead. He also established that mechanical energy could be converted into heat, paving the way for the development of the science of thermodynamics and the invention of the first heat engines.

Center: Thompson's own drawings of the apparatus for his cannon-boring experiment.

Below: model of Thompson's cannon-boring experiment on the nature of heat.

for new scientific ideas to this day. Still unable to settle down, he left England again and after some further travels, spent the rest of his life in France.

One of Thompson's responsibilities in the employ of the Elector of Bavaria was armaments, and it was while watching the manufacture of cannon barrels that he began to formulate his theory of heat. To make the barrels, a solid block of metal was bored out with a large slow-turning drill. As the drill bit into the metal, so much heat was generated that workmen had to continually douse the block in cold water. Thompson knew the conventional scientific explanation. The motion of the drill was releasing a fluid called "caloric" from the metal, and this showed itself as heat in the atmosphere. Thompson realized that heat continued to be released as long as the drilling went on, and he felt that much more caloric was being released than could possibly have been contained in the metal. He concluded that it was the mechanical action of the drill which was being converted into heat, and there-

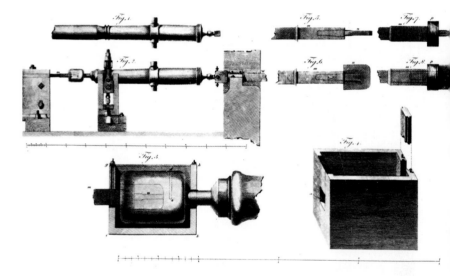

Born in Woburn, Massachusetts, Thompson spent most of his early life as a store clerk. When the American Revolution broke out, he sided with the British and, leaving his wife and child, went to England to work as a government official. Victory for the American revolutionary forces meant that Thompson could not easily return, and he reconciled himself to the life of an exile. Leaving England to travel through Europe, Thompson found work as an administrator in the government of the Elector of Bavaria. Trying to forget the events of the war, Thompson worked with a single-mindedness that was rewarded in 1780 when the Elector made him a count.

It was during his stay in Bavaria that Thompson formulated his theory of heat. His scientific reputation established, he returned to England as Count Rumford. In the years that followed, he founded the Royal Institution, a body that remains one of the world's most important forums

fore that heat was itself a form of motion.

It was the first time heat had been regarded as mechanical energy in a different form, but Thompson did not stop there. He extended his work by trying to calculate exactly how much heat is produced by a given amount of mechanical energy. The experimental problems were immense and Thompson's results were wildly inaccurate. However, by establishing the idea of what is now called a "mechanical equivalent of heat," he helped to found a branch of engineering that in later years found numerous practical applications in the interconversion of heat and mechanical energy. Best known of these are the steam engine and the internal combustion engine. Thompson's theory of heat also helped to found a new branch of physics that concentrates on the nature and effects of heat, today called "thermodynamics." Thompson's view of heat as a form of motion still plays a part in the subject although heat energy is now regarded as the motion of atoms and molecules.

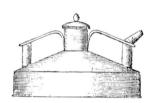

Above: Royal Institution Library.

Left: Thompson warming himself before a Rumford stove.

Center: Thompson's kettle.

Above right: Thompson's polyflame burners and spirit lamps.

Below right: Thompson designed a versatile range of cooking equipment. Top: a saucepan (C) on stewpot (A) heated by portable furnace (B); bottom: furnace without pot.

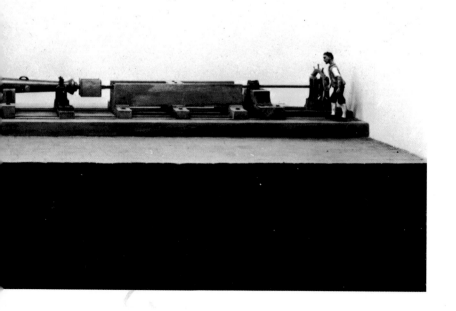

William Murdock

1754-1839

William Murdock said of himself: "I believe I may, without presuming too much, claim both the first idea of applying and the first actual application of . . . gas to economical purposes." In fact, all commercial and domestic uses of gas as a fuel and light source can be traced back to the experiments that Murdock carried out in England in the 1790s.

The son of a millwright, he was born in Ayrshire, Scotland and learned his father's trade. He moved south to Birmingham in 1777 to join the Soho manufactory, the engineering works owned by Matthew Boulton and James Watt. Two years later, Murdock was sent to Cornwall to supervize the installation of Watt steam engines to work pumping equipment in the tin mines.

After he settled in Redruth, where he married the daughter of a Cornish mine overseer, Murdock began to test his ideas on the possibility of harnessing the gas given off by burning coal. He tested the effects of different types of coal from all over Britain, setting up an iron retort in the backyard of his home from which a metal tube ran into the living room. On July 29, 1792 he presided at the lighting of a gas flame within the room. It was the birth of the gas industry, although at that stage he does not seem to have taken his invention much beyond the rudimentaries. After he returned to Birmingham in 1799, he continued his experiments. He knew he still had a long way to go in devising storage methods, mantles to give effective light, and gas purification systems, as well as safety measures.

Right: Regent Street, London, 1840. Within 20 years of its introduction, gas light illuminated most London streets.

Center: indoor lighting by gas, around 1870, in the Army and Navy Club.

Below right: *A Peep at the Gas Lights of Pall-Mall* (1809), depicting the introduction of gas for street lighting.

Boulton and Watt already included retorts and purifiers to make oxygen and hydrogen among their factory products, and they took a close interest in Murdock's progress. They held back from applying for patents, though, because litigation was already pending in the courts, and it seemed doubtful whether any patent could be made to stand up. Then, in 1801 they got word of experiments being carried out in Paris by the French engineer Philippe Lebon. In 1799 Lebon

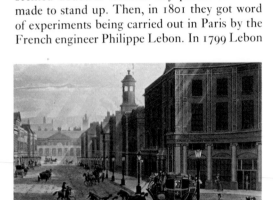

patented what he called his *thermlampe,* which burned gas obtained from wood distillation. The British made haste to bring their plans forward, and in 1802 placed and ignited two gas lamps outside each end of their Soho factory building to celebrate the Peace of Amiens. The following year, the foundry was entirely illuminated by gas. The "Soho stink," as Murdock himself called the odor of the gas, was eliminated after a time and factories as well as private homes began to install the system. The Soho manufactory then started to market its new line in lighting and heating equipment.

Murdock took little interest in developments after about 1810, by which time the infant gas industry was in the hands of businessmen scrambling for position and setting up rival gas companies in every city. In that year Murdock became a partner in the Soho company and remained so until he retired in 1830. After his death he was buried in the nearby Handsworth church, where Boulton and Watt are also interred.

Below: a model of the gas plant Murdock designed to light up his workshops in Redruth, Cornwall. The gas used was obtained from the distillation of coal.

Murdock was a man of great inventiveness. He even built model steam carriages, including one that terrified the vicar of Redruth one evening when he encountered it on a test run along the church path. Murdock's partners regarded all such applications of steam power as frivolous and irresponsible, however, and no one was able to make progress with a steam-driven vehicle as long as Watt controlled the patent.

The rotary piston gear that Watt patented in 1781 is actually thought to be of Murdock's devising. Certainly his invention of a slide valve simplified and improved the complex valve system on the Watt engine. Murdock was the first to make an oscillating engine, and the first to build a steam engine that was freestanding, independent of a building structure to keep it in position. His catalog of inventions include an iron cement, the basic formula of which is still in use today, a steam gun, and a method of harnessing compressed air that he used to work the bells in his home in Birmingham.

John Loudon McAdam

1756-1836

The Scottish surveyor John Loudon McAdam was the inventor of the 19th century's most widely used method of road construction: the macadamized road surface.

By the late 18th century, road building in Europe was beginning to reach a level of importance unknown since the Roman Empire was at its height. The growth of commerce and industry, and the increase in freight traffic between towns and cities, led to the greater utilization of navigable rivers and the building of canals. It also produced a consciousness of the need for good road surfaces. It was impossible to institute regular, reliable stagecoach services until there were decent tracks for them to travel over. The earliest stagecoaches barely managed to average more than a brisk walking pace.

The first leading pioneer of modern road-making techniques was the French engineer Pierre-Marie-Jérôme Tresaguet, who became inspector general of roads and bridges in France in 1775. He worked out a method of constructing a well-drained road with a strong foundation of flat stones hammered in edgeways to take the weight of the traffic, the crown of the road slightly raised, and a surface of broken stone. His efforts meant that, by 1800, France had one of the finest road systems in Europe.

Trésaguet's direct contemporary in England was John Metcalf, who, though blinded by smallpox in early childhood, engineered roads in the north of England. He used a system of ditches to provide drainage and layed brushwood foundations in swampy areas. His example, together with that of Trésaguet, provided the impetus for the next generation of road-builders. Their outstanding representatives were John McAdam and the great self-taught engineer and bridge-builder, Thomas Telford.

Telford, in his road-building operations, adapted Trésaguet's method in most of its essentials. McAdam, on the other hand, had his own theories on how the method could be improved. He saw the surface rather than the foundation as taking the brunt of the wear and tear of traffic. After returning in 1783 to his birthplace in Ayrshire, Scotland, from New York, where he had spent 14 years in the counting house of an uncle, he carried out some experiments in road-making at his own expense. Later he was able to continue these in Cornwall under government contract, but it was not until he was appointed surveyor general to the city of Bristol that he could put his ideas to the test on a large scale. The roads surrounding Bristol, then a rapidly growing port, were in a bad state of disrepair.

McAdam drew up a specification for a road with its bed raised slightly above the level of the surrounding land to facilitate drainage. Drainage ditches edged each side, and the roadbed consisted of large pieces of crushed rock laid com-

Below: a stage wagon on a macadamized road, 1840. McAdam's system of road building enabled heavy loads to be transported at fast speeds. His roads were similar to those built by the Romans in that the crown was above the level of the ground. The roads were thus kept dry, and this, rather than an elaborate foundation, was the secret of their success. The simplicity of McAdam's roads also meant that their construction was speedier and cheaper.

Roman pavement in section, showing local-stone wearing course (blue), cambered hard filling (green), Roman concrete (yellow), waterproof layer of stones (brown), compacted earth footing (red), retaining stones (A) and drainage ditch (B).

18th-century French engineer Pierre Trésaguet is credited with the first modern pavement design. Its 3¼-inch surface of small stones (blue) covers a 6¾-inch course of large stones (yellow), resting on a foundation of heavy stones (red) placed on a cambered footing.

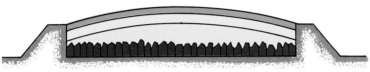

A road pavement design by British engineer Thomas Telford (1757–1834). Its 2-inch-thick gravel wearing surface (blue) rests on two layers of 2½-inch stones, forming a base course 20 inches deep in the middle (yellow). It rests on 6¾ inches of heavy stones (red).

MacAdam's road pavement was simpler than some other versions, but very effective. It comprised three layers—wearing surface (blue), base course (yellow), and footing (red)—the first two of 2-inch stones resting on a footing of compacted, cambered earth.

Above left: a comparison of some different methods of road building.

Above right: a space-saving, high-level stretch of Tokyo Expressway No. 4, an urban freeway of reinforced concrete on steel pillars. To enable them to carry heavy loads of traffic, modern highways have a gravel base several feet thick, and a surface of 10-inch thick reinforced concrete. Rural roads are still built on McAdam's principle.

Center left: *Mock-Adamizing – the Colossus of Roads* (1827), a cartoon depicting McAdam's ability to make money as well as roads.

pactly. The road was 18 feet wide and the crown in the middle rose 3 inches. The all-important surface layer consisted of broken angular pieces of granite or greenstone – no piece heavier than 6 ounces. Successive layers of stone were then laid as each preceding surface was compressed by the traffic. In this way, under pressure, the surface became virtually self-sealing. The iron rims on the wheels of carts and carriages, which previously reduced natural surfaces to a chaos of ruts and potholes, were now in effect put to work impacting the surface ever more tightly. McAdam described his methods in two books, *Remarks on the Present System of Road-making* (1816) and

Practical Essay on the Scientific Repair and Preservation of Roads (1819).

The main disadvantage of the new type of road was that in dry weather an excessive amount of dust was thrown up to cover travelers from head to foot. Its practical advantages, on the other hand, were obvious, and a parliamentary inquiry into road building in 1823 led to McAdam's system being officially adopted. In 1827, he was made surveyor general of roads in Britain, and since he combined a talent for organization and administration with his other gifts, he achieved remarkable feats of road construction.

There were in Britain by 1840 more than 22,000 miles of turnpike road, punctuated by almost 8000 tollgates. The fast new stagecoaches drawn by up to a dozen horses entered into their hour of glory before the coming of the railways made them extinct. McAdam's method was also quickly adopted in other countries, notably in the United States. It introduced a new verb, "macadamize," into the English language, and remained the standard method of road construction until the development of the automobile, whose rubber tires tore the small stones out of their bedding. This made necessary the use of a new, "tar macadam," and ultimately a further revolution in road engineering.

Robert Fulton

1765-1815

The American inventor Robert Fulton built the first steamship to operate as a commercial success. He was also responsible for a vital phase in the early development of the submarine.

Fulton started life as an artist and in 1787 he set out from his home in Pennsylvania intent on furthering his career in London. The reception of his artistic talent in England was polite rather than encouraging so he turned his attention to other possibilities, such as the new applications of steam power then being explored.

Fulton stayed in Britain for several years and occupied himself with designing a canal system

that avoided using locks by substituting inclined planes to lift boats onto different levels. Nothing came of his designs and in 1797 he left for Paris. Britain and France were then at war, a situation that gave Fulton the opportunity to put forward his idea for a submarine, which he thought could be used to place powder mines under the hulls of warships. It was another American, David Bushnell, who made the original submarine craft to be used in active warfare. His was a one-man capsule, the *Turtle*, which made several unsuccessful attempts on British warships during the American War of Independence.

At first the French authorities recoiled from

such a deceitful war tactic, but in 1801 they allowed Fulton to test his prototype, which he named the *Nautilus*. It was made from sheets of copper on iron ribs, and was capable of carrying four passengers for three hours under water. Its propeller was worked by hand, and it had a rudimentary conning tower. Fulton's submarine succeeded in sinking a derelict schooner, but when it came to trying to catch a real warship, it could not move fast enough. The French withdrew their support. In the meantime, however, he met Robert R Livingston, the US minister to France. Livingston already held business interest in steamboat navigation within New York State, and the two men agreed to collaborate.

Fulton designed a 66-foot craft with paddle wheels at the side and an engine of 8 horsepower. It was built in 1803 and tested on the Seine river. The hull proved to be too weak to support the engine, so the design was satisfactorily improved, and Fulton ordered a more powerful engine to be sent direct to America from England. He returned to New York in 1806.

The history of attempts to develop a viable

Right: the *Nautilus*, built for the French in 1801. On the surface of the water it looked like an ordinary boat, with a mast which folded away into a deck groove when underwater. There was a conning tower, ballast tanks that could be filled and emptied, and in the first model, room for four men to crank an endless belt that turned a propeller shaft. The submarine was designed to contain sufficient oxygen to support four men and two small candles for three hours, although Fulton later incorporated a brass globe of compressed air to act as a reservoir.

steam-driven ship went back over many years, though it was the improved steam engine designs produced by the Scottish inventor James Watt in the 1770s that finally made the idea workable. The American inventor John Fitch built a series of steamboats in the 1780s. First he tried one propelled by mechanical oars, then he turned to paddle wheels. His second and last paddle steamer made regular passenger trips on the Delaware river but was a financial failure, partly because of Fitch's unbusinesslike approach to the costs he incurred, and partly because public opinion thought it was an unnecessary novelty at that time.

Above: the launching of the *Demologos* at New York, October 29, 1814. It was formally christened *Fulton the First*, and was the first ever steamship of war. The *Demologos* was a floating fort with a paddle between double hulls. It was intended for use against the British in the War of 1812–1814.

Left: Fulton's steamboat, the *Clermont*. It was 150 feet long and traveled at a speed of 5 miles an hour.

In 1800 the Scots engineer Henry Bell, whom Fulton may well have met during his time in Britain, sent his proposals for a steamboat to the British Admiralty, though it was 1812 before Bell's *Comet*, which ushered in the steamship age in Europe, made its maiden voyage along the Clyde river in Scotland. In 1802 the British engineer William Symington launched his 56-foot paddle boat, the *Charlotte Dundas*. Since the *Charlotte Dundas* worked successfully as a tugboat on the Scottish canals for several years, it has an undeniable claim to being the first workable steam vessel.

The first passenger- and freight-carrying ship to show commercial viability, however, was Fulton's 150-foot *Clermont*, launched on the Hudson river in 1807. Its success was immediate, and before long – having modified and improved many aspects of his basic design – Fulton was building further paddle steamers to operate on other American rivers. He also built the first steam-powered warship, the *Demologos*, to protect the New York harbor during the British blockade of 1812–1814.

During his last years Fulton expended a considerable amount of energy and money on lawsuits to defend his steamboat patents against infringement, and on the ideas for submarines that had fascinated him from the beginning. He managed to persuade Congress to back a project for a steam-driven submarine that could carry a crew of one hundred. It was unfinished at the time of his death, and was never completed. Fulton's *Nautilus*, on the other hand, was commemorated in the name Jules Verne used for the undersea vessel in his science-fiction fantasy, *Twenty Thousand Leagues under the Sea*, and it was in turn the name given to the first submarine to be driven by atomic power.

Eli Whitney

1765-1825

When he invented the cotton gin, Eli Whitney created the basis for the wealth of the cotton plantations in the American South in the early 19th century. He later evolved the technical and labor systems on which every manufacturing industry has since been based.

The son of a Massachusetts farmer, Whitney was born in the town of Westboro where he received a primary education in the local school and developed an ingenuity for dealing with farm machinery. When the American War of Independence was over in 1783, he decided that he needed a college education if he was to fullfil the ambitions he had for himself. After a long period of preparation, he gained entrance to Yale College. By the time he graduated at the age of 27, he had an up-to-date knowledge of mechanics and technological developments in Europe.

Whitney left for Georgia hoping to become a teacher. In this he was unsuccessful but he did strike up a friendship with Phineas Miller, a plantation manager, and learnt some of the facts about the cotton trade. Following the innovations of the English inventor Richard Arkwright, the English spinning mills were hungry for raw cotton. The problem was to grow enough of a suitable variety. It was easy to clean the fibers off the seed-heads of the long-stapled kind, but this could be grown only in coastal areas. The variety that grew inland had short staples, and the fibers clung to the seed-heads, making the removal of the raw cotton fiber from them a difficult and time-consuming process.

Below: the cotton gin. Until its invention over three hours of hand work were needed to process 1 pound of the local cotton seed. In Whitney's machine a sieve of wires, stretched lengthwise, held the seed in place whilst a rotating drum with fine hooks pulled the lint away. A revolving brush cleaned the lint off the hooks.

Whitney at once visualized the sort of machine that might do the stripping, and almost within days produced his prototype. The idea was one of cunning simplicity. The seed-heads, fed into the machine by a hopper, were caught up by rows of wire hooks set on a cylinder which, as it turned, ripped the cases away from the fiber against a fixed wooden breastwork with fine grooves corresponding to the positions of the hooks. At the back of the machine another cylinder, set with bristles and turning in the opposite direction, then brushed the fiber from the hooks.

Whitney and Miller went into partnership to manufacture and market the new cotton gin. It provided the cotton plantation owners with the means to make quick fortunes, and they were not slow to take advantage. Unfortunately for Whitney and Miller, they were slow to honor the business agreements that should have given the manufacturers a share of the profits. It was also practically impossible to stop the machine being pirated, despite the patents that applied to it. Its very simplicity meant that any local blacksmith and carpenter could run one up without diffi-

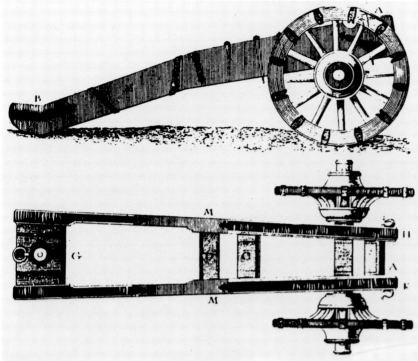

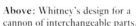

Above: Whitney's design for a cannon of interchangeable parts.

Above right: Whitney's patent milling machine, designed to cut metal to precise patterns. The machine had a toothed wheel, each tooth being sharpened to a cutting edge. The wheel was driven around the edge of a template clamped down on top of the metal which lay on a movable workbed. It did away with the need for each component part to be individually cut by a skilled workman with a chisel.

culty. Within five years the business foundered.

After long negotiations, Whitney and Miller were able in the 1800s to squeeze token compensations amounting to some $90,000 out of the states of South and North Carolina, and Georgia. In the meantime, Whitney turned his attention to a new horizon. In 1797, he contracted with the United States government to supply 10,000 muskets within two years, using a method where each piece of a musket would be interchangeable with a piece from any other musket similarly produced. Up to then it had been impossible for one armory to turn out more than about 250 muskets a year, because each weapon was individually built by craftsmen. Similarly, spare parts then had to be made for each particular weapon when anything went wrong.

Whitney saw that if each part of a musket could be manufactured according to a standard template pattern, using precisely designed guides and jigs, then not only would it be possible to dispense with the need for a highly skilled gunsmith, but the whole operation could be speeded up many times over. He set up his gun factory in Connecticut to demonstrate his point. There

were, however, many problems in the way of getting the system onto a working basis. It was 1801 before Whitney was ready to show the effectiveness of his method by assembling complete working muskets using pieces taken at random from piles of spare parts.

The system that Eli Whitney founded soon had an application in other processes, such as clock-making. Parallel developments in Europe led to the invention in 1797 of the metal lathe by the English engineer Henry Maudslay. This was particularly important to the early history of the machine-tool industry. On the one hand, there were new standards of precision in boring and screw-cutting equipment. On the other, there was Whitney's grasp of the principle of a manufacturing standard and the division of labor. The combination of the two laid the foundations for the mass-production manufacturing techniques of the 19th and 20th centuries, in which Whitney's gun factory was the true forerunner.

Joseph-Nicéphore Niepce

1765-1833

The first man to catch and fix a photographic image was the French inventor, Joseph-Nicéphore Niepce.

Photography has its origins in the camera obscura ("dark chamber") of the early Middle Ages, which was, to start with, a dark box or room with a minute hole in one side that projected an inverted image of a lighted scene outside the box onto the opposite interior surface or wall. The first person to test it with a lens in the hole is thought to have been the Italian scientist

Giambattista della Porta in the late 16th century. The addition of the lens sharpened the image. Later models incorporated a prism or mirror to turn the image the right way up, and the camera obscura was much used by both amateur and professional artists over the course of the next two centuries. By the early 19th century, various light-sensitive chemical solutions were known, and the idea of fixing the image became a practical possibility.

Niepce was the son of a French royalist family who had forfeited much of their wealth in the Revolution. He served in the Napoleonic armies until ill-health forced his retirement and he returned to the family estate at Châlon-sur-Sâone. There he gave his time to scientific inquiry, and in 1807 he and his brother Claude invented an early version of a piston-and-cylinder internal-combustion engine. In 1813 he turned his atten-

tion to lithography, developed by the German inventor Aloys Senefelder several years before. Lithographic stone was hard to obtain in the Sâone valley, and as Niepce had no particular talent for draftsmanship, he decided to try to find a way of using light to produce the picture for him.

By 1816, Niepce was making his first camera experiments in a process he named heliography, or "sun-drawing." He succeeded after a very long exposure in obtaining an image on paper sensitized with silver chloride. Attempts to fix the image failed, and he began to experiment with other materials such as glass and pewter that might form the basis for a photographic plate.

In 1822 he began to use a solution of a kind of asphalt called bitumen of Judea, which hardens on exposure to light. By 1826 he developed this to the point where he could produce a copy of an existing etching by mounting it on a sheet of glass and allowing sunlight to pass through it onto a copper or pewter plate coated in the asphalt

Above: View of the Bridge of Changes and the Notre Dame Bridge, Paris, 1820. In the right-hand corner can be seen the shop of Charles-Louis Chevalier, the optician who prepared lenses for Niepce in the years 1825-1835.

Right: *The Legend of the Unknown Inventor*, an apocryphal story of the invention of the photograph. One day an unknown man presented himself in the shop of optician Charles-Louis Chevalier and told him that he had discovered a means of fixing photographic images.

Photography

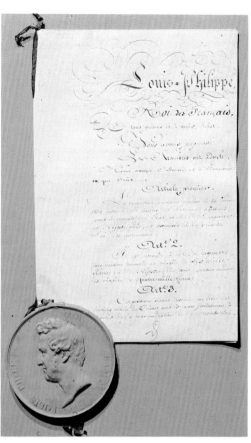

Left: the camera obscura.

Right: the original text on vellum of the law of purchase of the invention of photography to Niepce's son and Daguerre.

solution. The sunlight hardened the asphalt where it passed through the white areas, and the shaded areas could be gently dissolved away by a mixture of oil of lavender and white petroleum. The plate could now be etched and copies printed. The method lost a certain amount in definition and clarity over the original, but Niepce's heliogravure was the first decisive step

Below: the history and uses of the photograph, from the camera obscura and the discovery of light sensitive silver chloride, through Niepce's and Daguerre's innovations, to the portrait photograph.

along the road to an effective process of photo-engraving.

In the same year of 1826, he succeeded in producing the world's first acknowledged photograph. Using his camera, he submitted a sensitized pewter plate to an exposure lasting several hours and obtained on it a fixed negative image of the view outside his attic workshop. His objective was then to make a plate that could be etched and used to print off the image in positive form. This turned out to be impracticable. The length of exposure time it needed meant that the angle of the sun, and hence the surfaces illuminated and the shadows cast, changed considerably during the plate's exposure. Definition and contrast were consistently poor, and resulted in a good deal of visual indistinctness.

Niepce in fact had little further success in developing his system, and he tended to guard the secrets of his method with obstinate jealousy. When he addressed a paper on his method to the Royal Society in London, he omitted to give technical specifications to back his thesis and so members were unable to sum up his work properly; nor was it possible to have a fruitful exchange of ideas. In the meantime he found himself placed under siege by a young Parisian painter named Louis-Jacques-Mandé Daguerre who tried to persuade him that they ought to work together to perfect heliography. At last, in 1829, Niepce agreed to a partnership. A chapter was about to be added to the early history of photography even though it was not to be in Niepce's own lifetime.

John Dalton

1766 - 1844

by my own experience." Despite his insistence on direct observation of phenomena, Dalton's greatest achievement concerned invisible atoms. His formulation of the atomic theory, a masterpiece of intuition and deductive thinking, was a brilliant synthesis of knowledge and ideas stretching back to the times of the ancient Greek scientists.

Dalton published the atomic theory in 1808 in a book called *A New System of Chemical Phil-*

Drawing together the scientific work of centuries, English chemist John Dalton formulated the modern atomic theory of matter. His ideas established chemistry as a true science, producing greater understanding of the most fundamental chemical process—the way elements combine to form compounds. Dalton's particular emphasis on the weight of atoms as one of their main distinguishing features led to the first quantitative descriptions of basic chemical reactions.

Dalton was born of a devout Quaker family, and throughout his childhood in the northern English village of Eaglesfield where he was born, religion and education were the two most important features of everyday life. Dalton was so brilliant that he became a teacher when barely 12 years old. Influenced by a friend of his family, a wealthy instrument maker and amateur weather-observer, Dalton became deeply interested in meteorology. In 1787 he began a daily journal of weather observations that he painstakingly maintained for over 40 years until his death. He made many contributions to the fledgling subject and in 1793 published a definitive work called *Meteorological Observations and Essays*. It was

Right: Dalton's symbols of atoms of different elements together with their atomic weights, drawn up in 1808-1810. In his book *New System of Chemical Philosophy*, Dalton explained how chemical reactions took place by the union of atoms to form "complex atoms," which are now called molecules. Of the elements depicted, magnesia, lime, soda, potash, strontites, and barytes were shortly after discovered to be compounds.

ELEMENTS

	wt			wt
⊙ Hydrogen	1	⊕ Strontian	46
① Azote	5	✦ Barytes	68
● Carbon	54	Ⓘ Iron	50
○ Oxygen	7	Ⓩ Zinc	56
✶ Phosphorus	9	Ⓒ Copper	56
⊕ Sulphur	13	Ⓛ Lead	90
◉ Magnesia	20	Ⓢ Silver	190
⊖ Lime	24	ⓓ Gold	190
◐ Soda	28	Ⓟ Platina	190
◍ Potash	42	✺ Mercury	167

Below: *Dalton Collecting Marsh Gas (Impure Methane)*, a fresco by Ford Maddox Brown.

filled with Dalton's original and perceptive thinking, unhampered by prejudice or superstition.

Although Dalton's approach to science did not neglect the work of others, he always satisfied himself about other people's conclusions before accepting and applying them. In the course of a book describing the nature of the Aurora Borealis (the Northern Lights), Dalton wrote: "Having been in my progress so often misled by taking for granted the results of others, I have determined to write as little as possible but what I can attest

osophy, and the effect of his ideas on chemistry was as fundamental as the title suggests. His theory was based on three important propositions. The first of these was that all matter is composed of extremely small, indivisible, and indestructible particles called atoms. Secondly, that the atoms of one element are all exactly alike in every respect including weight but are different from the atoms of every other element. Thirdly, that when elements combine to form compounds, their atoms combine in simple numerical proportions such as one to one, two to one, and four to three.

Once explained by Dalton's characteristically lucid writing, atomic theory was accepted universally by chemists with virtually no opposition. The ideas of atoms had been suggested centuries earlier by the Greek philosopher Democritus, so the concept was not entirely unfamiliar. But Dalton's first complete formulation of a consistent theory was a breakthrough. One of the most important features of the theory was its proposal that atoms differed from each other by weight. This was something measurable, and therefore Dalton's was the first quantitative atomic theory ever advanced.

The theory also provided a clear explanation of why elements combine to form new compounds in definite relative weights. For example, it had long puzzled chemists why a substance such as copper carbonate, however prepared, always contained the same proportions by weight of copper (five parts), oxygen (four parts), and carbon (one part). Dalton's theory that elements combine atom by atom in simple numerical proportions explained it, because if all atoms of a

Below: some of the apparatus used by Dalton in his experimental work. Dalton made many instruments himself, for his own use and for other scientists.

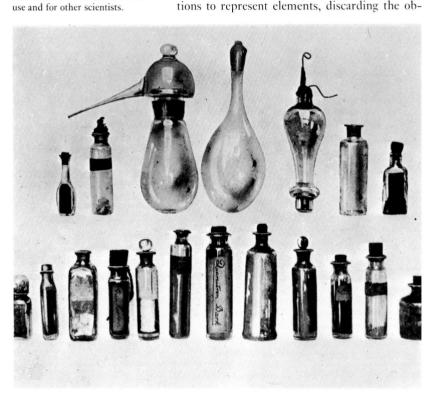

particular element have the same weight, they must have definite combining weights.

Dalton tried to work out the relative weights of different atoms from the proportions by weight of the elements in certain compounds, so becoming the first to prepare a table of atomic weights. In later years such a table enabled the first major periodic classification of chemical elements to be drawn up. Dalton also drew up a system of notations to represent elements, discarding the ob-

○ Oxygen
⊕ Sulfur
⊗ Aluminum (Alumine)
⦀ Potassium (Potash)

Above: Dalton's design for the potassium-aluminum-sulfur molecule (commonly known as alum), together with his key of the elements involved.

scure drawings that had been handed down from the alchemists of ancient times. He created clear symbols to stand for the atoms of different elements, and used them in drawings that showed what took place during chemical reactions. For example, molecules were shown as groups of atom symbols linked together.

Dalton was shy of the inevitable fame that his work earned him. As a Quaker, he shunned public acclaim, even refusing to be nominated for membership of the Royal Society. Finally, in 1822 his determined admirers elected him without his knowledge, and in 1832 he was persuaded to accept a Doctorate of Science from the University of Oxford. His colleagues also arranged for him to be presented to the king shortly afterwards. Dalton had long resisted such a presentation, refusing to wear the ornate court dress the occasion demanded. There was also a problem in wearing his Oxford gown, which would have been appropriate for meeting the king, because it was scarlet and Quakers wore no red. Dalton could not bring himself to disappoint his friends, however, and falling back on his congenital color blindness, remarked that the University gown appeared gray to him. It was probably the only deceit he ever permitted himself.

Georges Cuvier
1769 - 1832

The French zoologist Georges Cuvier played an important part in systematizing the classification of animals, considerably modifying the system evolved in the mid-18th century by the Swedish naturalist Linnaeus, while at the same time founding comparative anatomy as a modern science. He also, by his work on fossils, laid the basis for paleontology as an independent study.

Born at Montbeliard in France, Cuvier went to Stuttgart to study dissection and anatomy. After returning home, he wrote an important paper on mollusks and was given a post at the Museum of Natural History in Paris. He continued his zoological research at the Museum over many years, emerging as one of the most considerable scientific intellects of his genera-

Below: an anatomical study of a living hippopotamus, taken from Cuvier's *Researches on Fossil Bones* (1824). Cuvier believed that if the shape of each bone was studied in functional terms, in relation to the rest of the body, it should be possible to reconstruct correctly a whole animal from its parts. This was particularly important in the case of collections of fossil bones. However, the functional significance and relationship of many anatomical parts was not known. Cuvier therefore, had to rely more on his wide knowledge of the anatomy of living animals, than on the principle of functional coordination.

of squaring with the Genesis account of creation and with Archbishop Ussher's famous calculation, made in 1654, that the creation of the world occurred at 9 am on October 26, 4004 BC. According to the theory, Noah's flood was the cataclysmic agent that wiped out whole species and left their remains to form fossils in sedimentary deposits.

Cuvier developed catastrophism to new levels, of complexity. He did not accept for a moment the transmutability of species by which one species might in time develop into a new species. Every kind of animal was unchangeably as the Creator made it in the first place. The awkward fact that both freshwater and saltwater species turned up in the rocks around Paris could be skirted if it was assumed that a series of cataclysms was responsible for obliterating whole areas which were then recolonized by other creatures moving in from elsewhere. Each successive catastrophe had the effect of advancing the complexity of life since it was obvious that more recent creatures were advances on the ones that went before.

The fact that his basic thesis was such a blind alley did not detract from Cuvier's achievements in describing and classifying his fossils, and from

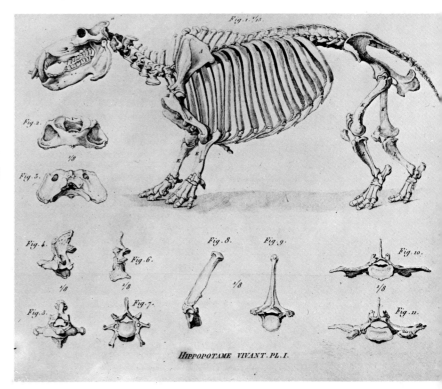

HIPPOPOTAME VIVANT. PL. I.

tion. By 1805 he completed his *Lesson in Comparative Anatomy*, and in 1810 he published his *Historical Report on the Progress of the Sciences*. Important as an educationalist, Cuvier helped to set up several French provincial universities. He organized the collection of a vast range of fossils (including the pterodactyl, which he discovered and named), and began their systematic study.

He soon noticed that the deeper down in the earth's crust a specimen came from, the more remote it seemed from existing animal forms. His contemporary Jean-Baptiste Lamarck evolved a simple basic theory of evolution, which he published in 1809 and which partly anticipated by 50 years the theory of the origin of species of Charles Darwin. Cuvier rejected any such notion. To account for the chronological sequence of his fossils he looked to the theory of catastrophism, which had been the common scientific belief since the 17th century. This had the advantage

there moving on to construct a concept of four major groups called phyla within the animal kingdom. These were *Radiata* (including jellyfish, starfish), *Articulata* (including worms, insects), *Mollusca* (including snails, cuttlefish) and *Vertebrata* (all the higher animals). Though they had to be discarded in time, Cuvier's classifications were transitional between old ideas and the new ones which would finally undermine the theory of a scale of creation. His book, *The Animal King-*

Biology

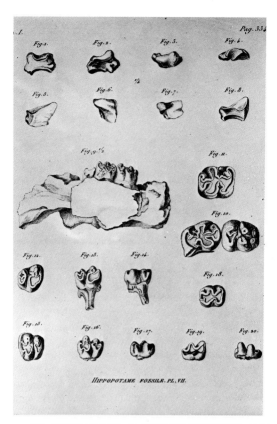

HIPPOPOTAME FOSSILE. PL. VII.

Left: fragments of hippopotamus fossils drawn by Cuvier. He identified the largest piece (9) as the broken fragment of the bottom left jaw and pieces 12–17 as teeth belonging to a species similar to the hippopotamus but smaller than a pig.

Below: a painting of the reconstruction of the dodo at the National Museum of Natural History, Paris, where Cuvier was curator of anatomical material. Although the dodo became extinct in about 1681, reconstruction was still possible from surviving skeletons and old descriptions.

dom, Distributed According to Its Organization (1817) was a decisive improvement on the Linnaean system.

Cuvier's other main contribution was his theory of the "correlation of parts." The implication of this principle was that all the anatomical structure and individual organs of an animal are the way they are and "collaborate" with each other, so as to adapt the animal to "the conditions of its existence." It thus differed from other prevailing theories of the time which held that an animal's anatomy governed its mode of living.

Cuvier died of cholera in the first epidemic to hit Paris. Despite his unshaken adherence to catastrophism, he was the first to achieve a comparison of living and fossil types. By his correlation of parts theory he claimed it was possible to project a complete reconstruction of a creature, given one part of it, such as a piece of bone. In putting his theory into practice he achieved some dramatic results. As the French novelist Balzac wrote of him:

"Our immortal naturalist reconstructs whole worlds out of bleached bones. . . . He fills the void; he examines a piece of gypsum, observes an imprint and lo! the marble becomes flesh, and the dead are quickened to life."

Thomas Johann Seebeck

1770 - 1831

The German physicist Thomas Seebeck was the discoverer of the "Seebeck effect," an apparently simple observation that has had far-reaching effects in modern industrial processes and temperature measurement.

As a young scientist, Seebeck collaborated with the great German writer and poet Johann Wolfgang von Goethe in formulating his theory of colors. (Goethe's theory of colors had some influence on contemporary European artists, but was not important scientifically.) After this Seebeck went on to discover the phenomenon that bears his name. This happened in 1821 when he saw by chance that the needle of a compass was deflected when it was placed close to a wire loop made of two different metals – a length of copper and a length of bismuth. He established that if a circuit is made of two different metals, and if the two junctions are kept at different temperatures where they join, then an electric current is created that flows around the circuit. The current is the result of a flow of heat from the hot to the cold junction.

His discovery was the basis for all future work in thermoelectricity, in which electricity is created by the direct conversion of heat into an electric current. In thermoelectric studies it is usually closely linked with another effect known as the "Peltier effect," which is in fact the reverse

Below: *Light and Colour (Goethe's Theory – The Morning after the Deluge – Moses writing the Book of Genesis*, by Joseph Mallord William Turner, 1843. The British artist Turner was greatly influenced by Goethe's theory of color, produced in collaboration with Seebeck. The English translation appeared in 1840 and Turner acquired a copy to which he frequently referred. According to Goethe's theory color consists of indivisible pigments, as did the degrees of light and shade. He considered that the splitting of white light by a prism into monochromatic beams of color was a trick to deceive the eye. His theory was formulated as a direct attack on Newton who had postulated that white light consists of a series of colors which are absorbed and reflected. Goethe's theory had little scientific value but considerable influence on the European Impressionists.

of the Seebeck effect. This was discovered in 1834 by Jean-Charles-Athanase Peltier, a French clockmaker who retired from his profession at the age of 30 to take up studies in physics. He found that if an electric current was passed through a circuit like the one made by Seebeck, then heat was either created or absorbed at the junctions of the metals, depending on the direction of the current. Where the heat was absorbed, it in effect created coldness.

For many years, the only practical outcome of either of these observations was the development of the thermocouple. This made use of the Seebeck effect, since the strength of the current indicates the temperature at the hotter part of the link. Thermocouples have been developed in recent years to the point where they are highly accurate heat-measuring devices, capable of measuring temperatures ranging from a few degrees above absolute zero to as high as 3100°F. The importance of such an accurate instrument, with such a wide temperature-measurement range is extremely important in modern industrial processes as well as in scientific experiments.

By the early 20th century, it was well known that in theory the Seebeck effect could be used to generate electricity for practical use and the Peltier effect to make refrigeration units. What the theories lacked to turn them into reality were certain kinds of metallic alloys that did not exist until the 1950s. From then on, research in the

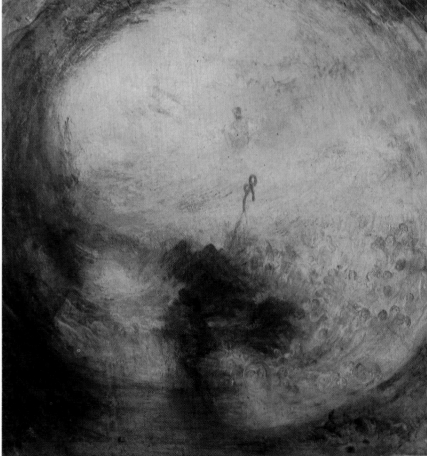

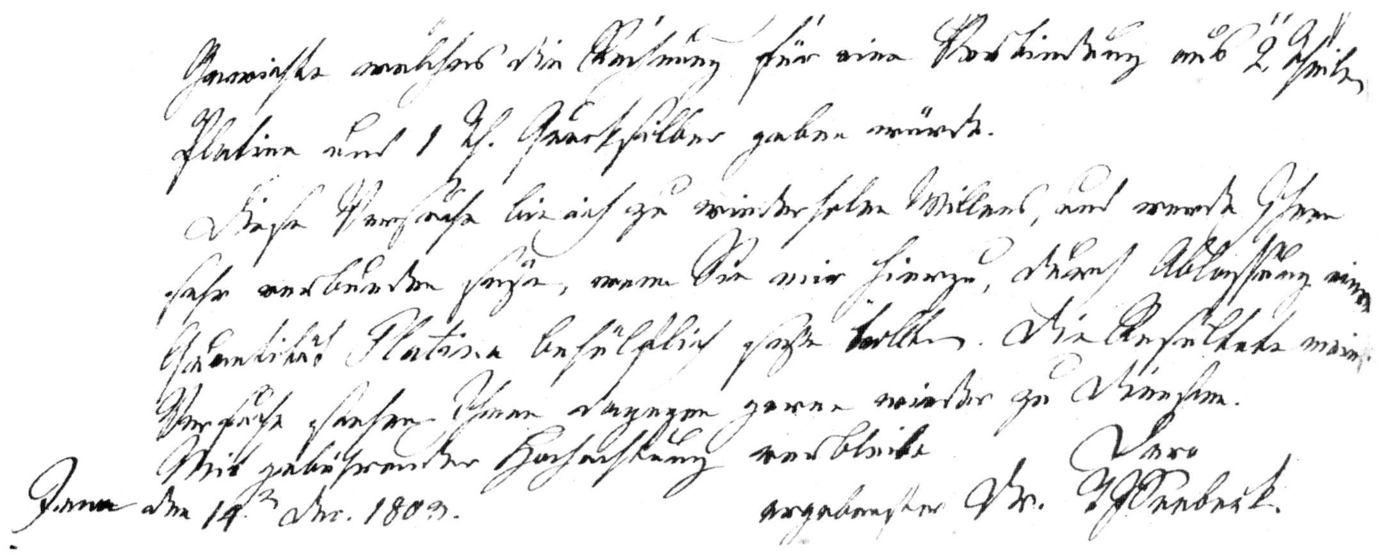

[Handwritten letter in German script]

United States, the USSR, and Europe led to various practical applications in thermoelectrics. These ranged from a Soviet kerosene-lamp generator capable of operating a radio set in remote areas, to radioisotope generators, where the radioactive material is utilized as the heat source. These have been used to power automatic weather stations in arctic conditions as well as to operate space equipment on satellites and the moon, and to transmit the information obtained back to earth. The main application of refrigera-

Above: Seebeck's letter describing experiments with platinum and mercury.
Below left: thermomechanical generator, a result of Seebeck's work. It uses waste gases to produce low wattage electricity for powering radio and television stations in underdeveloped countries.
Below right: the Seebeck effect is utilized in cryogenics to liquefy helium.

tion techniques has been in laboratory and technical experiments where it is essential to fix and maintain a specific low temperature.

Because of the expense and scarcity of the conducting alloys needed to make these techniques practicable, they have so far found few commercial and domestic applications. They are likely, however, to begin to move out of more specialized areas as time goes by. It seems probable that Seebeck's discovery of 1821 will belong firmly to the technology of the 21st century.

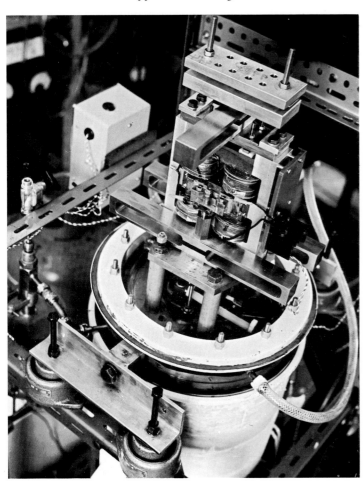

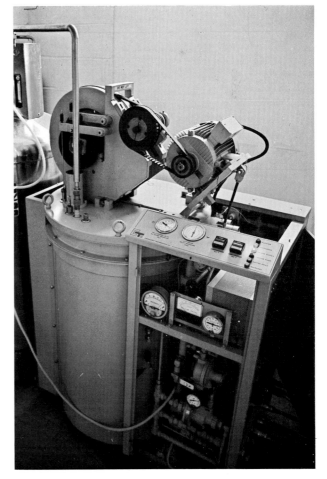

Aloys Senefelder

1771-1834

The principles of lithography, one of the most widely used methods of non-relief printing, were accidentally stumbled upon by a young and aspiring Czech writer named Aloys Senefelder.

Senefelder was born at Prague, the capital of Bohemia, which was at the time one of the states of the Hapsburg Empire. As a young man he wrote plays but was unable to have them published because he did not have enough money to pay for their engraving. He decided, therefore, to see to the engraving himself, and bought the copper plates on which to do it. The results were

ink or a grease crayon. The stone was then made completely wet, though the areas protected by the design repelled the water. When oily printing ink was next applied, it left the wet surfaces of the porous stone clean but adhered to the grease in the design drawing. The lithograph could now be made by a direct impression on a sheet of paper pressed on top of the stone.

There was no limit to the number of impressions that could be taken, and the results were remarkably sensitive in reproducing the original in all its details and idiosyncracies of line. A design transferred from the stone to the paper

Right: lithographic printing. The image is applied to the flat printing surface as a greasy film to which ink adheres. The nonprinting part of the plate is wetted and repels the ink.

level printing surface
nonprinting areas

Below: frontispiece plate of Senefelder's *A Complete Course of Lithography* (1818).

not encouraging. Then, one day in 1796, Senefelder happened to use a grease pencil to note down a laundry list on a slab of limestone. At first he thought that if he etched away the surface of the surrounding stone the markings would stand out in relief. This started off the train of thought that lead him on to establish the technique of lithography.

He laid his plays on one side and began to test out his idea in different ways. He spent two years over his experiments, using metal surfaces as well as various types of stone. By the end of the period he arrived at a flat surface method of printing – the classic method of lithography. It was based on the principle that grease and water are mutually repellent. The design to be reproduced was drawn directly on to the stone with a greasy

could, moreover, then be transferred in turn on to a clean stone, and the same thing done as many times as the designer liked. In this way, several copies of a design could be printed off simultaneously on one large sheet of paper.

The first applications of lithography were practical and commercial, but they became known to a wider circle after Senefelder pub-

Right: lithographic machine from German edition of Senefelder's book.

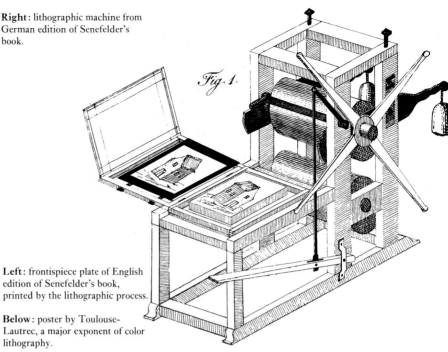

Fig. 1.

Left: frontispiece plate of English edition of Senefelder's book, printed by the lithographic process.

Below: poster by Toulouse-Lautrec, a major exponent of color lithography.

May Belfort

lished his book, *A Complete Course of Lithography* (1818). Later on a German music publisher invited him to go to Offenbach, near Frankfurt-am-Main, to set up a lithographic workshop where craftsmen could be trained to handle the process. It was always Senefelder's intention to develop a completely mechanized lithographic press, but this was not achieved until several years after his death in Munich.

It was in the 1820s that the French painters Théodore Géricault and Eugène Delacroix first saw the advantages lithography offered in directly conveying artistic intentions. Goya, in his old age, also took it up and produced a well-known series of bull-fighting subjects. The printmaker, caricaturist, and painter Honoré Daumier did much of his most important work in the form of lithographs, using an adaptation of the method whereby the picture was drawn in greasy ink on paper before being transferred to the stone – a method that greatly increased subtleties of textures. Color lithography, or oleography, was developed in the middle of the 19th century, using a whole series of different stones because one stone had to be used for each individual color. It was then necessary to print them off in turn in register. The most successful and best-known results of the technique were the posters of Henri de Toulouse-Lautrec.

From the Impressionists onward, through the main schools and movements of modern art, the lithograph has remained an important medium for artistic expression. Among the modern masters who have used it are Picasso and Henry Moore. The technical complexity, and hence the subtlety, of lithography has increased with the years, and the skill of an expert craftsman is needed to obtain the best results. It is still, in the second half of the 20th century, one of the most versatile and popular methods of print making.

Friedrich König
1774 - 1833

The steam-driven printing press, the invention of the German printer and engineer Friedrich König, brought about a far-reaching revolution in the techniques of printing that until then had remained unchanged for virtually 300 years.

The fundamentals of printing, established by Johannes Gutenburg in the mid-15th century, had gone through many phases of improvement and refinement, but by the end of the 18th century, the demand for printed information in the form of newssheets, as well as developing tastes in literature, had grown to the extent where existing hand-worked presses found it hard to cope. The problem of how to apply steam power, increasingly successful in various other industrial processes, to a printing machine, had become urgent. Between 1803 and 1811 König devoted himself to trying to perfect a press that worked by a series of gear wheels. These raised and lowered the flat platen (the plate that presses the paper to be printed against the type matrix) at the same time as the bed containing the type moved back and forth under the platen while inking cylinders applied ink to the type.

The mechanical platen press did not emerge as very successful in practice, and König went into partnership with another engineer, Andreas Bauer. Working together, they adopted the principle of using a cylindrical rather than a flat platen. As the platen turned, it carried the sheet

Below: König's machine built in 1814 for printing *The Times*. On this press the ink rollers were made from molasses and glue molded over a hard roll which gave continuous inking and much better coverage. This was a marked improvement over the old method of inking on hand presses which was done by leather-covered balls.

of paper with it and pressed it down against the type held in the flatbed, which moved to and fro in coordination with the cylinder. As the flatbed completed its forward movement, the cylinder's pressure was released and the printed sheet was delivered. The flatbed meanwhile returned under the inking rollers, ready to repeat the process. The first operating steam-powered press of this type was installed in 1814 to print *The Times* of London. By using two cylinders, so that two copies of each sheet could be printed with each backward-and-forward motion, it was able to print on one side over 1000 sheets an hour.

Four years later, König and Bauer built what they named as their "perfecting machine." This made double-sided printing possible as each sheet of paper was passed through a system of two cylinders. The paper still had to be fed in by hand, though in 1824 this part of the operation was also mechanized when the American-born British inventor William Church, who was also the first to develop a workable typesetting machine, introduced a system of grippers to lift and release the paper.

König's press entered into the final stages of its development with the innovation in 1846 of

Communication

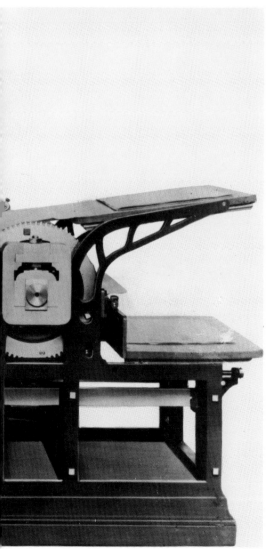

Below: König's first press, built at Suhl in 1811. It was the first steam-powered cylinder press and worked by moving a flat horizontal type forme back and forth under a revolving cylinder. König's steam-driven press could produce over 800 sheets an hour.

the all-rotary press, built by the American inventor and printer Richard Hoe, which replaced the flat typebed with a further cylinder. This exploited the use of stereotypy, a process used in printing since 1790, when stereotyping text blocks of type by clay or soft-metal molds had been one method of increasing rates of production. In rotary printing, the type was, by a system of molds, transferred onto metal plates that were curved to fit the cylinder. By running it between the platen cylinder and cylinder on which the type molds were locked, the paper could be printed off in one swift operation, giving up to 8000 one-sided printed sheets an hour. In its later version it could produce 18,000 sheets an hour, printed on each side.

Finally, in 1865, William Bullock, another American inventor, adapted the press to take paper on a continuous roll and incorporated an automatic guillotine to cut it to shape. It then became possible to produce 12,000 copies of a newspaper in one hour. The growing newspaper industry possessed the technological basis on which to expand as the rapid communication of information became an essential feature of modern life.

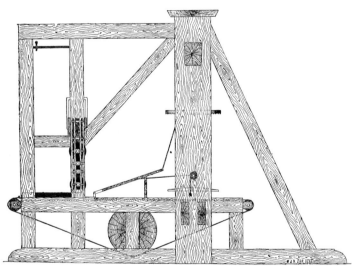

Right: the Hall of Presses at Times Newspapers, with the printing plates locked in position.

André-Marie Ampère

1775-1836

The French physicist and mathematician André-Marie Ampère was the first to establish the importance of the relationship between electricity and magnetism. He devised the earliest form of an electromagnet and suggested a theory to explain magnetic effects. This theory foreshadowed the discovery of the electron and its role in the modern atomic theory of matter.

Born in the village of Polémieux on the Rhône river, Ampère's early life was marred by a double tragedy. His father, a dedicated monarchist, was involved in the city of Lyon's rebellion against the Republican government of France. Convicted of treason, he was publicly executed. Ampère, only 18 years old, had barely recovered from this ordeal when, a few years later, his young wife died of a sudden unidentified illness. The blow was almost too much for Ampere and for some years he lived alone, seeing no one and fighting against a depression that threatened to destroy his sanity. Slowly, however, his interest in science and mathematics reasserted themselves and, as he returned to his academic work, his mental anguish began to subside. In 1809, his intellectual powers fully restored, he secured the important post of Professor of Mathematics in Paris.

In 1820 the scientific world was excited by a momentous discovery. A little known Danish physicist named Hans Øersted had noticed by chance that a compass needle was deflected when brought close to a wire carrying an electric current. It was the first suggestion of a link between magnetism and electricity, the two most mystifying phenomena of the time. Ampère immediately repeated Øersted's experiment under carefully controlled conditions; within a week of Øersted's original announcement, Ampère had worked out a rule relating the direction in which the compass needle was deflected to the direction in which the electric current flowed along the wire. The "swimmer's rule," as Ampère called it, states that if an observer were to swim along the current-carrying wire in the direction of the current and facing the compass needle, the north pole of the needle would be deflected toward the swimmer's left hand.

Ampère is also credited with another version of the rule, called the "right-hand grip" rule. The observer's right hand is imagined gripping the wire through which the current flows, with the thumb pointing along the wire in the direction of the current. The fingers, curling around the wire, indicate the direction in which the compass needle will be deflected. This concept anticipated the theory of electromagnetic force, formulated some years later, which showed that

Below: L'Ecole Polytechnique, Paris, where Ampère was appointed Professor of Mathematics in 1809, and where he performed his most important works.

Electricity

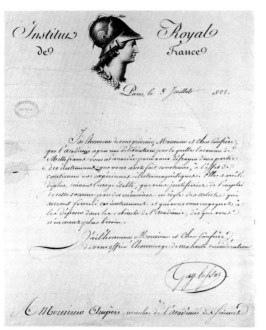

Left: letter to Ampère from Gay-Lussac of the French Royal Institute. It announced that the French Academy of Sciences was prepared to award him 1000 francs so that he could continue his research into electromagnetism.

Right: windings for a linear induction motor. Ampère defined the relationship between electricity and magnetism discovered by Øersted. The movement of a magnet due to the flow of an electric current was in fact the first electric motor, the predecessor of one of man's most important sources of power. Electric motors vary greatly in size and can be classified into different categories. Their uses are numerous. Linear induction motors, for example, are found in high-speed ground transportation, textile looms, and aircraft and missile launchers.

a magnetic field encircles an electrified wire just as do the fingers of the hand in Ampère's right-hand rule.

Continuing his investigations, Ampère found that wires could be made to behave like magnets by passing currents through them, and that the polarity of their magnetism depended upon the direction of the current. In his best-known experiment, Ampère arranged two parallel wires, one fixed, the other moveable. When Ampère placed the wires end to end and passed a current in the same direction through them both, the moveable wire was attracted toward the fixed one. When current was passed through the wires in opposite directions, the wires repelled each other. Their behavior was the same as two ordinary bar magnets in which like poles repel each other and opposite poles attract. Ampère's experiment established beyond doubt that the phenomena of magnetism and electricity were inextricably bound up together. On a practical level, the rudimentary electromagnets that he built were fore-runners of more sophisticated and powerful models which today find a wide range of industrial uses.

Having explored the way in which electricity and magnetism were linked, Ampère was convinced that electric current was somehow the actual origin of the phenomenon of magnetism. In 1823 he published a remarkable mathematical theory showing that the properties of a magnet could be explained by assuming that innumerable tiny electric currents were circling within it. But Ampère was ahead of his time and his contemporaries received this theory with undisguised skepticism. It was not until about 60 years after Ampère's death that his theory was shown to be substantially correct. It had to wait on the discovery of a negatively charged subatomic particle now called the electron.

Ampère's contribution to the understanding of electromagnetism has been recognized in one way by naming the unit of electric current after him. Appropriately, in view of Ampère's famous experiments, an *ampere* of electricity is formally defined as the amount of current in a wire that will exert a certain force on another nearby current-carrying wire.

Sir Humphry Davy

1778-1829

Known widely as the inventor of the miner's safety lamp, Humphry Davy also made important discoveries about the properties of gases, especially nitrous oxide which is sometimes called "laughing gas." His most important achievement, however, was to devise a means of isolating metals from their compounds by using a process called electrolysis.

Davy was born in the fishing village of Penzance on the southwest coast of England. As a child he planned to become either a poet or an artist, and he showed a real talent for both poetry and art. His parents insisted on a more practical career, however, and encouraged him to study medicine. So at the age of 17, Davy was apprenticed to a local surgeon and apothecary to train as a doctor. Within a few years his interest had strayed from medicine to chemistry, and he soon developed strongly independent views on some of the most important scientific issues of the day. He became especially interested in the study of gases, a field in which he quickly established an international reputation.

One of Davy's earliest discoveries was of a gas called nitrous oxide, a compound of nitrogen and oxygen. Davy, a great believer in sniffing and tasting unknown chemicals, found that the gas had some unusual properties. Inhaling it first gave him a feeling of euphoria. Then he began to lose control over his emotions, laughing and sob-

Center: Davy at work.

Below: early 19th century electrolysis apparatus.

lecturer at the Royal Institution in London.

While working at the institution, Davy heard reports of a newly discovered technique called electrolysis by means of which water could be decomposed into its elements hydrogen and oxygen. The technique involved immersing electrodes in a fluid and passing electricity through it. Davy wondered whether other compounds besides water could be broken down by passing electricity through them. In order to test his idea, he first constructed a massive electric battery, the most powerful ever built. He used it for a series of experiments with commonly available minerals, and the results were immediate and spectacular. When he passed a current through molten potash, globules of a metal appeared. Davy named it "potassium." Soon afterward he liberated sodium from soda, and in the year that followed he isolated strontium, calcium, mag-

bing until he almost lost consciousness. His reports of the effects of "laughing gas," as it became known, led to its use as one of the first chemical anesthetics. More immediately, its discovery won for Davy an appointment as

Chemistry

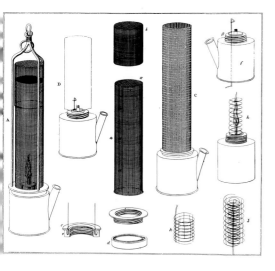

nesium, and barium. The discovery of so many new metals was an important enough achievement in itself, but Davy's work also helped to establish electrolysis as an industrial process. It is still widely used to extract metals from their ores, just as the method of extracting sodium from soda pioneered by Davy remains one of the most common methods of isolating that substance today.

Davy's scientific fame was assured, but his popular acclaim came for the invention of a new kind of lamp to be used by miners. One of the most common causes of deaths in mines during Davy's time was the explosion of pockets of underground gas ignited by the naked flame of miners' candle lamps. The most common killer was methane gas, undetectable by smell. Miners were totally unaware of their danger from methane until they encountered a critical concentration of the gas and were suddenly engulfed in flames. In 1815 a society that studied the problem of safety in mines approached Davy for advice. Davy realized at once that the source of the problem was the high temperature of the candle flame in the lamps. If a light had a temperature lower than the ignition point of gases such as methane, no explosions would occur.

Finally he hit upon a way of dissipating the intense heat of the flame by surrounding it with a metal gauze. Although enough oxygen could pass through the gauze to feed the flame, its surface always remained below the ignition temperature of the explosive gases. An added advantage was that the lamp flame burned with a bluish light when methane was present in any quantity, warning miners of potential danger. The Davy Lamp, as it became known, saved many lives and won for Davy the admiration of a public that knew little of his other scientific achievements.

Davy was less successful in caring for his own well-being. His lifelong practice of sniffing and tasting unknown chemicals played havoc with his constitution and by the age of 33 he was already a partial invalid. In a hopeless effort to recover his health, he made a number of trips to Europe. When in 1829 he settled for a while in Rome, he described himself with grim humor as "a ruin among ruins." A few months later he suffered a series of paralyzing strokes that killed him.

George Stephenson

1781-1848

The self-taught British inventor and engineer George Stephenson developed the steam-blast engine and thus made the steam locomotive practicable. His innovations over the whole range of railway technology initiated the railway age, and he was deservedly known as the "founder of the railways."

Stephenson, born at Wylam, Northumberland, was the son of a mechanic. George, likewise, went to work in the mines, operating a Newcomen engine. He received no formal education, but as a young man enrolled at night schools so as to learn reading and writing, and later basic arithmetic. In 1802 he was married,

and the next year his son Robert Stephenson was born, destined also to become one of the leading engineers of the 19th century. In 1806, George Stephenson's wife died, leaving him to bring up his young son alone.

Determined that Robert would not suffer from the same lack of early education, George spent his spare time repairing neighbors' clocks and watches, mending and making shoes, and even cutting cloth for work suits to raise money to send the boy to Newcastle for a proper schooling. The younger Stephenson would often bring home material relating to engineering for his father to study.

Right: Stephenson's steam locomotive, the *Caledonian*, pulling one of the first trains on the Liverpool-Manchester Railway in 1833.

The early years of Stephenson's life had witnessed the initial development of the locomotive. The first locomotive was the *New Castle*, built in 1804 by Richard Trevithick. Trevithick, a Cornish mine engineer, had introduced high-pressure steam into the steam engine, an innovation for which James Watt said that he "deserved hanging." Watt was adamant that a pressure of five pounds to the square inch, on which his own engines operated, was the reasonable safety limit. Trevithick achieved pressures of up to 145 pounds to the square inch in his mine engines, and at the same time gained the advantage of needing a much smaller cylinder, and consequently far fewer moving parts. Trevithick applied these principles to build a locomotive that would run on rails. The result was the *New Castle*. It was designed to run on an existing horse tramroad in a Welsh ironworks but unfortunately it was so heavy that it broke the cast-iron rails.

Subsequent development was slow. The locomotive's many problems included drive, suspension, and a strong and safe permanent track. There was also the difficulty of creating a speed

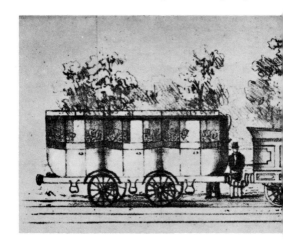

faster than horses pulling an equivalent in loaded wagons. Other early examples, such as William Hedley's *Puffing Billy* built in 1813, were used only for short-haul runs to carry coal between the minehead and warf.

Stephenson, by this time chief mechanic at Killingworth Colliery, had developed a reputation for being able to deal with recalcitrant machinery. He was commissioned by the colliery's owner to build a locomotive for carrying coal out of the mines. Stephenson improved on current designs, and in 1814 built the *Blücher*, which turned out to be the most successful "traveling engine" to date. Shortly after this, Stephenson made his key discovery: if the waste steam was allowed to escape through a narrow pipe by way of the chimney, the draft in the furnace was considerably reinforced. This, the steam-blast technique, was the single most important innovation in the history of the locomotive, since it opened up the possibility of a much faster traveling engine.

Over the next few years Stephenson used his spare time to work on many aspects of railway engineering, including rail joints, tracks, axles, and improvements in economies of engine design. Then in 1822 he was hired to be company engineer to the 12-mile-long Stockton and Darlington Railway, at that point in its planning stage. When the line was inaugurated in 1825, Stephenson's *Locomotion* drew the world's first passenger train at speeds of up to 12 miles per hour. The Stockton and Darlington Railway, however, was designed primarily for freighting. The first passenger service came five years later with the opening of the Liverpool and Manchester Railway, on which Stephenson also worked as engineer.

The directors of the new railway linking the two cities decided, a year before the opening, to hold a competition over a newly laid stretch of track at Rainhill to pick the most suitable locomotive. For the Rainhill Trials, Stephenson built the *Rocket*, a locomotive which incorporated all the lessons learnt during the previous two decades. In efficiency of performance it easily outstripped its rivals, achieving what was

Right: Stephenson's *Rocket*. This pioneer engine incorporated a revolutionary boiler design. Twenty-five tubes, each of about 3 inches diameter, ran at an angle from the firebox through the boiler shell. With a steam pressure of 40 pounds per square inch, it could travel 60 miles at 14 miles per hour. Its tubular boiler and direct piston-to-wheel drive set the pattern for the future.

then an amazing speed of nearly 30 miles per hour. The true inauguration of the railway age took place with the public opening of the line on September 15, 1830, when a majestic procession of eight brand-new locomotives left Liverpool, drawing trains which carried 600 guests.

The financial and technical triumph of the Liverpool and Manchester Railway triggered the intensive and rapid development of rail systems in Europe and the United States. Until his death George Stephenson continued to act as a consultant for many of the more important enterprises. By 1850 his son Robert could say in a speech in Manchester: "As I look back upon these stupendous undertakings, accomplished in so short a time, it seems as though we had realized in our generation the fabled powers of the magician's wand. Hills have been cut down and valleys filled up; and when these simple expedients have not sufficed, high and magnificent viaducts have been raised, and if mountains stood in the way, tunnels of unexampled magnitude have pierced them through."

Below: the opening of the Stockton-to-Darlington railway, 1825. It covered 37 miles and carried the world's first passenger train, drawn by Stephenson's *Locomotion*.

Joseph Fraunhofer

1787-1826

In the course of his short life, Joseph von Fraunhofer became famous throughout Europe as one of the finest lens and prism makers of the time. Today he is remembered as one of the founders of the science of spectroscopy, a method of analyzing the light radiated by planets or heated substances that enables scientists to identify the elements of which they are composed.

Fraunhofer was born in Straubing in Southern Germany, the son of a poor but talented glassmaker. Both his parents died while he was still a child and he received little formal schooling. When he was 14 he was apprenticed to a lookingglassmaker in nearby Munich. Fraunhofer had his father's instinctive gift for glassmaking, but nonetheless his employer ill-treated and exploited him, making his life a misery of virtual starvation and overwork. Then came a stroke of good fortune that changed Fraunhofer's life. The decrepit lodgings in which he lived suddenly collapsed, trapping him in the ruins. Miraculously unhurt, Fraunhofer found himself the center of a dramatic rescue operation. The Elector of Bavaria himself came to watch the rescue and was moved by Fraunhofer's plight. The ruler decided to help the boy by providing enough money for him to buy himself out of his apprenticeship and obtain a good education. It was a turning point for Fraunhofer. By 1806 he had been accepted onto the staff of the famous Munich Optical Institute.

In his new job, Fraunhofer's genius for making lenses and optically perfect prisms was quickly appreciated. Astronomers and scientists from all parts of Europe heard of his work and were soon applying to the institute for various kinds of lenses and prisms. Many important discoveries were made possible by the quality of Fraunhofer's lenses in particular. In 1817 he made a 9.5-inch object lens for the Russian Dorpat Observatory in Estonia. When the tele-

Above: the Utzschneider Optical Institute, Benedictbeuern, near Munich, where Fraunhofer perfected his techniques for grinding lenses and making prisms. In 1818 he became its sole manager.

scope was assembled, astronomers were able to identify over 2000 new double stars within a few years. In recognition of his fine work, Fraunhofer was appointed director of the Munich Institute in 1823.

Fraunhofer made his most famous discovery in 1814 while he was testing prisms. He noticed that the spectrum of colors into which the sunlight was broken by the prism was crossed by a large number of dark lines. Although a few such lines had been observed before by scientists, the superb optical quality of Fraunhofer's prism enabled him to identify over 500 of them. He

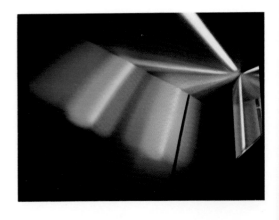

Right: diffraction grating, a series of parallel slits or finely etched rules. When light is directed on it at a particular angle it is diffracted or broken up into a series of spectra. The amount of diffraction depends on the wavelength of the light and the width of the opening. As different colors have different wavelengths, the light emerges in the form of a spectrum. Because of their superior efficiency in separating out colors, diffraction grating are nowadays used in spectroscopes in preference to prisms.

Spectroscopy

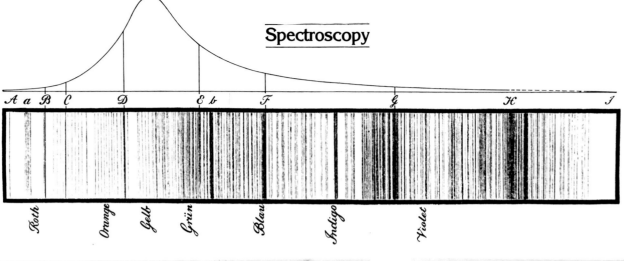

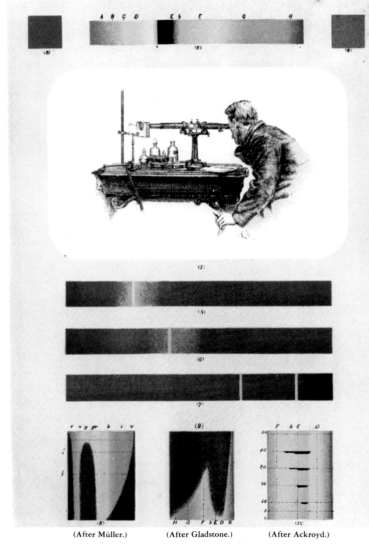

(After Müller.)   (After Gladstone.)   (After Ackroyd.)

measured the position and wavelength of the seven most prominent lines, naming them with the letters A to G by which they are still identified today. Later he succeeded in measuring the wavelengths of almost all the other lines, which became known as the *Fraunhofer Lines* in his honor. Intrigued by the meaning of the lines, Fraunhofer continued his research by analyzing starlight. He directed a telescope toward a star and placed a prism at its focal point. Split into a spectrum by the prism, the starlight also showed a number of dark lines although their positions were different to those in the solar spectrum.

Above: solar spectrum map.

Above center: spectroscopist (1) and his observations: magenta spectrum (2), its surface color (3), solution color (4). Emission spectra of sodium (5), thallium (6), indium (7). Absorption spectra of indigo (8), chromic chloride (9), magenta (10).

Above right: Fraunhofer's original spectroscope and prism.

Right: absorption spectrophotometer.

Tragically, Fraunhofer did not have time to complete his research by formulating an explanation of the significance of the lines. On the brink of a momentous discovery, he contracted tuberculosis and died at the age of 39. A few years later, Fraunhofer's remarkable work was brought to fruition when it was shown that the various spectral lines he had identified were in fact the "signatures" of particular chemical elements present in the atmospheres of the sun and stars. Today Fraunhofer's discoveries are the basis of the science of spectroscopy. Modern astronomers can make a detailed analysis of the composition of stars by identifying the spectral lines in the light they radiate. For example, it is now known that the sun contains at least 70 of the 92 elements occurring naturally on earth. Similarly, chemists can apply spectroscopy to the analysis of chemical compounds. By heating them until they glow they produce light which can be split up into a spectrum revealing the signatures of their component elements.

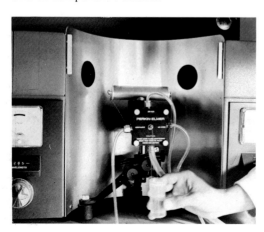

Georg Simon Ohm

1787-1854

Although he discovered one of the most fundamental laws of current electricity, German physicist Georg Ohm was virtually ignored for most of his life by scientists in his own country. However, his formulation of a simple relationship between electric current, voltage, and the readiness of a material to conduct electricity, helped to transform electrical studies into a quantitative science.

While still a child in his home in Erlangen in Southern Germany, Ohm's ambition was to become a scientist and to work at one of the great German universities of the day. Ohm's father, a mechanical engineer, taught him basic practical

skills that later proved invaluable to Ohm's experimental work, and encouraged his enthusiasm for science. However, the family was poor with no influential friends and Ohm had little success in securing a university post. Finally he accepted a job teaching in a local school, resigned to conducting private research and perhaps establishing his reputation through an important scientific discovery.

Ohm's main interest was current electricity, recently advanced by Alessandro Volta's invention of the battery, the first reliable source of a steady current. Unable to afford the necessary equipment for research, Ohm drew upon the skills taught by his father and spent long evenings making his own. He even made his own metal wire, producing a range of thicknesses and lengths of remarkably consistent quality.

Having heard of some important discoveries concerning the rate of flow of heat, Ohm felt intuitively that similar ideas should apply to electric current. He speculated that just as the flow

of heat between two points depended partly on the differences in temperature between the points and partly on the readiness with which heat was conducted by the material between, so the flow of electric current might depend on a difference in electric potential between the two points – today commonly called voltage – and the readiness of the intervening material to conduct electricity. He tested his hypothesis by passing current through wires of different thicknesses and lengths, painstakingly building up a vast store of experimental data. He discovered that for a given kind of metal, the current conducted increased as length and thickness decreased. The simple logic of this was that the more metal there was present, the more difficult it was for the electricity to pass through the wire. Ohm used his findings to describe a quantity that he called electrical resistance, defining it for a particular material in terms of a standard length and cross-sectional area.

In 1827 he was able to show from his experiments that there was a simple relationship between resistance, current, and voltage. Ohm's famous law states that the flow of current is

Below: original apparatus used by Ohm in his series of experiments between 1825 and 1840 which showed that the flow of an electric current depended on the resistance of the wire carrying it. Ohm's original source of electricity was not a battery but a set of Leyden jars connected by brass rods.

Left: Ohm's galvanometer, used for measuring extremely small currents.

Right: a toroidal rheostat, a modern example of the practical application of Ohm's law. Rheostats control the supply of current to electrical equipment by introducing a variable resistance. They are used for the starting of electric motors, the control of their speed, adjusting the field strength of generators, in radio receivers, and for varying light intensity. The toroidal rheostat, so-called because of the doughnut shape of the ring around which the wire is wound, is found in many laboratories. It is also used in a large number of industrial processes, in particular electroplating.

directly proportional to voltage and inversely proportional to resistance. Using this law, scientists could for the first time work out the amounts of current, voltage, and resistance in electric circuits, and the variations of one through changes in the others. By altering circuit components such as resistances, they could then design circuits to perform specific functions. Ohm's law not only made major advances in studies of electricity possible but also became the cornerstone of electrical engineering.

Ohm knew he had made a major discovery and was determined to use it to achieve finally his ambition of a university appointment. Fearing that the purely experimental basis of his work might undermine its significance in the eyes of the scientific community, Ohm made the disastrous decision to try to state his law theoretically. When he published his discovery, his brilliant experimental studies were mentioned only briefly and most of his paper was devoted to dubious mathematics. Far from establishing his reputation, publication did it untold harm. German scientists ignored the basic importance of Ohm's findings and concentrated on ridiculing his ram-

bling mathematical derivations. He was so strongly criticized that he was even forced to resign his school post.

In the years that followed, Ohm lived in poverty and isolation. Meanwhile, outside of Germany news of his discovery was spreading and steadily gaining recognition as an important breakthrough. To his delight, Ohm began to receive congratulatory letters from scholars in various parts of Europe, and in 1842 the Royal Society in London admitted him as a member. As the tide of opinion in Europe gathered in Ohm's favor, German scientists began to reconsider the experimental basis of his work. Slowly they came to accept that the vital importance of the discovery far outweighed Ohm's shaky mathematics. In 1849, just five years before his death, Ohm's lifelong dream was realized when he was given a professorship at the University of Munich.

Sir Edward Sabine

1778-1883

He was more successful in an experiment to determine the longitudinal distance between Paris and London by firing rocket signals. His results were accurate to within 0.6 of a second. His leave of absence from the army to engage in scientific research was broken briefly in 1830 when he was stationed in Ireland. Back in London in 1834, he became the leading architect of the first magnetic survey to be undertaken of Great Britain.

Sir Edward Sabine, an English astronomer and soldier, was the first scientist to plot the earth's magnetic patterns. He was also the first to link activity of sunspots with disturbances in the earth's magnetic field.

Edward Sabine managed to combine his work in science with a successful military career. He was born in Dublin, Ireland, and received his education at the Royal Military Academy, Woolwich, England, before becoming a subaltern in the Royal Artillery. Posted to Canada in 1813, he served at the siege of Fort Erie in 1814 during the American War of Independence. Already, however, he was developing a strong interest in science, especially in astronomy and terrestrial magnetism.

Sabine returned to England in 1816. In 1818 and 1819–1820, in his capacity as astronomer, he accompanied two official expeditions to the Arctic to search for the Northwest Passage. He soon demonstrated remarkable ability for recording and correlating scientific data and was commissioned to establish the shape of the earth. It was a long-term research program, involving the use of a sensitive magnetic pendulum at 17 selected sites over a wide area of the earth's surface. By 1825 he had published his results, though these were later found to be inaccurate because of variations in the earth's density which he could not have taken into account.

Above: Alexander von Humboldt, the German naturalist and explorer who laid the foundations of physical geography and geophysics.

Right: the earth's magnetosphere, a recent concept of the earth as the center of an extensive magnetic field. The magnetosphere forms a barrier against radiation, and resembles a teardrop in shape with the tail pointing away from the sun. As the solar wind (Y), a stream of atomic particles, comes toward the earth it meets the magnetic field and a shock wave forms, inside which there is a turbulent region bounding the magnetopause (Z).

Below right: the origin of the earth's magnetic field is still uncertain, but its direction and intensity near the surface can now be measured.

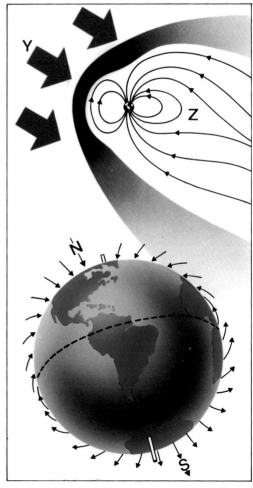

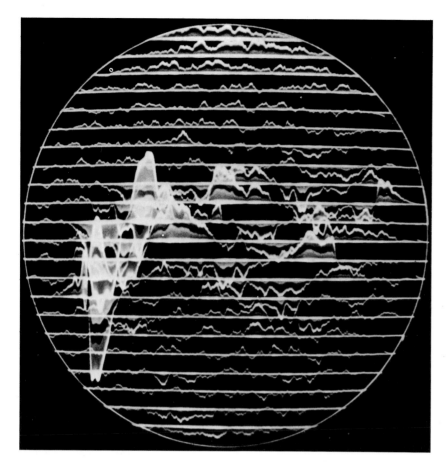

He discovered that sunspots (dark, relatively cooler areas on the sun) likewise, had a periodicity of intensity over a 10- to 11-year cycle. When Sabine saw the details of Schwabe's work he realized that the phenomena of sunspots and frequency of magnetic storms could be correlated.

It was a discovery of considerable scientific importance, and together with his momentous achievement of mapping the earth's geomagnetism, it established Sabine's fame. As a soldier, he retired from the army with a rank of general, and as a scientist, he held for 10 years the presidency of the Royal Society. Oxford and Cambridge universities both granted him honorary degrees, and he received many international tributes. During his last years, unfortunately his mental powers declined and he was forced to withdraw from public life.

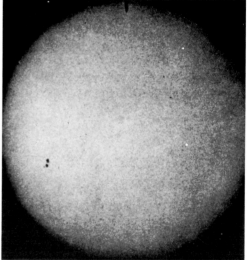

The cause of periodic fluctuations in the magnetic field of the earth had for a long time been the preoccupation of the German explorer and scientist Alexander von Humboldt. During these "magnetic storms," as they were called, compass needles fluctuated strangely and auroras, northern and southern lights, were seen. Humboldt suggested that chains of magnetic monitoring stations should be set up round the world, and appealed to Britain, whose imperial territories extended into both hemispheres, to cooperate. With Sabine's persuasion, this was adopted as official government policy in 1839, and by 1840 a whole network of stations was in operation.

To help Sabine process the vast quantities of information which now came back from the magnetic stations, the War Office agreed that he should be seconded a small staff of clerks at Woolwich. For 20 years this staff sorted and cataloged data. Sabine meanwhile tabulated and published his results in a vast range of scientific papers, starting with *Observations on Days of Unusual Magnetic Disturbance* (1843). His output of writing was formidable, a monument to his exceptional industry and ability to digest and marshal a multitude of facts. In particular he traced the pattern of magnetic storms and found that they followed a 10- to 11-year cycle.

In Germany, meanwhile, a chemist and amateur astronomer, Samuel Heinrich Schwabe, was meticulously plotting the number of sunspots seen each day, a task he had started in 1826.

Magnetic map (above) and photograph (right) of the sun taken on the same day. Magnetic activity is strongest near the spots.

Below: Aurora Borealis, the northern lights.

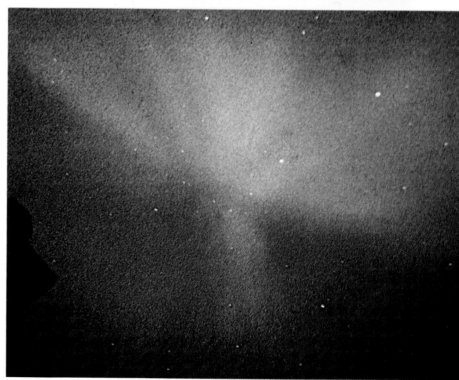

Louis-Jacques-Mandé Daguerre

1789-1851

Louis-Jacques-Mandé Daguerre invented, and gave his name to, the daguerreotype. This was the first practical form of photography, surpassing other methods of recording a permanent image by its speed of development and clarity of image. Until the mid-19th century the daguerreotype was the most widely used photographic process.

Daguerre began his professional life in Paris as a scene painter and designer for the stage. He introduced the Diorama, a display of views painted on transparent canvas. The views were arranged so that each appeared as a set on a stage, a series of which was arranged around a platform. The platform on which the audience sat then revolved, and Daguerre achieved subtle, illusory effects such as moonlight by changes in lighting. As a theatrical device it was short-lived, but it did have a long-term application for both peep-shows and three-dimensional museum reconstructions.

Daguerre had been interested in trying to fix, in some way, the image produced by a camera obscura. When he heard that Joseph Niepce had succeeded in producing the first photograph, he managed to persuade the older man, after much discussion, that they should collaborate in developing the invention. The central problem was

to reduce the time needed for exposure, as Niepce's method required seven or eight hours. Research continued until Niepce's death, and then Daguerre persisted on his own.

Using copper plates with silvering on one side, he exposed the silvered side to iodine vapor, and this produced a coating of light-sensitive silver iodide. Initially, when he tried these out in a camera, they emerged blank. However, he found that an image began to appear after some old plates were stored in a cupboard where some mercury had been spilt. Quite by accident he had discovered that mercury vapor could be used to develop the image. Later he found that a concentrated solution of sodium thiosulfate could be used to fix the image by washing out the unexposed silver iodide.

By 1837 Daguerre was obtaining remarkable results. The daguerreotype was extraordinarily faithful in the details and clarity of the image it recorded, and the exposure time was reduced to about 20 minutes.

In 1939 the French government granted

Below: la Place du Chateau d'eau, Paris; in the background can be seen the Diorama, Daguerre's exhibition of pictorial views painted on transparent canvas.

Right: three early daguerreotype cameras.

Daguerre and Niepce's son, who inherited his father's share in the partnership, life annuities in return for the publication of the invention "free to the world." Before the year was out, daguerreotypes were being made of the pyramids in Egypt and the antiquities of Greece as well as of scenes in the United States.

During the next few years the invention was developed further as the sensitivity of solutions was increased and improvements were made in camera lenses. Once the exposure time was reduced to well under half a minute, its use in portraiture became far more practicable and very widespread. It also made the photographing of moving objects a feasible proposition.

Above left: daguerreotype of Louis-Philippe of France printed on paper.

Above right: one of Daguerre's first successful exposures, taken of the Tuilleries in Paris, around 1839.

Center: early daguerreotypes, polished silver-plated copper plaques treated with iodine and bromine vapors.

Right: daguerreotype guarantee plaque, warning users to "beware of all imitations."

The daguerreotypes had several practical disadvantages. Because it was necessary to use a metal plate for each exposure the costs were high. Then, because daguerreotypes were made from a direct image, each individual picture was, in effect, a unique copy and not satisfactorily reproduceable. It came out, moreover, in reverse, as a mirror image, and by the 1850s the process had reached its limits of practical development. It was gradually displaced by the more flexible calotype system of obtaining positive prints from negative images, invented in Britain by William Henry Fox Talbot.

Michael Faraday

1791-1867

Michael Faraday, a physicist widely regarded as the greatest experimental scientist in history, made up for his lack of mathematical training with a genius for visualizing the physical mechanisms of nature. His fame rests mainly on his contributions to the understanding of the link between magnetism and electricity, and for formulating the quantitative laws governing electrolysis.

Faraday was born near London, one of 10 children in a poor working-class family. There was little chance of anything but the most basic schooling before he was apprenticed at the age of 14 to a firm of booksellers. His job, however, turned out to be a stroke of good fortune because his employer encouraged him to study. Faraday also went on visits to the Royal Institution in London to hear the principal lecturer Humphry Davy talk. Greatly impressed, Faraday kept careful notes of every lecture, later illustrating them with his own diagrams. Hoping for a job at

Below right: Faraday's laboratory.

Opposite left: Faraday's electroscope. When a negatively charged glass rod is brought near the knob of the electroscope, it repels the negative charges in the knob, forcing them down into the gold leaves, which therefore repel one another. When the glass rod is removed the negative charge redistributes itself, the apparatus becomes neutral, and the leaves hang limply. However, if the stem near the leaves is touched before the rod is removed, some of the negative charge escapes to earth. If the glass rod is then removed, the electroscope is positively charged and the leaves will repel each other.

cussions of some of Europe's finest scholars. When he returned to London, he determined to start his own research at the Royal Institution.

Building on the discovery by the Danish physicist Hans Oersted that a compass needle shows a deflection when brought close to a wire through which an electric current flowed, Faraday began experiments to explore the relationship between electricity and magnetism. His first major discovery took place a year later when he showed how electrical and magnetic forces could be converted into mechanical motion by placing a current-carrying wire between the poles of a horseshoe magnet. The interaction of forces caused the wire to rotate. Although Faraday took this line of research no further, he had in fact built the first rudimentary electric motor.

Although Faraday's discovery established his scientific reputation, he continued to assist Davy and, interested by his employer's experiments with electrolysis, began independent research into the phenomenon. It had been known for several years that when electricity was passed through water, the liquid decomposed into its constituent elements, oxygen and hydrogen. Davy showed that the phenomenon could be extended to solutions of various compounds and, from common chemical salts, managed to separate a number of hitherto unknown new metals. Faraday, using the results of his own painstaking experiments, reduced electrolysis to quantitative terms. His laws of electrolysis showed how the

the Royal Institution, he sent the notes to Davy. He was overjoyed when in 1813 Davy responded by offering him a position as his personal assistant. The salary was less than he received at the bookshop but he cared more about the chance to enter the world of scientific research, usually closed to someone without recognized educational qualifications.

Almost at once after his appointment, Faraday left with Davy for a grand tour of Europe. Although he was treated more as a servant than an assistant, he had the opportunity to see scientific research at first hand and to listen to the dis-

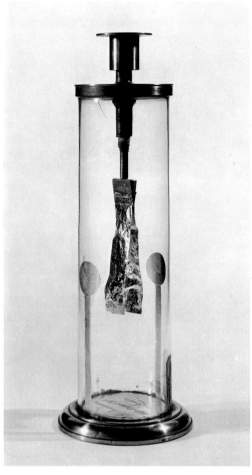

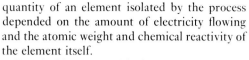

quantity of an element isolated by the process depended on the amount of electricity flowing and the atomic weight and chemical reactivity of the element itself.

Despite his success with electrolysis, Faraday's real interest lay in the link between magnetism and electricity. He was convinced that magnetism could be made to generate electricity just as electricity could create magnetism. In 1831, in a series of historic experiments, he discovered the phenomenon of electromagnetic induction – the production of electricity by means of fluctuating magnetic intensities. The most famous of his experiments used a ring of soft iron wrapped in two windings of insulated wire. The ends of one winding were connected to a galvanometer,

Below right: coil used by Faraday in his discovery of electromagnetic induction. When the coil was connected to a galvanometer and a magnet passed through it the galvanometer needle was deflected, indicating an electric current. However, the needle only oscillated when the magnet was moving. Thus Faraday showed that an electric field could be produced from a magnetic field, provided the magnetic field changed with time.

Above: Faraday's rod and coil used to demonstrate the production of electricity by a magnet. The rod is a cylinder of soft iron around which some silk-covered copper wire has been wound. One end of the wire terminates in a copper disk, and the other end is bent so that it is barely in contact with the disk. When the rod is placed on a strong magnet the two ends of the wire separate temporarily, and likewise when the rod is removed. The presence of an induced electric current, which causes the two ends of the wire to repel each other, can be observed by the bright electrical spark generated when the wires separate.

which measures current. When the other wire was connected to a battery, nothing appeared to happen although Faraday knew that the iron was temporarily magnetized by the current. But when the circuit was completed or broken the galvanometer recorded a pulse of electricity. Faraday realized that while the intensity of the iron's magnetism was rising or falling, an induced current was produced. In other words, a change in the degree of magnetism created induced electricity. Faraday used his discovery to build the first dynamo, the model for the powerful generators that today supply most of the domestic and industrial electricity.

Faraday's work led him to formulate the idea of "lines of force" to explain magnetism. He imagined magnetic force stretching out from the poles of a magnet in all directions, filling space with a kind of "field" of force. Lines could be drawn connecting all points where the strength of the force was equal. In this way the magnetic field could actually be mapped. After Faraday's death, his idea was extended to form the basis of the first full mathematical description of the nature and interaction of electricity and magnetism, now known as electromagnetic theory.

Always a modest man, Faraday accepted the honors and awards showered upon him with great reluctance. He even insisted that on his death his grave be marked with the simplest of headstones.

Samuel Morse

1791-1872

The first practicable telegraph system, so essential to the development of communications during the second half of the 19th century, was the work of a professional painter and amateur scientist, Samuel Morse.

Samuel Morse, the son of a Calvinist minister and distinguished geographer, began life as a painter. Shortly after graduating from Yale College in 1810, he left for his first visit to England to study art. On his return in 1815, he took up a career as a portraitist, and became one of the most stylish of portrait painters in early American art history. Those who sat for him included the Marquis de Lafayette and the inventor Eli Whitney.

From the beginning, side by side with Morse's preoccupation with art, there went an interest in science, and particularly in electricity. Returning in 1832 from a later visit to Europe, he overheard a shipboard conversation about Joseph Henry's development of the electromagnet. Henry was in fact the first to succeed in sending an impulse along a mile-long length of wire in 1831. The impulse was generated by a battery and rang a bell attached to a magnet armature at the other end. The idea of incorporating the electromagnet as a basis for working a wire telegraph system took root in Morse's mind. He began work on designs for magnetic transmitters and receivers,

Below center: Morse recording telegraph. When the operator depresses his key a current flows from the electromagnet (A) through an armature (B) which attracts the lever (C). The end (E) of its longer arm is pressed upward. The steel point on its end is pressed into a shallow groove in a metallic roller. Between the point and the roller a paper tape (K) unwinds and the message is thus embossed.

Below: Morse transmitting key.

and developed his prototypes in 1835. In 1837 he abandoned painting altogether to concentrate on his new invention, and within a year evolved the Morse code, the dots and dashes which correspond with the letters of the alphabet and numerals.

With single-minded persistence, Morse now began to lay the ground for the construction of the first long-distance telegraph line, and eventually persuaded Congress to back the project. The line, made of iron wire strung between posts, with glass doorknobs for insulators, was built between Baltimore and Washington, a distance of 37 miles. History was made on May 24, 1844 when it carried its inaugural message: "What hath God wrought!"

The spread of the telegraph encountered initial difficulties, for people still feared the effects that the electricity passing over their land might have. One group of farmers in the American South demolished a whole line, blaming it for upsetting the weather and causing a sequence of bad harvests. Nevertheless, the telegraph played a key role in opening up the American West.

Morse himself became embroiled in prolonged litigation to defend his patents and fight off rival claims. He triumphed ultimately in 1854, when the US Supreme Court upheld his patents rights. His failure to acknowledge the contributions of others to his invention, however, is usually seen as the most discreditable side of his character. In particular, without the system of relays to boost

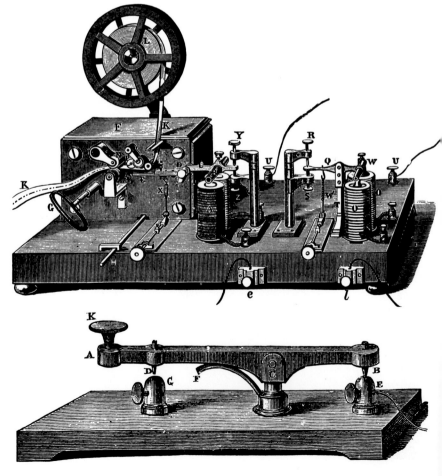

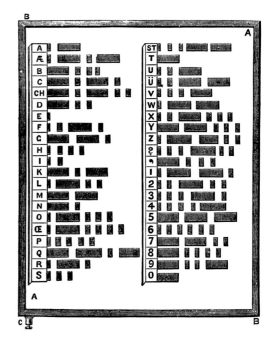

the signal at intervals that Joseph Henry invented but never patented, the whole project would have remained unworkable.

The Morse key for tapping out the code remained fairly consistent in its basic design, but the receiving register went through a series of developments, starting with a stylus that embossed the code on a continuous roll of paper. This was replaced by an inking device, and, in the mid-1850s, once it was found that trained operators could easily learn to "read" and note down the sound, by a simple sounder. In Europe, the Morse code was modified to take account of accents and other considerations when it was

Left London Telegraph Exchange, 1871. Within a very short time Morse's invention was being widely used, providing employment for many women.

Right: Morse's transmitting plate. The dots and dashes of the Morse code were transmitted by varying the time the transmitter key was depressed. Many operators found it difficult to learn to time the signals accurately, so Morse invented a transmitting plate. This was a tablet of nonconducting ivory, with strips of metal the lengths of which corresponded to the code. These were soldered to a metal plate underneath and flush with the surface of the tablet. A binding screw (C) connected the metal to a battery. The operator ran a rod, connected to the transmitter, along the tablet and each time it met the metal an electrical circuit was established.

Below: replica of Morse's receiver.

needed to convey an international range of languages.

Samuel Morse, in his old age, became a philanthropist in the American patriarchal mold. He contributed to the funds of educational establishments as well as to temperance and missionary societies. By the time of his death, the telegraph system to which he gave his name was in use throughout virtually the whole world.

Charles Babbage

1792-1871

The British-born mathematician Charles Babbage was a prolific inventor, being responsible for, amongst other things, the speedometer, locomotive cowcatcher, and an early opthalmoscope. But the major contribution of this technological visionary was a design for the first digital computer.

The earliest kind of calculating device known to man is the abacus, whose frame contains moveable beads on rods, each row of beads having a defined numerical value. It was probably invented in Babylonia about 5000 years ago, and is still used by merchants and shopkeepers in parts of the Far and Middle East. In skilled hands, the abacus can calculate complex additions with considerable speed.

It was the French mathematician and philosopher, Blaise Pascal, who in 1642 built the first adding and subtracting machine. It operated on a system of gears and numbered wheels, and he invented it to assist his father in his work as a

local tax administrator. The next stage – that of a machine which would also multiply and divide – was developed in 1694 by the German mathematician Gottfried Wilhelm von Leibniz, though it was not reliable enough for general use until improvements were made to it well over a century later.

These early devices were calculators rather than computers in the sense in which we use the word today. The first man to conceive of a true computer, and the tasks and functions of which it would be capable, was Charles Babbage, a mathematician whose genius turned out to be far in advance of its time.

Below: the Babbage "Analytical Engine," the forerunner of modern calculators and computers. The data was stored in columns of wheels, each wheel being capable of being moved to one of 10 positions. Each position thus corresponded to one decimal digit. The machine was programed by a series of punched cards. By moving a lever forward and back numerical problems could be computed in a cumulative manner by the series of wheels.

Babbage came from an affluent background, and studied at Cambridge. He became associated with a group of young scientists and mathematicians who felt that the cause of science in Britain was being neglected by both the government and the educational establishment. Mathematics was still being taught in the universities in accordance with a rigidly conservative adherence to the doctrines of Newton, and much of the work being done by a new generation of mathematicians in Europe was being ignored.

In 1830 Babbage published *Reflections on the Decline of Science in England*. It incorporated an attack on the Royal Society which he felt was then becoming too self-satisfied with its restricted membership. The next year he was one of the founder members of the British Association for the Advancement of Science, which swiftly became (and still is) an arena for advanced and controversial debate in every scientific area. It had considerable success in stimulating research as well as in promoting the academic status of science.

Babbage devoted many years to the problems of calculating machines. In 1823 he started on a calculating machine with a 20-decimal place capacity, and by 1834 his idea for an "Analytical Engine" was fully evolved. Babbage saw that the punched cards which Joseph-Marie Jacquard had developed for feeding complex patterns into his silk-weaving looms could be a basis for feeding instructions on complex mathematical and

Computers

algebraic problems into a calculating machine. This could then compute the answers more quickly and more accurately than a human being working alone.

He visualized his computer incorporating a memory bank, comparing results, and printing out required data. It was also to modify its own program and process data accordingly. The final 37 years of Babbage's life were largely given over to its development, a task (and eventually ob-

Below: computers being used to simplify the complicated procedure of airline bookings. This scene in the British European Airways reservations hall shows Uniset machines in operation, recording booking transactions for the airway's Beacon computer.

session) of bewildering complexity and monumental elaboration. Initially he received a grant of public money for his research, but the government withdrew its support in 1842 and Babbage had to carry on as best he could, using his own resources.

By the end of his life, Babbage was embittered by what he felt was a lack of recognition for the importance of his work and disappointed by his failure to bring his principles within sight of

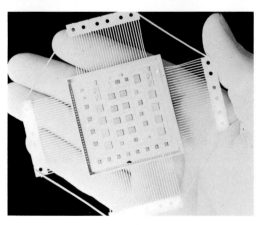

Left: microcomputer. Today's computers bear little resemblance to the cumbersome "Analytical Engine." In the early 1960s the reduction in size of electronic components and circuits enabled microcomputers to be built. With the increasing use of tiny silicon chips, the minaturization of circuits has reached the point where even the computer illustrated is large by comparison.

completion. The fact was that Babbage was attempting the impossible with the means at his disposal. The concept and the principles behind the "Analytical Engine," on the other hand, were absolutely sound.

The mechanical system of wheels, cogs, wires, levers, and cams, which Babbage built into his experimental models could never have, on their own, achieved the combination of accuracy and flexibility necessary to solve the kinds of advanced problems that he had in mind. But, when developments in electronics during World War II ultimately made the modern computer possible, Babbage's original ideas were vindicated.

Joseph Henry

1797-1878

A prolific and energetic American scientist, Joseph Henry's long life was crowded with invention and discovery. His most important achievements were the development of the first practical electromagnet (leading to a rudimentary electric telegraph), the construction of the earliest electric motor, and the discovery of "self-inductance," which had vital importance in the design of electric circuits.

Below: Charles Wheatstone's numeral receiver. The credit of inventing the electric telegraph resulted in a bitter legal battle between Samuel Morse and Henry. Wheatstone became involved because he himself had invented a needle telegraph in 1837.

order to make it possible to have a large number of turns without short-circuiting the coil, he struck upon the idea of insulating the wire using strips torn from his wife's silk petticoats. The results were spectacular. Europe's most powerful magnet could lift barely nine pounds. Henry's could lift over 2000!

Henry recognized that the practical uses of electromagnets were not confined to their strength. He explored the possibilities of using them to send messages over long distances. His plan was to connect a small electromagnet to a battery by wires over a mile long. An operator at the battery could make and break the electric circuit, thus switching the magnet on and off. The magnet could therefore be made to attract and release a metal bar in a sequence determined by the operator and so send messages in signal code. Henry soon put his idea into practice and by 1831 had built the first electric telegraph.

Henry's introduction to science came by accident at the age of 16. While staying with a relative near his home in Albany, New York, he chased a rabbit to ground beneath the floors of an old church. Losing interest in the rabbit, Henry began to explore the church and soon came upon a shelf of books. Among them was an old but beautifully illustrated volume on experimental science. Fascinated, Henry leafed through the pages and from that moment decided that his future lay in science.

Henry enrolled at the Albany Academy intending to study medicine, but changed to engineering. Soon after graduation he returned as a lecturer in science and mathematics. At about this time, Henry's main interest lay in European discoveries concerning electricity and magnetism, especially in the efforts being made to build electromagnets by winding a current-carrying wire around an iron core. In 1829 Henry set about improving the European design. He realized that the key to making a really powerful magnet was the number of turns of wire on the iron core. In

Electricity

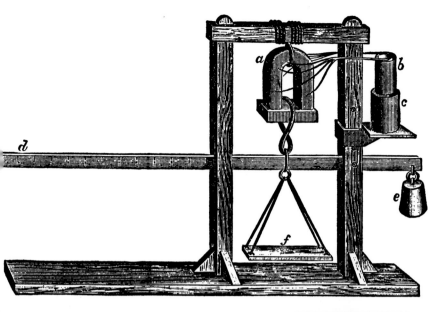

However, believing that scientific discoveries were the property of all mankind, he did not patent his invention and in 1844, with Henry's help, Samuel Morse set up the first patented telegraph. Morse avoided any public acknowledgement of Henry's contribution, taking all the credit and financial reward for the breakthrough.

Another of Henry's achievements was the discovery of self-inductance. In 1830 he published a paper describing how an electric current in a coil can not only induce a current in another coil but also in itself. The overall current in the coil is therefore a combination of the original current and the self-induced one. His discovery was to be of major importance in electric circuit design, especially where the maintenance of a particular level of current is crucial.

At about the same time, Henry drew together much of the current knowledge of electricity and magnetism to produce the design for the first

Above left: Henry's powerful electromagnet, capable of lifting a ton weight. The horseshoe magnet (a) was covered with a large number of turns of insulated wire around it, the ends of which were soldered to the galvanic element of the battery, which also contained a cup of dilute acid (c) on a movable shaft. The current from the battery made the horseshoe magnetic and it was able to support an armature from which hung a scale (f) for loading weights.

Above right: Samuel Morse. Henry's electromagnetic telegraph anticipated Morse's invention by six years.

practical electric motor. It was the first example of efficient conversion of electrical energy into mechanical energy, and created a revolution in everyday life. Henry's motor is the motive force of innumerable modern appliances such as refrigerators, vacuum cleaners, and electric shavers.

A dedicated scientist throughout his life, Henry also worked on the applications of science for the benefit of society. In 1846 he was elected the first secretary of the newly formed Smithsonian Institution and proved himself a brilliant administrator. He used his influence to set up a means of drawing together weather reports from all over the country using Morse's telegraph, a system upon which the present United States Weather Service is founded.

Henry's death was marked by public mourning throughout America. His funeral was attended by the President of the United States and many members of his Cabinet. A few years later, his memory was honored when the unit of self-inductance was named after him.

William Henry Fox Talbot

1800-1877

William Fox Talbot made the two most important contributions to the science of photography – the negative-positive method of print making, and the development of a "latent image" on a sensitized surface. These discoveries revolutionized photography. A subject could be recorded instantaneously and accurately, and reproduced indefinitely.

Fox Talbot, an English country gentleman, studied science at Cambridge University. He began his attempts to record an image with a camera obscura which he originally took to Italy on a drawing holiday. Knowing nothing of the work of the French pioneers Niepce and Daguerre at this stage, he began his experiments quite independently, using paper which he made sensitive to light by alternate soakings in solutions of silver nitrate and sodium chloride (common salt). The paper became impregnated with silver chloride, which darkened and hardened in those areas which were exposed to light. The amount of light passing through the lens depended on the subject at which the camera lens was directed. The darker a particular area, the less light passed through and consequently there was less blackening of the light-sensitive paper. When the unexposed silver chloride was washed away with a concentrated salt solution, a negative image was formed. From the negative it was now possible to obtain quantities of prints by placing

it against other sheets of sensitized paper and exposing it to strong light.

The results were coarse, and a 20-minute exposure time was necessary, but by 1835 Fox Talbot had a working system for his "photogenic drawing," as he called it. Early in 1839 he heard rumors of Daguerre's experiments in France and rushed to publish his own invention as well as secure his patents. In 1840, he discovered the principle of the latent image when he found that an initially invisible image could be formed by a much shorter exposure time. The negative picture could then be "developed" by bathing it in a chemical solution.

Fox Talbot called the end-product of his system a calotype (from the Greek for "beautiful picture"). At the family house of Lacock Abbey, Wiltshire, he continued his experiments, taking as his study any subject immediately available,

Right: Lacock Abbey, Fox Talbot's family home. It now houses the Fox Talbot Museum.

Below: the Oriel window at Lacock Abbey, taken by Fox Talbot in 1835. This is a positive print of the oldest negative in existence. The paper used to record the negative image was first bathed in solutions of sodium chloride and silver nitrate to precipitate silver chloride in the fibers. Twenty minutes' exposure time was required.

from bricklayers at work on the estate to his gamekeeper or coachman. Between 1844 and 1846 he published, in six parts, *The Pencil of Nature*, the first book to be illustrated by photographs. It was unfortunate that he did not as yet know how important it was to wash out all traces of the fixing agent, and as a consequence the quality of these calotypes deteriorated within only a few years.

Fox Talbot also had the distinction of taking the first flash photograph in 1851, when he used a Leyden jar battery to set off a spark.

After Fox Talbot, the next most important innovation in photography was the wet-collodion process, which in good light permitted almost instantaneous exposure. This was developed by an English silversmith and portrait sculptor, Frederick Scott Archer, who had tested out Fox Talbot's calotype as an aid to his professional

Above right: calotype of Lacock Abbey coachman, made in 1840 by Fox Talbot. The discovery of latent image and development enabled the exposure time to be drastically reduced – in this case to three minutes.

Above left: *The Pencil of Nature*, the first book to be photographically illustrated. Because the fixing solution was not washed out, the calotypes faded very quickly.

Above right: calotype of a boy with a hurdy-gurdy.

Left: wet-plate photograph of Abraham Lincoln, taken by Matthew Brady.

work. He soon realized that a completely transparent negative base would have enormous advantages, and succeeded in sensitizing a glass plate with a solution of collodion (gun cotton dissolved in ether and alcohol). Archer published his discovery in 1851.

Prints obtained from the wet-collodion negative were of exceptional quality, but the fact that the place had to be exposed and developed before it dried meant that a fully equipped darkroom had always to be close at hand. Even so, some of the finest and most famous early photographs were made by this method, including the series on the Crimean War by Roger Fenton, and those of the American Civil War by Matthew Brady.

Wet-plate photography remained in use up to and throughout the first half of the 20th century, particularly where excellence of graphic quality was a prime consideration. Side by side with it went the development of dry-plate photography, established in the 1870s and considerably improved upon over the following few years.

Friedrich Wöhler

1800-1882

The seemingly undramatic discovery by German scientist Friedrich Wöhler that it was possible to synthesize urea, an organic product, was one of the key contributions to revolutionizing the concepts of organic and inorganic chemistry.

Friedrich Wöhler was born at Aschersheim and educated at the grammar school at Frankfurt-am-Main. Even as a schoolboy his interest in chemistry was intense, and he devoted more time to collecting minerals and conducting experiments than he did to more general academic studies. At the University of Marburg he took his degree in medicine, but then decided to make chemistry his main subject, and in 1823 he left for Stockholm to work for a year with the Swedish chemist Jöns Jacob Berzelius.

Berzelius was by then one of the leading and most highly respected experimental chemists in Europe. He was a pioneer in determining the elemental constitutions of compound materials and introduced the system of notation still used for the formulae of chemical compounds. He discovered several elements and evolved a number of laboratory techniques and pieces of equipment that are still in standard use today.

In 1825 Wöhler returned to Germany to take up a teaching appointment in Berlin. He continued to combine experimentation with his other

duties, and to apply what he learned from Berzelius about the chemistry of elements. One day, in 1828, he was perplexed to find, after heating a compound of ammonium cyanate in a test tube, that the inorganic chemical appeared to have turned into urea, the main organic compound present in urine.

Like all chemists of his generation, Wöhler was trained to uphold the doctrine of "vitalism." According to this theory, the chemistry of life is quite distinct from inorganic chemistry, since a vital force or spirit governs its physical processes. An organic compound, it was therefore thought, could only be made by living tissue and in the case of urea, by the kidneys. Wöhler's discovery was a direct challenge to those beliefs and gave other scientists the impetus to synthesize a range of organic compounds. Vitalism was eventually discredited, and the way lay open for the new chemistry which recognized that fundamental laws applied equally to organic and inorganic substances.

In 1832, Wöhler's wife died. Partly to overcome his grief he accepted an invitation to work with Justus von Liebig in his laboratory at Giessen. Liebig's laboratory was famous as a center for the systematic teaching of research

Below right: Justus von Liebig in his laboratory, 1845. Liebig and Wöhler worked together on the analysis and synthesis of many organic chemicals.

Left: early portrait of Friedrich Wöhler.

methods. Despite a contrast in the two men's characters – Liebig was inclined to be dogmatic and irascible whereas Wöhler was gentle and reticent – the collaboration was a fruitful one.

The main direction of their investigation was

into molecular structure, and the study, then in its infancy, of the combinations of atoms which build up a molecule. They had previously become acquainted in 1824 when Liebig was working on the explosive compound, silver fulminate, while Wöhler was studying the stable substance, silver cyanate. These two distinct compounds contained the same elements in the same proportion. This discovery led on to the realization that the spatial organization of atoms within a molecule was important in governing the kind of sub-

the molecule accounting for the variations.

Another important study which Wöhler and Liebig made was into oil of bitter almonds (benzaldehyde). They found that even when the oil was put through a whole series of chemical reactions its basic group of atoms remained unchanged. Such groups of atoms they termed "radicals," and the theory of radicals was the first important attempt to explain organic chemical reactions.

Wöhler remarried in 1834. From 1836 until

Left: Liebig's appratus for galvanic analysis.

Right: samples of Wöhler's discoveries: synthetically manufactured urea (top) and pure metallic aluminum (bottom).

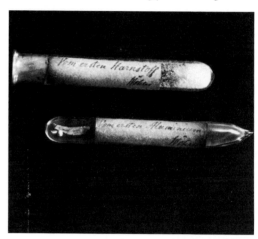

the end of his life he was Professor of Chemistry at the University of Göttingen. He continued to undertake important research, much of it in collaboration with Liebig, and in 1845 found a way of refining metallic aluminum that formed the basis for the first industrial process of aluminum production. He isolated a number of elements and investigated several physiologically important compounds, but above all he became a teacher of outstanding ability, and one whose influence was profound over the next generation of chemists.

Right: a range of modern drugs – synthetic organic chemicals. The pharmaceutical industry was one of the many important byproducts of Wöhler's initial discovery that an organic compound could be synthesized in the laboratory.

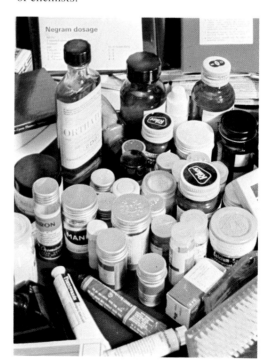

stance formed as well as its properties. Berzelius used this work to develop the concept of isomers: different compounds which possess the same constituent atoms but vary in their properties, the differences of atomic arrangements within

Christian Johann Döppler
1803-1853

Austrian mathematician and physicist Christian Döppler was the first to work out how the motion of a sound source affects the pitch of the sound as heard by an observer.

Born in Salzburg, Döppler's chief ambition was to make a career as an academic. Despite his outstanding abilities as a mathematician, however, he found it difficult to secure a university appointment. After much fruitless effort he despaired of ever finding a post in Europe and made plans to emigrate to the United States where more opportunities were available. A matter of days before he was due to leave, Döppler received an offer of the position of Professor of Mathematics in Prague. He immediately cancelled his plans to cross the ocean, preferring to remain near his homeland.

While in Prague Döppler became interested in finding an explanation for a commonplace but puzzling phenomenon concerning sound waves. For many years it had been known that a moving source of sound seems more highly pitched to someone whom it is approaching, and more deeply pitched to someone from whom it is mov-

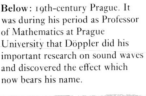

Below: 19th-century Prague. It was during his period as Professor of Mathematics at Prague University that Döppler did his important research on sound waves and discovered the effect which now bears his name.

ing away. A present-day example of this phenomenon is the falling pitch of a train whistle as it passes someone standing on a station platform. The pitch of the whistle remains high while the train approaches the station, and falls instantly as it passes the listener on the platform.

Döppler first explained the falling pitch qualitatively and then worked out the theory mathematically. A stationary sound source, Döppler said, can be imagined surrounded by successive spherical sound waves centered upon and moving outward from the source itself. The interval between the waves determines the pitch of the sound. If the source is moving, the wave fronts ahead of the source "crowd together" as each succeeding wave shares in the velocity of the source itself. Behind, the wave fronts become "stretched out," the intervals between them increasing as the source moves away from them. In front of the source, therefore, the intervals

Right: the Döppler effect is used to determine the movement of objects in the universe in relation to the earth. The wavelength of moving light is shortened in an approaching object and lengthened in a receding one. By observing light from celestial objects through a prism, light displaced toward the red end of the spectrum means that the source is receding; toward the blue end that it is approaching. A: light source from an object traveling at the same speed as earth; the spectral lines are in the normal position. B: light source approaching earth; spectral lines shifted toward blue end of spectrum. C: light source receding from earth; spectral lines shift toward red end of spectrum.

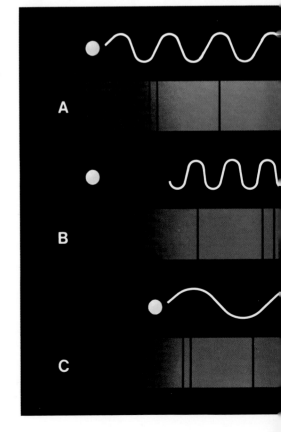

between successive waves reaching the listener's ear is smaller and the pitch higher than that of the waves behind the source.

In 1842 Döppler worked out the mathematical relationship between the pitch of the sound and the relative motion of the source and observer. He arranged to have his theory tested by some Dutch colleagues who planned one of the most bizarre scientific experiments in history. A number of trumpeters were persuaded to ride on a railroad truck as it was pulled to and fro at different speeds, and to play various notes on their instruments. Musicians with perfect pitch who could identify exact frequencies of musical notes sat at various points along the railroad track and recorded the notes they heard as the train approached or receded. This was done for two days. Despite the apparently crude technique, the results were a complete confirmation of Döppler's theory.

Delighted with his success, Döppler predicted that a similar effect would be found in light waves. Although he spent years working on the problem, he never succeeded in extending his principle. It was a few years later that the Döppler shift for light was worked out. It was shown that the frequency of light will be shifted toward the red end of the spectrum if a light source is receding rapidly from an observer, and toward the blue if it is approaching. Soon astronomers discovered that light from many stars and nebulae is red-shifted, indicating high velocities of recession from the earth. Further analysis of Döppler shifts helped to build up a picture of a universe expanding from a common point in space. This finding led to the formulation of the so-called "big bang" theory which holds that the cosmos was created when a single giant "molecule" of matter exploded, hurling its fragments apart to form the expanding universe.

Below left: Döppler radar is used to measure movement of rain or snow particles. Position, size, and movement of the rightmost pulse on the broad green line indicates the height, size, and numbers of particles, and their speed up or down. Speed is measured by noting the change in echoes, whose frequency varies in a similar way to the pitch of a moving train.

Right: sound waves of a reflected pulse, made visible by schlieren photography. This is an optical system which detects regions of varying refraction by their deflection of a beam of light.

Below: plot of sound waves reflected in the exploration of a seabed.

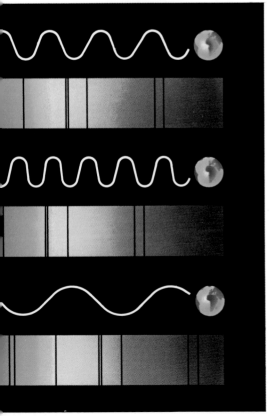

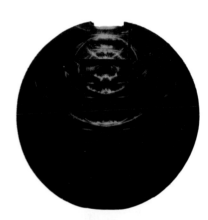

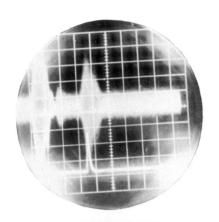

Sir Joseph Whitworth

1803-1887

Sir Joseph Whitworth's inventions represent an important development in the evolution of machine tools. He was, above all, the first engineer to make truly plane surfaces in metal, and he introduced the standardization of screw threads.

Joseph Whitworth was born at Stockport, near Manchester, where his father was a schoolmaster and congregationalist minister. At the age of 14 he was apprenticed to an uncle who was a Derbyshire cotton-spinner. Within a short time he had mastered all the machinery in his uncle's factory, but was critical of the rough standards of workmanship to which it was constructed. In 1821 he left Stockport first for Manchester, where he worked as a mechanic, and then in 1825, to London to train in Henry Maudslay's workshop. It was there that he perfected the technique for hand-scraping true metal plane surfaces to the point where the frictional resistance in the sliding parts of machines was largely overcome. In 1833 he returned to Manchester to set up his own machine shop.

By the 1850s, Whitworth's business had acquired a world-wide reputation for producing machines of unrivaled quality and precision. At the Great Exhibition of 1851 Whitworth emerged as the foremost manufacturer of machine tools in Britain. Precision was his keynote, and during his early years in business he devised a machine capable of measuring to an accuracy of

one hundredth-thousandth of an inch. He followed this with his plan to standardize screw threads at a time when each workshop operated to its own individual patterns. By 1860, his specifications for sizes, pitches, and a mean angle of 55° for all screw threads was in generally accepted use throughout Britain.

Like so many engineers of his generation, Whitworth applied his ingenuity across a wide spectrum of technology. He was among the first in Britain to point out the advantages of decimalization. His development of hard-wearing cutting edges greatly increased the efficiency of milling and planing machines. In 1835 he built a knitting machine and in 1842 he invented a machine for sweeping the streets.

The outbreak of the Crimean War in 1854 led

Below: Whitworth's drilling machine, still in use today. It is cheap to make but rather limited as the drill and bed can only move up and down.

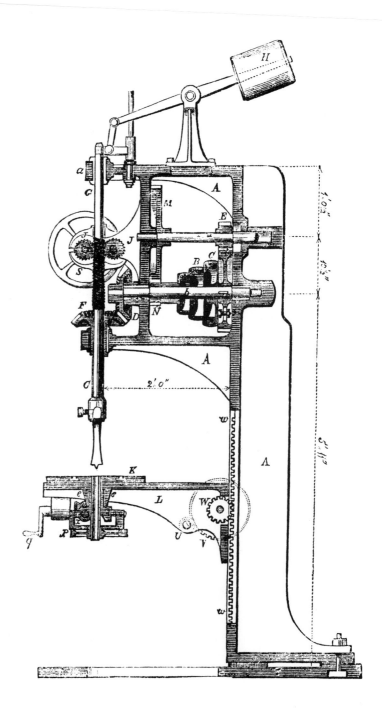

him to turn his attention to the problems of military weapons and equipment. The Enfield rifle then in use was not very reliable and Whitworth set out to establish standards for bore diameter and type of rifling. The War Office turned down his proposal of a rifle of 0.45 inch diameter with rifling that gave a rapid twist to the bullet. It was apparently rather quick to foul up. Even so, the National Rifle Association of Great Britain named the Whitworth rifle as the most accurate then in existence and the French army adopted it for use in target practice.

He also developed a rifled field gun capable of firing a shell up to six miles, but again, due to official procrastination, it was never exploited. He did, however, have success with his innovation in the manufacture of ductile steel for heavy

Above right: Whitworth's self-acting drilling machine. The drill and bed could be moved in and out, horizontally, and vertically.

Left: Henry Maudslay's lathe, the prototype of successive instruments.

Below left: Whitworth's planer, known popularly as a "Jim Crow."

Center right: Whitworth's screw-cutting lathe.

Below right: Whitworth's screw dies and tap.

field-gun manufacture. This was achieved by forging the steel under pressure to eliminate air pockets forming in the molten metal and creating weaknesses in the casing. It was enormously influential in the making of field weapons, and, in the view of an American commission which visited his factory, surpassed all other methods.

Whitworth's inventions earned him many accolades, including the French Legion of Honor from Napoleon III and a baronetcy from Queen Victoria. Though twice married, he died childless, and the bulk of his considerable estate went to further the progress of engineering by endowing scholarships and making funds for research available to technical colleges and institutes.

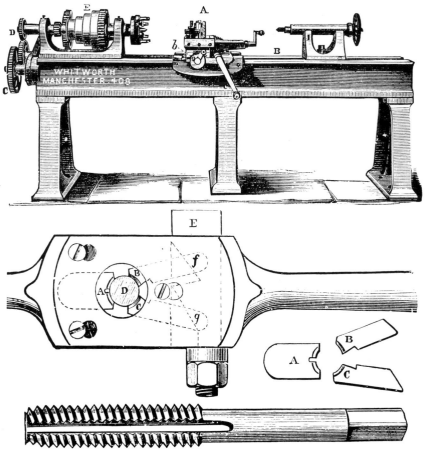

Isambard Kingdom Brunel
1806-1859

Few men embody so perfectly the restless energy and inventiveness of the 19th century as Isambard Kingdom Brunel – engineer, designer, surveyor, builder, and visionary. Brunel is best remembered for his three giant ocean-going liners which initiated the age of steamship travel. But throughout his life the grandeur, ambition, and range of his concepts challenged the technical resources of his time and overcame them brilliantly.

Brunel was born in Portsmouth, England, the son of Sir Marc Brunel, a French engineer whose royalist sympathies forced him to leave France in 1793. In 1799 Brunel senior settled in Britain, where he achieved fame for his inventions and a knighthood for building the first tunnel under

At this time he also designed and constructed a revolutionary "atmospheric" railway in which the train was drawn by suction by means of a piston in a conduit between the rails from which the air was pumped. Unfortunately the experiment was not a success, and the scheme was eventually abandoned.

Brunel's greatest achievements were in ship building. Here, radical ideas executed on an immense scale brought him two successes and

Above: the *Great Western*, Brunel first great liner launched in 1837 as an ocean extension to the Great Western Railway.

the Thames river, completed in 1843. From an early age Isambard showed a passionate interest in engineering, and at the age of 19 was in charge of construction on his father's Thames-tunnel project.

In 1833 the young Brunel was appointed engineer of the newly formed Great Western Railway. His mighty achievement was to design and construct the first railway from London to Bristol, with all its bridges, tunnels, and stations.

Right: the construction of the *Great Eastern*, at that time called the *Leviathan* because of its projected size and splendor. It was designed to carry 4000 passengers or 10,000 troops, and was powered by four paddle-engines of unprecedented size.

one disastrous failure. First, he built the *Great Western*, the first successful transatlantic steamship to extend the Great Western Railway "a bit further" as he put it. This wooden paddle steamer was, like the other two, the largest in the world at the time of its launch in 1837. The second giant, the *Great Britain*, was more revolutionary. It was the largest ship to be built of iron, and it was the first ocean liner to be powered not by paddle wheels but by a screw or propeller. Launched in 1843, the 3270-ton ship plied the Atlantic successfully until 1846 when it ran aground on the Irish coast. Even this did not dismay the traveling public, for while a wooden hull would have broken up, the *Great Britain* with its iron hull was undamaged. Iron ships had come to stay.

Brunel's third ship, the *Great Eastern*, was the most ambitious financial failure in steamship history. Designed to carry 4000 passengers in luxury and sufficient coal to sail to Australia and back, it incorporated both paddles and screw, and a revolutionary double iron hull which was to become the model for all future liners. Brunel was obsessed by this giant: "I never embarked," he wrote, "on any one thing to which I have so entirely devoted myself." Dogged by misfortune

Above: print of the Clifton Suspension Bridge with Brunel's original design for the towers. The bridge was completed after Brunel's death.

Right: the *Great Eastern*, 1857, on its maiden voyage.

and far ahead of its times, the great ship proved extremely difficult to finance, and almost impossible to launch. A failure as a passenger ship, the *Great Eastern* achieved fame by laying the first transatlantic cable. In 1872 it was docked in Liverpool, Northern England, where it rusted away until broken up for scrap in 1888. Ironically, the ill-fated ship was the prototype liner for an age that was yet to come.

Brunel never lived to see the final shattering of this last great dream. He died, worn out with overwork and financial worries, within days of its setting out on its disastrous maiden voyage, during which part of the ship blew up, killing the stokers. The power and construction of the engines was such that the *Great Eastern* still managed to steam into port for repairs. The failure of his last giant ship was an unhappy end to a brilliant career, but the sheer range of his achievements left a lasting memorial. Brunel built over 1000 miles of railway, numerous bridges including the magnificent Clifton suspension bridge, and a prefabricated 1000-bed hospital for use in the Crimean War. He also designed a multitude of other technical advances. His weaknesses were an inability to delegate and serious financial ineptitude. As a friend wrote: "By his death the greatest of England's engineers was lost, the man with the greatest originality of thought and power of execution, bold in his plans but right. . . . great things are not achieved by those who sit down and count the cost of every thought and act." It was an accurate tribute to an outstanding man.

James Nasmyth

1808-1890

The Scottish engineer James Nasmyth was the inventor of the steam hammer, a machine of primary importance in the development of large-scale engineering.

James Nasmyth was one of the group of brilliant young engineers who refined their craft in the London workshop of Henry Maudslay, the "father of the machine-tool industry." It was Maudslay who, in response to demands for precisely constructed components, invented the first screw-cutting lathe in 1797. This was powered by a steam engine, and had a slide rest to hold the cutting tool firmly in position. Maudslay also introduced one of the earliest examples of mechanized mass production when, in 1799, he built a series of machines for the Anglo-French engineer, Sir Marc Brunel, to manufacture wooden pulley blocks for the British Royal Navy. This innovation corresponded directly with that of Eli Whitney in the United States.

James Nasmyth became interested in engineering while he was still in his teens in Edinburgh. He was the son of Alexander Nasmyth, a Scottish portraitist, landscape painter, and architect, and in later life he said that his father's artistic influence was invaluable to him in engineering design. By the age of 17, James was

Below: Nasmyth's steam hammer in operation. The anvil projects through a large base plate which has two standards as guides for the hammer. A cylinder enclosing a piston is also supported by the standards. The hammer head, attached to the piston, is lifted when steam enters the cylinder, and drops when the steam escapes.

capable of building model steam engines to illustrate lectures at mechanics' institutes. At 19 he was invited to build a full-sized steam carriage, which he did and, to judge by contemporary accounts, it performed very well. In 1829, two years before Maudslay's death, he went to London to be his assistant and to learn the latest techniques in machine-tool manufacture. Returning to Edinburgh in 1834, he undertook some local commissions, but within three years made the decision to move to Manchester, a city then consolidating its position as an important industrial center.

On six acres of land at Patricroft, on the outskirts of the city, he built the Bridgewater foundry as it later became known. Here he manufactured steam locomotives and engines, hydraulic presses, and pumps. He devised many improvements to existing machinery and methods of construction, but it it was in 1839 that he built the invention for which he is chiefly remembered – the steam hammer. This massively powerful piece of equipment was built in

Engineering

Left: a smaller version of Nasmyth's steam hammer.

Below: Nasmyth using his telescope, an instrument which could be pointed to any part of the heavens without the observer having to move. It combined the principles of the Newtonian reflector and the Cassegrain telescope, named after the 17th-century French astronomer. Nasmyth's telescope formed the basis of the modern coudé system, in which the eyepiece, at the upper end of the polar axis, rotates to make changes in right ascension. Changes in declination are made by the rotating plane mirror in front of the object glass.

response to a request from Isambard Kingdom Brunel that he should forge a drive-shaft to drive the huge paddle wheels of the projected iron ship, the *Great Britain*. In the event, this aspect of the plan was scrapped and Brunel used screw propellers instead. The steam hammer, however, with its ability to apply tremendous forces under controlled conditions, at once found a whole range of applications in heavy industry.

"The steam hammer is capable of adjustment of power in a degree highly remarkable," said the description in the catalog for the Great Exhibition of 1851. "While it is possible to obtain an enormous impulsive force by its means, it can be so graduated as to descend with power only sufficient to break an egg shell." It was also the direct predecessor of the pile driver, and with its upright, inverted cylinder was adapted as the basis for a standard design in marine engines.

For the last 30 years of his life, Nasmyth, having retired from business, devoted his time to a life-long interest, astronomy. He made important contributions to lunar cartography, using

Right: Part of Nasmyth's 20-inch Cassegrain-Newtonian telescope, showing the position of the eyepiece in relation to the mounting.

a telescope which he built himself, a combination of the Newtonian reflector and the French Cassegrain instrument, and in 1874 he wrote *The Moon Considered as a Planet, a World and a Satellite*. His invention of the steam hammer, however, was his lasting monument. It resulted in the development of many large-scale industrial processes and brought the industrial trend full circle, to the point where the making of machines was itself the work of machines.

Louis Braille

1809-1852

Blinded himself at an early age, the Frenchman Louis Braille developed the system which revolutionized reading and writing for the blind. Based on a system of raised dots, with a total of 63 characters, it combined speed with simplicity of learning, and its use is now world-wide.

Braille, the son of a leather-worker, was blinded at the age of three when a knife with which he was cutting leather in his father's workshop slipped and injured him in the face. As he grew up, his natural intelligence went a long way toward overcoming his disability, and he became a talented musician, playing the cello and the organ. At the age of 10 he obtained a scholarship to the National Institute for Blind Children, in Paris. The founder of the school, Valentin Haüy, had introduced a system of embossing paper with normal roman type, but it proved to be a slow and tedious solution to the problem of blind reading. Nor did it offer any hope of teaching blind students to write.

Right: before Braille's invention blind people were usually kept in asylums, earning their living by crafts.

Below: first embossed Bible, 1840, by Scotsman James Alston.

Braille's system was first published in 1829, and was improved and elaborated over the next eight years. It was introduced for informal use in the National Institute, where Braille had become a teacher, but at the time of his death from tuberculosis it was still a long way from being generally accepted.

Meanwhile other systems of reading for the blind were being tried and tested. In the 1860s

In 1819, a French army captain, Charles Barbier, invented a system called "night writing" to enable messages to be read and written on battlefields at night. This used variations on a basic pattern of 12 raised dots. When he was still only 15, Braille came across Barbier's system and began to adapt it for use by the blind. He reduced the 12-dot code to one of six dots and worked out a basic alphabet and a series of contractions to speed up the rate of reading.

BRAILLE ALPHABET

A	B	C	D	E	F	G	H	I	J
K	L	M	N	O	P	Q	R	S	T
U	V	X	Y	Z	and	for	of	the	with

| W | Oblique stroke | Numeral sign | Poetry sign | Apostrophe sign | Hyphen | Dash |

| Lower signs | , | ; | : | . | ! | ( ) | ? | " " |

Above: the Braille alphabet.

Above left: stamp commemorating Braille's invention.

Right: Braille typewriter.

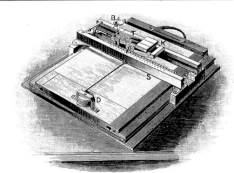

140

the "New York point" dot system was invented in America, and in the 1870s a system called "American Braille" was adapted from Braille's original by a blind teacher in Boston. Both these systems were kept in use for many years. Gradually the basic clarity and effectiveness of Braille's concept won through and as time went by there was a return to his original method. All future modifications and improvements were based firmly on his guidelines, and in 1932 an international conference agreed on the Braille code being adopted as the standard in the English-speaking world.

The Braille system has since been adapted for many of the world's languages, musical notation, and a form of shorthand, as well as science and mathematics. It is possible for the blind to write with Braille, using a stylus to press out the raised

Above: Dussaud's writing apparatus for the blind which employed Braille's alphabet.

Below: Moon type, invented in 1845 for people who have been blinded late in life.

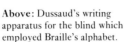

about half the average speed for sight reading. The one remaining disadvantage of Braille is the difficulty in learning it encountered by people who have gone blind relatively late in life. For this reason one alternative early method remains in occasional use – the embossed Moon type, invented by an Englishman, William Moon in 1845. This is easily learnt, being based on modified outlines of roman letters, and is satisfactory for the purpose of straightforward reading.

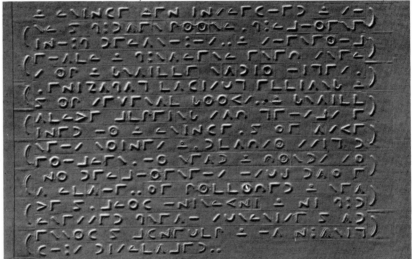

dots on paper clamped between a pair of metal plates that have a system of guides. The writer works from right to left, so that when the indented paper is reversed the dots can be read from left to right.

There are also various Braille writing machines, the earliest of which, invented in 1892, laid down the principles for all subsequent models. The printing of texts in Braille is achieved by using stereograph zinc plates which press out the Braille writing on paper, and it is possible to emboss sheets of paper on each side without the sequence of dots conflicting.

The skilled Braille reader can read a text at

Left: scanning the raised braille text, embossed on manilla paper.

Right: Braille model of a Picasso sculpture and layout of a plaza in Chicago.

Charles Robert Darwin

1809-1882

When the amateur naturalist and geologist Charles Darwin published *On the Origin of Species*, he did more than just overturn current biological beliefs. The theory of evolution by natural selection had resounding effects on philosophical and religious thinking, and paved the way for the modern sciences of ecology, anthropology, and genetics.

Darwin was born in Shrewsbury, Shropshire, the son of a doctor. His maternal grandfather was the industrialist and potter, Josia Wedgwood, and his paternal grandfather was the scientist and philosopher, Erasmus Darwin. Among leading men of science, however, Darwin was a notorious late developer. He was rebuked by the headmaster for wasting time on such trivial pastimes as collecting plants, birds' eggs, and minerals.

His father's attempts to steer him first into medicine, and then into the Church, were likewise failures, but during his time at the Universities of Edinburgh and Cambridge he met teachers who further stimulated his interest in natural history. Then, in 1831, Darwin accepted an invitation to be honorary naturalist on a round-the-world expedition in the government survey ship, the *Beagle*.

The *Beagle* sailed first to the Cape Verde Islands, then on toward South America. In Brazil, he walked in the rain forests, and near Bahia Blanca he found his first fossil, the skull of the extinct giant sloth called megatherium. For three years the ship cruised back and forth along the coasts of South America gathering data, while Darwin made geological and biological observations and records, and collected specimens of every kind.

In 1835 the *Beagle* landed in the Galápagos Islands. The four weeks spent there were the most significant of the expedition. Darwin noted that on the Galápagos there were around 14

Above: the *Beagle* at anchor in Sydney Harbor, Australia.

Right: skeleton (top) and bony armor (center) of the extinct glyptodon compared to the armadillo (bottom). Darwin found the fossil remains of the glyptodon in South America and concluded from its resemblance to the armadillo that the two must be related. This similarity between extinct and existing species was one of the factors which pointed to a process of evolution.

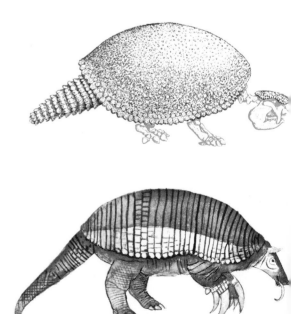

species of finch, each species having adapted to a particular form of feeding: the seed eaters had powerful parrot-like beaks while the insect feeders had sharper, finer beaks, more suited to stabbing at their prey. These important differences between obviously related species seemed to indicate that one species had given rise to several others. There were comparable differences between the tortoises of each island.

On his return to Britain in October, 1836, Darwin began to synthesize a theory to explain how one species could change or evolve into another. Theories of evolution had been put forward before, most notably by the French biologist, Jean-Baptiste Lamarck, who believed that animals and plants acquired and passed on characteristics in response to conditions they encountered. However, the predominant belief of the time was in the immutability of the species, each species being the direct result of Divine Creation.

Darwin began a series of notebooks called *The Transmutation of the Species*. He noted that in areas separated by geographical or physical barriers, such as the Galápagos, there existed related but different species. Meanwhile, animals in different geographical regions had adapted in similar ways. This was most striking in Australasia where the marsupials such as the Tasmanian

Below left: three of the species of palm trees observed by Darwin in his journey along the South American coast.

Below right: the evolutionary development of the mammalian hand. A: opossum; B: tree shrew; C: colugo; D: tarsier; E: baboon; F: orang-utan; G: man. The ability to grasp – the primate's distinctive feature – is small in the lower mammals (A, B, C, D) and increasingly more developed in higher primates. Note that man has relatively short fingers and a long thumb, for good opposition.

wolf and spiny anteater had developed along similar lines to higher mamals elsewhere. In addition, the fossils which Darwin had collected resembled existing species.

All this, however, was strong evidence for the existence of a process of evolution but did not explain its mechanism. Darwin solved the problem after reading Thomas Malthus' classic text *An Essay on the Principle of Population*, which predicted that the human population would outgrow its food supply unless birth was strictly controlled. The basic fallacy of the book was that man could increase his food supply according to his needs. Plants and animals, on the other hand, could not and their growth in number was therefore subject to environmental conditions. Darwin reasoned that those plants and animals with the most favorable characteristics for say, obtaining food, would have the best chance of surviving and breeding, their offspring inheriting

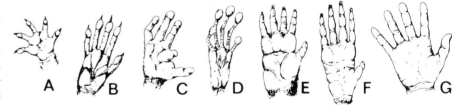

these features. In other words they were subject to natural selection.

For the next 20 years Darwin continued to accumulate evidence that species were indeed mutable. He remained cautious about publishing any of his findings until, in 1858, he suddenly received from Malaya a paper by the naturalist Alfred Russel Wallace. This, he was startled to find, outlined his own theory with remarkable clarity. Mutual scientific friends arranged for a joint paper to be read to the Linnean Society, and the next year Darwin brought out his great book, *On the Origin of Species by Means of Natural Selection*. The first printing sold out on the day of publication. Few books have caused such a storm. Eminent scientists, statesmen, and leading figures in the church engaged in furious debates, and the controversy soon spread abroad. Darwin was fortunate in having among his champions prominent and articulate scientists who eventually insured that the theory of evolution by natural selection was accepted.

Darwin continued his work on evolution, and pursued the then unacceptable possibility of man's own evolution from ape-like primates. He studied the similarities in structure and behavior between men and other animals, and in 1871 published *The Descent of Man*. It was this aspect of evolution which many found heretical, ridiculous, or simply distasteful.

But Darwin's theory won the deserved recognition of the scientific establishment. Throughout the world he was venerated and it was fitting that on his death in 1882 he was buried in Westminster Abbey beside Sir Isaac Newton.

Cyrus Hall McCormick

1809 - 1884

McCormick took out his first patent in 1834 but made little attempt to exploit his invention until the bank failure of 1837 threatened his family business. Over the next 10 years he introduced various improvements to his reaper and built up a small-scale manufacturing business, eventually selling about 50 machines a year. In 1844 he realized that the future of the reaper lay with the opening up of the vast, flat Midwestern prairies with their potential for wheat cultiva-

The mechanical reaper was an innovation of primary importance in the mechanization of agriculture. It made possible the large-scale cultivation of the wild lands of North America and Australia, and was the invention of a Virginian farmer's son, Cyrus McCormick.

The Industrial Revolution produced a considerable build-up in urban populations which had to be fed. Despite this, the pace of mechanization in agriculture hung well behind that of industry. The conservatism and traditional outlook of farming practice were partly responsible, though improved systems of crop cultivation did lead to bigger yields in European countries as well as in the United States. In North America, the need for mechanization was particularly urgent as new areas of virgin land were opened up to agriculture. More efficient types of horse plough were evolved, and a threshing machine

Right: farming the prairies with a McCormick reaper, mid-19th century. Until the invention of the reaper farmers grew only as much wheat as they could feasibly reap themselves with a scythe. Additional grain has to be imported from Europe. McCormick's invention opened up the prairie lands to agriculture and was a major contributing factor to the prosperity of the United States and Canada.

Below: advertisement for McCormick's reaper.

was developed. But it was during harvest-time, with its sudden requirements for many extra workers to hand-reap the grain crops, that the need for mechanization was most crucial.

From the late 18th century onward there were various attempts to build a mechanical reaper, but success evaded would-be inventors. One of these was Cyrus McCormick's own father, a Virginian farmer and blacksmith, and the son picked up his mechanical skills in the father's workshop. In 1831, at the age of 22, he built his first reaper. It had all the features of later reapers, but there were still defects to be ironed out. For instance, it created a tremendous racket, making the horses difficult to control.

McCORMICK'S
PATENT
VIRGINIA REAPER.

The above cut represents one of McCORMICK'S PATENT VIRGINIA REAPERS, as built but the body of it...

D. W. BROWN,
OF ASHLAND, OHIO,

Having been duly appointed Agent for the sale of the above valuable labor-saving machine (manufactured by C. H. McCormick & Co., in Chicago, Ill.,) for the Counties of Seneca, Sandusky, Erie, Huron, Richland, Ashland and Wayne, would respectfully inform the farmers of those counties, that he is prepared to furnish them with the above Reapers on very liberal terms.

The Wheat portions of the above territory will be visited, and the Agent will be ready to give any information relative to said Reaper, by addressing him at Ashland, Ashland County, Ohio.

Ashland, March, **1850.**

144

tion, and he founded a factory in Chicago. In the first year of trading 800 machines were sold.

Within the year, however, McCormick's original patent ran out, and a group of business competitors got together to challenge its renewal. Among these was Obed Hussey who, beside inventing a corn grinder and a sugar-cane crusher, also had a form of reaper to his credit, first tested out in 1833 and patented in the same year. While not so satisfactory as McCormick's design for

Above right: Obed Hussey's reaper, the first to be patented (1833).

Below left: public test of McCormick's reaper at Steele's Tavern, Virginia, July 1831.

Below right: a combined harvester, 1890, which required a large team of horses to haul it. This huge machine was a later development of McCormick's original reaper. It combined reaping with the binding of the wheat into bundles.

reaping grain, his machine was more efficient at mowing hay.

McCormick lost this particular legal battle and there followed an era of fierce competition between the rival companies. McCormick was in the vanguard with his vigorous sales techniques, intensifying his mass-production methods and extending credit to purchasers. He advertised widely, put on working displays, and soon outstripped his rivals. In 1851, at the Great Exhibition in London, the McCormick reaper made a considerable impression, and in 1855, at the Paris International Exposition, it took the Grand Medal of Honor. By the late 1850s the McCormick reaper was known to farmers in every country with a developed or developing agriculture. The Chicago factory was producing over 4000 machines a year to keep up with the demand.

During this period Chicago was going through a period of explosive expansion, both as a commercial center and as the focal point of the new national railroad networks. On each side of the Chicago river there arose haphazard complexes of wood-built warehouses, factories, and workers' dwellings, and these eventually provided the fuel for the disastrous fire which swept through the city in 1871 and burnt out four square miles at the center.

McCormick's premises were among those destroyed. Undaunted, he reconstructed the business and, at his death, the McCormick Harvesting Company was one of the great commercial enterprises of industrial history. During his last years he received many awards, including the French Legion of Honor, presented to him personally by Napoleon III. McCormick was an example of a man who combined inventiveness and business drive to serve humanity. In the words of a citation from the French Academy of Sciences, he did "more for the course of agriculture than any other living man."

Sir Isaac Pitman

1813-1897

use. Samuel Pepys in the 17th century wrote his classic diary in a shorthand devised by Thomas Shelton, the first translator into English of Cervantes' *Don Quixote*. The relative secrecy of the method meant that Pepys wrote down many entertaining indiscretions that might otherwise have gone unrecorded. An alternative system, invented by William Mason during the same period, was the first to be adopted for recording English parliamentary proceedings.

Unfortunately, all the early systems had a

Right: early 19th century system of shorthand. From the mid-18th century onward, a large number of shorthand systems were devised in Europe and the United States, mainly designed for personal use. Most were more cumbersome than the longhand they intended to replace, and few survived any length of time.

There has always been a need for shorthand systems of writing and their use can be traced back to antiquity. It was Sir Isaac Pitman, however, who in response to a rapidly expanding business world invented the first system which could be easily learnt and fluently written.

The history of shorthand is said to originate in Greece, where, in the 4th century BC, Xenophon used a Greek system when writing his memoirs of Socrates. There was also a Latin system, the "Tironian notes," invented by a freedman named

Marcus Tullius Tiro in 63 BC. It remained in circulation throughout the early Christian period, but by the Middle Ages was associated with heretical or magical cults and so was discouraged.

From the 16th century onward, various systems were devised for both public and private

Above: the Tironian alphabet, devised to record speeches in the Roman Senate. Each letter was abbreviated into a stroke which could later be joined.

large number of symbols, many of them awkward, and it took a long time to learn them effectively. The growing complexity of business routines in the early 19th century resulted in a steadily more urgent need for a system in which stenographers could be trained quickly. One stenographer, Samuel Taylor, adapted one of the earlier systems in 1786, and it was this method which Isaac Pitman, a schoolmaster and educator from Trowbridge in Wiltshire, first learned.

Pitman saw the difficulties and weakness of Taylor's script, and set out to make a scientific analysis of the basic sounds used in speech and language, and to match these with phonetic symbols. He evolved a system that could record 16 vowel sounds, 25 single and 24 double consonants. The consonants were formed from straightforward geometric shapes combined with shallow curves and straight lines. The vowels were indicated by dots or dashes placed in juxtaposition to the consonant signs.

In 1837 Pitman published *Stenographic Sound-Hand*, the first textbook to explain and teach his technique. The Pitman shorthand system was quickly adopted in Britain, and Pitman followed up his initial publication with others, including *Phonetic Journal*. He also founded a

Communication

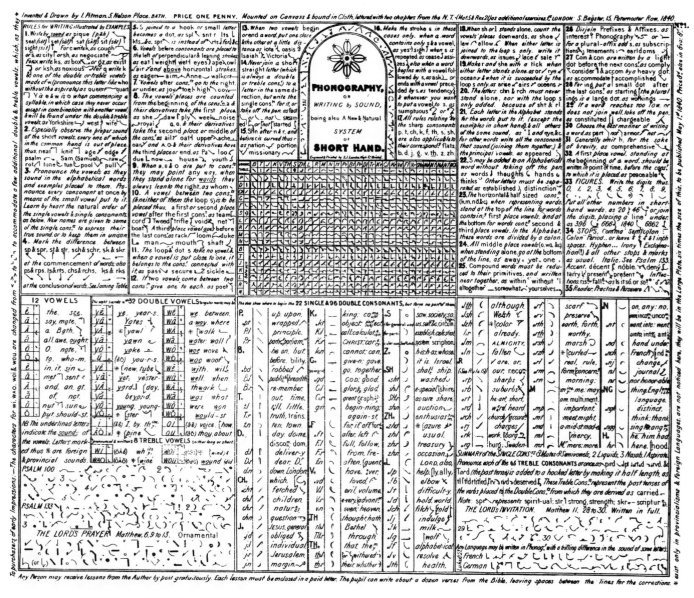

Above: the "Penny Plate," the second edition of Pitman's *Phonography*, published in 1840. It was published as a companion to the penny postage stamp, which Pitman originally submitted to the British Treasury as the first means of sending prepaid letters including enclosures. The "Penny Plate" condensed all of Pitman shorthand notation into a space of 6.5 inches by 8 inches. He also offered shorthand lessons by post, the first correspondence course. The pupils submitted verses from the Bible, with spaces left for corrections, on condition they were sent by penny post.

Left: stenographer, 1922

shorthand institute. In 1852 his brother, Benn Pitman, introduced the system to North America, where it underwent some practical variations. By 1889 a survey showed that over 95 percent of those who used shorthand in the United States, used a system based on the Pitman notation. It was also adapted to the European Romance languages and several of the more widely used languages in the Near and Far East.

The only modern oral shorthand to rival Pitman's is that of John Robert Gregg. Gregg, an Irishman, formulated a system of curved and hooked symbols that avoided the more angular features of the Pitman method. Today the Gregg system predominates in the United States. Nevertheless, Sir Isaac Pitman's invention has continued to demonstrate its value and effectiveness down to the present day. He received his knighthood from Queen Victoria in recognition of his achievement, though his other enthusiasm, the rationalization of English spelling by a system of phonetic writing, never caught the public imagination or even found a practical application.

Sir Henry Bessemer

1813 - 1898

The British inventor and engineer Sir Henry Bessemer patented the first successful method of mass-producing steel. The Bessemer converter was able to meet the needs of a rapidly-advancing technology, producing cheap steel of a high quality.

The art of converting iron into its harder and more durable alloys of steel has been known since antiquity. By the early 19th century, the ironmasters and steelworkers were able to produce a wide range of steel alloy for a variety of uses, but the amounts which could be produced were strictly limited.

In fact, Bessemer's invention was anticipated in the United States, where an ironmaster from Pittsburg, William Kelly, had arrived at an identical solution six years earlier. The technique was based on the principle of blowing a blast of cold air upwards through a bath of molten pig iron in a converter vessel. The oxygen in the air combined with the impurities in the metal to form an oxidized slag which could be easily removed. Carbon was burned off as carbon monoxide. The blast considerably increased the temperature of the metal, so prolonging and intensifying the process.

Bessemer, knowing nothing of Kelly's work, came across the problem when he invented a new type of rotating shell for use in the Crimean War.

The cast-iron cannons of the day did not have enough strength in their barrels to take the shell without bursting, and so he turned his attention to providing a stronger type of cast iron. The experiments he carried out led directly to the steelmaking process which bears his name. The Bessemer converter produced a mild steel superior in use to wrought iron and the English ironmasters were quick to take out licenses when these were offered to them.

Unfortunately, Bessemer worked with samples of iron ore containing very little phosphorus and sulfur. In Britain and Western Europe the ores had a high amount of phosphorus and sulfur which were not removed by the process as it then stood. Facing the indignation of the ironmasters and temporarily losing their confidence, Bessemer was obliged to call in the licenses. He did, however, set up his own steelworks, for which he imported phosphorus-free ore from Sweden, and where he manufactured steel at a competitive price.

The phosphorus problem was finally solved in

Below: a Bessemer steel converter operating during the "fining" stage, at the Bessemer Steel Works, Sheffield, late 19th century.

148

commercial quantities of the alloy. In 1866 the Kelly Pneumatic Process Company joined forces with a rival company which was operating with Bessemer's patents, revolutionizing steel production in the United States.

The availability of cheap, high-quality steel had far-reaching consequences. Steel superseded timber as a large-scale construction material, revolutionizing bridge, railway, and marine engineering. Meanwhile, Bessemer, who was honored with a knighthood in recognition of his process, continued to exercise his inventiveness. At the end of his life he had 114 inventions to his credit, ranging from a method of manufacturing "gold" paint out of brass to a solar furnace, and a stabilized cabin for use on ocean liners.

The Bessemer converter, although gradually losing ground to the open-hearth or Siemens-Martin process, still has its uses, especially as a preliminary stage in the processing of iron ore. The air blast has now been replaced by one of oxygen which removes nitrogen to produce a more ductile and malleable steel.

1878 when a young British metallurgist, Sidney Gilchrist Thomas, discovered that it was possible to remove sulfur and phosphorus from the molten metal if it was heated in a furnace lined with limestone and magnesia. This method became known as the basic Bessemer process.

In the United States, meanwhile, William Kelly continued to work on his own version of the process, though he did not take out a patent until 1857, when he heard about Bessemer's developments. In 1862 he started to build his own steel plant and two years later was producing

Above: the stabilized Bessemer saloon steamer.

Right: William Kelly, an American contemporary of Bessemer's who also invented a steel converter.

Below: model of Bessemer's steel apparatus. Liquid pig iron is conveyed to the converter (A) by means of a trough (C) lined with infusible clay.

Carl Zeiss

1816-1888

Carl Zeiss was a German industrialist who specialized in optical instruments. In association with the scientist Ernst Abbe, he was responsible for the leading advances in microscopy and lens manufacture made during the second half of the 19th century.

Carl Zeiss, born at Weimar in Germany, set up his workshop for building optical instruments at Jena in 1846. He was one of the most progressive manufacturers of microscopes and lenses of his day, and he realized that scientific research was going to be essential, both for the improvement of his instruments and for building up a

reputation for unrivalled excellence. It was for this reason that he sought to employ the optical physicist, Ernst Abbe, who was then rapidly becoming the foremost expert in the field.

Abbe, who was born at Eisenbach, took an appointment at the University of Jena, where, by 1870, he had become Professor of Physics and Mathematics. In the meantime he agreed to work with Zeiss, and in 1866 he became the company's research director.

The development of microscopy was slow after the pioneering work of Leeuwenhoek in the Netherlands in the late 17th century. The problem of chromatic aberration (colored haloes) in particular continued to plague lens makers, and the utmost skills of the lens grinders could not guard against distortions and inadequacies

Right: Ernst Abbe, pioneer of modern high-power microscopy and research director of Zeiss's optical works. He introduced the use of the condenser into microscopy. This is a system of lenses that focuses light from a source such as a tungsten filament onto the field of view, and matches the illumination to the requirements of the objective lens. Abbe's other developments included apochromatic lenses (free from color distortion) and oil-immersion lenses which greatly increased the resolving power of the microscope.

Right: section of Holophane globe and Welsbach mantle, two pieces of apparatus which were developed to enable light to be distributed more evenly. Holophane glass has a lens-like pattern on its surface. The Welsbach mantle contains a mixture of thorium nitrate and cerium nitrate which glow brightly when exposed to gas and thus increases the light output from gas lamps.

in the glass available to them. Achromatic lenses were first developed in the Netherlands, but there were still difficulties in using them for high magnification. One solution was discovered by the English wine merchant and amateur microscopist, Joseph Jackson Lister, father of the surgeon Joseph Lister. He worked out a scientific basis for making achromatic lenses, stating that if two such lenses were put together to make, in effect, a single lens, both the

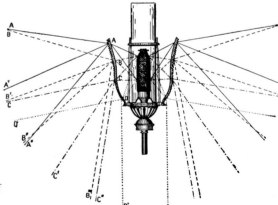

chromatic aberration and the distortions caused by the curvature of the lens could be largely neutralized.

This was the point which the science of optics had reached when Ernst Abbe, the first true optics engineer, began his researches. He laid on one side the traditional, and often inaccurate, methods of instrument making and instead introduced into the Zeiss works the principle that all optical instruments should be carefully planned on paper and worked to a blueprint which took full account of the latest scientific and empirical knowledge.

Optics

The work of Otto Schott, a research chemist who took charge of the glassworks side of the company, was also an important ingredient in the firm's success. Schott developed close to 100 types of glass for use in optics, as well as a type of heat-resistant glass.

Abbe continued to occupy an important place in the academic world, becoming director of the university's astronomical and meteorological observatories in 1878. He combined this with his

the formula for the resolution of a lens (its ability to produce the sharpest possible image). He also invented the oil-immersion lens, where a drop of oil situated between the object and the lens had the effect of improving image quality at the same time as it enhanced magnification. The first *apochromatic* microscopes (microscopes with lenses entirely free from color distortion), were the product of the Zeiss optical works.

After Zeiss's death, Abbe became the pro-

association with Zeiss, the partnership leading to some of the most important innovations in the science of microscopy. It had profound effects as well on the development of lenses for telescopes, cameras, and various other kinds of optical instruments.

Among Abbe's related achievements were the working out of a comprehensive theory of image formation in a microscope and the definition of

Above left: Dr Otto Schott.

Below left: view of the head office of the Zeiss Works, showing the Zeiss Observatory.

Below right: modern optical glass: photochromic glass with solar leaf pattern.

prietor, but three years later he donated his ownership to endowing the Carl Zeiss Foundation, which had as its objective research into science and social improvement. The company itself was later reorganized as a cooperative on a profit-sharing basis between the university, the management, and the work force. After World War II, Jena fell within the East Germany, but the company, its research staff, and the Zeiss Foundation were evacuated and reestablished in West Germany by the US forces of occupation.

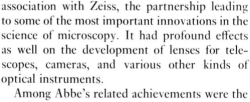

James Prescott Joule

1818-1889

The English physicist James Joule holds the reputation of being one of history's most dedicated men of science. Yet Joule in fact did not come to science through the academic establishment and he remained a lifelong amateur. His habit of painstaking research was rewarded by the vital discovery of the mechanical equivalent of heat that today plays an important role in thermodynamics and many branches of engineering. He also worked out the principle later used to create extremely low temperatures and opened the way for the modern science of low-temperature physics called cryogenics.

Joule was the son of a successful brewer from Salford in northern England. Because of his father's wealth Joule was able to devote himself to his main interest, experimental science. After studying briefly at the age of 17 under the English chemist and physicist John Dalton at Man-

Above: the apparatus used by Joule to determine the mechanical equivalent of heat. Two weights, suspended alongside measuring scales, operated a paddle wheel in a boiler, and thus raised the temperature by a measurable amount.

used wooden paddles to churn the water violently, measuring its temperature before and after. He drove water through small holes in an effort to heat it by friction. In every experiment he worked out the amount of heat that had been produced.

In 1843 he published the results of his experiments. He stated that a particular quantity of work always generated a certain fixed amount of heat. He called the amount of work needed to

chester University, he soon began to teach himself. His interest was quickly fired by the physics of heat – an interest that would grow into a lifelong obsession. In the history of science Joule is known as almost a fanatic for the measurement of the heat produced by different processes. He even spent most of his honeymoon measuring the difference in water temperature between the top and bottom of a waterfall near the resort at which he and his wife were staying. His idea was one that dominated all his research: that heat and energy are basically the same and can be changed into one another. He was trying to find out if the falling water of the waterfall was being converted into heat as it crashed into the pool at the bottom.

Joule devoted years to measuring heat changes caused by every mechanical process he could think of. In those experiments with water he

Right: Joule's electromagnet. He used it in his first experiment to determine the mechanical equivalent of heat by suspending it in water between the poles of another magnet and measuring, from its rotation, the rise in temperature, the current, and the mechanical work produced.

produce one unit, or calorie, of heat the "mechanical equivalent of heat" and calculated it as 41,800,000 ergs (an erg is the work done in moving a mass of one gram a distance of one centimeter). It was a major achievement, but to Joule's frustration few scientists took the slightest notice of his work. His paper was actually rejected by several learned journals and Joule had to announce his discovery at a poorly attended public lecture in Manchester and afterward persuaded

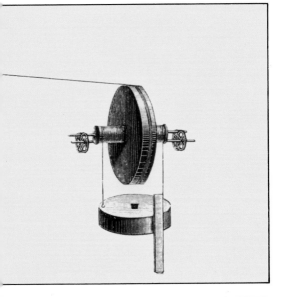

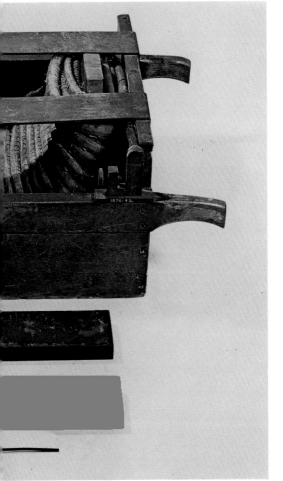

Below: apparatus Joule used to establish the relationship between work and heat. It consisted of a shaft of paddle wheels inside an insulated container of water. A falling weight turned the crank; the friction of the paddles created heat and caused a rise in the water temperature, which could be measured. The work done was then equated with the heat that had been produced.

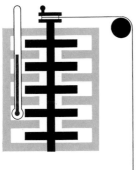

Above right: an example of heat from chemical reaction. Safety matches usually contain antimony sulfide and various oxidizing agents such as potassium chloride. The special striking surface contains red phosphorus. Nonsafety matches contain phosphorus sulfide and do not need a special striking surface.

a local newspaper to report his words. The reason for the lack of response to such important discoveries was that Joule was not a known member of the scientific circles of his day. He was merely a wealthy amateur, and although the history of science had been filled with the successes of such men, Joule's scientific contemporaries knew how notoriously difficult it was to make accurate measurements of heat changes. Joule's luck changed, however, when a young but well-respected physicist called William Thomson, later Lord Kelvin, showed an interest in Joule's work. He examined Joule's methods and results and announced that in his opinion they were both impressive and eminently sound. Soon the situation began to change and the scientific community started taking Joule seriously. Before long his work was accepted by scientists everywhere and a new unit, equal to 10,000,000 ergs, was named in his honor. The mechanical equivalent of heat could now be said to be 4.18 joules.

Thomson's interest in Joule's work led to an important collaboration between them. Together they showed that when a gas is allowed to expand freely, its temperature falls slightly. The phenomenon, now known as the Joule-Thomson effect, is due to the slight attraction gas molecules have for one another. During expansion, a small amount of heat energy is taken up by molecules moving apart and overcoming this attractive

force. Joule and Thomson announced their discovery in 1852. By the end of the century, their findings were being used to found a whole new refrigeration industry. Using the Joule-Thomson effect gases such as hydrogen and eventually helium were liquified and the extremely low temperature produced was the starting point of an entirely new branch of science, low-temperature physics or cryogenics.

Throughout his life Joule never accepted a teaching post in any academic institution. But, despite the early difficulties in achieving recognition for his work, he enjoyed the admiration of some of the greatest scientists of the day. In his later years he was elected to the Royal Society in London and became president of the Association for the Advancement of Science. A dedicated amateur, Joule enjoyed the satisfaction of having made a greater contribution to physics than most professional scientists of his day.

Elias Howe

1819-1867

The sewing machine was the first mass-produced appliance to find a wide domestic as well as industrial use. The inventor of the first model capable of practical development was Elias Howe, an American machine-shop engineer.

Despite the industrialization of so many of the processes of spinning and weaving during the late 18th century, the sewing of garments continued to be done entirely by hand. One of the earliest attempts to build a workable sewing machine was a single-thread stitching model patented in France in 1830 by Barthélemy Thimonnier, a Parisian tailor. Thimonnier set up a workshop containing 80 machines to meet an army contract to manufacture uniforms, but a mob of tailors and seamstresses, fearful for their living, broke in, destroyed every machine, and almost lynched their inventor.

Sixteen years later in the United States, Elias Howe, an engineer in a cotton machinery factory, completed his plans for a more sophisticated machine. It had a lock-stitch mechanism and used two threads, one housed in a shuttle and the other fed through a needle. He patented it, but was unable to persuade members of the tailoring profession to invest in the new machine. So, with his family, he left for Britain where, to raise funds, he sold the English patent rights for £250.

An unhappy period followed as Howe's financial circumstances deteriorated and he continued to try to extend the range of tasks of which his invention was capable. He sent his family back to the United States, and in due course, having

reached the brink of ruin, followed them himself. He returned only to find that his wife was mortally ill and that, during his absence, many others had pirated his invention. The initial resistance of the clothing manufacturers, on the other hand, was by now overcome.

Howe launched into a period of litigation to establish his rights. Among those against whom Elias Howe's litigation was directed was Isaac Merrit Singer, whose name has become virtually

Right: in 1845 Howe entered a contest at the Quincy Hall Manufacturing Company, Boston, with five top seamstresses. Howe finished his five seams before the girls and his work was declared superior, but the manufacturers did not buy any machines.

Below: the chain stitch machine, devised in 1856 by the American James Gibbs.

synonymous with the domestic sewing machine. Singer, an engineer, went into partnership with Edward Clark. He designed and marketed an improved version of the sewing machine, which finally established the design on which all subsequent models have been based. It introduced great flexibility into sewing with its long horizontal arm to hold the needle unit. This created a wider flat surface on which cloth could be manipulated. The machine also incorporated a foot treadle, making it suitable for workshop use. shop use.

In its final form, the Singer and Clark machine incorporated a dozen new patents and by 1860 the company was the world's largest manufacturer of sewing machines. They were also pioneers of schemes to buy on credit and pay by instalment, an innovation that was to have a profound influence over modern sales techniques.

For Elias Howe, however, there was a happy ending. In 1854 he won his patent infringement suit against Singer. While he did not prevent any other such machines being marketed, Howe received, until his death in 1867, royalties on all sewing machines sold in the United States.

The social consequences of the sewing machine were also considerable. Tailors and seamstresses, having previously worked as individuals with an apprentice system, began to set up clothing workshops and factories and to employ semi-skilled machine operators. By the turn of the century, the "sweatshop" aspect of the industry was notorious. In the United States especially, the clothing trade became a focus for radical reform and the drive to unionize labor to improve pay and work conditions. On the other hand, in the home, the sewing machine was one of the earliest labor-saving devices for women.

Above left: the cover of *le Petit Journal*, celebrating the invention of Barthélemy Thimonnier's sewing machine, a single-thread model.

Above right: Howe's first successful lock-stitch machine, built in 1845. The needle moved horizontally and the machine was powered by a hand crank.

Right: cover of Singer sewing machine instruction manual. The foot treadle was one of Singer's innovations.

Below: the original Singer sewing machine, constructed in 1854. Unlike Howe's machine, the needle moved up and down so that the work could be turned more easily and it could therefore sew curved seams.

Jean-Bernard-Léon Foucault

1819-1868

The French physicist Jean Foucault was the first to provide direct experimental evidence of the earth rotating on its axis. He also made the earliest accurate measurements of the velocity of light, proving that the velocity varies and the variation depends on the medium through which the light passes.

Foucault grew up in a comfortable home in Paris and, like many middle-class children of the day, became a doctor. As a newly qualified physician he made a chance friendship that changed the course of his life. It was with Armand Fizeau, a distinguished young physicist who had an infectious enthusiasm for science. Their friendship deepened, and Foucault's interest began to turn away from medicine and toward physics. Encouraged by Fizeau, Foucault began his own scientific research, tentatively at first but with increasing confidence. No doubt remained in his mind that his future lay in physics rather than medicine and, as if to confirm the promise of that future, he achieved an immediate major success in his research.

Soon after meeting Fizeau in the early 1840s, Foucault had assisted him in experiments designed to measure the velocity of light. By modern standards, Fizeau's results were only moderately accurate. However, Foucault's im-

agination was caught by his friend's experiments and he decided to devise his own technique to measure the velocity. He realized that because the velocity of light was so huge, it was important to measure accurately the time taken for light to travel a very long distance. Over a short distance, the time taken was so small that no means existed to measure it accurately. To reduce these requirements to a manageable experiment, Foucault struck upon the idea of using two mirrors, one stationary and the other revolving. His idea was to bounce a light ray back and forth between the mirrors, simulating a long-distance journey. Foucault's technique was a brilliant success, enabling him to calculate the velocity of light in air to within 1 percent of the most accurate figure known today.

Foucault took his research even further. He used the same basic technique to investigate the velocity of light as it passed through media other than air. In particular, he showed that light travels more slowly through water. This result was a breakthrough in the arguments raging on the nature of light. The variation in velocity was powerful evidence that light was a kind of wave and Foucault's work was a sharp setback for physicists who, since the time of Isaac Newton, had argued that light consisted of a stream of luminous particles.

Foucault's best-known research came after 1851 when he started the work for which he is most popularly remembered today. In a dramatic experiment he produced the first direct evi-

Above right: the Panthéon, Paris.

Above center: Foucault's regulator, which enabled electricity to supplant gas in providing lighting.

Physics

Left: Foucault's pendulum, which he used in 1851 to show that the earth rotates on its axis. It weighed 11 pounds and was suspended by a steel wire 195 feet long.

Right: the Foucault's telescope. In 1857 Foucault introduced the modern technique of silvering glass to make mirrors for reflecting telescopes. The silvered glass proved to be superior to the speculums previously used in reflecting telescopes because it was easier to manufacture. Also the surface could be resilvered if it became tarnished or damaged.

Below: cover of *le Petit Parisien*, showing Foucault's pendulum experiment in the Panthéon.

dence that the earth rotates on its axis. Foucault had studied simple pendulums and had noticed that no matter how the point of the pendulum's suspension was moved, the pendulum always tended to keep swinging in the same plane. With brilliant insight he theorized that if a very large pendulum were set in motion, its plane of motion would remain fixed while the earth moved be-

neath it. Many scientists had speculated about such a movement of the earth, but Foucault had conceived a direct means of investigating it. He believed that if the earth rotated, all the observers watching the pendulum would rotate with it and only the plane of the pendulum's motion would remain fixed. Theoretically therefore, the plane of the pendulum's swing should appear to the observers to change direction slowly. In fact, they would actually be watching the effect of the movement of the earth itself.

Foucault's idea caught the public imagination. Emperor Napoleon III gave him permission to attempt the experiment in the Panthéon, one of the churches of Paris having a large dome. Foucault suspended a large iron ball by a 200-foot steel cable from the center of the dome and attached a spike to the lowest point of the ball just touching the floor, which had been lightly sanded. Any movement of the plane of the pendulum's swing were recorded by the marks in the sand.

A large audience gathered to watch the momentous experiment, and for about an hour before Foucault started the pendulum they remained silent and motionless in order to eliminate vibrations and air movements in the church. Then Foucault quietly set the great pendulum swinging. For some time, no change in the plane of motion was apparent. Then, very slowly, the hushed crowd saw the track in the sand changing. The pendulum's plane of motion was visibly rotating. For the first time, the movement of the world around its axis was witnessed.

Christopher Latham Sholes

1819-1890

In association with a friend, Samuel W Soule, he took out a patent for an automatic numbering machine in 1864. It was then suggested to him by a fellow-inventor, Carlos Glidden, that he might utilize the principle involved to make a letter-printing machine. Glidden also brought to his attention an article in the magazine *Scientific American* which described a writing machine recently designed in London by an inventor called John Pratt.

The first workable and commercially viable typewriter was invented by the American printer and newspaper editor, Christopher Latham Sholes. Its social effects were considerable, since it revolutionized office and administrative routine and, it has been said, opened up the business world to women.

The earliest known attempt to build a typewriter dates back to a patent, taken out in Britain in 1714, for an "Artificial Machine or Method for the Impressing or Transcribing of Letters Singly or Progressively." Unfortunately, no details of its proposed or actual mechanism have survived. There were intermittent attempts to build workable writing machines over the next 150 years, but the results were unwieldy or slow to operate. The practical origins of the modern typewriter lie with Sholes' invention in 1867.

Sholes became a printer after completing an apprenticeship, then moved to Wisconsin, where he took over the editorship of the *Wisconsin Enquirer*. During the early 1860s he was editor, successively, of the *Milwaukee News* and the *Milwaukee Sentinel*, and by this stage had also gained some experience in local politics. In due course he accepted an appointment as a port official in Milwaukee, and took advantage of the spare time left over from his duties to exercise his inventive faculties.

Communication

Sholes evidently decided that he might be able to improve on the design, and he set out to make a machine that was reasonably compact, efficient, and quick to use. His first patent for a typewriter was taken out in 1868, the year after the prototype, and was held jointly with Soulé and Glidden. By this time he had a working model with which it was possible to write faster than with a pen. During the next five years he continued to work on improvements, adding other features to

Right: a Burt typewriter, 1830. Austin Burt was the first to be granted a US patent on the typewriter. In his typographer the letters were mounted on plungers held in springs on a circular carriage. This was rotated by hand and depressed against the paper.

his basic design, and he took out two further patents.

When it came to exploiting his invention beyond this point, Sholes found that he was unable to raise the necessary capital. In 1873 he therefore decided to dispose of the patents to a firm of gunsmiths in Ilion, New York, called E Remington & Sons. The first commercially produced typewriter, which was put on the market in 1874, was thus the *Remington* – a name that would become familiar to generations of typists. It embodied most of the features of the modern typewriter, and the arrangements of characters on the keyboard has, in most part, remained unchanged. The keys worked the type-bars on levers, and the letters were printed by striking the bars against an inked ribbon. It was capable of consistent line and letter spacing, and a cylinder carried and held the sheet of paper in position.

The main feature lacking as yet was the shift-bar, and so the first Remingtons could only type capital letters. Another aspect of the design was that the keys struck on the underside of the

Above: early typewriters. Left: *Lambert*, 1900; center: *Columbia*, 1886; right: *Blickensderfer*, 1893-1910. The *Columbia* had a type disk instead of keys, and proportional spacing for letters of different widths.

Opposite above: the ornate Sholes and Glidden typewriter, the keyboard of which operated in a similar way to that of the piano.

Opposite below: an early Sholes typewriter, 1868.

cylinder, and this made it impossible to check back on the line of text being typed without raising the carriage. Nevertheless, with the vast increase in business activity taking place in the later 19th century, the machine was an immediate commercial success. On the literary front, Mark Twain invested in a model and became the first writer ever to submit a typed manuscript to a publisher.

During his remaining active years, Sholes continued to be associated with his invention and to contribute to its improvement. One attempt to provide both capital and lower case letters was a double-keyboard machine. However, it was the shift-key mechanism, introduced in 1878, which solved the problems and also made possible the development of touch typing.

By 1890 another American inventor, John N Williams, developed the front-stroke machine, which enabled the typing to be seen as it was being done. The principle was adopted in all the leading makes of machine, and the manual typewriter was complete in all its essential details.

Gregor Johann Mendel

1822-1884

The science of genetics has its origins in a program of research carried out between 1858 and 1866 in the vegetable garden of an Austrian monastery by one of the monks, Gregor Mendel.

He was born Johann Mendel, the son of a farmer at Heinzendorf, then in Austrian Silesia. He seems to have developed a broad interest in the natural sciences from quite an early age, though he was also conscious of his own lack of a formal, systematic education. To gain an education was evidently a factor in his decision to become a monk when he entered the Augustinian Order and took the name of Gregor. The Augustinians were known as teachers, and Mendel was sent to study for his teacher's certificate. He took the examination in 1850, but the examiner commented that he lacked "insight, and the requisite clarity of knowledge."

Center: Mendel's Second Law of Independent Assortment, illustrated by genes for rounded (R), wrinkled (r), yellow (T), and green (y) seeds. Each gene is inherited independently of the others.

kitchen garden, he quietly began a methodical investigation into the nature of heredity which took him eight years to complete. Mendel was primarily interested in the hybridization of plants. He was aware that in all the breeding experiments carried out so far nobody had taken their research to the extent where there were enough results to make any statistical analysis. As the subject of his study he chose the cultivated pea, and he defined seven characteristic variations which were likely to occur.

These variations included, for example, the color of the pea (green or yellow), its appearance (smooth or wrinkled), and the length of the stems (long or short). Mendel conducted his experiments with care, pollinating the flowers himself and guarding against chance cross-fertilization.

male gametes

female gametes

Below: Mendel dealt only with genes showing complete dominance or recessiveness. Some plants however appear to show blending of characters due to incomplete dominance. A recessive character is actually an absence of dominance.

Mendel never did succeed in gaining a teacher's diploma, though he went to the University of Vienna for a further period of study, mainly in science, before returning to the monastery at Brunn in Moravia (today Brno in Czechoslovakia) in 1854. Two years later, in the monastery

He kept meticulous records of the results. Sexual reproduction in plants was known about since the 17th century, but it was thought that hybridization between different types would give characteristics lying midway between the two crosses. Mendel soon proved that this was not the case. He found that if short-stemmed peas were hybridized with long-stemmed peas, the first generation turned out to be not an intermediate length but exclusively long-stemmed. In this case, using Mendel's description, the long-stem character was *dominant* and the short-stem character *recessive*. If these hybrids, which Mendel called F_1, were allowed to cross-fertilize amongst themselves the latent characteristics reasserted itself in the subsequent generation and a proportion of short-stemmed varieties reappeared. Mendel found that this proportion of short-stemmed and long-stemmed plants was always in the ratio of one to three. The proportions of varieties were likewise calculable over several generations since they observed simple statistical rules.

With inspired insight Mendel advanced the theory, now known as Mendel's first law, that each characteristic was governed by a pair of corresponding units from each parent, one of which was contributed at fertilization by the male cell (pollen) and one by the female cell (ovule). These units, or factors, which contained the blueprints for hereditary characteristics, were later, in 1909, christened "genes" (derived from the Greek for "give birth to") by the Danish biologist Wilhelm Ludvig Johannsen. Mendel meanwhile published his findings in two scienti-

Above: anticipated result of selective breeding in man.

Left: polyploidy (multiple of normal number of chromosomes) in tomato plants. 1. Normal diploid leaf and 24 chromosomes.
2. Triploid with 36 chromosomes.
3. Tetraploid with 48 chromosomes. Polyploid plants are usually larger and hardier than normal diploids.

fic papers in 1866, though in doing so he attracted almost no attention whatsoever. His discovery of the basis of genetic inheritance was nevertheless of a magnitude to rank with that of natural selection. So far as is known, he was unaware of the work of Charles Darwin when he began his experiments, though he did obtain a copy of *On the Origin of Species* in its third (1863) edition. In this he carefully marked the passages concerning variations and hybrids. For theological reasons, however, he never accepted Darwin's arguments on the mutability of species.

In 1869 Mendel was elected abbot of his monastery, and the rest of his life was given over largely to administrative problems and official duties. His years of scientific research became a forgotten episode until 1900, when the texts of his articles were stumbled upon virtually simultaneously by botanists working independently in Germany, Austria, and the Netherlands. The three scientists concerned were all engaged in plant-breeding experiments, and were astonished to find that their results had been anticipated by an obscure Austrian cleric over 30 years before.

The impressive accuracy of Mendel's workings was demonstrated and justified, and it was shown that the same principles were equally valid for hereditary animal characteristics. It is a mark of his posthumous status that the term "Mendelian genetics" is virtually synonymous with the study of heredity. His discoveries became the bedrock of all later developments in genetic understanding, and were profoundly influential over all modern biological studies, especially biochemistry, physiology, medicine, and evolution.

Louis Pasteur

1822-1895

fermenting wine, the other racemic acid, an industrial byproduct. They were identical in chemical composition and structure, but when dissolved in water they differed in a curious way. When a beam of polarized light was passed through tartaric acid, the light was rotated. Racemic acid had no such effect.

Pasteur established that the difference between these two was due to their crystal structure. Those of tartaric acid were exclusively

Above: sodium tartrate crystal. The crystals are exclusively right-handed and optically active.

Below: apparatus which enabled Pasteur to prove that microbes in the air can be responsible for food spoiling. Sterile broth kept in the swan-necked flasks, whose curved necks trapped bacteria, went bad if microbes reached it. Pasteur later found that bacteria causing the spoiling of wine could be destroyed by heating the wine, before fermentation finished, to a temperature between 130° and 140°F. A similar process, pasteurization, is now used to kill bacteria in milk.

Both science and mankind are indebted to the French chemist Louis Pasteur. Through his pioneering work, which established the existence of germs as the agents of fermentation and disease, he founded the science of microbiology. But he is perhaps best remembered for discovering a way to cure one of the most horrifying diseases known to mankind – rabies.

Pasteur was born in Dole, eastern France, the son of a tanner. The family was not rich and his father often had to struggle to keep his small business from collapsing. At school he proved a conscientious student, though not outstanding, with drawing and sketching as his major talents. In 1844 he went to a teacher's college in Paris to study chemistry. Looking for a suitable thesis subject, Pasteur turned to crystallography. Being a keen draughtsman, he was attracted by the beauty and structure of crystals.

After the completion of his thesis he received a post as a physics teacher, but his interests centered on crystallographic research, in particular on the behavior of two substances. One was tartaric acid, which developed in the vats of

right-handed, while those of racemic acid were a mixture of right- and left-handed ones, mirror-images of one another or *stereoisomers* as they are now called.

Pasteur's work on stereoisomers established his scientific reputation. He then turned his interests to fermentation and putrefaction, on the invitation of a distiller who was having problems distilling alcohol from sugar beet. At that time the cause of fermentation was un-

Left: Pasteur working in his laboratory.

Below: Pasteur (seated center), his nursing staff, and some of the children he inoculated successfully against rabies.

known. It was only differentiated as "good," for instance in the production of wine or beer, or "bad," as when milk went sour. Pasteur discovered that in "good" fermentation only yeast cells were present. In "bad" fermentations, in addition to yeast, there were rodlike organisms. Different types were responsible for different kinds of fermentation.

Pasteur's work had several important consequences. By heating the liquid, be it wine, beer or milk, to a sufficiently high temperature he killed the organisms and improved the keeping power of the product. This process is now known as pasteurization.

He then proved that these organisms resided in the air and were not spontaneously generated. He boiled up various liquids in swan-necked flasks so that the steam expelled the air, and then sealed the necks. The liquids remained clear indefinitely. When the necks were broken, and air rushed in, there was subsequent clouding and fermentation.

Pasteur's work on fermentation also lead him to suspect that microbes were responsible for

diseases. In 1865, at the request of the French Government, he investigated two silkworm diseases, then threatening to destroy the French silk industry. He established germs as the cause and introduced preventative measures. During this period he also suffered a stroke which left him partially paralyzed, but this did not prevent him from continuing his work.

Pasteur produced vaccinations against anthrax and chicken cholera, but his most famous work was directed against rabies. He believed that vaccination could be effective even if the disease was already present, and performed his dramatic experiment on Joseph Meister, a nine-year-old boy who was bitten 14 times by a rabid dog. Sixty hours after the bites had been inflicted Pasteur injected the boy with the pulverized spinal cord of a rabbit that had died from rabies. After a series of injections the boy recovered. It was a mark of Pasteur's confidence that he used his own new method in preference to the usual cure – cauterization with carbolic acid. This was occasionally successful but agonizingly painful.

The work of Louis Pasteur encountered much opposition during his lifetime. In particular, his pioneering work in microbiology was treated with hostility by conservative scientists who believed that their theories were unassailable. Pasteur was able to vindicate his results because he always maintained that any scientific fact must stem from observation, not mere hypotheses or preconceived ideas. He received many honors, but his biggest reward was probably the establishment of the Pasteur Institute in 1888, which he headed until his death.

Etienne Lenoir

1822-1900

The French engineer Etienne Lenoir designed the internal-combustion engine. He is also credited for having built the first vehicle which ran on the principle of the internal-combustion engine – the direct forerunner of the modern automobile.

One of the ironies of the early history of the self-propelled road transport is the fact that Britain, the country with the best-developed technological expertise and knowledge at that time, did more than any other to retard its progress. This was a direct result of the Locomotives on Highways Act, passed in 1865 and popularly known as the "Red Flag Act." While it was in force, and it was not fully repealed until 1896, any self-propelled carriage on an English

French artillery engineer, Nicholas-Joseph Cugnot. It could reach a speed of 2.25 miles per hour, but its small boiler meant that repeated stops had to be made to refill it with water. With the building of lighter and more efficient steam engines, steam carriages became more effective as modes of transport. On the other hand, while they could achieve speeds of up to 30 miles per hour, they remained noisy and dirty to drive. They also damaged the road surfaces.

highway was obliged by law to have a crew of three, one of whom had to walk in front with a red flag as a warning of its approach, particularly to horse-carriage drivers. The maximum speed limit was 2 miles per hour in urban areas and 4 miles per hour on country roads. As a consequence of this inhibiting legislation, designed to apply primarily to steam carriages, early work on the internal-combustion engine was almost entirely carried out in France, Germany, and Austria.

The first true automobile was the three-wheeled road steamer, invented in 1769 by a

Above: The Highways Act of 1865 in operation. A man precedes a car with a red flag to warn horse-carriage drivers and other road users of its presence. The Act was in force for 31 years in Britain and effectively prevented the development of the British motorcar.

The thermal inefficiency of the steam engine, plus its needs for cumbersome pipes, cylinders, and boilers, encouraged attempts by would-be inventors to produce an engine which used the fuel directly. In this the fuel would be burnt, not in a separate container, as in the steam engine, but within the engine cylinder itself. In other words, the combustion of the fuel would be internal. The fuel had to be fed into the engine in the form of a gas or vapor, then burnt explosively to give an impetus to the piston within the cylinder. A patent exists for a vehicle built by a British engineer called Samuel Brown, which

164

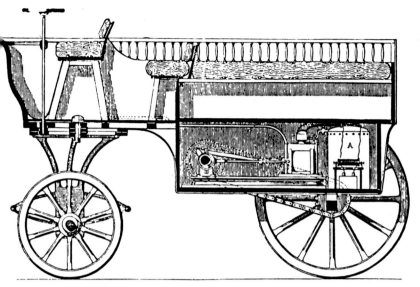

ran on a mixture of air and hydrogen and was apparently tested out on a hill near London some time in the 1820s. During the same period, the French physicist Sadi Carnot wrote his important book, *Reflections on the Motive Power of Heat* (1824), which outlined the basic theory of the internal-combustion engine. The first ancestor of the modern automobile, however, was

Above: Lenoir's first gas and gasoline engine, built between 1860 and 1863.

Below: internal components of Lenoir's first gas engine (1860). It developed little power and had a thermal efficiency of only 4 percent.

the car built in France in 1862 by Etienne Lenoir.

Lenoir, a prolific inventor, was born at Mussy-La-Ville, Belgium. It was he who constructed the first successful engine which worked on the internal-combustion principle. Lenoir's engine was in essence a converted steam engine and worked on a two-stroke cycle. The mixture of air and coal gas was drawn in by the withdrawal of a piston operated by a flywheel. When the piston had been partly withdrawn, the gas supply was cut off and an electrical spark ignited the fuel mixture. The piston was forced by the resulting explosion to complete its stroke. It was then drawn in again by the momentum of the flywheel. Slide valves on either side of the piston acted as inlets for the air-fuel mixture and outlets for the exhaust products.

The engine was widely marketed to perform small-scale tasks. Lenoir then adapted it to run on a liquid fuel such as turpentine and incorporated it into a vehicle. In this carriage he took almost three hours to make a journey of six miles from Paris to Joinville-le-Pont. However, having made his invention, Lenoir seems to have foreseen little further prospect of its exploitation, though some years later he did adapt his engine to power a motorboat.

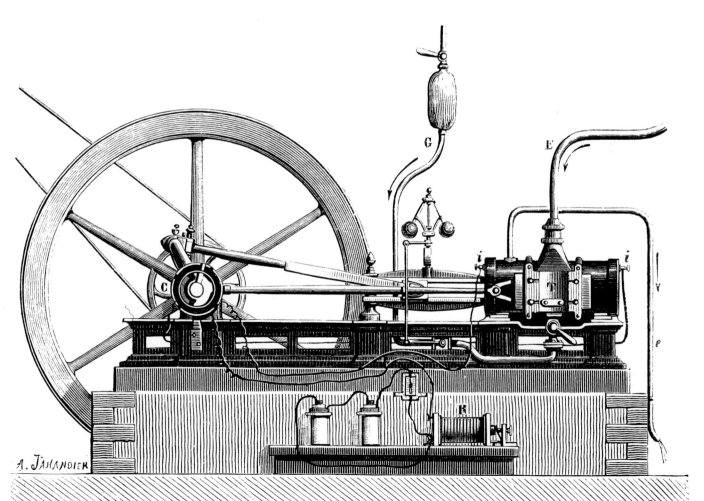

Sir William Siemens

1823-1883

The German-born engineer Sir William Siemens was the originator of the Siemens-Martin open-hearth method of steel refinement. The process, which was superior to the Bessemer converter both in its efficiency and the quality of steel it produced, became the main method of manufacturing steel in the late 19th and early 20th centuries.

William Siemens was born Karl Wilhelm Siemens in Lenthe near Hanover, the second of four brothers who were all distinguished scientists and inventors. When their father died in 1840, the eldest brother, Werner, took over responsibility for the family's upbringing. Werner was trained as an engineer in the Prussian artillery, and was an expert in telegraph engineering. He instituted the use of guttapercha as an insulator on underground and underwater cables, and built the first telegraph line in Germany, running from Berlin to Frankfurt-am-Main.

Their parents originally intended that Wilhelm should be given a commercial training, but

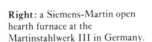

Right: Siemens' electric furnace, London. It consisted of a carbon crucible connected at one end to the electricity supply by a copper wire. The current flows out through a water-cooled metal electrode. The flow of the current, through loosely packed material of high resistance and low conductivity, created a temperature high enough to melt a pound of iron in an hour.

Right: a Siemens-Martin open hearth furnace at the Martinstahlwerk III in Germany.

water meter. This was successfully marketed and began to bring in royalties. From 1847 he had the help of a younger brother, Friedrich, and they began to look together for applications of the so-called "regenerative principle." In this, the idea was to capture and use the heat which normally escaped with the waste gases in industrial processes. The hot gases were passed through an open-brickwork chamber. The air for combustion was then drawn through the chamber and

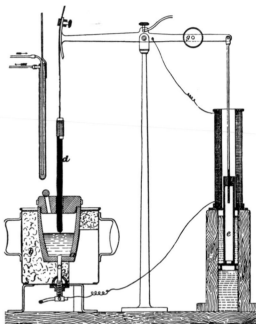

Werner decided that a more likely future for his brother lay in engineering, and he sent him to a technical school in Magdeburg. After he finished his training, Wilhelm traveled to London in 1843 to try to sell an electroplating process that Werner had invented. He was successful and as a result decided to move to Britain to settle and try his chances as an inventor.

There followed a period of hard work and financial struggle until 1851, when he invented a

heated up. This improved the efficiency of the furnaces, raising the temperature dramatically.

In 1856, the same year in which Henry Bessemer took out a patent for his steel-refining process, the Siemens brothers took out their first patent for a regenerative chamber for use in metal processing and refining. Two years later they applied the regenerative principle to a steel-refining open-hearth furnace which William had patented. The open-hearth furnace was so-called because it was open to the flames above it and the molten metal lay on the bottom or hearth. It was to form the basis of the most widely used method of mass-producing steel. As it stood then, the process had some shortcomings. Its system of ducts conveying the hot gases from the solid-fuel, shallow-hearthed furnace to the regenerative chambers, and then returning the hot air to the furnace, was complicated and not completely effective.

Below: Siemens' electric railway, 1879. The open coaches were driven along by a locomotive containing a small electric motor. The current was supplied by two outer noninsulated rails, and a central insulated one. It eliminated the dangers of fire in the coaches by dispensing with the need for a boiler and inflammable fuel. If it was derailed it came to an immediate standstill as the current supply was cut off.

A solution was found in 1864, when the French engineer Pierre-Emile Martin adapted the furnace to fuel gas and positioned a pair of Siemens chambers at either end of the furnace. One member of the pair heated air and the other fuel gas. This reinforced the heat in the furnace raising it to a temperature where it was capable of melting scrap steel. The Siemens-Martin process gradually supplemented the Bessemer converter in industrial use. It was cheaper, produced a better quality steel, and was able to consume the vast amounts of scrap which had resulted from the growing steel industry.

William Siemens took British citizenship in 1859, the year of his marriage. From 1850 onwards he controlled the London branch of Siemens & Halske, a company founded in Berlin by his brother Werner. The company specialized in electrical equipment and telegraph engineering, and acquired a world-wide reputation. It was responsible for laying the first transatlantic cable in 1875. In 1878, William was the first to use an electric arc to melt steel, though the first commercial electric furnace did not come into general use until 1899.

In the year of his death, Siemens was given a knighthood, which was a culmination to many international honors. During his final years he added to his list of inventions various improvements in electric lighting and he contributed to the foundations of electric locomotion by building the Portrush electric railway in Northern Ireland.

Right: turbines on the Portrush electric railway, the first to be powered by hydroelectricity. The railway was completed in 1883, and the electrical work was carried out under Siemens' direction. The water turbines drove a Siemens dynamo which then powered a motor on the tramcar.

Gustav Kirchhoff

1824-1887

The German physicist Gustav Kirchhoff founded the modern science of spectroscopy. His invention of the spectroscope and his explanation of the significance of the spectral lines it produced created a powerful new technique for analyzing chemical compounds. Kirchhoff also showed how this new technique could be extended to an examination of light from stars, enabling astronomers to identify the elements of which they are composed.

Born in Königsberg in eastern Germany, Kirchhoff was one of the star pupils at the town's university. He made his first big contribution to physics shortly before graduation by showing that electrical impulses in circuits travel at the speed of light. His reputation insured for him rapid success in an academic career, and he was appointed Professor of Physics at the famous University of Heidelberg in 1854 at the age of 30. By that time Kirchhoff's main interest in

Below: an early spectroscope consisting of a collimator (a tube with a slit through which the light enters), a viewing telescope, and a tube with a micrometer for measuring the spectral lines.

through a narrow slit. This meant that the spectrum produced was in fact a large number of variously colored images of the slit. These appeared as easily identifiable lines, each representing a particular wavelength in the light being analyzed. Kirchhoff's simple technique resulted in the first practical spectroscope and was the key to a wide range of important discoveries.

Bunsen played his part by inventing in 1857 his famous burner, now named after him and one of the most basic pieces of apparatus in every chemical laboratory. For Kirchhoff its important feature was that the burner's flame produced very little light of its own despite being an effective means of heating chemicals. Its dim flame created virtually no background lighting to confuse the spectrum of lines produced from the light of a glowing chemical.

Kirchhoff quickly found that each chemical he examined with his spectroscope produced its own distinctive pattern of colored lines. The metal sodium, for example, produced a double yellow line and any compound containing sodium would have a spectrum containing such lines. Kirchhoff realized, therefore, that he had stumbled on an important new method for determining the composition of unknown substances. By simply heating them and examining the spectra produced, the elements of which substances consisted could be identified by spotting their characteristic "spectral signatures."

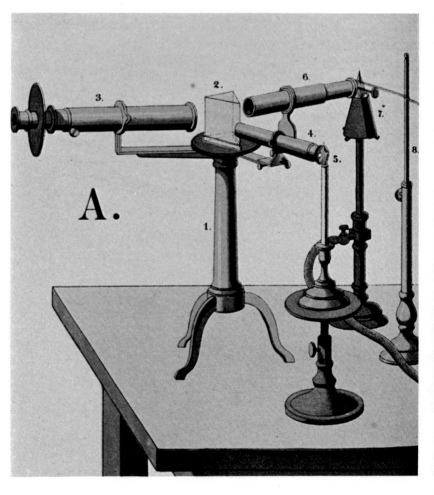

research was the way substances behaved when heated to incandescence. Assisted by the distinguished chemist, Robert Bunsen, Kirchhoff began an important series of experiments to analyze the light emitted by the heated chemicals. Kirchhoff planned to break the light into a spectrum using a glass prism. The technique was not new – Isaac Newton had used it almost 200 years earlier – but Kirchhoff decided first to pass the light

Spectroscopy

Kirchhoff was refining his technique when in 1859 he found by chance a mineral which displayed spectral lines unlike any of the known elements. It was a totally new element, the first to be discovered by spectroscopy. Kirchhoff announced the discovery in 1860 naming the new element "caesium" from the latin for "sky blue," the color of its most prominent spectral line. Soon afterwards he discovered another new element which he named "rubidium," the latin for

"red." With remarkable insight Kirchhoff began to speculate on whether he could extend his technique of analysis to the light from the stars. He began studying the work of Joseph von Fraunhofer who had classified spectral lines in the light from the sun and stars. Fraunhofer had not grasped their significance, but Kirchhoff realized that the lines were exactly like the "signatures" of elements he had produced through his spectroscope. This meant that the same means of analyzing compounds in his laboratory could be used to probe the composition of the stars themselves. Kirchhoff immediately set to work examining the solar spectrum and soon identified a number of elements including one of the most valuable, gold.

The story is told how Kirchhoff, who was frequently short of money, was asked by his impatient banker what was the use of discovering gold in the sun when Kirchhoff had no way of bringing it back to earth. A few months later Kirchhoff's work was recognized in Great Britain with an award to Kirchhoff of a medal and a sizeable sum in gold sovereigns. When he deposited the money he presented the coins to the banker with the wry comment: "Here it is – gold from the Sun."

In the years that followed Kirchhoff's pioneering work, spectroscopy became a standard technique in analytical chemistry while enabling astronomers to explore not only the composition

of stars but also of distant galaxies. One of the most exciting discoveries of recent times was of the spectral "signatures" of some of the complex organic molecules fundamental to life, drifting among the glowing clouds of gas which form nebulae. Spectroscopy has therefore brought us a step closer to finally resolving one of the most fascinating enigmas of the universe: is there life beyond the earth?

William Thomson, Lord Kelvin

1824-1907

A prodigious scientific genius, William Thomson was made Lord Kelvin in 1892 in recognition of his many contributions to science and engineering. Best known of these is his invention of a new temperature scale based on the concept of an absolute zero of temperature at −273°C (−460°F). The Kelvin scale enabled scientists to make major advances in the study of heat, and furthered the understanding of the physical behavior of matter at very low temperatures.

Thomson was born in Belfast, Northern Ireland. His early life was influenced by his brilliant but domineering father, a distinguished mathematician and author of many successful textbooks. Thomson inherited his father's intellectual gifts and soon showed a genius for mathematics. So great were his abilities that when the family moved to Scotland, William entered the University of Glasgow at the age of 10. While still a child he graduated with honors and immediately took up postgraduate research in France. In 1846, when barely 22, he was appointed Professor of Mathematics at Glasgow University where he was to remain for the rest of his career.

Thomson's unabiding curiosity led him to study many different areas of science and engineering. He made contributions to geology with controversial estimates of the age of the earth, and through his lifelong passion for sailing, invented many nautical implements including new kinds of compasses, sounding gauges, and tide predictors. He received a knighthood for his work on submarine cables, which included the patenting of the submarine telegraph receiver. His most important discoveries, however, concerned heat and temperature.

Thomson was among the first scientists to recognize the importance of James Joule's work in calculating a mechanical equivalent of heat. In fact, it was Thomson's influence which eventually won Joule the deserved recognition of the scientific establishment. In the years that followed, Thomson's interest in the nature of heat was stimulated by working with Joule and discovering how gases could be cooled by expanding them into a vacuum. This phenomenon, now called the Joule-Thomson effect, led directly to the first successful liquefaction of gases such as hydrogen and helium, and the development in later years of the modern science of low temperature physics, known as cryogenics.

Thomson was especially interested in a law discovered in 1787 by French physicist Jacques Charles. Charles had found that when a gas was

Below: laying the first transatlantic cable in 1866 from the *Great Eastern*. Kelvin made many contributions to submarine telegraphy and was the electrical engineer in charge of the project. Top: splicing the cable after its first break. Bottom: passing the cable out.

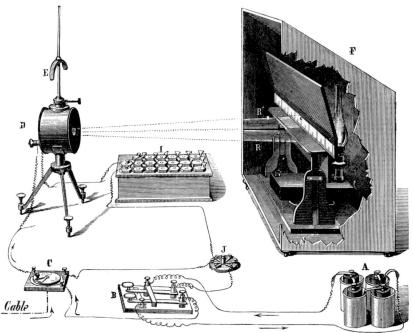

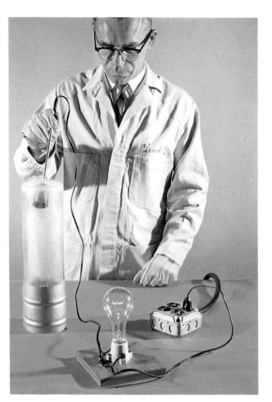

cooled, it contracted by 1/273 of its volume as measured at 0°C (32°F), for every drop of one degree centigrade in temperature. Scientists had for years been puzzling over the implications of this law. Did it imply that at −273°C the gas would cease to have any volume? The concept seemed meaningless and yet Charles' law was a fact that could not be ignored. In 1848, Thomson solved the problem by proposing that it was not the volume but the energy of motion of the gas molecules that reached zero at −273°C. Thomson went on to suggest that this held true for all matter, and that because the movement of its molecules was the source of a substance's temperature, when they ceased moving no further

Above: Kelvin's receiving apparatus at Brest Harbor, France, which made long-distance telegraphy possible. It included his mirror galvanometer, a tiny magnet attached to the back of a convex mirror and suspended inside a coil of very fine wire. A lamp directed on the mirror reflected a spot of light on a scale, moving from left to right as the electric current deflected the magnet. The telegraph message, in Morse code, could thus be recorded. It was later superseded by his siphon recorder, by which the cable wrote its own message.

fall in temperature could occur. He proposed, therefore, that −273°C was the absolute zero of temperature.

Using his idea he devised a new temperature scale with its zero point at absolute zero and its degrees equal to those on the ordinary centigrade scale plus 273. The new scale became known as the absolute scale or, in honor of Thomson, the Kelvin scale. Temperatures referred to the scale are denoted by the letter K and are called "degrees Kelvin."

The concept of an absolute scale of temperature proved a major advance in the study of heat. It enabled the laws governing heat engines to be worked out and provided the Scottish mathematician James Clerk Maxwell with the basis for formulating the kinetic theory of gases, which used Thomson's concept of the energy of the moving molecules of substances to describe their overall properties and behavior.

Thomson's achievements won him international acclaim. But despite the brilliance of his life work, his later years were spent resisting change and progress. In the 1880s he was the leader of the school of thought in Victorian science which believed that all the basic work in physics had already been completed and little new remained to be discovered. The pioneering research on radioactivity in the early 1900s, and the promise of a new era in science, did nothing to shake his reactionary beliefs. To the end of his life Thomson maintained fierce opposition to the idea that the energy emitted by radioactivity came from within the atom. One of the greatest scientific discoverers of the 19th century, Thomson died opposing one of the most vital innovations in the history of science.

Superconductivity, a discovery made possible through Kelvin's absolute temperature scale. **Left:** in this coil of wire at room temperature the electrical resistance is high. Only a small current flows around the circuit and the bulb glows dimly. **Right:** the coil is lowered into a jar of liquid nitrogen and cooled to well below 100 K. Electrical resistance drops and a much higher current flows around the circuit with the result that the bulb glows brightly.

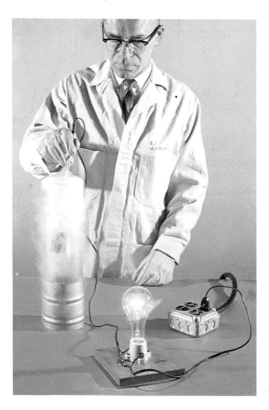

Joseph Lister

1827-1912

mortality rate. Wounds very rarely healed cleanly. Usually they festered, and this led to gangrene or blood poisoning. Consequently only simple operations were ever contemplated. Although every surgeon had his favorite method of attempting to reduce infection, few connected disease with hygiene.

A notable exception had been Ignaz Semmelweis, an Austro-Hungarian obstetrician who became known as the "savior of mothers."

Right: German woodcut, 1528, of a wound being cauterized with fire. Before Lister's time, surgery was a primitive technique with a high fatality rate. The lack of antiseptics and rudimentary hygiene meant that gangrene inevitably followed. Death also resulted because of shock during the operation. In England surgery was carried out by "barber-surgeons."

The British surgeon Joseph Lister pioneered the introduction of antisepsis into hospital routine. This was one of the major advances in medicine: surgery was converted from a technique with a high incidence of death into a method for actually saving lives.

Joseph Lister was born in Essex, the son of a Quaker wine distiller. His father, Joseph Jackson Lister, was also an amateur microscopist who invented the achromatic microscope – one which eliminated color distortion. By the time he was 16, Joseph Lister was skilled in animal dissection and microscopy. He had also decided to make surgery his vocation.

In 1848 he enrolled at University College, London to study medicine. He was an outstanding student and graduated in 1852 to become a Fellow of the Royal College of Surgeons. The next year he moved to Edinburgh to take up a position as assistant to James Syme, the foremost surgeon of his time. The move was fortunate in another way, for he fell in love with Symes' daughter, Agnes, and three years later they were married.

Lister's career as a surgeon advanced rapidly and in 1861 he was appointed surgeon to the Glasgow Royal Infirmary. He proved to be an innovative surgeon, devising many new appliances and perfecting operating techniques. He was, however, dismayed at the high rate of septicemia and gangrene. At that time surgical operations were accompanied by a very high

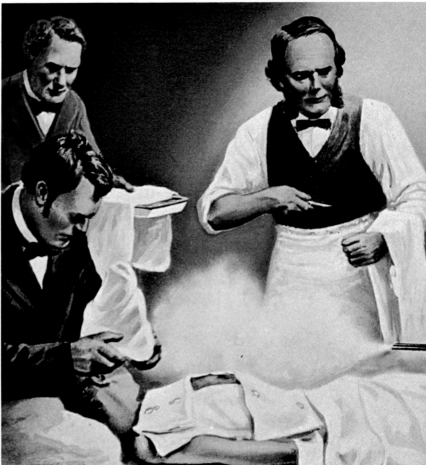

Semmelweis correlated the high incidence of puerperal fever in his lying-in wards with the unhygienic conditions of the doctors and medical students who usually spent the mornings dissecting corpses. In 1846 he introduced a program of thorough washing with chlorinated water and the incidence of puerperal fever dropped dramatically. Unfortunately, Semmelweis' fanatical denouncements against those of his colleagues who ignored his methods made him many enemies. His work at the time was largely ignored and Semmelweis died in a mental institute, ironically of blood poisoning.

The idea of antisepsis first came to Lister in 1865 when he read about the work of the French chemist and pioneer microbiologist, Louis Pasteur. For a long time Lister had been puzzled by the fact that simple fractures always healed quickly and cleanly, while compound fractures, in which the bone pierced and wounded the skin, invariably festered. Pasteur had shown that fermentation is caused by microbes which abound in the air. It occurred to Lister that fermentation and putrefaction were phenomena similar to the suppuration of wounds. The answer, therefore, was to protect the wound from the air and destroy the airborne microbes.

For this purpose Lister chose carbolic acid, which had been used successfully to cleanse sewers. In August, 1865, Lister performed the first antiseptic operation. Everything that came

Above: early 19th century operating theatre in St Thomas' Hospital, London. Surgeons dressed up in frock coats for the occasion and were observed by an audience of medical students.

into contact with the wound was sterilized with carbolic acid. The regimen was extended throughout the male surgical ward which Lister took charge of, and included the dressing and cleansing of wounds. The rate of festering, blood poisoning, and gangrene fell dramatically, and in 1867 Lister published his results. The paper, which included some observations on wound and tissue healing, announced how one of the unhealthiest and insanitary wards in Britain had become the safest.

A large proportion of the medical profession remained unimpressed. Many surgeons found Lister's techniques too cumbersome, while nurses resented the interference with their routine. In addition, many were unconvinced of the germ theory of infection and considered festering to be the result of contact with the miasma – "bad" air. It was also unfortunate that carbolic acid was an irritant, especially in the high doses used by Lister.

Lister, however, persevered. He lectured on his techniques at home and abroad, at the same time preaching the theories of Pasteur. The two, in fact, became great friends. In 1877, having received the chair of Clinical Surgery at King's College Hospital, London, Lister received the chance to make the most dramatic demonstration of his techniques. He introduced the operative technique of wiring up a fractured kneecap. This involved converting a simple fracture into a compound one, which would have normally festered. Thanks to Lister's antiseptic routine the fracture healed cleanly.

Lister received many honors for his work, the culmination being a baronetcy in 1883. It is to his credit that although he was responsible for the widespread use of antiseptics, he always acknowledged the pioneering work of others, in particular that of Ignaz Semmelweis.

Left: Lister directing the use of a carbolic-acid spray, the first widely-used antiseptic technique.

Sir Joseph Wilson Swan

1828 - 1914

The British chemist, Sir Joseph Swan, made an important contribution to photography in inventing the dry plate. He also anticipated the industrial method of manufacturing the first synthetic fiber, but he is remembered above all for the role he played in the early development of the domestic electric-light bulb.

The development of electric generators in the mid-19th century resulted in a search for different ways to exploit the potential of electric power. As yet, there was no practical way of using it to work a domestic light source. The carbon-electrode arc lamp was already in existence, but needed constant skilled maintenance. It was also extremely large and threw a light, which although very flattering, exceeded any normal requirements in its brightness. The incandescent lamp, which utilized the light from

were started around 1860, using carbon as the filament. He took a piece of burnt paper and placed it between two wire electrodes inside a glass bulb in which a vacuum had been created. The purpose of the vacuum was to prevent the filament from being rapidly oxidized.

At once he ran into practical difficulties, the major one being the problem of making an effective vacuum inside the glass bulb. The lack of a steady and reliable electric power source

Right: the Swan electric lamp, consisting of a carbon filament inside an evacuated glass container.

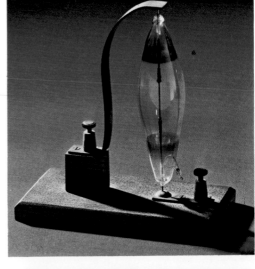

Below: a private residence illuminated by Swan's electric lighting system. Left: the library; center: bay window in the library; right: the staircase.

a glowing wire, was the ancestor of the modern light bulb. Early experiments were carried out, notably in France and Russia, to find a material that did not burn up so readily. One of the first and most important experimenters in this area was the English physicist and chemist, Joseph Swan.

Born at Sunderland, in the north of England, Swan began his career as a chemist's apprentice. He later joined a firm of photographic-plate manufacturers at Newcastle-upon-Tyne. His first attempts to make an incandescent light bulb

Engineering

Above: electric street lighting in 1881, at Mansion House, London.

Below right: printing room of *Paris Match*, which is produced by high speed rotary photogravure. In this printing process the image is etched out by acid on copper cylinders. As the cylinders rotate they are covered with ink which transfers the design etched on them onto a moving ribbon of paper. The paper takes the imprint of four successive cylinders, each using a different color. The gravure process, particularly suited to printing heavily illustrated magazines with a very high print run, owes its development to another of Swan's inventions—carbon tissue. This gelatine medium is coated with a photosensitive solution and exposed to light passing through a positive of the image to be printed. The gelatine hardens in proportion to the light passing through. The tissue can then be wrapped around the cylinder, unexposed gelatine washed away, and the etchant applied.

also contributed to the bulb's having a short life. Nevertheless, Swan continued to make progress with his idea, and in 1878 he brought his carbon-filament bulb to the point where it was both efficient and practicable, displaying it to a meeting of the Newcastle-upon-Tyne Chemical Society on December 18.

In fact, his progress by this stage was running almost parallel with that of Thomas Alva Edison, who illuminated his own first successful light bulb on October 21, 1879. Unlike Edison, Swan was slow to put his invention into commercial production, and he did not do so until 1881. The electric-light bulb, however, was established in its basic practical form by the work of Swan and Edison. It only remained for later workers to introduce tungsten filaments, and to use the inert gas nitrogen instead of a vacuum, for the light bulb to assume its modern form.

In his search for a better filament, Swan had become interested in nitrocellulose, an unstable substance which was discovered in the 1840s and subsequently formed the basis for the manufacture of explosives. It could be made into strongly bonded fibers, but was extremely flammable. Swan developed a method of forcing a solution of nitrocellulose through a grid of small holes so that it formed into filaments. These were then treated chemically to transform the explosive nitrocellulose back into inert cellulose. Although Swan made some articles from his fabric he did not exploit the idea. The principles were later applied to the manufacture of rayon, the first synthetic fibre to be manufactured commercially.

Another of Swan's innovations was in photography. Following the pioneering achievement of William Fox Talbot, the wet-plate process had become the commonly used method of taking photographs. Swan observed that if a silver bromide solution was heated, its sensitivity was increased. By 1871, he succeeded in producing an effective dry plate. It was the initiation of a new era in photography, and in 1878 he patented his invention of bromide paper, which is still the most widely used material for the printing-off of photographic negatives.

Friedrich Kekule

1829 - 1896

The German chemist, Friedrich Kekule, founded the modern structural theory underlying organic chemistry. His most famous discovery was that of the unique structure of the benzene molecule, one of the most important compounds in the synthetic dye industry, and widely used in chemistry for the synthesis of other more complex compounds. Though refined and modified over the years, Kekule's ingenious explanation of chemical structures is still used today to depict organic molecules.

Born in Darmstadt, Kekule was fascinated by structures even as a child. His interests centered on buildings and he planned a career as an architect. He entered the University of Giessen to follow its well-known course in architectural studies. By a chance meeting he became friends with the brilliant young chemist Justus van Liebig who persuaded Kekule to change to chemistry. Kekule's decision to give up architecture

Right: Justus von Liebig, in his laboratory. Liebig, one of the founders of modern organic chemistry, persuaded Kekule to give up his architectural studies and turn to chemistry.

Below: the snake with its tail in its mouth inspired Kekule to formulate a circular structure for benzene. In Kekule's words: "I turned the chair to the fireplace and sank into a half-sleep. The atoms flitted before my eyes . . . wriggling and turning like snakes. And see, what was that? One of the snakes seized its own tail and the image whirled scornfully before my eyes. As though from a flash of lightning, I awoke. I occupied the rest of the night working out the consequences of the hypothesis." Kekule concluded this account with a recommendation to his scientific colleagues: "Let us learn to dream, gentlemen, and then we may perhaps find the truth."

proved a turning point, both in his life and in the history of chemistry.

After receiving a doctorate in 1852 he traveled widely in England and France, meeting scholars and seeing some of the latest chemical research in progress. Returning to Germany in 1856 he took a post lecturing at the famous University of Heidelberg and set up his own private laboratory. Kekule's travels and discussions had generated an interest in the concept of valency, the means

by which individual atoms and molecules form bonds with each other to build up chemical compounds. Up to the 1850s chemists had denoted the atomic make-up of molecules by simply listing the numbers of atoms of each element in a certain conventional order. Using this approach, water is represented as H_2O, meaning two atoms of hydrogen (H) linked with a single atom of oxygen (O). Kekule, however, wondered whether these fixed combinations of atoms might be represented more usefully as patterns of atoms linked to one another. Such representations, if they were feasible, would tell chemists much more about a given molecule and could even suggest how molecules combine with one another to form new compounds.

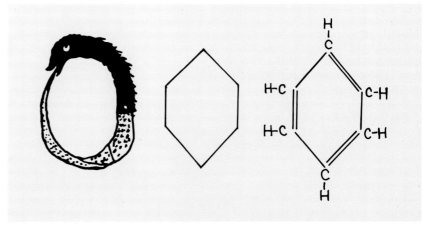

To test his idea, Kekule began by studying the chemistry of carbon, the fundamental element in organic chemistry. In 1858 he published his historic paper describing the valency of the carbon atom. It was, he explained, tetravalent. In other words, one atom of carbon could combine with up to four others. More important still, Kekule showed that up to three of the four available carbon atom bonds could be attached to other carbon atoms so that long chains of these

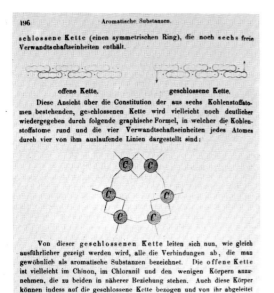

atoms could be formed. The Scottish chemist, Archibald Couper, an admirer of Kekule, suggested that the bonds themselves might be written down as short dashes, and immediately the idea of "Kekule Structures" became universally accepted by chemists.

It was now a simple matter to describe compounds structurally. Water, for example, changed from the uninformative H_2O to a representation

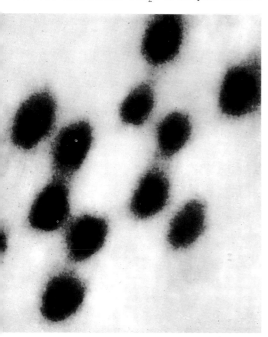

Left: the hexagonal structure of benzene as revealed by modern techniques. This is an X-ray photograph of hexamethylbenzene, consisting of six carbon atoms linked together to form a hexagon, each carbon atom being attached to another carbon attom carrying three hydrogen atoms, which are too small to show up in the picture.

Left: a drawing of the benzene molecule, taken from Kekule's *Textbook of Organic Chemistry* (1861).

showing that a single chemical bond links each of the two hydrogen atoms to the single oxygen atom. A molecule of water is therefore depicted as $H-O-H$. In more complicated structures, double and triple bonds (shown as double and triple dashes), first suggested by Kekule, help to elucidate the structure. Take the example of acetic acid ($C_2H_5O_2$): in the case of one of the carbon atoms, only two of the four carbon bonds are used singly, so a double bond (making up the total of four available bonds) exists as well. Acetic acid is therefore written structurally as:

Despite the enormous advances made possible by "Kekule Structures," a major problem remained unsolved. The structure of an important hydrocarbon called benzene was baffling chemists and its importance in the development of the first synthetic dyes made the problem an urgent one to solve. Chemists knew that its formula was C_6H_6 but not how the twelve atoms were connected to each other.

It was left once again to Kekule to make the breakthrough. He hit upon the answer by a flash of pure intuition. One day in 1865 while dozing he had a dream in which he saw the atoms wriggling about like snakes. One of the snakes bit its tail, forming a whirling circle or ring. Starting from his sleep, Kekule realized he had the solution to the problem of the benzene molecule. The key was the idea of a ring of six carbon atoms, each itself linked to a single atom of hydrogen. Kekule represented the molecule as:

Since Kekule's ideas were published far more sophisticated theories of valency have been developed. Highly complex mathematical formulations exist to explain the simple dashes of Kekule's structural formulae. Nonetheless, modern chemists still use Kekule's approach, finding it a simple but powerful means of depicting molecules. The additional information which Kekule's formulae provided has enabled chemists to work out how new compounds can be formed and, from this, to develop techniques to tailor-make specific new kinds of substances.

James Clerk Maxwell

1831-1879

Renowned as one of the finest mathematicians in history, James Clerk Maxwell is nonetheless best-known for his contributions to physics. Most important among his many achievements was the formulation of the field theory of electricity and magnetism which led directly to modern electromagnetic theory. He also made major contributions to the kinetic theory of gases, showing how their behavior could be reduced to a statistical interpretation of the random, ceaseless movements of individual gas molecules.

Maxwell's father inherited a substantial estate near Edinburgh, Scotland, and although educated in the city, Maxwell spent most of his childhood in the country. His town-bred classmates tormented Maxwell mercilessly for his country clothes and unsophisticated manners, even inventing the nickname of "dafty" for him. No less appropriate a description can be imagined. Maxwell was a brilliant pupil, a mathematical prodigy who had contributed an original paper on geometry to the Royal Society of Edinburgh when he was barely 15. But the cruelty of

Below: diagram of lines of force in a disturbed field, taken from Maxwell's *Treatise on Electricity and Magnetism.* Maxwell showed that the quantities which oscillates in a light wave are the electric and magnetic fields. Electric field (moving electric charge) and magnetic field (changing magnetic intensity) are inextricably linked and cannot act independently. Electric and magnetic fields have peaks of maximum and minimum strength, analogous to the crests and troughs of a water wave, but there is no vertical motion. Maxwell's equation overthrew the theory that a light wave oscillated by the displacement of particles in the ether.

his fellow pupils left its mark on Maxwell. He remained a shy introspective character throughout his life, uncertain in the company of strangers and only really at ease when absorbed in the problems of mathematics and physics. Nonetheless, Maxwell's modest nature and his absolute integrity won him many close friends and countless admirers.

Maxwell studied mathematics at Cambridge University, scoring record grades in all his examinations. On one occasion he answered all the questions with great speed and spent the rest of the allocated time translating the examination paper into Latin, just for the intellectual exercise. His reputation as a mathematical genius secured him professorships first at Aberdeen University and then at Kings College London, only a few years after his graduation. Although still a young man, Maxwell was at the height of his powers. During the 10 years following his appointment at Aberdeen in 1856, he made his most important contributions to physics.

He first brought his mind to bear on the behavior of gases. It had long been known that gases consisted of tiny particles – atoms or molecules – in constant motion. Maxwell assumed that their motion was random, and applied powerful statistical techniques to prove this idea of their behavior. He worked out a now famous equation describing the distribution of velocities among the various particles, showing how an "average" velocity could be identified for the

gas as a whole. A rise in temperature, Maxwell explained, could be interpreted as a rise in this average velocity, and a fall as a fall in the velocity.

Maxwell's work finally disposed of the old notion of heat as a kind of fluid and put the kinetic theory of moving molecules on a firm footing. But his work also had important philosophical implications. Maxwell had shown that gas behavior was governed by the statistical behavior of gas molecules. Since statistics is based on the law of chance, Maxwell had in fact proved that the laws and ideas of heat transfer in gas were not absolute. Although there was always a high probability that the laws would hold true, a small but significant probability had existed that they would be broken. It was a major step away from the deterministic thinking of classical physics toward the probability-based ideas underlying much of modern physics.

Soon after his work on kinetic theory, Max-

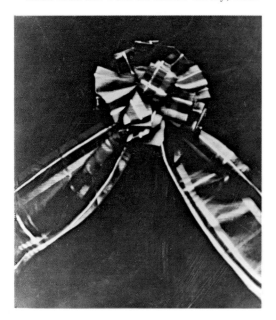

well made his supreme achievement. It involved extending the ideas of the physicist Michael Faraday and interpreting them in rigorous mathematical terms. Like Faraday, Maxwell visualized the space surrounding charged bodies as filled with lines of force carried in a field of electricity and associated a field of magnetism with it. In a few equations based on this concept of fields, Maxwell devised a mathematical expression of all the varied phenomena of electricity and magnetism. It proved beyond doubt the indissoluble link between electric and magnetic fields, and added the term "electromagnetism" to the vocabulary of science.

Using the equations, Maxwell showed that the oscillation of an electric charge would produce an electromagnetic field radiating from its source at a constant velocity. He worked out the velocity to be 186,300 miles per hour, roughly the velocity of light. Maxwell immediately suggested that light was therefore a kind of electromagnetic radiation and that visible light was only a small

Above: double refraction through Iceland spar crystal illustrates the theory that light vibrates in several planes.

Left: first color photograph, 1861, made by Maxwell to illustrate the trichromatic theory of vision – that the eye has separate receptors for red, blue, and green light.

Above: photograph of English countryside taken with infrared light, part of the wide radiation of electromagnetic spectrum initially postulated by Maxwell. In aerial photography it can penetrate atmospheric haze, discriminate between healthy and diseased vegetation, and pick out concealed bodies. Invisible to the eye, it can also be used for night photography.

part of a much wider electromagnetic spectrum. Today Maxwell's remarkable work is verified by the wide use made of the spectrum he described. From the long wavelengths of radar and radio to the ultrashort wavelengths of X-rays, the laws governing the behavior of the radiation are expressed with brilliant simplicity by Maxwell's equations of the electromagnetic field.

In the few years before his tragically early death, Maxwell was invited to become the first Cavendish Professor of Physics at Cambridge. He helped to design the now world-famous Cavendish laboratory and recruited its first staff. Despite a painful illness and the knowledge of its terminal nature, Maxwell continued his work with quiet efficiency. Although widely respected throughout his life, his true greatness was only recognized after his death, and the full significance of his work became apparent from later discoveries and developments. Today he is widely regarded as secondary only to Isaac Newton and Albert Einstein in the world of science.

Nikolaus Otto

1832-1891

The first four-stroke internal-combustion engine established the principles on which all later automobile engines have been based. It was built by the German engineer Nikolaus Otto and has hence been known as the "Otto engine."

The term "internal-combustion engine" arises from the fact that the fuel which powers the engine is burnt internally. This is in contrast to the steam engine, which might be called an "external-combustion engine" since its fuel is burnt outside in a separate compartment, the firebox. As a rival source of power to the steam engine, the internal-combustion engine soon made headway since it required a smaller, more compact machine structure.

The four-stroke internal-combustion engine is so-called in turn because the piston goes through a cycle of four movements, unlike the two-stroke engine built by Etienne Lenoir. At the start of the cycle, the piston is pushed outward, so drawing a mixture of (originally) air and domestic gas into the cylinder. With the next movement, the piston is forced in again, compressing the gas in the cylinder. The moment it

Below: Otto and Langen two-stroke gas engine. A mixture of gas and air was drawn into a vertical cylinder as the piston moved up. The mixture was then ignited, forcing the piston to complete its upward stroke. Atmospheric pressure then forced the piston down, causing a toothed rack to engage a gear and move the rotating shaft.

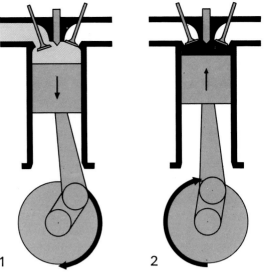

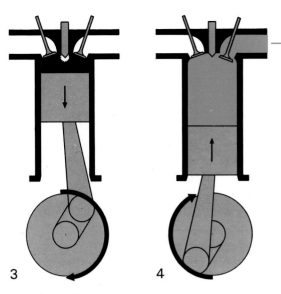

1   2   3   4

is fully compressed, an electric spark ignites the vapor and the resulting explosion forces the piston out again. Then, as the piston returns to its original position, it forces out the spent gas into the exhaust. The cycle then restarts.

The principle of the four-stroke engine was first defined by Alphonse-Eugène Beau de Rochas, a French engineer who realized that the.

Above: the four-stroke cycle in a diesel engine. 1. The induction stroke: the piston draws air into the cylinder through the open inlet valve. Once the piston is at the bottom of the cylinder the inlet valve closes. 2. The compression stroke: the piston then rises, compressing the air and causing it to heat up. 3. The firing stroke: at maximum compression, fuel is injected and the mixture ignites, and the exploding mixture forces the piston down. 4. The exhaust stroke: when the piston is at the bottom of the cylinder, the exhaust valve opens so that as the piston rises the burned gases are forced out of the cylinder.

technique of compressing the gaseous fuel was a vital element to its success. He never, in fact, built an engine himself, though he did take out several patents. Nikolaus Otto, the self-taught son of an innkeeper at Holzhausen, Germany, seems to have begun his own experiments independently. He built a simple two-stroke gas engine in 1861 and added improvements over the next few years. In 1867 he entered an engine at the Paris Exhibition, and it took the gold medal, knocking Lenoir's engine into second place. The Otto model was more than twice as economical on fuel consumption.

Five years later, in 1871, Otto set up a gas-engine factory at Deutz in partnership with a fellow engineer, Eugen Langen, who later was the first man to put forward the idea of an overhead, suspended monorail. As their technical manager, they took on another engineer, Gottlieb Daimler, and Otto and Langen turned their attention to putting the four-stroke engine onto a practical working basis.

The first Otto four-stroke engine was built in 1876, and its German patent was registered in the following year. Although by present-day standards it was noisy and voracious in its fuel consumption it very quickly proved its worth. Over the course of 17 years nearly 50,000 Otto engines were sold, mainly for use in small light-engineering factories. Improvements naturally continued to be made, and the addition of other cylinders to work in series enhanced its smooth running. Later there were experiments to get it to run on gasoline.

In the meantime, Beau de Rochas entered into litigation to uphold his own patent rights in the French courts, and in 1886 the German High Court ruled that Otto's patent should pass into the public domain. The possibilities which the four-stroke engine presented were thus opened up to other inventors. Its adaptation to the automobile was only a question of time, and the working principles of the Otto engine established the operating structure of the automobile engine in almost all its details. Foremost among those who exploited the possibilities were Daimler himself, after he had left Otto and Langer, and another German engineer, Carl Benz.

Left: Duryea automobile, an early four-stroke motorcar first operated in 1893. Its 4-horsepower engine had friction drive, and a single cylinder.

Sir William Crookes

1832-1919

he inherited a large fortune from his father and returned to London, where he established a private laboratory and set himself up as a chemical consultant.

Following Faraday's advice, Crookes turned to spectroscopy and began studying selenium compounds and minerals. The result of his research was that in 1861 he discovered a new element, thallium, a metal similar to lead. He concentrated his efforts on this new element and

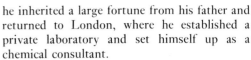

Right: thallium and its salts.

Below: Crookes' radiometer. It consists of a paddle-wheel assembly of vanes with one side polished and the other blackened, mounted in a quartz or glass bulb. Radiation from a hot source causes the wheel to revolve in the direction toward which the polished surfaces of the vanes are directed.

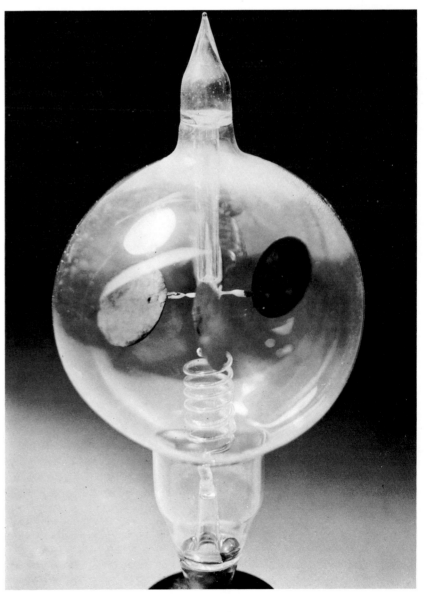

The Crookes tube was fundamental to the discovery of X-rays and the electron. Its use in the study of cathode rays was initiated by the British chemist and physicist, Sir William Crookes, who in addition discovered the element thallium and invented the radiometer.

William Crookes was born in London, the son of a master-tailor and eldest of 16 children. He became a student at August Wilhelm von Hofmann's Royal College of Chemistry in London, and then took up an appointment as Hofmann's personal assistant. In connection with his duties he attended meetings at the Royal Institution where he met the British physicist Michael Faraday. Faraday persuaded Crookes to change the direction of his studies from traditional chemistry to chemical physics, which at that time centered on optics and spectroscopy.

In 1854 Crookes was appointed superintendent of the meteorological department at the Radcliffe Observatory, Oxford. Two years later

its properties. A byproduct of his studies was his invention of the radiometer, an instrument consisting of sets of vanes with one side of each vane darkened and the other side polished. When light is directed on the vane more light was absorbed by the blackened side, activating the molecules. The vanes then start spinning. The instrument is thus a sensitive meter of the intensity of incident light.

Another of Crookes' inventions was the spin-

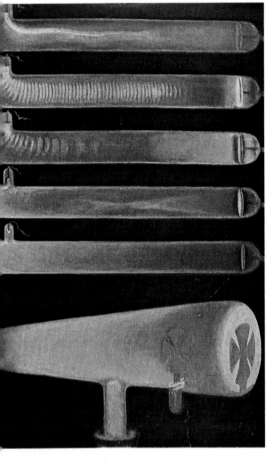

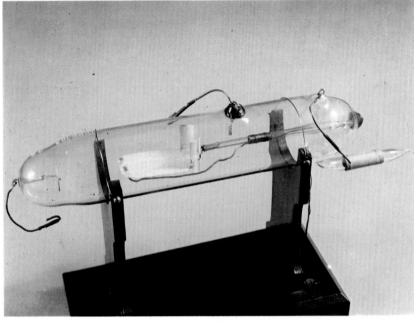

Above: Crookes' focus tube. A concave cathode focuses the electron beam on a target inside.

Left: as the pressure inside the Crookes' tube is decreased the color of the gas changes and the glow separates into bands. The metal cross inside the bottom tube obstructs the cathode rays and produces a shadow.

thariscope, an instrument for observing the scintillation produced by alpha particles, and the British physicist Ernest Rutherford used it for his studies on radioactive decay. A large-scale modification is used nowadays to measure the emission of alpha particles from radioactive substances.

Crookes' greatest achievement, however, was in his work on cathode rays. In 1887 he began to investigate the behavior of electricity generated across two electrodes in an evacuated glass tube. For this purpose he designed the Crookes' tube, a piece of apparatus which could sustain a very high vacuum. He applied a high voltage and turned on the vacuum pump. As the pressure inside decreased a green glow began to form in the tube and an electric current began to flow. The glowing gas separated out into bands, and a space formed in the region of the cathode (negative electrode). This space is now known as "Crookes' dark space." Inside the tube a small

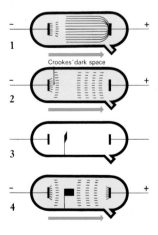

Above: on evacuating the electrified tube the glow (1) disappears to leave a dark space (2). A vane in the space (3), struck by particles from the cathode, pivots (4).

vane began to pivot, obviously deflected by particles traveling from the negative to the positive electrode.

Crookes used his results to postulate a fourth state of matter, not solid, liquid, or gaseous, but ultragaseous and arising under the conditions of a high vacuum. He assumed the particles to be of the same dimensions and mass as the original gas molecules, but in an electrified state. In fact, in 1897 the British physicist, J J Thomson, announced that these particles were electrons, minute particles 1/1800th the weight of a hydrogen atom. It was also while using the Crookes tube to study cathode rays that Wilhelm Röntgen, the German physicist, discovered X-rays.

Although Crookes' experiments on cathode rays and the designing of the Crookes' tube were his most important contribution to science, his work was, in fact, very diverse. He became widely regarded as a brilliant experimenter, although towards the end of his career his work became more theoretical. He edited many publications and lectured on the threat of mass starvation as a result of the world population outgrowing its food supply. His diversity was partly motivated by his belief that scientific endeavor should be financially rewarded. It was an understandable viewpoint as he had 10 children to support.

It was unfortunate that Crookes' work became tainted by his association with spiritualism. He devoted much of his time to investigating mediums and occult manifestations. He also joined both the Institute of Psychical Research and the Theosophy movement at their inceptions. By the time of his death he had established a reputation as an eccentric Victorian sage. However, some of his instruments are still in use today. The Crookes' tube, in particular, gave rise to the television tube.

Gottlieb Daimler

1834-1900

engine to run on gasoline, basing it on the Otto four-stroke cycle. The gasoline engines which Daimler built earlier for Otto achieved speeds of only 130 revolutions per minute. The new engine, with its efficient ignition system and surface carburettor, designed to vaporize the petrol and mix it with air, reached speeds of 900 revolutions per minute. In 1885, later during the same year in which Carl Benz made his historic run with his three-wheeled vehicle, they

Along with Carl Benz, Daimler has an assured place as one of the founding fathers of the automobile age. He invented the carburettor, which made possible the first high-speed gasoline engine, and his contributions were basic to the evolution of the car in all its practical early phases.

Gottlieb Daimler, born at Schorndorf in Germany, decided to become an engineer after an initial training as a gunsmith. He traveled abroad to study in Britain, France, and Belgium, and at the age of 38 was appointed technical director to the gas-engine company which Nikolaus Otto founded at Deutz. One of his research assistants was a young engineer called Wilhelm Maybach. Daimler and Maybach both saw the potential of the internal-combustion engine for propelling road vehicles. Otto, on the other hand, was skeptical about its development in this direction. Their mutual disagreement came to a head in 1882. Daimler and Maybach resigned and Otto declared that nothing could be done with so "indescribably thick-headed" a man as Daimler.

Daimler and Maybach then set up their workshop at Bad Cannstatt. They concentrated on developing the first light-weight, high-speed

Above: Daimler and Maybach's workshop at Bad Cannstatt, Germany.

Right: Daimler compound gasoline engine developed in 1879 at Nikolaus Otto's gas-engine factory.

mounted the new engine on a wooden bicycle and tested it. This mechanical contraption has a well-justified claim to being the world's first motor-bike.

In the autumn of the following year, Daimler and Maybach incorporated an engine into a horse carriage, and drove this, the first Daimler car, along the road between Cannstatt and Esslingen. Achieving speeds of 11 miles per hour, they created a considerable sensation for they were literally driving a "horseless carriage." The Daimler model of 1889 was then the first four-wheeled automobile to be built as such, and it incorporated some innovative features. These included a belt-drive mechanism to turn the

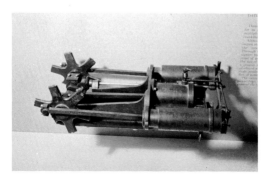

wheels, a tiller to steer with, and a four-speed gearbox. In addition it was built on a tubular steel frame.

The automobile was now a commercial proposition, and it was at last possible to think in terms of manufacturing and marketing this new invention. Therefore, in 1890, Daimler and Maybach set up the Daimler Motor Company. The quality and efficiency of their product was soon established. In 1894, the road from Paris to

Above: Daimler and Maybach in the first four-wheeled Daimler automobile.

Right: Daimler car works at Bad Cannstatt.

Below: Daimler automobile built in 1899.

Rouen witnessed the first international "race for horseless carriages." Out of the 102 cars which started only 15 finished the course, but it was significant that each one of these was powered by a Daimler engine. Daimler engines were also chosen by Ferdinand Graf von Zeppelin when he was carrying out his first tests on rigid airships in the 1890s.

In 1896 the Daimler Company produced the first road truck, but the culmination to their enterprise came in 1900, the year of Daimler's death, with the production of what is generally seen to have been the first true modern automobile – the Mercedes. Its design was a brilliant concept, and it incorporated an engine of 24 horse power, which was the most advanced then available. It was named "Mercedes" after the daughter of its owner.

The Daimler Company started various subsidiaries under license in other countries, including Britain. Eventually, in 1926, it merged with the Benz Company, the name of its product thus becoming the Mercedes-Benz. Maybach himself continued to be an influential engineer and designer, and in 1909 he set up a factory with his son to manufacture aircraft engines as a subsidiary to the Zeppelin organization.

Dmitry Mendeleyev

1834-1907

The Russian chemist Dmitry Mendeleyev discovered a fundamental interrelationship among chemical elements based on their atomic weights. He formulated his discovery in a periodic table of elements, now regarded as the backbone of modern chemistry. His work enabled chemists to identify "families" of elements with similar chemical and physical properties, and to predict the existence of hitherto undiscovered elements by identifying gaps in the family structures. The fundamental importance of atomic weight which Mendeleyev's work revealed, led physicists toward a new understanding of nuclear structure and the significance of such structure in determining the behavior and properties of matter.

The youngest of a family of 17 children, Mendeleyev was brought up in Tobolsk, Siberia. His father, a local teacher, lost his sight while Mendeleyev was still very young and much of his childhood was therefore spent against a background of financial difficulty. His mother became the family breadwinner but in 1849, when Mendeleyev was just finishing school, a double tragedy struck. Mendeleyev's father died and his mother's small business was destroyed by

Gold	
Silver	
Copper	
Iron	
Lead	
Sulfur	

Above: alchemist using mercury in an effort to produce gold. The symbol for mercury appears on the flask. Before the concept of the atom and its indivisibility, it was believed that one substance could be transmuted into another through magic and mystisism. The search for the philosopher's stone, which would change substances such as mercury into gold, occupied alchemists for over 600 years.

Above right: the alchemists used drawings as symbols for the substances they regarded as elements (right). The symbols are astrological, corresponding to the planets, and formed part of the alchemist's hidden knowledge, available only to the initiated. These were replaced by John Dalton who devised the symbols on the left when he postulated the atomic theory. Even these proved too clumsy and were eventually replaced by the now-familiar chemical notation of alphabetical letters.

fire. With the older children already independent, Mendeleyev's mother set out to organize her youngest child's education. Her remarkable determination was rewarded when, a matter of weeks before her death, she succeeded in finding Mendeleyev a place in the science faculty of St Petersburg University (now Leningrad).

A brilliant student, Mendeleyev made the best of his opportunity, graduating top of his year and pursuing postgraduate studies in France and Germany. In 1866 he returned to Russia, a respected chemist, and became professor at his old university. His dissatisfaction with existing textbooks led him to write his own, *The Principles of Chemistry*, published in 1870 and now a great classic. While researching the book he probed the relationship between different chemical elements, searching for signs of a unifying pattern in their properties. Other chemists before Mendeleyev had attempted this and since English chemist John Dalton had established the concept of atomic weight, many had sought arithmetic links between the atomic weights of the elements, hoping to reveal some basic pattern. It was Mendeleyev, however, who saw the key and so established the periodic classification of the elements.

By listing the 63 elements known in his day in order of their atomic weights, Mendeleyev did no more than several of his predecessors. His historic achievement lay in recognizing in the list that certain properties of the elements recurred periodically. In particular, he spotted a regular rise and fall in the elements' valencies, an integral measure of their power to combine chemically with others. He discovered that if he arranged elements of similar valency in columns,

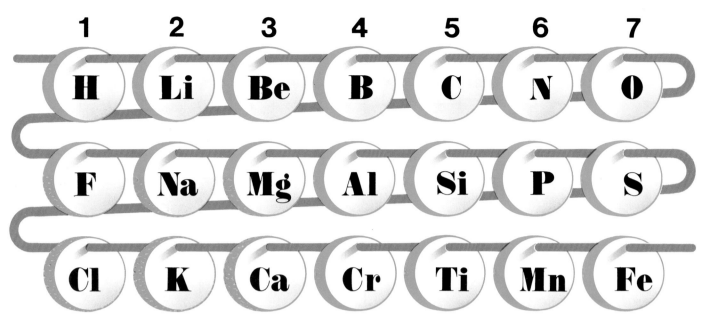

1	2	3	4	5	6	7
H	Li	Be	B	C	N	O
F	Na	Mg	Al	Si	P	S
Cl	K	Ca	Cr	Ti	Mn	Fe

the members of particular columns would show similarities in many other chemical properties. Because of the periodic way the properties recurred, Mendeleyev called his classification the *Periodic Table of the Elements*, a name by which it is still known today.

Despite Mendeleyev's reputation in academic circles, his periodic table was greeted with skepticism. Too many scientists had already announced supposedly unifying arrangements of the elements only to have their work discredited later. But in 1871 Mendeleyev provided the crucial proof which was soon to make his work universally accepted. In an historic paper published in the *Journal of the Russian Chemical*

Above: the "Law of Octaves," proposed in 1865 by British chemist J A R Newlands. Elements with similar properties were spaced out at intervals of eight when arranged in a table based on their atomic weights.

Below left: reproduction of Mendeleyev's chart, with the elements arranged according to atomic weight. Elements side by side in adjacent columns behaved in the same way. The question marks represented hitherto-undiscovered elements.

had therefore passed the test which every scientific theory must face – it had successfully predicted new verifiable facts.

Suddenly Mendeleyev became a worldwide celebrity. Honors were showered upon him and he made many overseas visits. Abroad he was a popular figure. His long hair and flowing beard gave him a patriarchal appearance which appealed to the public. In Russia he was less well liked, especially by the government who were suspicious of his liberal and egalitarian ideas.

Mendeleyev died only a few years before the Russian revolution. In 1955, in belated recognition of his vital contribution, a newly discovered element, mendelevium, was named after him.

			Ti=50	Zr=90	?=180.
			V=51	Nb=94	Ta=182.
			Cr=52	Mo=96	W=186.
			Mn=55	Rh=104,₄	Pt=197,₄
			Fe=56	Bu=104,₄	Ir=198.
		Ni=Co=59		Pl=106₆,	Os=199.
H=1			Cu=63,₄	Ag=108	Hg=200.
	Be=9,₄	Mg=24	Zn=65,₂	Cd=112	
	B=11	Al=27,₄	?=68	Ur=116	Au=197?
	C=12	Si=28	?=70	Sn=118	
	N=14	P=31	As=75	Sb=122	Bi=210
	O=16	S=32	Se=79,₄	Te=128?	
	F=19	Cl=35,₅	Br=80	I=127	
Li=7	Na=23	K=39	Rb=85,₄	Cs=133	Tl=204
		Ca=40	Sr=87,₆	Ba=137	Pb=207.
		?=45	Ce=92		
		?Er=56	La=94		
		?Yt=60	Di=95		
		?In=75,₆	Th=118?		

Eka-Silicon	Es	Germanium	Ge
(as predicted by Mendeleyev in 1871)		as discovered in 1886	
Atomic weight	72	Atomic weight	72.3
Atomic volume	13	Atomic volume	13.2
Specific gravity	5.5	Specific gravity	5.47
Dirty gray element forming white oxide	EsO_2	Grayish white element forming white oxide	GeO_2

Society, he identified gaps in the periodic table, suggesting that they represented elements still to be discovered. He went further, announcing that the position of the gaps in the table indicated that the new elements would have properties similar to those of their neighbors in the table. He actually gave fairly detailed descriptions of the new elements. Four years later, the first of these, gallium, was discovered and others quickly followed. Mendeleyev's predictions were found to be accurate. His periodic classification

Above right: the properties of germanium, discovered in 1886, compared with the predicted properties of Mendeleyev's eka-silicon.

Right: crystalline gallium phosphide. Gallium is a silvery metallic element, the first of the missing gaps to be discovered (1875). Its properties were correctly predicted by Mendeleyev using his periodic table.

Johannes Diederik Van der Waals

1837-1923

A self-taught scientist, Dutch physicist Johannes Diederik Van der Waals, won the Nobel Prize for Physics in 1910 for his work on the behavior of gases. By formulating an equation accurately relating basic properties of gases such as pressure, volume, and temperature, he enabled physicists for the first time to make detailed predictions about the way in which gases behave under different conditions. Such predictions are now

Below left: Johannes Van der Waals (right) and Heike Kamerlingh Onnes (seated left).

Right: the Van der Waals equation can be used to determine the physical structure of gases on the giant planets such as Jupiter.

put to practical use in almost every engineering situation in which gases play a significant role. Well-known examples are refrigeration and the freezing of foods. The deeper understanding that Van der Waals' work provided also made possible the first successful efforts to liquefy gases such as hydrogen and helium.

Van der Waals was born in Leiden of a poor family, which meant that he had to rely largely on his own resources for his education. He spent

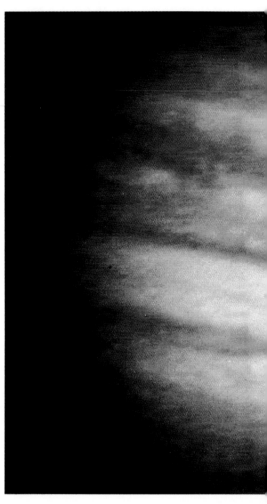

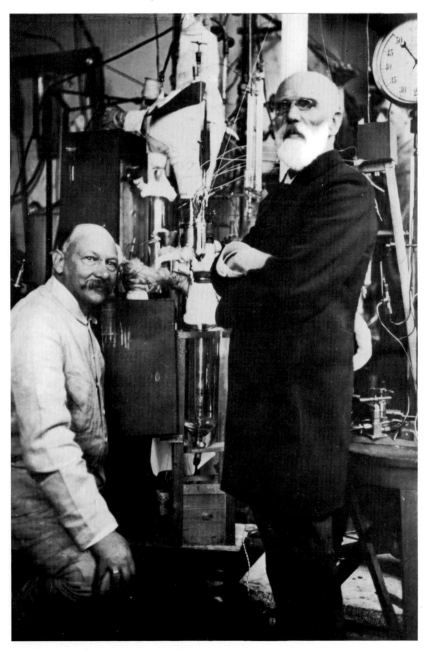

long solitary hours studying mathematics, physics, and chemistry without formal instruction, and made enough progress to win a place at Leiden University in 1862. Van der Waals had a rare talent for visualizing the physical processes underlying scientific phenomena, combined with outstanding mathematical powers. His postgraduate work at Leiden on the behavior of gases and liquids caused a minor sensation by the powerful and original insights it contained. It was a foretaste of the vital discovery on which Van der Waals later made his reputation.

The favorable reception of his postgraduate thesis fired Van der Waal's interest in trying to improve on the somewhat crude descriptions of gas behavior than available to science. All knowledge rested basically on a single principle called Boyle's Law which linked together changes in the pressure, volume, and temperature of a gas.

Physics

First worked out in 1662 by English physicist Robert Boyle, the law holds up fairly well in most situations. In a simple gas such as hydrogen or nitrogen, it gives a good approximation but it is not entirely accurate in any case. Scientists, aware of the limitations of Boyles' Law, tended to regard it as accurate for a so-called "ideal gas" and tried to ignore the fact that no such gas existed.

Van der Waals devoted himself to working out

Below: foliated graphite. The layers of carbon atoms are held together by weak Van der Waals forces. This accounts for graphite's greasy texture.

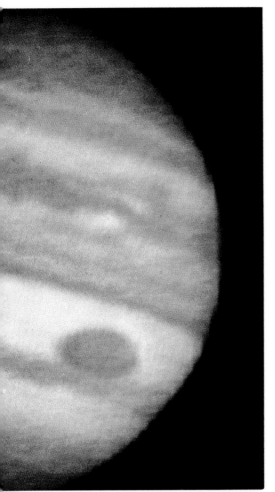

why the Ideal Gas Law, as it is known, did not hold exactly true for real gases. He knew that the main theoretical basis of the law was the kinetic theory of gases, which made two important assumptions necessary. One was that there were no attractive forces between gas molecules, and the other was that the molecules themselves had location but no actual size. Neither assumption made good sense as far as Van der Waals was concerned, knowing as he did that small attractive forces did exist between molecules and that, although molecules were extremely small, they had size.

In 1873, after several years of painstaking work, Van der Waals finally formulated the mathematical equation that explained the behavior of gases. Far more complicated than the Ideal Gas Law, his new law was a spectacular success in accurately predicting the way pressure, volume, and temperature varied.

An immediate result of Van der Waals' breakthrough was the discovery, by the Dutch physicist Heike Kamerlingh-Onnes, that hydrogen and helium could not be liquefied by means of the Joules-Thomson effect – which states that gases cool when they are allowed to expand fully – until they had first been cooled by other means below a certain temperature. This discovery opened the way for scientists to liquefy hydrogen and helium, which produces temperatures approaching absolute zero and marked the beginning of the science of low-temperature physics, known today as cryogenics.

Below left: helium liquefier at the Cavendish Laboratory, Cambridge. Kamerlingh Onnes used Van der Waals' equation to establish the necessary data for liquefying the so-called permanent gases (hydrogen and helium), and initiated the science of cryogenics or low-temperature physics. Apart from its obvious use in refrigeration, cryogenics is being applied in surgery, pollution control, radiation detection, and energy supply.

Right: launch of Apollo II, powered by liquid hydrogen fuel. Space technology is particularly dependent on cryogenics: liquid oxygen and hydrogen, used in combination as rocket propellants, provide greater thrust than solid fuel and need less storage space. In space life-support systems, liquid hydrogen can be used to recover oxygen from expired carbon dioxide.

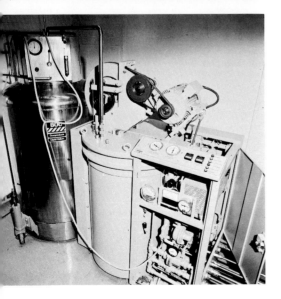

Sir William Henry Perkin

1838-1907

Hofmann's that it might be possible to synthesize quinine from the byproducts of coal tar.

At that stage, while the composition of quinine was known, its highly complex molecular structure was far from understood. Perkin's ambitions to synthesize it were not as yet a practical idea. In his attempts to make quinine by passing aniline through a series of chemical reactions, he instead produced a dark, nondescript, and sticky liquid. It did, however, have a purplish glint, and he speculatively added some alcohol. The

Right: the original dyes prepared by Perkin. Left: bottle of alizarine, which replaced the red dye obtained from madder root. Center: mauveine, the first man-made dye. Right: mauveine-dyed yarn.

The dyeing of cloth by means of vegetable and other naturally occurring dyes such as indigo was known at least since the days of ancient China and Egypt. The development of the vast range of synthetic dyes used in the modern textile industry, by contrast, stems from one event: the discovery in 1856 of the synthetic dye, aniline purple or mauveine, by a young British chemist, William Henry Perkin.

When the Royal College of Chemistry was founded in London in 1845, the man chosen to be its first director was August Wilhelm von Hofmann, a specialist in organic chemistry whose own discoveries included formaldehyde. In particular, he carried out extensive research into the nature and products of coal tar, among which was the compound known as aniline.

As a student of 17, William Perkin arrived at the Royal College of Chemistry in 1853, and Hofmann quickly saw in him the potential of a brilliant researcher. He made him his laboratory assistant, and the next year Perkin took up a research program, acting on a suggestion of

Right: the production of aniline blue, 1870. Perkin's discovery of mauveine in 1856 prompted other chemists to investigate aniline. Advances in organic chemistry enabled many new dyes to be discovered and they formed the basis of a new chemical industry.

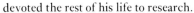

sticky liquid at once took on a majestic bluish-purple color.

Perkin lost no time in exploiting the commercial potential of his discovery. He sent a sample off to be tested for its properties as a dye and as soon as he received an encouraging reply, set about obtaining a patent. This he managed to do, though he was still only 18 and there was some bureaucratic disagreement over whether a patent could legally be issued to anyone under 21. In 1857, the year after he first made his aniline dye, he left the college and set up in business with his father and his brother, Thomas, manufacturing aniline in a chemical factory at Harrow, Middlesex.

The enthusiastic response of the French dyers meant that the company's output rapidly increased. The color was called "mauve," from the Latin *malva* for mallow, and mauveine dye became a basic feature of the high fashion of the day. By the age of 23, Perkin was a man of considerable wealth as well as the leading authority on artificial dyes. His success opened up a whole new area to commercial research, and many chemists, especially in France and Germany, set out to emulate his example. Even his old teacher, Hofmann, joined in, and succeeded in creating a reddish-purple dye, whose color was christened "magenta" in celebration of a French victory over the Austrians at the Italian town of that name in 1859.

The industrial applications of chemical research still tended to be regarded with suspicion by the conservative-minded entrepreneurs of British industry and it was Germany which became the center of world chemical research. Many of the present massive German chemical industries were thus founded on Perkin's achievements. Perkin himself was able to retire from the world of commerce at the age of 35, and he devoted the rest of his life to research.

Within a year of his retirement, Perkin had synthesized coumarin, an aromatic substance known for its pleasant scent of new-mown hay. This discovery initiated the synthetic perfumes industry, and again it was on the European continent rather than in his homeland that Perkin's work was taken up and continued. In 1906, the year before his death, and fittingly on the 50th anniversary of his first chance discovery, he was knighted.

Below: the subtlety of color that man-made dyes can produce is shown in this detail from a 1961 tapestry by the French artist Jean Lurçat.

Above: paper-chromatography test on mixture of dyes. When a special solvent is added the various dyes spread out at different rates and can thus be analyzed.

His other discoveries included the synthesis of tartaric acid and what is known as the "Perkin effect," a method of altering the atomic structure of certain organic compounds. The 3500 synthetic dyes in constant use today are a fitting monument to his enterprise.

Ernst Mach

1838-1916

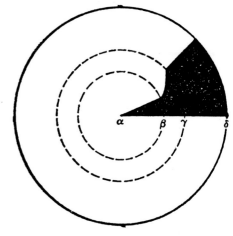

The Czech-born physicist and psychologist Ernst Mach was one of the pioneers in the study of aerodynamics. His work had important consequences in the development of aeronautics and supersonic aircraft. His biggest contribution to the field of science was in reviving and expanding the philosophical school of scientific positivism. This consisted essentially of rigorously verifying basic principles and assumptions, rather than working from hypotheses and suppositions.

Mach was born in Turas, now in Czechoslovakia, and became a professor of mathematics at the University of Graz, Austria, in 1864. In 1867 he went to Prague as professor of physics, and remained there for 28 years. His most influential book, *The Science of Mechanics: A Critical and Historical Account of Its Development*, was published in 1883, and in it he argued that the concepts of mechanics were only valid in so far as they could be verified by empirical observation. To fall back on imaginative or intuitive reasoning was, for Mach, to become involved in metaphysics. He took his arguments a stage further in *Contributions to the Analysis of Sensations* (1886), asserting that the experimental data from which we develop ideas and construct theories are in themselves neutral. Hence, in the psychology of observation, the phenomena being

Above right: when Mach spun a white disk with an irregular black nick two colored bands appeared. He postulated that these "Mach Bands" were due to neurological inhibition in the subject viewing them, not the result of a physical phenomenon, because photometric instruments could not detect them. They were subjective rather than objective.

Below: Mach photographs of shock waves. Left: cardboard; right: bullet.

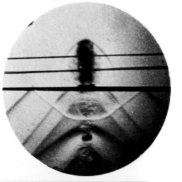

investigated can be investigated and understood only in terms of the experience which the investigator is undergoing.

In the positivist tradition, hypotheses and theories thus became "convenient fictions" which might or might not be useful tools in the assembling of objective knowledge. At this stage of scientific history no one had as yet observed an individual atom. To the positivist, therefore, atomic theory was only a "convenient fiction."

Mach himself became one of the most determined opponents of the atomic theory of matter. Until there was empirical evidence for the existence of atoms, his view was that their objective reality should be denied. For similar reasons he rejected the concepts of absolute time and space in Newtonian physics. He considered such speculations not to be the true concern of science.

His denial of Newtonian space and time did, however, have a positive influence on the thinking of the young scientist Albert Einstein, who at that time was in the process of formulating his theory of relativity. Mach's intellectual stature and his critically uncompromising stance before all projected theory make him a significant figure in the evolution of modern scientific thought. Future developments in physics and psychology, as well as the modern empiricist schools of philosophy, owed much to his theories. Critics of Mach's viewpoint, on the other hand, have pointed out that positivism in its ultimate form represents a flight from reality rather than a coming to terms with it: in the end all observed

Philosophy-Aerodynamics

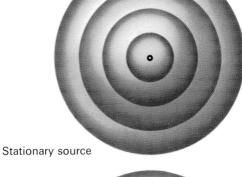

Stationary source

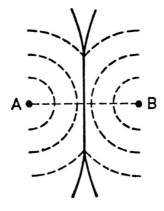

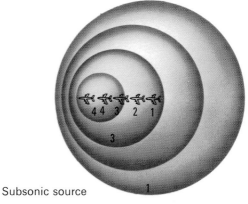

Subsonic source

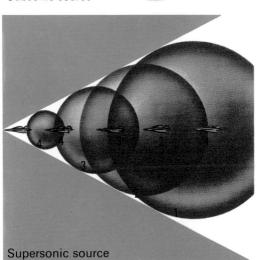

Supersonic source

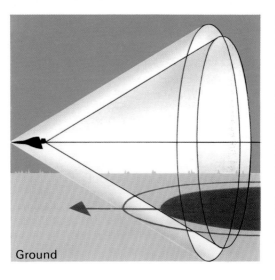

Ground

Above: shock wave from two electric sparks (A, B) exploded simultaneously.

Left: a static source radiates sound waves as concentric spheres. The subsonic source radiates spheres successively displaced by the source's motion, sphere 1 being caused by the source at position 1 (drawing shows jet traveling at Mach 0.8, so it will never catch up with any of its sphere surfaces). The supersonic source, however, leaves all its spheres behind.

Right: schlieren photograph of waves produced by aircraft flow.

Below left: the nose and tail of an airplane act as sonic airsources, producing conical shock waves. Everyone within the colored area will hear two sonic booms, the first being on the outer line.

Below right: aerodynamics test on hypersonic airplane in wind-tunnel.

truths have a significance and validity only as phenomena of the mind.

The term "Mach number" was coined in recognition of Mach's pioneering work in studies which he made of the behavior of objects in wind tunnels, working out the ratio between the speed of sound and the speed of a body in undisturbed air. These were a primary influence on the development of the theory of aeronautics. The Mach number is now used in modern aeronautics to express the velocity of an aircraft or projectile in relation to the speed of sound within the environment in which it is traveling. Thus Mach 1 is a velocity equal with the speed of

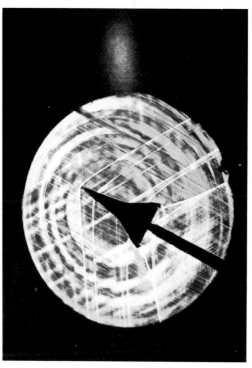

sound, and any speed above that becomes supersonic, Mach 2 representing twice the speed of sound, and so forth. The characteristic "sonic boom" from a supersonic aircraft is created by sound waves hitting the ground when the aircraft slows down or turns.

Ferdinand Graf von Zeppelin

1838-1917

The rigid airship, which made the dirigible balloon a practicable and commercial vehicle for long-distance passenger transport, was largely the brainchild of Graf von Zeppelin, a former German army officer who came from Constance, in Baden.

After the development of lighter-than-air balloons by the Montgolfier brothers and J A C Charles in the 1780s, there was a long search to find a dirigible form of balloon craft – one that was capable of being steered and navigated, and would not need to remain at the mercy of wind direction and other climatic factors. Many suggestions were made, some more practical than others, but the most prophetic of the early designs was that of General Jean-Baptiste-Marie Meusnier, a French military engineer, who was unfortunately killed in the battle of Mayence. Meusnier's design, dating from 1785, showed all the essential elements of a navigable airship – the ellipsoid shape, the car hung underneath from regularly slung lines, and a rudder. All it lacked was the motive force.

At the Paris Hippodrome in 1850, a French clockmaker demonstrated a model that was propelled by a pair of airscrews worked by clockwork. But the first powered airship to be built and to get off the ground was that of the French engineer, Henri Giffard, who used a lightweight, coke-fired steam engine to turn the propeller, and after ascending from the Hippodrome on September 24, 1852, made a journey of 17 miles out of Paris and landed safely at Trappe. Even so, Giffard's airship could only cope with the calmest weather conditions. The invention of an engine with a far more effective power-to-weight ratio was required before further progress would become possible.

The invention by Gottlieb Daimler of the four-stroke gasoline automobile engine in the 1880s gave a boost to the next wave of practical experiments. There then followed a series of different types of airship, the Brazilian aviation engineer Alberto Santos-Dumont favoring the nonrigid (soft fabric) kind. He built his airships on a relatively small scale and had considerable personal success with them. In October 1901, with his "No. 6" machine, he won a prize of 100,000 francs for being the first aeronaut to leave the French Aero Club at Saint-Cloud, head for the Eiffel Tower, circle it, and return to Saint-Cloud, all within 30 minutes. His "No. 9" was small enough to be used as personal transport. On one occasion he parked it in a Paris

Above: French cartoon, 1908, commenting on the growth of German air power. It reads "Wilhelm II on his new war horse . . . our future is in the air! (Watch out moon.)"

street while he stopped off at the *Cascade*, his favorite café.

The future lay, however, with large-scale rigid airships. The construction of these was made possible by the increased availability of aluminum for the construction of the frame. The frame was then covered by a light fabric, and the gas was contained in a series of cells or compartments, constructed of rubberized fabric and inflated within the frame. Zeppelin, who was in the United States at the time of the American Civil War to observe the use of balloons in military intelligence work, patented his initial design for an airship in 1898. He spent the next two years building the first Zeppelin airship in a floating hangar on Lake Constance. His name became virtually synonymous with

Transport

Left: the *Deutschland*, an early Zeppelin.

Below left: *Lieutenant Warneford's Great Exploit*, painting of the first Zeppelin to be brought down by Allied aircraft, 1915. Six bombs were used to bring the airship down in flames, over Belgium.

Right center: the *Graf Zeppelin*.

Below right: Goodyear advertising blimp. The Goodyear Tire and Rubber Company acquired the German Zeppelin patents in 1924.

this type of craft. The inaugural flight on July 2, 1900 was a historic event, but there were still many problems to be ironed out in the decade which followed.

World War I gave a strong impetus to the development of Zeppelins and about 100 were built. Many of them carried out bombing raids over eastern England and some even reached London itself. They caused much damage and some loss of life, but became steadily more vulnerable targets as aircraft defence tactics improved, and many were shot down. Their inventor was dead before the return of peace to Europe. He did not see the extensive building of large rigid airships and the inauguration of

regular long-distance passenger services which took place after 1918.

Of the great passenger airships between 1918 and 1937, the most famous was the *Graf Zeppelin*, which during the course of its working life made 144 transatlantic crossings and logged more than a million miles, with a perfect safety record. There were accidents, however, and 12 airships crashed or were lost at sea during these years. The most spectacular disaster occurred with the *Hindenburg*. It was the largest dirigible ever built, 803 feet long, and capable of carrying 70 passengers together with large quantities of freight. In May 1937 it went on fire at its moorings after being in service for only a year. Of those on board at the time, 35 were killed, and the event marked the end of the airship era. The *Graf Zeppelin* itself was quietly retired.

John Boyd Dunlop

1840-1921

changes of climate. He had no scientific training, but persisted with his experiments nonetheless. His first attempt, using nitric acid, was not effective. Then, in 1839, he stumbled on the solution when he accidently dropped a mixture of sulfur and rubber on to the top of a hot stove. Hastily scraping it off, he was amazed to find that it had lost its stickiness. He then tested the lump for its reactions to hot and cold conditions. The sample remained consistent.

The Scottish-born veterinarian John Boyd Dunlop invented the rubber pneumatic tire. The social consequences of this included the perfection of the bicycle as a means of popular recreation, and a rapid acceleration of motorized transport.

When the Spanish conquistadors arrived in South America, they found the Indians in the Amazon basin using the liquid latex gathered from cuts in the bark of a certain tree to make bouncing balls with, to brush onto cloaks as a form of weatherproofing, and to mold into footwear. The tree was *Hevea brasiliensis,* the rubber tree, and as Europe began to find an increasing number of uses for its product, rubber became a very important crop. The first leading advance in its application was made early in the 19th century when a Scottish chemist, Charles Macintosh, discovered that coal-tar naphtha dissolved the rubber. The solution was used to waterproof overgarments and thus the mackintosh was invented.

The trouble with rubber, however, was its tendency to harden and go brittle in cold weather, and to soften during a heatwave. Charles Goodyear, the son of a storekeeper at New Haven, Connecticut, became interested in finding a way of treating rubber to remove its tackiness and stop it reacting so drastically in

Above: Goodyear accidentally drops some sulfur-treated rubber on a stove and discovers that the stickiness disappears. As Goodyear did not have any scientific training, most of his experiments were done by trial and error, and dogged persistence. His obsession with rubber – he believed that it could form the basis of virtually any product – brought him to near financial ruin several times.

The process of adding sulfur to rubber under heat became known as "vulcanization," from Vulcan, the Roman god of fire, and its product as "vulcanite." It was the beginning of the modern rubber industry, and Goodyear took out a patent in the United States in 1844. In his own country, however, he found that his patent was constantly being infringed and he entered into long battles in the courts in an attempt to defend his patent rights. There were problems also to establishing firm patent rights in Europe. As a result, while others made considerable fortunes out of his discovery, Goodyear himself died deeply in debt, any money he made having been dispersed in litigation. His method, on the other hand, remains essentially the same to this day, and is capable of producing variations in texture from the toughest and most hardwearing to the softest and most elastic types of rubber.

Solid rubber tires were soon installed on the wheels of the first bicycles, and as early as 1845 a patent was taken out in London for an air-filled tire to cushion the cyclist from the inevitable jarring of rough road surfaces. This was never developed, but in 1887, John Boyd Dunlop, a Scottish-born veterinarian who subsequently moved to Belfast, made a pneumatic tire for his

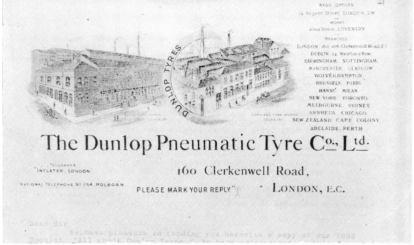

Above: Dunlop tire advertisement, 1898. The pneumatic tire soon became a standard feature of the automobile.

Right: Dunlop displaying the pneumatic tires fitted onto his bicycle. The pneumatic tire, essentially an inflatable tube inside a rubber and canvas cover, rapidly superseded the solid rubber tire.

Left: fitting a Dunlop tire onto the rim of an automobile wheel, 1910. The rapidly expanding automobile industry made huge demands on the supplies of natural rubber latex. These proved adequate until World War II when most of the rubber producing countries came under Japanese occupation. This forced the United States into developing a synthetic rubber.

son's bicycle. The next year he took out his own patent for a tough outer casing containing a soft, inflatable inner tube. By 1890, the pneumatic tire was in full-scale production at a Belfast factory.

The pneumatic tire immediately made bicycling fashionable and resulted in the design of a bicycle with wheels of equal size at the front and rear. This has since become established as the standard model. It was also swiftly adopted for use on the wheels of the new automobiles, which in turn gave rise to demands for improved road networks with better surfaces. The advance of the age of the automobile owed as much to Dunlop's invention as it did to any other factor. The Dunlop Rubber Company became, as it still is, one of the world's best-known rubber manufacturers.

Robert Koch

1843-1910

By establishing that infective diseases were caused by parasitic organisms, and not invisible forces, the German physician Robert Koch helped found the science of bacteriology. Through his meticulous experimental methods he isolated and identified the causes of some of the most devastating diseases. His work paved the way for modern immunization programs.

Koch was born in Klausthal, near Hanover, one of 11 children. His father, a mine-overseer, inspired in Koch a desire for travel which he was never to lose. From his mother he learnt to love and respect nature, and this interest shaped his subsequent career. Koch studied medicine at the University of Göttingen. At that time medical faculties did not teach bacteriology, but the discoveries of Louis Pasteur were provoking a lot of interest and discussion. After graduating in 1866, Koch practiced successfully as a doctor, eventually establishing a surgery in Wollstein. It was here that he equipped himself with a small laboratory and began the research destined to change medical science.

Koch focused his attention on anthrax, a disease which each year decimated sheep and

Right: Koch's laboratory at the Institute for Infectious Diseases, Berlin.

Below right: if these sheep were to graze on land contaminated by anthrax microbes, they would be dead in a day or two. The bacteria multiply rapidly in the blood of the infected sheep and form resistant spores. If a contaminated carcass is buried, the spores can survive for several years and then infect another animal. Consequently the only safe way to dispose of the carcasses is to burn them.

cattle. It had previously been shown that anthrax was probably caused by the presence of microscopic, rodlike organisms. The seasonal nature of the disease and its sudden new outbreaks remained a mystery. Koch cultivated the organisms and studied them under the microscope. He discovered that the anthrax bacillus formed spores which could remain dormant in unused pastures for several years and then infect hapless grazing stock. He also infected mice both with

the blood of anthrax-diseased sheep and with a pure culture of the bacterium, and passed the infection on from mouse to mouse several times. Each time he was able to demonstrate the presence of those rodlike organisms in the blood of infected mice. Healthy mice had no such organisms present. Also, microorganisms from infected blood which closely resembled, but were not identical to, anthrax did not produce the disease. In some cases a different disease was induced.

The results, which correlated the outbreaks of anthrax with the presence and lifecycle of the microbe, were published in 1876 and made a great impression on the medical establishment. From this and subsequent work on the transmission of disease from infected wounds Koch was able to derive the criteria which had to be satisfied before a microbe could be identified as the cause of a disease. "Koch's Postulates," as they became known, stated that the organism

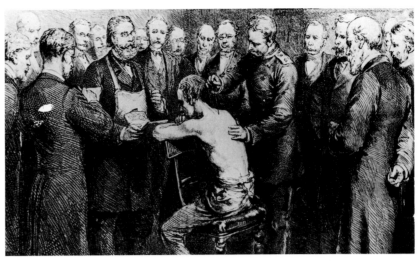

Above: Koch supervising inoculations against tuberculosis. He discovered the bacterium responsible for tuberculosis in 1882, and it was his work in this particular field that gained him the Nobel Prize for Medicine.

Above: photomicrograph of the tubercule bacillus.

Right: Koch on a medical expedition in Africa, 1907. He is shown dissecting a crocodile, the blood of which contains the antidote to sleeping sickness.

had to be present in every case of the disease, that it could be cultured for several generations (thus establishing that the cause of the disease was a living entity), and that, when introduced into a healthy subject, the organism should induce the same disease. His work finally established the parasitic theory of infection over the then-held view that infections were due to invisible beings. With a few exceptions, Koch's postulates still form the basis of bacterial diagnosis.

Koch's growing reputation secured him a post in the German Health Office. He established a laboratory in Berlin, and with his wife and daughter as assistants he pioneered many microbiological techniques, including culturing methods and using live steam to sterilize equipment. It was here that he isolated the organism

responsible for tuberculosis.

News of Koch's achievements spread abroad. He was invited by many governments to tackle crippling diseases endemic to those areas and so finally achieved his desire to travel. In Egypt he discovered the cause of amoebic dysentry; in India he managed to establish the bacterial origin of cholera, and also the transmission and sources of the disease. He also isolated the organisms responsible for rinderpest, sleeping sickness, and African relapsing fever. In 1905 his dedication to the elimination of these scourges gained him the Nobel Prize for Medicine.

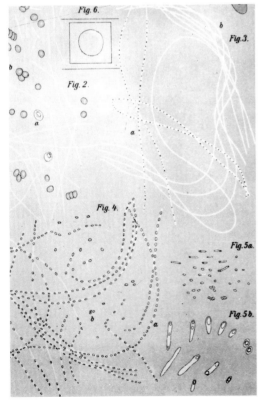

Left: drawings made by Koch to show the anthrax bacillus in various stages of development. 2. Bacteria growing in threads. 3. Threads elongating and minute spores developing. 4. Threads breaking to release mature spores. 5a. Stages in formation of new bacteria. 5b. The same under greater magnification.

Carl Benz

1844-1929

The first practical car to make a successful test run was the three-wheeled vehicle which the German mechanical engineer Carl Benz built at his factory in 1885.

Born at Karlsruhe, Benz was the son of one of the first engine drivers in Germany. He studied at the Polytechnic College of his home town and then worked as a technical designer. When he set out to build his first self-propelled vehicle, he was consumed with the idea and vision that the future lay with such inventions, and with the internal-combustion engine to drive them.

Right: the first three-wheeled vehicle, built by Benz in 1885.

Below: Benz at the first four-wheeled vehicle.

In 1883 he founded a factory at Mannheim to manufacture two-stroke gas engines which he designed himself. He continued to work on ways of adapting his engine to run a vehicle and to transform it into a gasoline engine, despite the severe criticisms from his business colleagues and the fact that his obsession was bringing him close to financial ruin. The vehicle that he eventually produced was based on a horseshoe-shaped steel frame, mounted on two large chain-driven wheels, with a smaller wheel to steer at the front.

One day early in 1885 he wheeled out this strange construction, rather resembling a giant perambulator, onto the cinder path which ran around the piece of land at the side of his factory. The car started, and it made four circuits, cheered on its triumphant way by his wife and a crowd of his employees, before one of the chains snapped and it came to a standstill. Later in the same year Benz achieved history's first automobile accident when, in his excitement, he forgot to steer his improved model during a public display and it collided with a brick wall.

In the Grand Duchy of Baden, in which Mannheim lay, there was a statute barring from the roads "conveyances driven by prime energy." Benz therefore had to press the authorities for permission before he could take his car out onto the streets. When they finally agreed, he created a sensation by driving through the town at 9 miles per hour. At this early stage he was unaware of the experiments of Gottlieb Daimler at Bad Cannstatt, and Daimler was unaware of Benz's achievement until he saw a Benz car in Paris late in 1885. For the rest of their lives there was a bitter rivalry between the two men as to which of them was the originator of the motor car. In 1926, however, the two companies merged to manufacture Mercedes-Benz cars.

In fact, where Daimler seems to have visualized the automobile as a kind of motorized horse carriage, Benz's conception was of an entirely new kind of vehicle. It was Daimler's engine, on the other hand, which finally made automobiles practicable, and motoring historians are inclined

Above: Benz's first four-wheeled vehicle, built in 1893.

Below right: front page of the French publication *La Locomotion Automobile*, 1896. The illustrations depicted, from left to right, are of an electric three-wheeled vehicle, a gasoline four-wheeled motorcar, and a four-wheeled vehicle with chimney, pulling passengers.

had been pending since 1879, taken out by a lawyer and inventor, George Baldwin Seddon, who never actually built a vehicle. The first native American gasoline-driven car to be built was quite possibly the one which the Duryea brothers, Charles Edgar and James Frank, constructed and ran through the streets of Springfield, Massachusetts, in 1893, though there are other claims to this distinction.

to see the claims as being equal. Benz made his first commercial sale in Paris in 1887. By the next year he was employing 50 men in his factory to work on constructing the three-wheeled model. His first four-wheeled vehicle was constructed in 1893.

During the late 1880s and the 1890s, many of the great manufacturing names in automobile history became established throughout Europe. In the United States, a patent for an automobile

Below: four-wheeled car with a woman driver.

Wilhelm Röntgen

1845-1923

The discovery of X-rays by the German physicist Wilhelm Röntgen revolutionized medical therapy and diagnosis. In addition, X-rays became an important analytical tool in many fields of science and industry.

Born in the small German village of Lennep, Röntgen's sole ambition was to study science. He believed that the application of science to everyday life would benefit all nations and that the fruits of scientific discovery were the property of all men. Röntgen's heady ideals were put to the test in later years, and despite his own difficult circumstances, he remained true to them.

Röntgen had his formal education broken by being expelled from school. As a result he was unable to attend university, and instead studied engineering at the Polytechnich of Zurich. However, his intention to continue as an engineer was soon forgotten when he became an assistant to

the distinguished German physicist August Kundt. Röntgen was introduced to many branches of physics and decided that his future lay in the study of pure rather than applied science. He eventually secured an appointment at the University of Würzburg in Bavaria. It was in 1895, while head of the physics department there, that Röntgen made his momentous and historic discovery.

He was investigating the behavior of cathode rays. These were produced at the negative electrode of an electric discharge tube when a high

Right: one of the first X-ray pictures to be taken – that of Röntgen's wife's hand. The rays pass through the skin but are impeded by the bones and metal rings. Röntgen's radiographs foreshadowed one of the most important uses of X-rays – that of medical diagnosis. Within a few months of their discovery, X-rays were being used in dentistry, to detect broken bones, and locate foreign bodies such as bullets. By using an X-ray opaque liquid, photographs could be taken of the stomach and intestines, and tumors could also be identified.

Below: German postcard at the end of the 19th century showing skeletal bathers on a beach. X-rays captured the popular imagination and were credited with many powers, including the ability to transmute base metals into gold and imprint diagrams on students' brains to aid learning.

voltage was placed across its two electrodes. Röntgen was particularly interested in the faint luminescence these rays produced in certain chemicals. In order to observe the glow more easily he darkened his laboratory and enclosed the cathode ray tube in black cardboard. When he switched on the tube he was startled to notice that some traces of a chemical called barium platinocyanide on the other side of the room were glowing. The chemical was known to

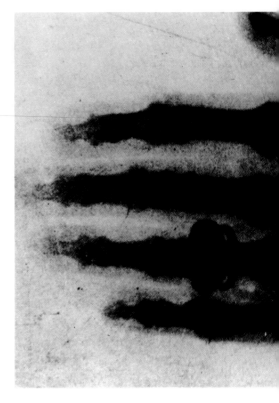

fluoresce when exposed to cathode rays. Yet Röntgen knew that these rays could not possibly be penetrating the cardboard enclosure surrounding the discharge tube.

Testing the phenomenon further, he found that even if he removed the chemical to the next room, it still glowed when the tube was activated. Röntgen realized that in addition to the well-known cathode rays, another form of radiation was being emitted by the discharge tube. It was obviously highly penetrating and yet invisible to the eye. By experiment he found that the mysterious rays could pass through a consider-

able thickness of cardboard and even through thin metal plates. He named them X-rays because of their unknown origin.

Röntgen discovered that X-rays had the property of producing a dramatic type of photographic image. He used it as the center-piece of his first public lecture on X-rays in 1896. After describing his experiments he called for a volunteer and before the audience took an X-ray photograph of the man's hand. When it

Above: Röntgen orthoradiogram, 1903, which used parallel X-rays for delineating organs in the body and their material size.

Right: Röntgen's first X-ray machine.

was developed, to the audience's astonishment, a perfect image was revealed of the bones in the man's hand. The X-rays, which passed easily through the soft flesh of the hand, were absorbed by the denser bone matter, allowing the photographic image of the bones in the hand to form. Röntgen's demonstration was a huge success and within days, X-rays were used in America to locate a bullet in a man's leg.

In addition to the importance of X-rays in medical diagnosis, investigations by scientists of their behavior led directly to the discovery of radioactivity. Röntgen's work therefore not only helped to found a major new medical technique, but played an important role in revealing the secrets of the atom and its nucleus.

Although prepared to accept scientific honors, including the Nobel Prize for Physics, he steadfastly refused to patent any aspect of X-ray production. True to his ideals, he regarded it an adequate reward to see the enormous value his discoveries had for the world. Sadly for Röntgen, the world treated him less kindly, and during the hyperinflation which destroyed the German economy in the 1920s Röntgen died in total poverty.

Above: German soldier being screened by X-rays during World War I.

Right: tomography, or radiographic analysis of the whole body. The apparatus is so designed that the radiographer can take shots of the patient at various angles.

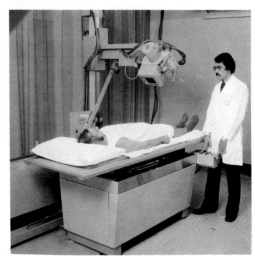

Alexander Graham Bell

1847-1922

A gifted and prolific inventor, Alexander Graham Bell is best known for his design and development of the telephone, probably the most revolutionary device in the field of communication.

Alexander Bell (the name Graham was given to him later) was born at Edinburgh into a family of noted elocutionists. His father, Alexander Melville Bell, was the author of the *Standard Elocutionist* and *Visible Speech*, the latter being a system of teaching speech to deaf people. The young Alexander and his two brothers were educated to follow in the family tradition, but both the brothers died as young men from tuberculosis. The elder Alexander decided in 1870 to move his home and business to North America in an attempt to protect the health of his only surviving son. They settled near Brantford, Ontario, and the young Alexander soon showed a remarkable gift for teaching the deaf to speak, using and adapting his father's system. At the age of 25 he opened his own school in Boston, Massachusetts, to train teachers to work with the deaf. Only a year later, the University of Boston appointed him to be Professor of Vocal Physiology.

failed to find a means of making it sensitive enough to transmit comprehensible sound.

The work of Elisha Gray was developing along similar lines to Bell's, and their technical devices were so close in principle that eventually there was a controversy over patent rights. Both Bell and Gray arrived at the notion of a telephone initially by trying to solve the problem of sending several telegraph messages simultaneously on one wire. Although their systems were unwork-

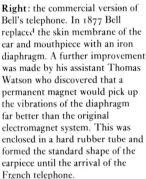

Right: the commercial version of Bell's telephone. In 1877 Bell replaced the skin membrane of the ear and mouthpiece with an iron diaphragm. A further improvement was made by his assistant Thomas Watson who discovered that a permanent magnet would pick up the vibrations of the diaphragm far better than the original electromagnet system. This was enclosed in a hard rubber tube and formed the standard shape of the earpiece until the arrival of the French telephone.

Below left: Bell investigating the telephone link between New York and Chicago, 1892.

Above: testing a Bell telephone. The mouth- and earpiece were similar in construction.

Bell's interest in speech and communication therefore seemed to extend naturally into finding ways of transmitting the human voice. He was not the only scientist researching in this area. One of the earliest was Philipp Reis, a German inventor who built a transmitter and receiver but

able, the fact that several harmonics could be transmitted through a wire indicated that it might be possible to do so with the human voice.

In the shop where he used to purchase his electrical components, Bell met a young and brilliant electrical engineer called Thomas Wat-

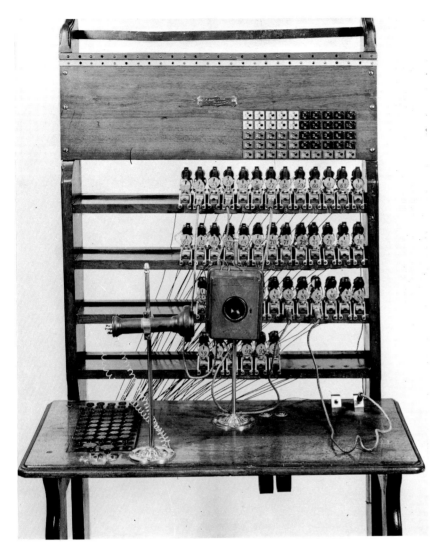

spilt acid from a battery down his trousers.

It was also on February 14 that Elisha Gray lodged a "notice of invention" for his device with the patent office. In one respect, Gray was ahead of Bell in that his patent specified the use of a metal diaphragm, which proved to be more effective. Bell, however, was far more aware of the wider possibilities of an effective telephone system and its commercial value.

After several more months of work, he and Watson were ready to start exploiting its potential, having replaced the skin membrane with a steel diaphragm. The transmitter alone was still creating difficulties, though these were eventually solved with the invention of a carbon microphone for which Thomas Alva Edison held the patent. It consisted of a pack of carbon granules, the resistance of which altered according to the pressure of the diaphragm.

Bell was obliged to fight for his own patent rights, even taking on the considerable vested interests of the Western Union Telegraph Company. After a series of court hearings over a long period, Bell's patents were upheld by the US Supreme Court in 1893. By that time the telephone was already established as a means of communication in many countries.

With his prolifically inventive mind, Bell made contributions to the study of flight, building large tetrahedral kites and helping to found the Aerial Experiment Association in the United States. He designed a hydrofoil boat which took the world's water speed record in 1918. He also invented the graphophone, an early device for recording sound. His work with the deaf remained of prime importance to him throughout

son, and the two men entered a collaboration which would establish the main working basis for the telephone. Bell was a specialist in acoustics rather than electrical engineering and he needed Watson's technical expertise to turn his ideas into realities.

The basic problem was to transform the vibrations of the human voice into electric signals, to pass these signals along a wire from a transmitter and to change the electric pulses back into sound vibrations at the receiving end. Bell and Watson experimented with a skin membrane that had a piece of iron attached to the center. Sound waves struck the membrane which vibrated, oscillating the piece of iron. This then induced an electric current in a magnetic coil. At the receiving end an electromagnet caused a diaphragm likewise to vibrate and reproduce the original sound.

Success eluded them initially, but they felt themselves to be on the right track. By early 1876 Bell was confident enough to draft out patent specifications, and to lodge them as an application on February 14. The patent was granted on March 7, and three days later Bell was able to send his assistant the first telephone message: "Mr Watson, come at once. I want you." He had

Above left: an early telephone switchboard, a crude system with few connections.

Above right: courting by telephone, one of the predicted uses of the instrument.

his years of success, and he used his royalties from the graphophone to found the American Association to Promote the Teaching of Speech to the Deaf, known today as the Alexander Graham Bell Association for the Deaf. He once said that he would sooner be remembered as a teacher of the deaf than as the inventor of the telephone.

Thomas Alva Edison

1847-1931

The name of Thomas Alva Edison is virtually synonymous with invention. By the end of his life there were 1093 patents in his name, including those for the electric-light bulb, the carbon-resistance telephone transmitter, the Phonograph, and the Kinetograph, the first fully effective moving-picture camera. He also built the first establishment devoted to invention – the industrial-research laboratory.

During the whole of his life Edison received only three months' formal schooling, and this ended abruptly when he was dismissed from school as being retarded, though in fact a childhood attack of scarlet fever had left him partially deaf. He was born at Milan, Ohio, but his family later moved to Port Huron, Michigan, and it was here that his brief experience of schooling occurred. Thereafter his mother took his education in hand, and succeeded in inspiring in him the limitless curiosity which was to be a constant feature of his character. He set up his first laboratory in the cellar of his parents' home when he was only 10 and taught himself the rudiments of chemistry and electricity.

His first earnings were from selling news-

papers at the age of 12 on the local rail link with Detroit. By 16 he had taught himself the techniques of telegraphy, and he spent several years picking up casual telegraphic work where he could find it. Meanwhile he seized every opportunity he could to experiment and to catch up with the latest technical information. He became known as someone who possessed a magic touch for putting right a faulty instrument. One day in 1869 he was summoned from his lodgings to the

Right: Edison's vacuum lamp, 1879. Forty years of experimenting preceded the arrival of the practical filament lamp. The development of a special vacuum pump was as vital as the reliability of the carbonized filament. Otherwise the filament would have oxidized and burnt out. Vacuum-tight connections also had to be developed.

Gold Exchange on Wall Street, New York, to look at the new gold-price telegraphic indicator, which had just broken down. Edison was promptly put in charge of the machine. He improved it and received an additional commission from the Western Union Telegraph Company to build an effective stock printer. His response was his first major invention: the Edison Universal Stock Printer. Western Union then retained his services and he made several improvements to telegraphic techniques.

By 1876 Edison was in a position to set up his own laboratory, or "invention factory" as he called it, where he could carry out research, either on commission or in those areas which interested him. This he built at the village of Menlo Park, New Jersey, and it was here, in what is said to be the world's first industrial-research laboratory, that he made his most famous inventions. First, in 1876, there was the carbon-resistance transmitter, which improved the audibility of the telephone, introduced only that year by Alexander Graham Bell. The Phonograph – the first working gramophone device – came next in 1877, the sound being recorded by a steel stylus and a diaphragm onto a cylinder covered in tinfoil. The later developments of wax cylinders

and disks were the work of other inventors.

Then he turned his attention to developing an "incandescent lamp," a field in which the British inventor Sir Joseph Swann had begun investigations almost 20 years earlier. For over a year Edison made a comprehensive search for a suitable filament which would not burn up so quickly, and eventually settled on scorched cotton thread. Swann was the first to produce a practical working bulb, but it was Edison who

Above right: Pearl Street power station, New York, 1884. It was based on Edison's direct-current electricity supply system.

Left: Edison at work.

Below: Edison's Home Phonograph, 1896. It could be used for recording as well as reproducing sound from disks.

saw the need for a parallel system in the wiring so that the circuit would not be broken if one lamp was switched off. Above all, he also saw the need for a comprehensive system of electrical supply. When the world's first power station was built at Pearl Street, New York, it was based directly on Edison's plans.

In 1887, Edison built the Edison Laboratory at West Orange, New Jersey. In this technological powerhouse, 10 times the size of the village laboratory at Menlo Park, he consolidated his earlier discoveries and made new ones. It was here that he perfected the Kinetograph, the first practicable moving picture camera, patented in 1891. It used the flexible celluloid film developed by George Eastman, which was run through horizontally and after developing could be viewed on the Kinetoscope, a type of peepshow. The Kinetograph, however, was soon outstripped in cinema history by the work of the Lumière brothers in Paris.

During his career, Edison made and lost fortunes on a prodigious scale. He set up many subsidiary companies to market both his own and other people's innovations. In some areas he has been accused of developing the ideas of others, merely adding the finishing touch and gaining the patent.

In essence Edison was a supremely practical inventor with a reputation for achieving results. Although he despised the theorists of science, he did have one abstract discovery to his name: the Edison effect. This was a phenomenon which occurred when a current flowed between two electrodes in a light bulb, one of which was heated, and it later formed the basis for the development of the electron tube.

Ivan Petrovich Pavlov

1849-1936

The Russian physiologist Ivan Petrovich Pavlov made many contributions to medical knowledge, in particular to the study of digestion. He is best known for his discovery of the conditioned or learned reflex, a concept which has profoundly influenced the study of behavior and learning.

Pavlov was born in Ryazan, a small village in central Russia. His family intended that he should become a priest, like his father, and Pavlov enrolled at a theological seminary. But his interests and attitudes were scholarly rather than religious, and in 1870 he left the seminary for the University of St Petersburg (now Leningrad). Pavlov studied chemistry and physiology, receiving his doctorate in 1879. He then spent two years in Germany studying the blood system and the physiology of digestion. It was these two aspects of bodily function which interested him most, and in particular the way they were controlled by the brain.

On his return to Russia Pavlov began his own researches, initially on the cardiovascular system. His work attracted much attention and in 1890 he was appointed Professor of Physiology at the Imperial Medical Academy. It was here that Pavlov started on his now-famous series of experiments with dogs. He introduced tubes into the dog's foodpipe and stomach. When the dog was fed, and the food dropped out through the

tube in the foodpipe, the stomach still secreted gastric juices, which could be collected from the tube in the stomach. Food placed into the dog's stomach without its knowledge took a much longer time to be digested than food entering in the normal way.

Fascinated by the way one physiological process was necessary to stimulate another, and anxious to find the way in which processes such as salivation and digestion are controlled, Pavlov

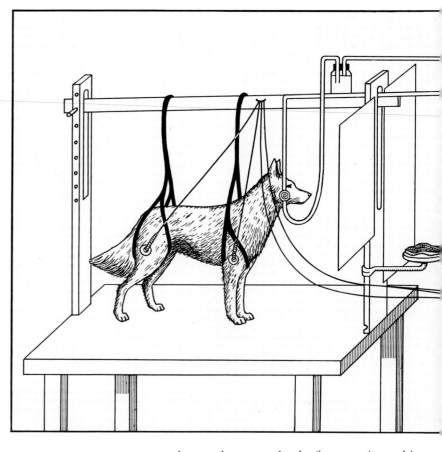

began what was to be the first experimental investigation of higher nervous activity in animals.

He found that if a dog was given food and simultaneously a bell was rung at several-minute intervals, the dog eventually salivated at the sound of the bell, even if no food was present.

Below right: Pavlov (center) with his laboratory assistants and dog.

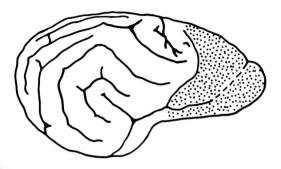

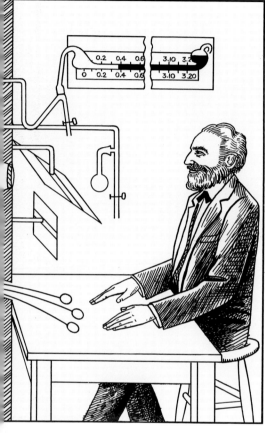

Left: Pavlov used the conditioned salivation reflex to map out the areas of higher nervous activity in the brain. After removal of the frontal lobes (shaded area) reflexes conditioned by tactile stimulation disappeared and could not be reestablished. On the other hand previously established visual and auditory reflexes returned soon after the operation and new ones could be established.

Left: Pavlov's experimental setup for measuring the amount of saliva produced during a conditioned reflex. The apparatus consists essentially of two parts: the dog's chambers where the reflex is induced, and the observation section where the dog's saliva is pumped out, collected, and measured.

Right: the isolation and despair of a mentally depressed patient. Pavlov believed that psychoses were the result of shutting out a world associated with harmful stimuli that had previously caused excitement. The Russian system of treating psychiatric patients in unstimulating conditions with no external excitement is based on Pavlov's ideas.

Below: Pavlov in his later years, in conflict with the Soviet Government.

salivating. The response was not forgotten but suppressed.

One of Pavlov's most important discoveries in this field was that the area of the brain responsible for this reflex is one found only in animals higher up on the evolutionary scale. He thus tried to apply his theories to human behavior in an attempt to explain psychotic and neurotic conditions. He considered that psychotic people, who shut out the rest of the world, behave in that way because they associate all excitation with possible injury or threat.

Pavlov's work has often been confused with brainwashing, but in fact many everyday responses are conditioned reflexes, from the blink of surprise to stopping a car at a red light.

Pavlov continued his laboratory studies until his death. An outspoken and vehement critic of Marxism and the Soviet system, he nevertheless was so highly regarded in Russia that he remained at liberty, despite his theological background. He received every possible Russian scientific honor, and also the Nobel Prize for Medicine, in 1904, for his work on digestive physiology.

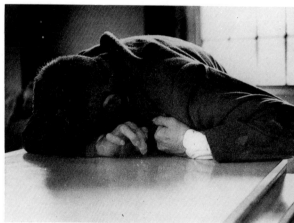

The dog's nervous system had learnt to associate the sound of the bell with food. Pavlov called this behavior the "conditioned" reflex and the process of learning it "conditioning." The conditioned reflex differs from an innate reflex such as the rapid withdrawal of a limb from a painful stimulus in that it has to be learned. A dog salivating when eating meat is exhibiting an unconditioned reflex. If it salivates at the sight of meat, on the other hand, the reflex is conditioned. As Pavlov demonstrated, a dog reared without ever seeing meat will show no response to it, not having learned to associate it with food.

Continuing his studies into the psychology of learning, Pavlov found that learning the reflex would be hindered by interruptions. The "external inhibition," as it is now called, is similar to the need for peace and quiet when studying or learning any process. He also discovered "internal inhibition," which occurred if, after a conditioned reflex such as response to the bell had been learned, the food stopped appearing when the bell was rung. The dog eventually stopped

Antoine Henri Becquerel

1852 - 1908

By discovering the phenomenon we now call radioactivity, the French physicist Antoine Henri Becquerel helped found the nuclear age. His historic experiments using compounds of the element uranium led directly to mankind's first hint of a vast new storehouse of energy lying in the heart of the atom itself.

Becquerel's discovery of radioactivity and his later research showing that the radiation emitted by uranium atoms contained tiny charged particles, was the starting point for modern theories of atomic structure.

Becquerel was born in Paris and brought up in a family dedicated to scientific research. His grandfather had been a distinguished physicist in the time of Napoleon Bonaparte and his father had continued the family tradition. Becquerel's

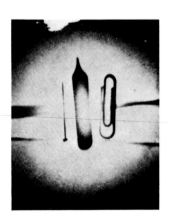

Above: shadow photograph produced by the Becquerel rays emitted by radium. The lighter portions are those where the rays are most intense.

Above right: discharge tube experiment, 1857, by Becquerel's father, a physicist who devoted much of his time to studying fluorescence. A voltage was applied across the electrodes at either end of the tube, high enough to ionize the gas inside. When the pressure inside was reduced the gas began to glow. Fluorescent tubes such as neon and mercury-vapour lights are modern examples of discharge tubes.

Below: crystals of potassium uranyl sufate.

penetrate materials such as cardboard and metal foil. Unable to think of a suitable name for the phenomenon, he called them X-rays. Intrigued by Röntgen's discovery, Becquerel wondered whether the fluorescence he was himself studying might contain X-rays as well as visible light. At the time, he was examining a compound of uranium called potassium uranyl sulfate and to test the idea Becquerel exposed some to sunlight and then wrapped it in metal foil. He then placed

father specialized in the study of fluorescence, a phenomenon in which certain chemical compounds exposed to sunlight would in turn emit a visible glow. Not surprisingly, the young Becquerel's future was virtually settled from the day of his birth and once his education was complete he began his own research, continuing his father's investigations into fluorescence. In 1896, almost by chance, Becquerel stumbled upon a mystery that held the deepest implications for science and the future of mankind.

A few years earlier, the German physicist Wilhelm Röntgen had discovered a new kind of radiation that seemed to have the power to

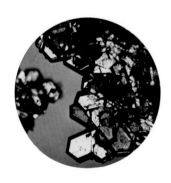

it in a dark room next to an unexposed photographic plate. Becquerel reasoned that if, in addition to the visible light in the fluorescence, some X-rays were emitted, they alone would be able to pass through the foil wrapping and imprint themselves on the photographic plate.

To Becquerel's delight, the plate, when developed, was heavily fogged. With mounting excitement he prepared to repeat the experiment and confirm his findings. But a series of overcast

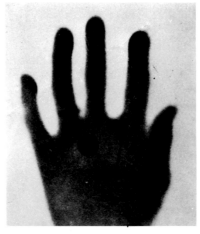

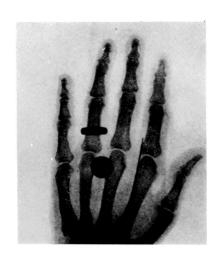

Above: radiographs of the hand. The one on the left is taken using Becquerel's gamma rays, and the one on the right by Röntgen's X-rays. Initially it was thought that gamma rays could be used instead of X-rays to examine the internal structure of the body. Their production would only require a small piece of radium, as opposed to the complicated apparatus needed to generate X-rays. Unfortunately, as the picture shows, Becquerel's rays pass through bone almost as readily as flesh.

Below: deflection of radium rays by a magnet. A: radium rays passing out of the slits at either side of the source tube, with no magnet present. B: electromagnet directly below the source. C: stronger magnet.

Left: Becquerel in his later years.

A
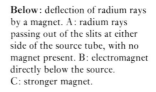

B
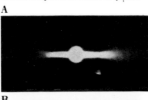

C
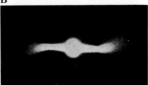

days meant he could not expose the fluorescent compound to sunlight. Too impatient to wait longer, Becquerel decided to see whether he could at least detect a slight fogging of a photographic plate caused by the weak fluorescence which was all that he could achieve without strong sunlight. To his astonishment, the fogging was as complete as before. Hardly daring to consider the implications, he put some of the uranium compound into a sealed box so that absolutely no light could reach it and activate its fluorescence. Again he placed a photographic plate nearby and again it was completely fogged. Becquerel realized that the radiation was being emitted by the substance independently of its fluorescence. Further research showed that apparently only chemicals containing uranium were natural emitters.

In 1899 Becquerel showed that the radiation could be deflected by a magnetic field and that therefore it consisted, in part at least, of tiny charged particles. This meant that the radiation was not the same as Röntgen's X-rays. In the years that followed, other elements were discovered which emitted the mysterious radiation. The most important of these was radium, discovered in 1898 by Marie and Pierre Curie. It was Marie Curie in fact who named Becquerel's radiation "radioactivity."

Becquerel's work began an exciting sequence of discovery. Once it was clear that Becquerel's rays were not X-rays, physicists, Becquerel among them, concentrated on finding out what they were. Soon it was apparent that they contained two kinds of tiny charged particles together with an electromagnetic radiation, similar to X-rays but more powerful, what we call today gamma radiation. The discovery implied that the atoms of radioactive substances were themselves the source of the emitted particles and energy, and that therefore the atoms must have some kind of internal structure. This was the vital link in the chain of scientific progress which has extended to the present day. It was the beginning of our modern understanding of the atom and the harnessing of its limitless energy in nuclear reactors.

A A
Michelson
1852-1931

Above: A A Michelson.

The German-born American physicist A A Michelson made a fundamental contribution to modern physics by providing an accurate measurement of the speed of light. He also discredited the theory that light waves were carried through space by "ether." His experiment of 1887, carried out with Edward W Morley, is famous in scientific history, and provided the theoretical basis for later work on relativity by Albert Einstein.

In 1850, when Michelson was barely two, his family left Strelno (then part of Prussia) to emigrate to the United States. They settled in Nevada where his father soon established a successful business. When Michelson was 17 he entered the United States Naval Academy and proved brilliant in mathematics and science. He showed little talent for seamanship, however, and following graduation remained at the Academy to lecture in science. Having developed a fascination for trying to measure the velocity of light, he decided to leave the Academy and learn more about the latest theories of optics. Michelson studied widely in Europe, especially at universities in France and Germany, and then returned to the United States to start his experiments.

With his first series of tests in 1882, Michelson's gift for accurate measurement came fully into play. He measured the velocity of light as 186,320 miles per second, a result that remained the best estimate available for 50 years. Even then, the only person who could improve on it was Michelson himself.

In connection with his experiments, Michelson built an instrument called an interferometer. This device split a light beam into two, sent the parts along separate paths, and then brought them together again. Michelson believed that if the two parts of the beam traveled different distances at the same velocity, they would be out of phase when recombined, in which case they would produce a series of light and dark bands called an interference pattern. An interference pattern would also be produced if the two parts of the beam traveled the same distance at different velocities. Michelson decided to use this idea to measure the velocity of the earth compared to ether, the medium that was sup-

Left: Edward Morley, the American chemist and physicist who collaborated with Michelson in his experiment to detect the movement of the earth relative to the ether.

Right: Michelson (second left) with Albert Einstein (right). Einstein acknowledged his debt to Michelson whose experiment had considerable influence on Einstein's Special Theory of Relativity.

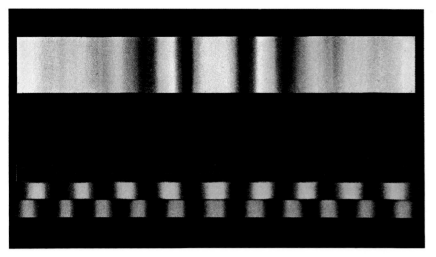

posed to fill all space. This ether was believed to be stationary, and light was thought to be a vibration in the ether.

Michelson conjectured that if he sent one part of a light beam in the direction of the earth's motion through the ether and the other at right angles to the earth's motion, one would have a greater velocity than the other. If he then recombined the beam after the parts had traveled the same distance, the degree to which they were out of phase would show in the interference pattern formed. This in turn would provide a measure of the speed of the earth's rotation through the ether.

Michelson's first experiments showed no interference pattern. After repeated failures, he joined forces with his friend and colleague Edward Morley in 1887. They took rigorous precautions to avoid experimental error. Again there was no pattern. Puzzled and confused, Michelson had to regard his efforts as a total failure. But the celebrated experiment became an example of how negative results can some-

Above: as the earth rotated through the ether, there would be a point at which light traveled with the ether, and at other times against it. The resulting differences of velocity should have been detected as shifts in the interference pattern. The lack of any noticeable shift convinced Michelson that his apparatus was inadequate.

Above right: diagram to show how light from L was partly reflected and partly passed by mirrors (at M and G) in criss-cross beams. Readings taken at T indicated that there was no appreciable change in the speed of the light beams whatever the observer's position.

Right: drawing of the rotating table mounted with mirrors that was set up by Michelson and Morley for their experiment to establish the velocity of light.

times be as valuable as positive ones. Scientists soon realized that the most likely explanation for a failure to detect the earth's motion relative to the ether was because ether did not exist. This radical idea raised other difficult problems. Light was regarded as vibration in the ether. Could there be a vibration without something in which to vibrate? Michelson had begun a chain of speculation about the nature of light and space that culminated in Einstein's theory of relativity 18 years later. Einstein drew directly on the results of Michelson's experiments, using the idea that the velocity of light is constant as his basic premise.

In the years following the famous experiment, Michelson returned to his lifelong interest and began to work on ever more accurate methods of

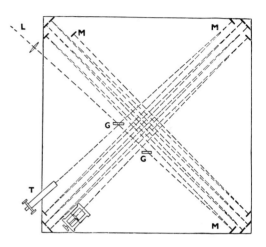

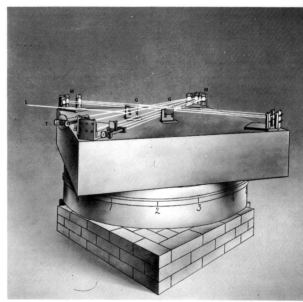

measuring the velocity of light. Sadly his health failed and he died before he could carry out the key experiment. It was left to his assistants to complete his work, which they announced in 1933 as 186,271 miles per second. This was a mere 11 miles per second less than the best estimate of today. For a man devoted to precise measurement, the accuracy of his last work was a fitting epitaph for Michelson.

Alphonse Bertillon

1853-1914

The French police clerk Alphonse Bertillon invented the first widely-used systematic method of criminal identification. Because it was based on sound scientific principles, it revolutionized inadequate, unjust, and often corrupt police methods of arrest.

Alphonse Bertillon was born in Paris, the son of a doctor. His father had initially wanted to be an engineer, and this interest was reflected in Dr Bertillon's medical work. He bought and designed many instruments to provide an accurate measurement of the human frame. Bertillon's maternal grandfather was a demographer who wrote a book on human statistics.

Bertillon himself did not show initial promise. He was an unruly student and expulsions from various schools led to his being educated at home. The nearest he displayed to scholastic interest was a pssion for collecting and arranging objects of natural history.

In 1879, with no specialized training, Bertillon took the only job he could get: that of a clerk in the Prefecture of Police. His duties were to fill in and copy out forms. At that time there was no systematized method of crime detection or identification. Descriptions such as "ordinary" and "average" for height and build abounded. Although photography had been introduced to record offenders, the quality was very bad and did not take into account disguises or prominent changes of expression.

Bertillon was disgusted by the unscientific methods used. They went against all he had been taught by his father and grandfather. Using his knowledge of measurements and statistics, he

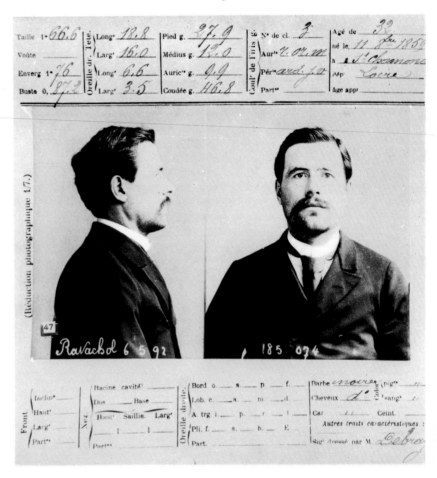

Above: the *portrait parlé*. Bertillon introduced the use of the profile photograph to overcome facial distortions often made by suspects.

Left: Bertillon lecturing on his anthropometric system, surrounded by the wealth of evidence that he had amassed.

devised a method of his own. He discovered that if a series of 11 measurements is made, the chances of two individuals corresponding exactly in all measurements was 4,194,304:1 against. The measurements that Bertillon chose were the length and breadth of the head and right ear; the length from the elbow to the middle finger; the length of the left foot; the lengths of the middle and right fingers; the height; the length of the trunk; the distance between the middle-finger ends of the outstretched arms.

To supplement the measurements Bertillon also devised the *portrait parlé*. This was a photograph of the full face and profile, with attached notes on any special marks, the color of the eyes, the color of the hair and its manner of growth. The introduction of the profile photograph was important because it was less affected by distorting expressions.

Bertillon submitted his method to the Prefect of Police. The response was a letter to Dr

214

Bertillon suggesting that perhaps his son was mad. Advised by his father to wait until a new Prefect was appointed, Bertillon eventually got a chance to prove the usefulness of his system. He was given three months to provide a correct identification. Bertillon built up a filing system so that his records could be easily traced, and in February 1883 made his first identification. A man called Dupont was brought in for questioning and was found to be identical to one called

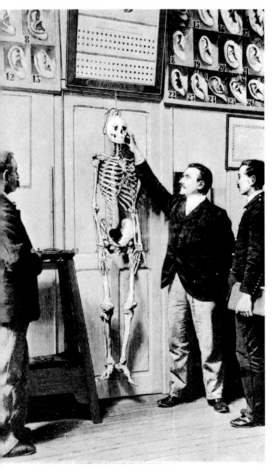

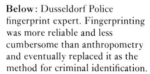

Left: instruction in anthropometric measurements at the Paris Police Headquarters, 1899.

Below: Dusseldorf Police fingerprint expert. Fingerprinting was more reliable and less cumbersome than anthropometry and eventually replaced it as the method for criminal identification.

Martin, previously convicted for attempting to steal empty bottles.

Anthropometry, or *Bertillonage* as it became known, was soon adopted throughout Europe and the United States. In 1888, when the Department of Judicial Identity was formed, Bertillon was appointed its head. He became a pioneer in the use of scientific method rather than speculation in crime detection. He developed the use of metric photography in recording scenes of crime. By placing measuring scales at selected points the relative sizes and distances of corpses, footprints, stains, and other clues could be accurately recorded. Before the only method possible was sketching. He also introduced the use of contact photography in the analysis of documents. A photographic plate was placed against the document and the two were exposed for a few seconds to a gas light. When the plate was developed it showed up erasures and changes made on the paper.

One of the unfortunate aspects of Bertillon's career was his involvement in the notorious Dreyfus case. Bertillon tried to apply the anthropometric system to handwriting, and on the basis of his supposed expertise he was called to give evidence. He used a very unsound method to prove that Dreyfus wrote the treasonable document, and mainly on this evidence Dreyfus was convicted. Subsequently the document was shown to be a forgery.

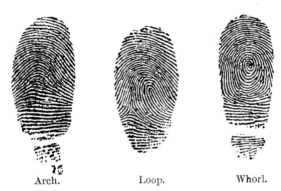

Right: fingerprints are classified by grouping the patterns into arches, loops, and whorls. The system was introduced by Sir Francis Galton.

Arch.   Loop.   Whorl.

Bertillon's anthropometric system was eventually replaced by fingerprint identification. The use of fingerprints in identification had been discovered 14 years before anthropometry by Sir William Herschel of the British Indian Civil Service. It did away with the cumbersome measurements of anthropometry but required a system of classification before it could come into general use.

Curiously enough, although Bertillon never quite understood fingerprinting and resented the possibility that it could supplant his own system, he did include fingerprints in his *portrait parlé*. He thus had the distinction of being the first detective in Europe to have a suspect convicted on fingerprint evidence alone.

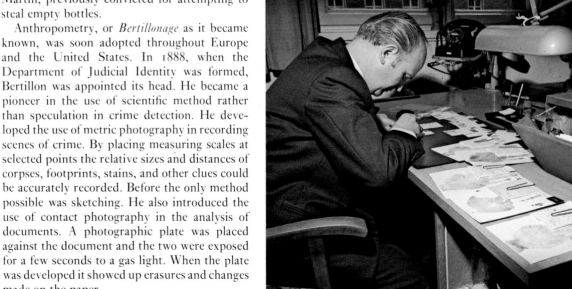

Ottmar Mergenthaler

1854 - 1899

The Linotype typecasting machine was the invention of a German-American engineer, Ottmar Mergenthaler. It was the first automatic typesetting machine, and its introduction revolutionized newspaper production, and the printing and publishing industries.

While König's invention of the steam-powered printing press in the early 19th century was successful in mechanizing the printing process itself, the actual setting up of type remained largely a manual operation. In 1822, William Church, a printer in Boston, patented a type-selecting machine with a keyboard. However, it was only a partial solution. It selected individual pieces of type from a magazine pool and placed them in order. These, however, needed to be composed by hand, and they could not be re-used until the whole printing operation was finished.

There were several practical difficulties to be overcome in designing a fully automated type-setting machine. Apart from being able to mold individual letters, it would also need to produce lines of type, *justified* (that is, filled out) to column width, with the words equally spaced within the line. In addition the typesetting operations would need to be done at a much faster speed than hand setting if it was to have any commercial advantage.

Ottmar Mergenthaler, who was born at Hachtel in Germany, served an apprenticeship to a watchmaker. At the same time he studied engineering in night classes. After he emigrated

Right: Mergenthaler demonstrating the operation of the linotype keyboard in the plant of the *New York Tribune*. In the year that linotype was invented a cartoon appeared in a British printing journal depicting a robot setting type. Many printers feared that the linotype would take away their livelihood. Today computer-assisted typesetting presents the same threat.

Right: a finished line or slug of type cast off the linotype.

to the United States at the age of 18, he became interested in the technical problems of building an automatic typesetting machine while working in the machine shop of a relative in Baltimore, Maryland. After a false start, when he tried to mold type from papiermâché impressions, he produced the Linotype machine in 1886.

In this, each line of type was produced as a separate unit or slug. As the operator worked the keyboard, similar to that of a typewriter, the

machine selected the copper type matrices for individual letters in their correct order, and as he came to the end of each line, a system of wedges adjusted the word spacing to fit it to the correct column width. This line of type then served as a mold for a molten but rapidly cooling alloy of lead, and a slug of type was cast. The individual type matrices were then returned to their correct places in the matrix magazine, ready for reuse.

The influence of Mergenthaler's invention

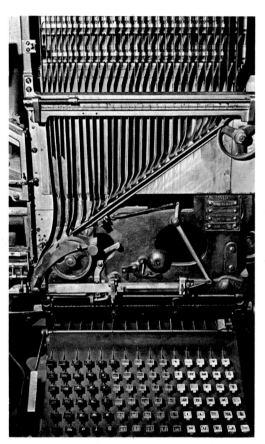

Right: a linotype machine, 1911, with four magazines – storage units holding matrices of a particular type face and size.

Below: apart from revolutionizing the printing industry, automatic typesetting had important social consequences. For the first time newspapers became widely available to the public.

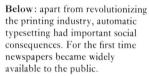

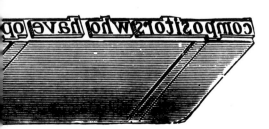

was immediate. It became possible to produce over 5000 pieces of type an hour, as opposed to about 1500 by the traditional hand methods. Its only main rival was the Monotype machine, patented in 1887 by Tolbert Lanston, an American inventor, though the two systems have subsequently coexisted as the leading and most widely used methods of typesetting down to the present day.

In the Monotype machine individual pieces of type are cast for each letter, and each line is then justified by a drum which calculates the spacing according to the total number of units in the line. The keyboard operator punches out a paper tape which is then run through a type-caster. The Monotype caster was eventually capable of producing over 10,000 pieces of type an hour. The flexibility and adaptability of both hot-metal systems in fact ensured their surival into the second half of the 20th century, where a newly sophisticated printing technology was increasingly making use of computer programing and electronic controls.

Paul Ehrlich

1854-1915

The German bacteriologist Paul Ehrlich pioneered the technique of chemotherapy in medicine. From his discovery that certain tissues have a specific affinity for chemicals, he reasoned that organisms causing disease could be selectively killed with chemical drugs. This led him to produce arsphenamine, the first synthetic drug, and highly effective against syphilis.

The son of a lottery-office keeper, Paul Ehrlich was born in Strehlen, Eastern Prussia (nowadays Strzelin in Poland). He chose medicine as his career, and by the time he had graduated from the University of Leipzig in 1878 he had already began research into the effect of chemicals on the cells of the body. His interest in this aspect of medicine had been stimulated by reading an account of the way tissues are affected by lead. It had been shown that the cells of those

Below right: photomicrograph of *Treponema pallidum*, the spirochaete responsible for syphilis. In the later stages of the disease chronic abscesses appear in various parts of the body, compressing healthy tissue. The valves of the heart may start to leak and prevent it from acting as an efficient pump. Attacks on the nervous system can lead to loss of coordination, personality changes, and general paralysis of the insane. The organism can also pass through a mother's placenta to infect the infant.

organs most affected during lead poisoning also absorb lead in test-tube solutions. That is, certain cells had an affinity for inorganic substances.

After graduating, Ehrlich was appointed head physician at the Charité Hospital in Berlin, where he continued bacteriological research in preference to clinical practice. His work impressed the German microbiologist, Robert Koch, who offered him a post at his Institute for Infectious Diseases. With a laboratory at his disposal, Ehrlich turned his attention to diphtheria.

Another German physician, Emil von Behring, had shown that the toxins produced by certain bacteria such as tetanus and diphtheria stimulate the cells of the body to produce antitoxins which then neutralized the poison. On the basis of these discoveries large amounts of antitoxin could be produced in animals and the serum used for therapeutic purposes. Ehrlich participated in these researches and pioneered the large-scale production of diphtheria antitoxins in horses.

The German government, greatly impressed, appointed Ehrlich to be Director of the Royal Institute for Experimental Therapy in Frankfurt-am-Main. He was given a free hand to pursue any research of his choice. His colleagues, who thought that serum banks had commercial potential, were disappointed when Ehrlich an-

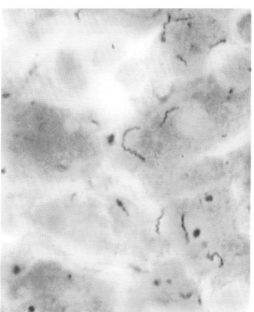

nounced that he did not wish to concentrate on serology. Ehrlich realized that antitoxins had limited uses and almost no effect against syphilis or diseases caused by protozoans, such as the African sleeping sickness.

Ehrlich considered that if an organic substance such as an antitoxin could have a prophylactic effect, it should be possible to make a synthetic drug with a similar antimicrobial activity, especially if the microbe showed an affinity for that chemical. He was particularly interested in finding a drug to cure syphilis, then

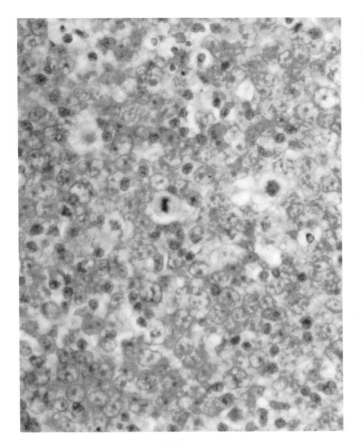

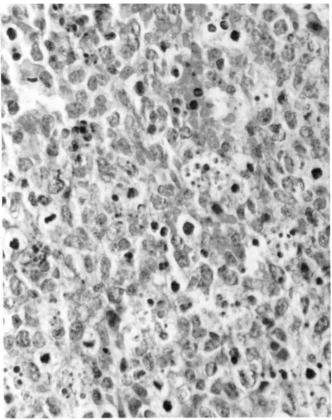

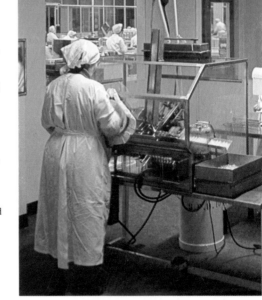

Above: the use of chemotherapy in the treatment of cancer. The photomicrograph on the left shows the cell of a malignant lymphoma (cancer of the lymph gland) before treatment. On the right is a picture of cells from the same tumor after chemotherapy. Many of the cancer cells have died or are shrinking and rupturing.

Left: Erlich with his colleague Sahachiro Hata. The two collaborated closely in the development of Salvarsan 606.

Right: synthetic drugs are prepared under conditions of scrupulous cleanliness. Here drugs are being packed in a sterile room at a large modern pharmaceutical factory, where every care is taken to insure that contamination by micro-organisms does not take place.

a prevalent and crippling disease. Ehrlich read reports of the successful use of arsenic compounds against the African sleeping sickness trypanosome, an organism resembling the syphilis spirochaete (so-called because of its spiral shape). Because arsenic compounds are generally poisonous to man, Ehrlich began to look for one which, while innocuous to man, would destroy the spirochaete. In 1910, after testing over 600 compounds, Ehrlich found one which fitted the bill. The name of the drug was arsphenamine and it proved to be a remarkable success. Marketed

under the name of "Salvarsan" it sold all over the world and made a fortune for Ehrlich, a matter of indifference to him. It also provided the starting point for the development of the synthetic drugs industry, in which the German chemical plants became leaders.

Ehrlich received numerous honors from virtually every developed country, including the highest one possible in Germany – that of the title "Excellency." Two years prior to his discovery he had already received the Nobel Prize for Medicine, for his work in immunology.

Sir Charles Algernon Parsons

1854-1931

Sir Charles Parsons may be regarded as the last of the great 19th-century engineers, men who combined imaginative scope with bold practical achievements. His contribution to technology was the invention of the steam turbine. With its ability to generate vast amounts of power, it was the most efficient machine to utilize the heat energy of steam.

Parsons was born into an aristocratic Irish family of distinguished scientific amateurs, his father being William Parsons, third Earl of Rosse, who in 1885 built what was at the time the world's largest telescope. Charles Parsons studied at Trinity College, Dublin, and Cambridge University, graduating in mathematics in 1877. He then served a four-year apprenticeship in an engineering works. In 1884 he joined a company at Gateshead, Northern England, as a junior partner. The company specialized in manufacturing electric dynamos, at that stage still driven by a belt run by the flywheel of a traditional steam engine.

Right: the first impulse turbine, devised in 1629 by the Italian Giovani Branca. It was designed to power a pounding machine through a system of wooden gears. Heat from the fire under the globular boiler produced a jet of steam from the pipe held in the mouth of the carved filler cap. By expanding the steam to a lower pressure in the stationary nozzle in the cap, the steam acquired a high velocity. The jet was directed onto the blades fixed to the wheel and when it hit the blades, its velocity decreased suddenly. The blades experienced an impulse, causing them to rotate and do work.

200 AD. However, a steam turbine would not have been practicable until the late 19th century when steel alloys tough enough to withstand the heat of the steam became available.

Parson's steam turbine was built in 1884. It consisted of a rotor in which a series of vaned wheels was attached to a shaft. As the steam entered, it expanded and caused the shaft wheels to rotate. In order to absorb as much of the steam's energy as possible, a series of stationary blades, alternating with the moving wheels, was attached to the rotor casing. These deflected the steam onto the vanes of the rotating wheels. Also, because the steam expanded as it passed through the turbine, the exhaust end was made wider than the intake end, and the wheels were made correspondingly larger. This was another

Parsons saw that a considerable increase in efficiency would be gained if the energy of the steam could be utilized directly within the dynamo. He decided to build a machine operating on the turbine principle – that is, one which is powered by the movement of a fluid such as water (as in a waterwheel) or air (for example the windmill). In Parson's machine the motive force was steam. The exploitation of the turbine principle dated back to Hero of Alexandria at around

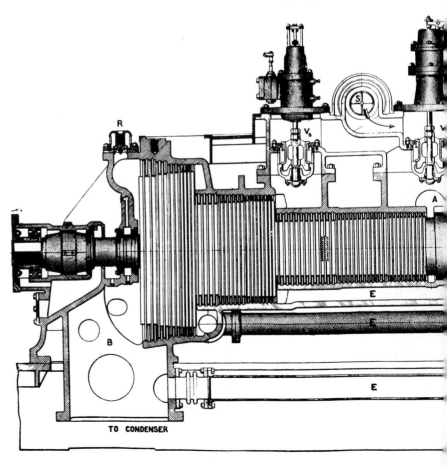

TO CONDENSER

way of utilizing the energy of the steam to a maximum.

The steam turbine achieved a speed of 18,000 revolutions a minute as compared to a previous maximum of 1500, and an output of 7.5 kilowatts at 100 volts. Parsons was fully aware of its potential in generating electric power. In 1889 he founded his own company, at Heaton, Newcastle-upon-Tyne, to gain full control over future developments. Two Parsons turbo-alter-

nators were installed at the Forth Banks power station at Newcastle. This became the world's first power station to be driven by a steam turbine when it commenced operation in 1900. The city public-light corporations turned increasingly to Parson's equipment for their generating stations. Larger, more powerful, and more efficient steam

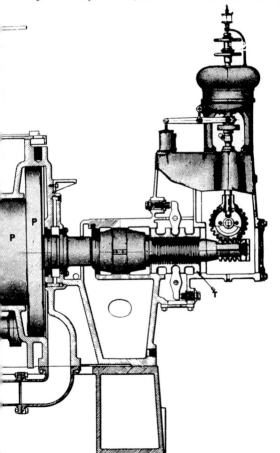

Above left: the *Turbinia*. Powered by a steam-turbine engine, it was the fastest ship of its time.

Above right: one of four 500 MW turbogenerators under construction at a new nuclear plant. Turbogenerators are now a basic power-producing machine of the electrical age.

Left: the Westinghouse-Parsons multistage reaction steam turbine. A, S: steam inlets; B: exhaust; P: balance piston; T: adjustment bearing; R: relief valve; V: primary admission valve; V_s: secondary admission valve.

turbines were built and they became the most widely used method of providing electricity for all large-scale processes.

From the beginning, Parsons was also aware that the steam turbine could provide a new method of marine propulsion. He set up a separate company at Wallsend to concentrate on this aspect, and built the *Turbinia*, an experimental vessel 100 feet long. By trial and error he found the right combination of propeller shafts which could be driven directly by steam-turbine engines, and in 1887 Parsons put on a public demonstration at the Spithead naval review for Queen Victoria's Diamond Jubilee. The *Turbinia* swept past the fleet at 34.5 knots, seven knots faster than any other ship then in existence.

By 1905, the steam-turbine engine had become established as the most efficient method of marine propulsion for both battleships and passenger liners, the latter including the *Lusitania* and the *Mauritania*. Further modifications produced a turbine which could be scaled down to operate smaller cargo vessels.

During his lifetime, Parsons took out more than 300 patents. He was also interested in optics and developed companies specializing in producing lenses for scientific instruments. The steam turbine, however, was his most important contribution to industry and the invention by which he will be remembered.

George Eastman

1854-1932

fully exposed, the camera was returned intact to the Eastman factory. There the roll was extracted and the negative images on the emulsion developed. The gelatin film was then stripped off its paper backing and the negatives remounted onto transparent backings.

A year later Eastman introduced an improved version of flexible film, which replaced the paper backing with a transparent support of nitro-cellulose, so dispensing with the need to remount

With his inventions of the flexible roll film and the Kodak camera, the American manufacturer George Eastman effectively placed photography at the disposal of the man in the street. The celluloid roll film was also crucial to the development of motion pictures.

As a young man, Eastman worked in banking and insurance before, in 1880, going into the business of manufacturing and marketing dry photographic plates. At that time photography was still a specialized occupation, in which the photographer needed the skill, equipment, and experience to develop his own plates and process his own prints. Eastman, realized however, that it should be possible to make photography accessible to the public if the developing and printing side could be provided as a service. His first innovation in simplifying the taking of photographs was the introduction of flexible film. Initially this consisted of a strip of paper coated with a gelatin-based photographic emulsion. The sensitized strips were wound onto spools, which could be turned inside the camera to give a whole series of exposures.

"You Press the Button, We Do the Rest" was the trade slogan adopted by the Eastman Dry Plate and Film Company, when in 1888 Eastman put on the market his Kodak box camera. This simple and justly famous device was sold with its roll of film incorporated and ready for use. Each roll gave 100 exposures, and once the roll was

Above: George Eastman (left) with Thomas Alva Edison, 1928. Edison used Eastman's flexible film in his moving-picture camera and made cinemaphotography a practical proposition.

Right: early advertisement for a Kodak camera, showing the "Kodak Girl."

Below: the Kodak no. 1, Eastman's first camera.

the gelatin negatives. It was now possible for anyone to take clear photographs by using little more than common sense. Eastman's developments heralded the age of the amateur snapshot and his factory had to expand rapidly to keep pace with the demand it created. In so far as he could, Eastman adopted mass-production methods in his factories, and he was ahead of Henry Ford in pioneering the introduction of industrial production lines.

When the Kinetograph, the earliest effective moving-picture camera, was developed in Thomas Edison's laboratories, it was Eastman's flexible film which made it practicable. Eastman thus made an important incidental contribution to the history of early cinema. The Eastman Kodak Company, as the company was renamed in 1892, continued to be one of the most important suppliers of film as well as becoming one of the world's foremost manufacturers of photographic equipment. The Brownie, a simple box camera, designed for children, was put on the market in 1900.

Eastman created a vast fortune through his inventions and industrial methods. He donated half of it to educational foundations, including the Massachusetts Institute of Technology and the University of Rochester, New York. After his death, by suicide at the age of 77, his home, Eastman House in Rochester, was made into a film-archive and photographic museum. Eastman's nitrocellulose film continued to be used in the cinema until 1951, but its preservation has, in fact, presented film archivists with some considerable problems because of its tendency to deteriorate suddenly and become an imminent fire hazard. The only safe way of preserving the old film has therefore been to copy originals onto nonflammable types of film stock.

Eastman Color, today the most widely used type of colour-film negative, was developed by the laboratories of the Eastman Kodak Company in 1952.

Above: a photograph taken with the first Kodak camera, 1888. Notice the shadow of the photographer at the bottom.

Left: detail from an advertisement, showing instructions for operating a Kodak, 1889.

Below right: glass tables, 200 feet by 42 inches, for making nitrocellulose film.

PHOTOGRAPHY REDUCED TO THREE MOTIONS.

1. Pull the Cord.   *2. Turn the Key.*

3. Press the Button.

Uncapping for Time Exposures.

Nikola Tesla

1856-1943

alternating current system was considered by many to be unsafe because of the high voltages it produced. Tesla, on the other hand, envisaged fantastic developments in electrical engineering which only the alternating-current system, more versatile than its direct-current counterpart, could produce.

In 1882 Tesla went to Paris as an engineer for the Continental Edison Company. In the following year, while in Strasbourg on a project, he

Right: Tesla reads while artificial lighting is generated.

Below: a demonstration of Tesla's "Light of the Future" in the Urania, Berlin, 1895, in the presence of the court. The engraving shows Prince Heinrich completing a broken circuit and causing the Geissler tubes in his hands to be illuminated.

The eccentric and brilliant Croatian-born electrical engineer, Nikola Tesla, contributed much to our understanding of magnetism and electricity. A prolific inventor, he is best known for building the first induction motor, based on his discovery of the rotating magnetic field.

Tesla was born in Smiljan, Yugoslavia, the son of an Orthodox priest. His mother, although illiterate, was a highly intelligent woman who invented several domestic and farm implements.

Fascinated by science from an early age, Tesla enrolled as an engineering student at the Technical University in Graz, Austria. While an undergraduate he saw the Gramme dynamo in operation. It had earlier been discovered that this dynamo could be reversed to work as an electric motor, though in doing so it sparked rather violently. This set Tesla thinking along the lines of building an improved motor and it is said that the solution came to him in a flash of intuition, one day in 1881, while he was taking a walk in the park.

Tesla conceived of using an alternating current – one which changed direction continually – to produce a rotating magnetic field which could then drive a motor. At that time the

built his first induction motor, the beginning of an alternating current system which was to include generators, dynamos, and transformers to change the voltage of the current without altering the frequency.

In 1884 Tesla left for the United States, reputedly arriving in New York with a few cents in his pocket, a working knowledge of 12 languages, and a letter of introduction to Thomas Alva Edison. Edison gave Tesla a job as

Above: an experimental Tesla induction motor. Unlike the direct-current motor it has no electrical connection to the armature (rotor). Instead an alternating current creates a rotating magnetic field in the stator which induces a current in the armature.

Below: a modern linear induction motor, the motive force of a portable compressor. In essence it is very similar to Tesla's original design.

wide, was abandoned when the financial backers withdrew their support.

Tesla made little money from his projects and in many cases did not even bother to seek patents. He was more interested in publicity and became a favorite with newspaper reporters for his eccentric behavior, controversial predictions, and flamboyant demonstrations. Many of his inventions had a science-fiction quality to them and some, such as his death ray, were, to say the least, bizarre.

In 1917, Tesla received the Edison medal for his work in electricity, the highest American honor in that field. He will always be regarded as a visionary and genius of physics, and scientists still consult his notebooks for possible new discoveries and inventions.

a research assistant in his industrial-research laboratory, but the association was not to last. Edison was a firm protagonist of the direct-current system and the following year Tesla sold his entire alternating-current system to the American industrialist George Westinghouse. This precipitated a monumental conflict between Edison and Westinghouse, each committed to his own current system.

The superiority of the Tesla-Westinghouse alternating-current system in generating large amounts of power was demonstrated in 1893 when alternating-current generators were used to light up the World Columbian Exposition in Chicago. As a result it was chosen to power the Niagara Falls hydroelectric station.

Tesla established his own laboratory where he was free to exercise his creativity. His inventions included a teleautomatic boat, a system of arc lighting which dispensed with wiring, and the Tesla coil, a high-frequency induction coil still used for long-distance radio and television transmission. Not all his projects were successful. Tesla's most ambitious venture, a world-wide communication system, initiated in 1900 and designed to transmit sound and vision world-

Sir J J Thomson
1856-1940

through electric fields of known strength and measuring the resulting deflection of the rays. In 1897 he announced that cathode rays were definitely streams of minute negatively-charged particles which he named "corpuscles." These were later to be called "electrons."

By measuring the ratio of their electric charge and mass, Thomson showed that these electrons were much smaller than individual atoms. If they were subatomic in size, Thomson reasoned that

The English physicist J J Thomson revolutionized our understanding both of electricity and atoms by explaining the nature of the electron. This fundamental unit of electric current also plays a vital role in the structure of the atom and thus in all the properties of matter.

J J Thomson was born in Manchester, the son of a book-seller. When he was only 14 he entered a local college intending to take up engineering. Within a few years he had become more interested in experimental physics and in 1876 won a science scholarship to Cambridge University where he was to remain for the rest of his life. In addition to his formidable gifts for mathematics and physics, Thomson was a brilliant administrator and his rise in Cambridge was meteoric. When barely 27 he succeeded the

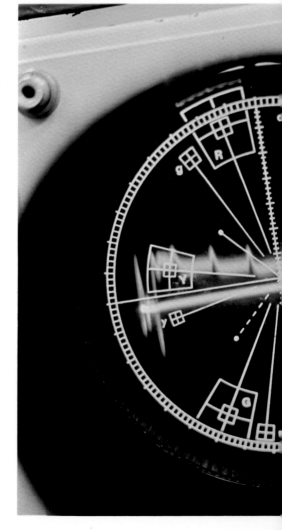

Above: a discharge tube designed by Thomson, in which cathode rays were allowed to travel past electrically charged plates. The deflection of the cathode rays by electric and magnetic fields convinced Thomson that these rays consisted of particles, which we now know as electrons.

distinguished physicist, John Rayleigh, as Professor of Physics, and took over the running of the famous Cavendish Laboratory. Under his inspired leadership the Cavendish became one of the most respected centers in the world for research into atomic physics.

The starting point of Thomson's great discovery was his interest in cathode rays. It had been known for some years that if an electric current was passed between two electrodes in a glass tube from which most of the air had been removed, a mysterious radiation was produced around the cathode (the negative electrode). Thomson suspected that, unlike light or X-rays, this radiation was not electromagnetic in origin, and began a series of experiments to determine its nature. This involved passing the rays

Right: polar coordinates in a television transmitter test. Thomson's work with cathode-ray deflection led ultimately to the many present-day applications of cathode-ray tubes, such as television, radar screens, and computer imaging.

electrons might well be actual components of atoms. Using this idea he suggested that the atom consisted of a mass of positive electricity containing numerous electrons studded around its interior. Thomson's atom resembled a cookie, with electrons embedded like chocolate chips in a mass of positively-charged dough. Although his model was soon replaced by the more accurate solar-system model formulated by Ernest Rutherford, Thomson's concept was the first

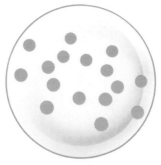

modern effort to represent the atoms in terms of positive and negative electricity, and as such, was the forerunner of the complex mathematical theories of the present day.

Exciting confirmation of Thomson's ideas about the electron and its role in atomic structure came a few years after its initial discovery. The German chemist Eugen Goldstein showed that in an electrified vacuum tube there were rays, additional to cathode rays and traveling in an

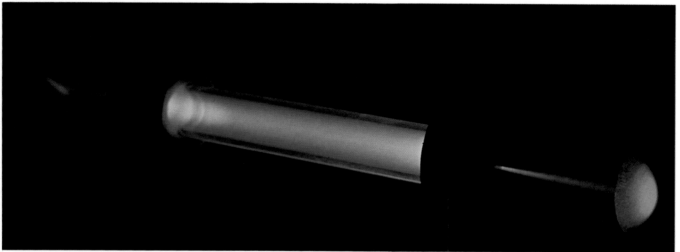

Above center: a "Thomson atom." It was pictured as "corpuscles" of negative charge (electrons) embedded in a sphere of positive charge.

Center: inside a discharge tube. The brightest discharge is the stream of electrons, traveling from the cathode to the anode. In 1886 Eugen Goldstein discovered that if he used a cathode with a hole cut in the center, rays streamed through to form a luminous spot on a screen behind the cathode. These rays were traveling in the opposite direction to the cathode rays. He named them, "canal rays." These were found to be positively charged atoms of the gases present initially in the tube – atoms stripped of their electrons.

Above right: Thomson (left) with Sir Ernest Rutherford, the New Zealand-born nuclear physicist who split the atom. Rutherford was one of Thomson's former students at the Cavendish.

opposite direction to them. He called them canal rays after the experimental equipment he had used to detect them. Proof soon followed that canal rays were positively-charged atomic particles, the residues of atoms stripped of their electrons. The picture confirmed Thomson's view of the electron as a "subatomic particle."

Thomson's importance to science was due as much to his influence on others as to his own research. He was a brilliant teacher and gathered around him at the Cavendish Laboratory some of the finest young minds of the day. Of those who worked under him, most went on to become professors in the world's leading universities and seven won Nobel prizes. Thomson taught elementary classes in the mornings, postgraduate classes in the afternoons, and despite his heavy administrative workload still found time for a wide range of personal interests. He read widely, argued politics, and was an enthusiastic follower of sports. He remained, until his death in 1940, one of the great intellectual celebrities of British science.

Heinrich Rudolf Hertz

1857-1894

In his tragically short life, the German physicist and engineer Heinrich Hertz laid the foundation of the greatest of all revolutions in human communications. In a series of brilliant experiments he discovered the existence of radio waves and showed how they could be transmitted and received. Within 50 years of his discovery, radio had become the first means of immediate global communication.

Hertz was born in Hamburg and trained to be an engineer. Then, whilst still a young man, he met the great physicist Ferdinand von Helmholtz. With the older man's encouragement, Hertz abandoned his engineering studies and turned to physics. Under Helmholtz's guidance, Hertz made excellent progress and by 1883 had secured an academic post in the University of Kiel where he devoted himself to research. His special interest was the electromagnetic theory which had been worked out by James Clerk Maxwell a few years earlier.

At about this time the much-respected Berlin Academy of Science was offering an attractive prize for some specialized work on electromagnetism, and at Helmholtz's insistence Hertz agreed to try to win it. His decision had historic consequences for, by chance, his investigations led him directly to the discovery of radio waves and how to transmit them.

The research needed for the Berlin prize involved the study of oscillating electric currents. In 1888, Hertz had a brilliant insight linking the idea of oscillating charge and the predictions of Maxwell's famous electromagnetic equations. The apparatus Hertz had built consisted of a circuit connecting two metal spheres. An electric current passing backward and forward in the circuit caused each sphere alternately to become charged. Hertz observed that when the charge

Right: Hermann von Helmholtz, the German scientist who made many contributions to optics, meteorology, and electricity. It was in response to his prize competition on electromagnetism that Hertz, a a pupil of his, devised his oscillator. The apparatus established electrically the existence of James Clerk Maxwell's postulated electromagnetic waves.

Below right: the basis of radio. A spark jumping the gap between the transmitter spheres (bottom) produces waves which make a spark jump the gap in the receiver (top).

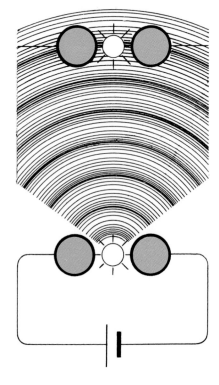

reached a maximum a spark leaped the gap between the two spheres. His mind immediately returned to the electromagnetic equations with which he was so familiar. He knew they predicted that an oscillating electric charge should emit electromagnetic radiation. He realized that by chance he had devised a circuit that could produce a constantly oscillating charge. Was it possible, he wondered, that as the spark leaped backward and forward, invisible waves of radiation were pulsating through the laboratory?

To test the idea Hertz constructed a simple wire loop with an air gap at one point. If an oscillating current could create electromagnetic radiation, he reasoned that the radiation might in its turn create an oscillating current in his wire loop. Moving the loop to various points in his laboratory, Hertz found to his excitement that not only could he detect the radiation by a small spark that jumped the air gap of the loop but he could "map" the intensity and shape of the radiation by watching how the strength of the spark varied with position. He worked out that the wavelength of the radiation was just over two feet – a million times greater than the wavelength of visible light.

Hertz's discovery was a dramatic confirmation of Maxwell's theory of electromagnetism. But the most spectacular application of "Hertzian waves," as they were called, came eight years later in 1894 when Italian engineer Guglielmo Marconi used them to communicate across long distances. On December 12, 1901, Hertzian waves spanned the Atlantic sending a message from England to Newfoundland. The occasion marked the birth of radio communications but Hertz, whose work had made the event possible, did not live to share in its excitement. He had died seven years earlier when only 36 from a chronic blood disease.

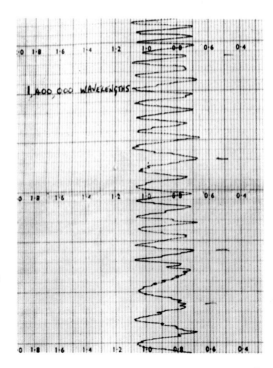

Above: listening to wireless time signals, 1913. The signals, in Morse code, came from the Eiffel Tower which tapped out a signal for each second.

Left: modern radio wave reception – a West German radiotelescope.

Right: radio emission from the quasar 3C273 as recorded with the 250-foot radio telescope at Jodrell Bank, Britain. Quasars (quasi-stellar sources) are small celestial objects that send out large amounts of radio waves. The intensity of this particular quasar's emissions, together with its apparent distance from the earth, seems to indicate that it is as bright as 200 galaxies combined.

Rudolf Diesel

1858-1913

The diesel engine improved on the efficiency of previous internal-combustion engines by dispensing with an external ignition source. With its ability to run on cheap, unrefined oil, the engine became widely used in industry and transport. It was named after its inventor, the German-born engineer Rudolf Diesel.

Diesel was born in Paris, the son of an immigrant German leather worker. When he was 12, the Franco-Prussian War broke out and the family, branded as "undesirable aliens," were deported to London. He was able to complete his education in Germany with the help of a cousin's patronage, and he emerged from the Technical College in Munich as a machine designer and thermal engineer. Returning to Paris, Diesel worked for a refrigeration company, but in addition to his talents in engineering, he became a man of broad cultural interests and deep social convictions.

In about 1885 he first conceived of an engine which would be an improvement over the Otto

engine by dispensing with the need for an external ignition source. In the earliest gasoline engines this was initially a heated filament, and later an electric spark. Diesel's idea was to compress the air-fuel mixture in the driving cylinder to a point where it was hot enough to ignite itself. He started a program of research which was to last for more than a dozen years. Yet there was more to his motivation than technical curiosity. He also had a firm social objective.

Such an engine, he reasoned, would provide working people with an independence they had not possessed since the onset of the Industrial Revolution. Its versatility and its ability to use a variety of cheap fuels would lead to a scaling down of many industrial and workshop pro-

cesses. Men would no longer find themselves serving the needs of massive capital investment. The craftsman would be able to reestablish contact with the products of his labor.

It was 1892 before Diesel was even in a position to register a preliminary patent, and the next year he built his first prototype. The tremendous pressure in the cylinder caused an explosion, nearly killing him, and consequently some aspects of the design needed to be reconsidered. Diesel had initially seen cheap industrial byproducts such as coal dust or even animal fat as a possible source of power. He then switched his

Right: two-cylinder Diesel motor, 1897. This was the first factory-manufacture Diesel motor, built at the Matchwood factory in Kempten, Bavaria.

attention exclusively to crude fuel oil. The following model which Diesel built proved its worth and ran for one minute. By this stage he was attracting the interest of several manufacturers, and successive improvements produced an engine vastly superior to the steam engine in fuel consumption and mechanical efficiency.

Diesel's engine was quickly adopted as a leading industrial power source, and it was the basis for many later developments where heavy-duty engines were required. It was used in marine engineering, trucks, buses, tractors, other agricultural machinery, and the post-steam genera-

Above: Diesel engine designed for steam cargo and passenger ships. The double-headed motor is operated directly, without the use of a steering wheel. The propellers are controlled by pumps on either side of the motor which move independently of one another. The motor has an efficiency of 7300 horsepower, and a speed of 132 revolutions per minute.

tion of railway locomotives. Later it was used to power submarines. Because a diesel engine will run on cheaper crude fuel oil, it has retained its economic advantage over gasoline-powered internal-combustion engines. On the other hand it is much heavier and noisier, and its exhaust gases can be a serious pollution hazard. Nor did the engine fulfill Diesel's idealistic hopes for the beneficial social effects which he thought would follow from its availability.

To the end of his life Diesel remained preoccupied with the dilemma of reinstating the self-determination of the individual within an industrial society. As a result of his invention he became a millionaire, but because of his disinterest in wealth, he made no attempt to manage his fortunes efficiently and invariably found himself in financial difficulties.

Eventually his financial situation became desperate; he also became severely depressed by the movement towards war in Europe and these two factors drove him to suicide. He disappeared without trace during a crossing of the English Channel on the night ferry, on his way to attend an engineering congress in London where he was to have been guest of honor.

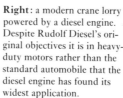

Right: a modern crane lorry powered by a diesel engine. Despite Rudolf Diesel's original objectives it is in heavy-duty motors rather than the standard automobile that the diesel engine has found its widest application.

Max Planck
1858-1947

The German physicist Max Planck was the architect of the modern quantum theory. In the early 1900s the quantum theory, together with Einstein's theory of relativity, presented a radically new view of the universe. Planck's hypothesis was a straightforward one. Instead of regarding electromagnetic radiation such as heat and light in the classical manner as a continuous wave, he assumed that it was in fact discontinuous, made up of tiny particles or "quanta" of energy. This deceptively simple idea concealed a complex and fundamental new approach to atomic science.

The son of a cultivated southern German family, Planck grew up in Munich where he pursued a wide range of cultural interests. For a time he seriously considered devoting himself to music but, encouraged by his professors at the University of Munich, he chose a career in theoretical physics instead. His outstanding abilities in mathematics and physics brought him a great deal of world recognition even before he completed the work that made him famous

Center right: the quantum theory. It states that all processes consist in series of jumps. Matter absorbs energy and loses it in quanta. The energy of a particular quantum is obtained by multiplying the frequency of radiation by h, the "quantum of action" known as Planck's Constant. Consequently, the quanta of high-frequency radiation such as X-rays will have more energy than the quanta of low-frequency radio waves.

Planck reached the hypothesis that is at the heart of quantum theory in 1900 while he was Professor of Physics at Munich University. He had spent several years studying the way in which heated bodies emit energy as radiation. Classical physics, with its rigid ideas, was at a loss to explain the anomalous way in which this energy was distributed among the wavelengths of the radiation. Several distinguished physicists had proposed elaborate equations to approximate the observed energy distribution. Although Planck was as traditional in his scientific outlook as most of his contemporaries, he was at least prepared to experiment with bold new ideas. One idea that appeared impossibly far-fetched provided the key to the problem.

Planck decided to reject all previous assumptions about the nature of radiation and started from a completely new premise. He postulated that radiation consisted of tiny energy "particles" which he termed quanta. He applied this

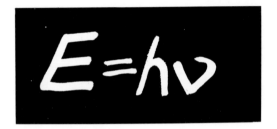

revolutionary idea to the problem of heated bodies and immediately found an exact and straightforward description of the energy distribution. Instead of the complicated formulae devised previously, Planck reduced the problem to a simple relationship: the emitted energy is

world-wide. Planck's standing in German scientific circles owed much to his strong personality which, although conservative, was always tempered by humor and a sense of humanity. In later years when Hitler rose to power, Planck courageously opposed the Nazi regime and defended Jewish colleagues from persecution as best he could, His own son was executed for being implicated in a plot to kill Hitler.

proportional to the wavelength of the radiation. He showed that energy and wavelength were linked by a special number that he named Planck's constant. Although to Planck his constant was no more than a number important to the mathematics of his theory, scientists were soon to discover that it played an important role in basic laws governing some of the innermost mechanisms of nature.

Physics

Quantum theory was not accepted at once. Planck himself could hardly believe its basic assumption, so it is scarcely surprising that it was met with much skepticism. But quantum theory did what every valid new theory sets out to do: it explained observable facts. Scientists could not

Above: the quantum theory can be used to calculate the energy radiated and absorbed by celestial bodies such as the Orion Nebula pictured here.

starting point of modern theories of the atom.

From this point on, scientists made rapid progress in applying quantum theory. Although its ideas and mathematics were often very difficult, scientists recognized a powerful new tool to help them explore the subatomic world. Previously the microworld of atoms had seemed strange and unpredictable, governed by unfamiliar and obscure laws. Planck's theory revealed that the apparent mystery stemmed from trying to use laws of the everyday world in a region in which they did not hold true. A new set of laws, based on quantum theory, were needed to describe the subatomic world. Once this was grasped, tremendous progress was possible in investigating the true nature of atoms and molecules.

The birth of quantum physics meant that for the first time scientists could build up theories about the everyday world from a detailed and accurate knowledge of the subatomic world. Today quantum physics is applied to a wide range of things. Atomic scientists use it to refine their understanding of the tiniest particles in nature, those involved in the inner structure of atomic nuclei. Astrophysicists use the same theory to describe the behavior of atoms and molecules in the huge accumulations that form stars and galaxies, Planck's great achievement, therefore, lies in founding a theory that contributes to the understanding of all natural phenomena, from the smallest to the largest conceivable.

therefore afford to discount it. In 1913 the Danish physicist Neils Bohr applied quantum theory to ideas of atomic structure and achieved spectacular results. The discontinuity Planck revealed in radiation extended to the way in which electrons could only orbit the nucleus of an atom in certain "permitted" energy levels. The new quantum model of the atom explained a wide range of atomic phenomena and was the

Above: the first Solvay Physics conference, Brussels 1911. Planck is in the back row, second from left. Ernest Rutherford, Marie Curie, and Albert Einstein (second from right) were also present.

Svante August Arrhenius

1859-1927

The Swedish chemist Svante Arrhenius was one of the founders of the modern science of physical chemistry. He was the first to suggest that electrolytes – chemicals which dissolve in water to give solutions that conduct electricity – were made up of tiny charged particles called ions Arrhenius' ionic theory was a vital contribution to the understanding of the structure of chemical compounds and their behavior in solution.

Born in Vik and educated in nearby Uppsala, Arrhenius began to formulate the ionic theory while still an undergraduate. He concentrated on studying a phenomenon called electrolysis. Nearly a century before Arrhenius' birth,

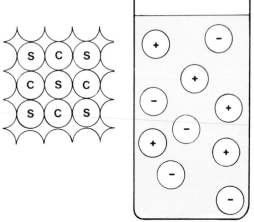

Right: sodium chloride as visualized by Arrhenius. In a solid crystalline state (left) the sodium and chlorine are held together by attractive forces between the positive sodium ions and the negative chloride ions. In solution (right) the ions dissociate and drift freely in the fluid.

scientists had discovered that certain chemical compounds when dissolved in water could conduct an electric current. More remarkable was the discovery that under the effect of the current the solutions decomposed, often yielding the constituent elements of the dissolved compound. Today electrolysis is widely used in industry for the extraction of elements from their compounds. But in Arrhenius' time electrolysis was a mystery, and despite the fact that scientists

had worked out the laws governing its effects, no explanation existed for the phenomenon itself.

Arrhenius posed a fundamental question. What property of a compound determines if it conducts electricity when dissolved in water? Intuitively Arrhenius believed the answer must have something to do with the structure of the compound. He experimented with hundreds of different solutions, studying how their properties varied with the amount of compound dissolved, measuring boiling points and freezing points and applying electric currents in order to study the effects of electrolysis.

By 1883 Arrhenius had devised a simple but revolutionary answer. Compounds that conduct electricity in solution, the so-called electrolytes, differed in structure from other compounds. Electrolytes, Arrhenius proposed, were composed of tiny charged particles called ions. In solid form, the electrolyte was held together by the attractive force between positively and negatively charged ions; but in solution, the ions dissociated and drifted freely throughout the fluid. When, during electrolysis, a positive and negative electrode were introduced into the solution, positive ions drifted toward the negative electrode and negative ions toward the positive electrode. The movement of the ions constituted the electric current characteristic of electrolysis.

However, Arrhenius still had to explain how electrolytes decomposed during electrolysis. To do this he made a bold assumption about the nature of ions. He asserted that ions were in fact electrically charged atoms and that when, during electrolysis, an ion reached an electrode, its charge was neutralized to leave a normal uncharged atom of the element.

Arrhenius' theory was received with frank disbelief. Most scientists regarded it as unsubstantiated guesswork. They pointed out that Arrhenius could not explain why an ion showed none of the chemical characteristics of the corresponding uncharged atom. Why should the presence of an electric charge have such a powerful effect? Neither could Arrhenius explain the mechanism by which an atom could acquire a charge. However, despite the storm of criticism, Arrhenius was convinced of his theory's validity and in 1884 he submitted it as part of his examination for the degree of Doctor of Philosophy at Uppsala University. One of the examiners was Arrhenius' tutor, the distinguished chemist Per Cleve. Cleve had already made up his mind against the ionic theory and used his influence to insure that Arrhenius received the lowest possible pass grade – a cruel humiliation for Arrhenius. In effect, the university had publicly proclaimed its rejection of the ionic theory.

However, Arrhenius was not easily silenced. He had prudently sent copies of his thesis to the most prominent chemists of the day, and among them he found a few with the imagination and

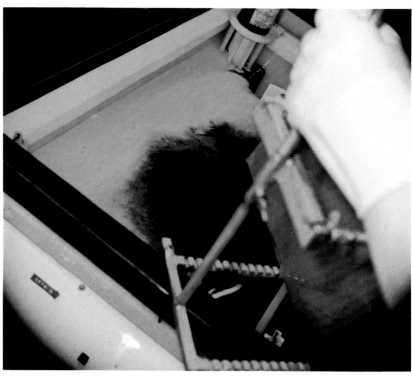

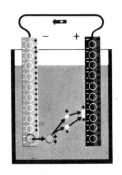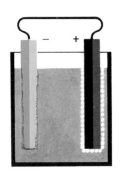

courage to support his unpopular ideas. With their help Arrhenius was able to secure a series of posts in various universities, which gave him the time and the facilities to refine and develop his theory. In 1897 events took a dramatic turn. J J Thomson, an English physicist, discovered the electron, identifying it as the basic particle of electronic charge. At about the same time, Henri Becquerel in Paris discovered radioactivity, showing that atoms of certain elements spontaneously decay emitting, among other radiations, electrons. For the first time it was clear that atoms were not solid particles like tiny billiard balls, but had some kind of internal structure. Becquerel's discovery showed that this structure relied on the presence within atoms of electrons.

At last an explanation existed for Arrhenius' idea of charged atoms. For example, if an atom of the metal sodium were to lose an electron – that is, one unit of negative charge – the atom would assume an overall positive charge. Conversely, if an atom of chlorine acquired an extra electron, it would assume an overall negative charge. Common salt, a compound of sodium and chlorine, could therefore be regarded as an accumulation of sodium and chlorine ions

Above: removing a copper-plated sheet on a plating jig. The principle of electroplating depends on the movement of charged ions toward the electrode of the opposite charge. In copper plating, the anode is made of pure copper, and the metal to be plated acts as the cathode. The two are immersed in a solution of a copper salt, when a current is forced through the cell, the copper dissolves from the anode, passes through the solution as positively-charged copper ions, and is deposited as a fine coat on the cathode.

Above left: a simple electrolytic cell commonly known as a battery. It consists of one zinc and one copper rod in dilute sulfuric acid. **Far left:** When the rods are connected the current flows as indicated by the upper arrow, while hydrogen ions flow to the copper in the direction shown by the lower arrows. **Right:** eventually hydrogen bubbles insulate the copper completely and stop the flow of current. This is known as polarization.

Right: part of the electrolytic refinery at the James Bridge Copper Works of Imperial Metal Industries Ltd, Birmingham, Britain.

bound together by the electrical attraction of positive and negative charges. Since electrons were involved in the internal structure of atoms, it was no longer surprising that their gain or loss by an atom should alter the properties of the atom. The dissociated ions of sodium and chlorine in salt water, therefore, show none of the properties of sodium, which reacts vigorously in water, or of chlorine, which is a poisonous greenish gas.

Years of persistence were rewarded by sudden public acclaim for Arrhenius. The ionic theory became respectable and the scientific establishment in Sweden hastened to congratulate the man it had once rejected. In 1903 he was awarded the Nobel Prize for Chemistry. For Arrhenius the prize had a special satisfaction. Among the panel of scientists who judged the ionic theory worthy of the supreme scientific accolade was his old tutor, Per Cleve, who in previous years had done so much to humiliate Arrhenius and oppose his ideas.

Willem Einthoven

1860-1927

To assist in his studies of the heart's electrical behavior, Dutch physician Willem Einthoven invented the electrocardiograph. This highly sensitive instrument, essentially a galvanometer, has become the standard apparatus used in the examination and diagnosis of heart disease.

Willem Einthoven was born in Semarang, Java, (now Indonesia). Following in his father's footsteps, he enrolled to study medicine at the University of Utrecht and graduated in 1885. Later that year he was appointed Professor of Physiology at Leiden University, Netherlands.

Einthoven's major interest was the heart, in particular the electrical activity of cardiac muscle. When a nervous impulse passes through the heart, causing it to contract and pump blood out, the electrical potential of the muscle changes. Einthoven read about various attempts to record these changes in animals and man, but the instruments available at the time were not sensitive enough. Einthoven himself tried to improve on the results, first using a capillary electrometer and then a mirror galvanometer.

Eventually, in 1903, he arrived at the concept of the string galvanometer. His invention was a highly sensitive instrument which could detect changes in electric potential of the order of a fraction of a millivolt. The "string" was a silver-coated quartz wire suspended between the poles of an electromagnet. Electrodes were attached to the limbs of the subject. These picked up the current caused by the ion flow preceding and following cardiac muscle contraction, and passed it through the wire which was deflected to one or other of the poles, depending on the strength and direction of the current. It was able to record the

Right: an electrocardiograph made in 1911 by the Cambridge Instrument Company.

Below right: a demonstration of Einthoven's string galvanometer at the Royal Society, London. A battery circuit was established by the bulldog having one foreleg and one hindleg each in a pot of salt solution. The thread of the galvanometer vibrated with each heartbeat which apparently was not very steady.

Below: Einthoven posing beside his string galvanometer.

distinct changes which occurred as the heart contracted and relaxed. He called the instrument the "electrocardiograph."

Einthoven saw the need for a permanent record of the changes which occurred as the heart pumped blood and arranged the string in such a way that when it was deflected it interrupted a beam of light and left a shadow on a moving strip of photographic paper. This record – the "electrocardiogram" – was a repeating sequence

Below: the PQRST complex of a normal electrocardiogram (top) compared with that of a complete heart block (ventricles and auricles beating independently). The P waves arise normally but because the conducting network is blocked, their stimulus never reaches the ventricles, which contract autonomously. The remedy in such a situation is a cardiac pacemaker.

Below left: Einthoven's triangle is a convention used for interpreting electrocardiograms (the cardiologist carries it in his head rather than on paper). Electrical activities in the heart are assumed to start at the triangle's central point and move outward. Movements in one direction along an axis are called "positive" (shown as heavy arrows in the diagram), in the opposite direction, "negative." Positive reading give an upward deflection of the electrocardiograph writer, negative readings a downward one. Movements directly toward an axis do not affect the writer. A displaced or damaged heart will be spotted by an abnormal deflection of the writer.

Below right: a patient rigged up for an electrocardiogram recording. The lead on the right leg is an earth.

of a wave pattern which corresponded to the contraction and relaxation of the heart. Einthoven labeled the distinct points of the wave P, Q, R, S, and T. R is the now-familiar spike of the electrocardiogram which occurs when the inlet valve of the heart closes and contraction begins, forcing the blood out.

The electrocardiograph does not measure the actual muscular contraction of the heart but the polarization and depolarization of the muscle membrane – the change in the concentration of the ions on either side of it. Polarization spreads from the heart's built-in pacemaker, the sinu-atrial node. To monitor the spread of the wave several electrodes are attached, across the chest and to the leg, and the readings combined into a graph known as "Einthoven's triangle."

On an electrocardiogram, the wave pattern and frequency produced by a healthy heart is standard. Consequently, any deviations indicate an abnormality, such as coronary thrombosis, thickening of the cardiac muscle, heart block, or an anatomical displacement of the heart.

Because of its sensitivity, the electrocardiograph soon became established in hospitals as an invaluable diagnostic instrument. It was eventually modified into an electronic device, using amplifier tubes and a cathode-ray oscilloscope, but the principle remained the same. Einthoven himself did many studies on standard and abnormal electrocardiogram patterns. In 1906 he set up a system called the "telecardiogram," whereby electrocardiograms recorded in his local hospital could be transmitted by cable to his laboratory, enabling him to study changes in patients with heart disease. In 1924 he received the Nobel Prize for Medicine.

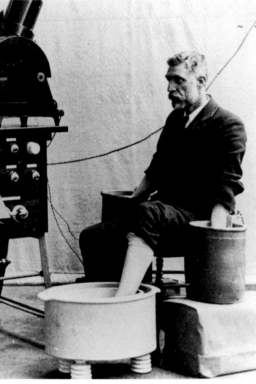

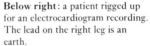

F(oot)

Normal

Axis deviates to left

Axis deviates to right

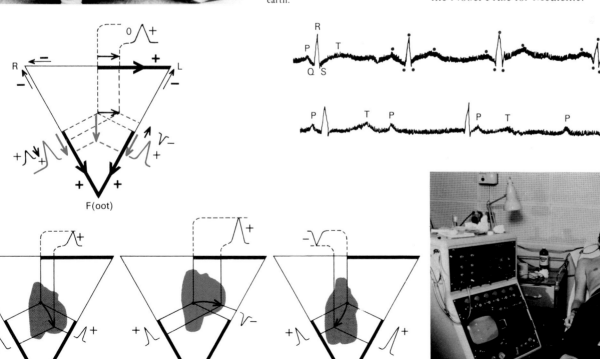

Paul Nipkow
1860-1940

The Nipkow disk, invented by the young German scientist Paul Gottlieb Nipkow, was so far ahead of its time that no one could think of a practical use for it and its inventor spent the rest of his working life as a railway engineer. The disk overcame the problem of transmitting an image of light and shade by scanning it and breaking it up into discrete units. It thus formed the basis of television transmission.

Once it was possible to transform the human voice into electric signals and send it through a wire, scientists began to explore the possibilities of doing so with a visual image, hence the word "television" – to see at a distance. There were, however, three practical difficulties involved: the analysis and conversion of the image into electrical impulses; the transmission of those impulses; and the reconversion of the image at the receiving end. The image, in particular, presented problems because it consisted of varying gradations of light and shade.

Various attempts were made to bypass these difficulties. For example, it was suggested that the whole picture might be transmitted simultaneously by a complicated cable system, each component wire of the cable being responsible for conveying its own fraction of the picture.

In 1873, George May, a British engineer, discovered that the metallic form of the element selenium is photoconductive, its conductivity varying according to the amount of light striking it. Selenium is also capable of transforming light energy into electrical energy, and it formed the basis for the invention of the photoelectric cell,

which was to be an essential component in television transmission.

The first basic step towards a practicable television was taken with the discovery of a mechanical way of scanning the subject. The device which made this possible was the Nipkow disk, invented in 1884 by Paul Gottlieb Nipkow, a student engineer from Lauenburg (nowadays Lębork in Poland). This rotating metal disk had a series of square apertures arranged in a spiral

Right: an early scanning device, designed by George Carey, 1880. The image was scanned by a selenium cell which traveled across it in a spiral path, and the signal currents were transmitted through a single line-wire. The system lacked any synchronization between scanning, transmission, and reception.

Below right: each aperture of the Nipkow disk scanned a small area of the subject. The image areas overlapped to form a composite 20-line picture.

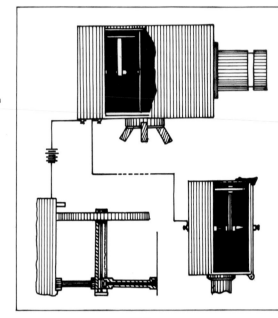

Below: Nipkow's patent, 1884, showing the scanning disk, transmitter (center), and receiver (bottom right). The transmitter contained a light-sensitive selenium cell, while reception was achieved by the rotation of the plane of polarized light in a magnetic field.

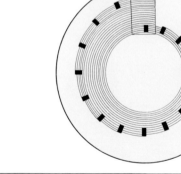

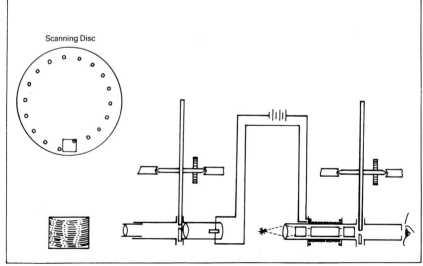

Scanning Disc

Communication

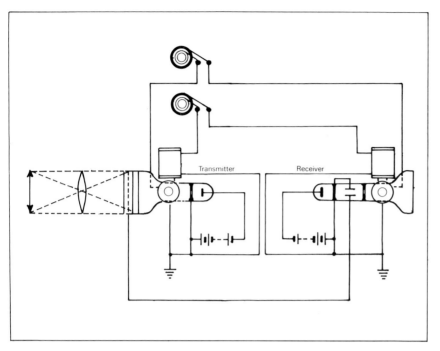

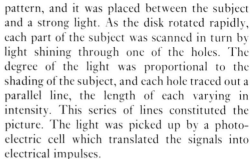

pattern, and it was placed between the subject and a strong light. As the disk rotated rapidly, each part of the subject was scanned in turn by light shining through one of the holes. The degree of the light was proportional to the shading of the subject, and each hole traced out a parallel line, the length of each varying in intensity. This series of lines constituted the picture. The light was picked up by a photo-electric cell which translated the signals into electrical impulses.

The production of the picture was similar to the scanning. The impulses of the cell generated a corresponding emission of light from a bulb. The beams passed through another disk rotating in synchromy with the one at the transmitting end and the picture was reconstituted.

Nipkow went so far as to patent a comprehensive television system developed around his invention but the technology to make it a working reality did not as yet exist.

The first practical application of the scanning principle was the transmission of photographs by

cable telegraph. A variety of techniques was used, varying from systems of turning drums to an arrangement of rotating mirrors. "Wire" pictures were being sent between London and Paris as early as 1907. The replacement of selenium by other materials which were far more rapidly light-sensitive was a major improvement in the transmitting system, and eventually electronic scanning methods replaced mechanical ones. It became possible to transmit a standard picture, consisting of about 200,000 picture elements, over a simple cable in 7·5 minutes.

Above: A A Campbell Swinton's scanning device, 1911. It employed a mosaic screen of photoelectrical elements onto which the image could be focused. A cathode-ray beam scanned the back of the screen and was synchronized electro-magnetically with a cathode-ray beam in the receiver. This system paved the way for present-day high-definition television.

Above right: television components.

Left: TV-camera tube (left) produces an "electronic copy" of the scene. The television tube (right) deciphers the image.

Below right: television scanning is discernible on the screen by a series of horizontal lines.

Below: Isaac Shoenberg, the Russian-born scientist who developed the first 405-line television system.

Vilhelm Bjerknes

1862-1951

The Norwegian physicist Vilhelm Bjerknes placed the study of meteorology on a firm scientific basis. With his son Jacob, he formulated the concepts of dynamic air masses and fronts from which modern practical systems of weather prediction have been derived.

Meteorology is the science of weather behavior and the way that it is influenced by atmospheric changes. Its most important application is in weather forecasting, on which so much human activity, in particular agriculture, fishing, and marine navigation, has depended for many centuries.

Until the early 1920s, when more became known of the structure of the upper atmosphere and the nature of its temperature changes and wind currents, there was very little data from which meteorologists could define weather patterns. Most of the pioneering work in this as yet not very scientific field was undertaken by a group of Norwegian meteorologists, notably Vilhelm Bjerknes.

Born at Christiana (now Oslo), Bjerknes was the son of a mathematics professor at the local university. He was greatly influenced by his father's own work on hydrodynamics and initially they collaborated. He then went to

Germany to assist the German physicist Heinrich Hertz in his work on electrical resonance and the dampening of Hertzian waves. Bjerknes returned to Scandinavia in 1893 to take up an appointment, first as a lecturer in and then as professor of mechanics and mechanical physics at Stockholm University. He began to apply his knowledge of hydrodynamics and thermodynamics to the study of the movements of vast air masses in the earth's atmosphere. He saw the

Right: pioneering weather researchers, 1862. The British scientist James Glaisher is shown sprawling unconscious from lack of oxygen while his pilot opens a control valve with his teeth. Glaisher fainted at 29,000 feet, after recording a barometer reading of 9.75 inches.

Below right: the Bergen Weather Service, 1919, with Jacob Bjerknes seated on the left. On the right is Tor Bergeron who discovered the phenomenon of occlusion – the coinciding of two fronts, pushing a pocket of warm air upward.

Meteorology

oceans and atmospheric masses as thermodynamic systems, moving because of heat from the sun and generating heat because of friction. Movement of air and water masses also occurred because of the earth's rotation. Bjerknes also applied hydrodynamic principles to the circulation of air and sea currents, and found that they explained the formation of land and sea breezes, mountain and valley winds, and the development of cyclones and anticyclones.

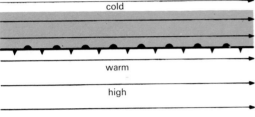

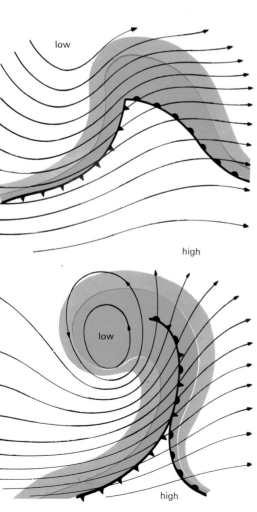

Left: the formation of a cyclone. This event frequently occurs when a warm air mass is adjacent to a cold one, with wind-shear at the discontinuity. Usually both air masses are moving in the same direction, but the effect is similar if they are traveling in opposite directions. A small bulge of warm air develops, and begins to push into the colder air. An area of slightly lower pressure forms near the wave's apex. The bulge invariably increases in size. The wave becomes wedge-shaped (third diagram) and the rear cold front (left) gradually gains on the slower-moving warm front (right). The cold air pushes the warmer air upward, and clouds form, resulting in snow or rain. When the two fronts coincide (bottom diagram), the warm air is displaced upward, and an occlusion is formed. Air rotates (anticlockwise in the Northern Hemisphere) around the low-pressure area (center top). Such a cyclone may have a diameter of 1000 miles.

In 1904 he drew up a plan to apply these theories to practical weather forecasting. This included making observations at all heights in the atmosphere at short intervals in time which would enable meteorologists to build up a picture of the changing structure of the atmosphere. Bjerknes realized that this was only possible if there was a coordinated, world-wide system of meteorological stations supplemented by aeronautical observations.

In 1912 Bjerknes became director of the Geophysical Institute at Leipzig, Germany, a position which in five years he had to abandon. With the German mobilization for war, Bjerknes' position and working conditions deteriorated. He left to direct the Bergen Geophysical Institute, Norway, taking with him his son Jacob, also a prominent meteorologist.

Because of the war, Norway found itself cut off from many sources of essential information including meteorological readings. To compensate for this, Vilhelm and Jacob set up a tight-knit system of meteorological stations across the Norwegian countryside. The data that they obtained from the use of these weather stations enabled them to give their theories a practical basis, and the two men collaborated in formulating what was to be the most important concept in weather forecasting.

They analyzed the airflow across the latitudes into the component air masses – large uniform bodies of air coming in from either the tropics or the arctic. The air masses were separated by sharp boundary surfaces which they called fronts, a now-familiar term in weather reporting because fronts are often associated with changes in the weather. The reason for this is that when two air masses of different temperature meet, the warmer mass slides over the colder one. The movement of warm air upward along the front causes water to be precipitated out.

The analysis of fronts thus provided a method of weather forecasting. By plotting and linking similar readings of temperature and pressure, (warm air weighs less and therefore creates low pressure) a front can be mapped. Its nature and direction indicates the type of weather one can expect. A warm front, where warm air pushes out cold air, invariably brings overcast skies and continuous rain or snow. A cold front, cold air pushing out warm air, is often accompanied by showers of squalls.

The Bjerknes theory of fronts, although subsequently modified, has provided the basis for modern weather forecasting. Vilhelm held a professorship at the University of Oslo until his retirement in 1932. Jacob, stranded in the United States in 1940 when Norway was invaded by the Germans, established a training school for Air Force Weather Officers at the University of California. Jacob also contributed much to our understanding of the nature and structure of cyclones (large areas of low pressure, in which winds spiral inwards) and depressions.

Lumière Brothers Auguste and Louis

1862-1954 1864-1948

The birth of movies and the motion-picture industry took place in 1895 at a cafe in Paris where the Lumière brothers put on a program of short films. They were demonstrating their new invention, a motion-picture camera and projector called the *cinématographe*.

The technique of the animated image goes back to man's earliest attempts to play with shadows on walls by firelight. More recently, the Victorian magic lantern developed sophisticated effects of movement with slides which turned in circles when cranked by a handle or which incorporated moving parts. The Zoetrope, the nursery toy where an image pictured in stages of movement took on the illusion of animation when viewed through slots in a turning drum, was the direct ancestor of the cinema image. Its rapid, successive presentation of images, which the eye then transformed into apparently continual movement by the phenomenon known as the "persistence of vision," was the basis of the Kinetoscope, invented by Thomas Alva Edison as the viewing counterpart of his Kinetograph camera. However, it was the Lumière brothers, Auguste and Louis, who could be called the true pioneers of the motion picture.

The Lumière brothers, both born at Besançon, were the sons of a painter who turned to photography, and both developed scientific interests and talents. As young men they founded and ran a photographic plate factory which was a con-

siderable commercial success. Their main interest was improving photographic techniques and developing an effective method of color photography. One day in 1894 their father came back from Paris and described a demonstration he had seen of the Edison Kinetoscope. This inspired them to build an improved film projection system which they called the "*cinématographe*," from which the word "cinema" derives. Where Edison's system had a speed of 46 frames

Above: preparation of light-sensitive emulsion at the photographic plate factory founded by the Lumière brothers at Lyon, France.

Right: the Lumière's *cinématographe*, 1896. It combined a motion-picture camera, printer, and projector, but its major innovatory feature was the system of claws which moved the film.

a second, they reduced the speed to 16 frames a second, which resulted in less film being used. A pin mechanism both advanced the film and held it stationary for exposure in front of a shutter. The *cinématographe* could be used both as a camera and a projector.

The first movie or projection of animated photographs onto a screen introduced an entirely new dimension of experience. This historic event occurred on December 28, 1895, in the Grand Café on the Boulevard des Capuchines, Paris, when Auguste and Louis mounted the first public showing of the *cinématographe*. They featured a 20-minute program of 10 films, showing such scenes as workers outside the Lumière

Left: the Lumière brothers, August (left) and Louis (right).

Photography

Left: the *cinématographe* used for the first nightly cinema shows in Britain.

Right: a scene from Georges Méliès film "*Rip Van Winkle.*" Méliès was by profession a magician, who attended the first public showing of the Lumières *cinématographe*. He discovered the possibilities of trick photography to create magical effects when the shutter of his camera jammed while he was filming a street scene. Some of the illusory tricks in his films still baffle experts.

factory gates during the lunch break, or a baby being fed. The program included *Teasing the Gardener*, a brief comedy film in which a gardener is tricked into being drenched by his own hosepipe. The films themselves were cut and perforated by hand.

Among the earliest Lumière films was one of a train advancing into a station toward the camera. The realism of this, when it was first shown, took the audience entirely by surprise. Several women are said to have fainted and there was a general panic. Apparently, however, not even this tribute to the power of their invention convinced the Lumière brothers that it could be more than a nine-days' wonder.

Present in the audience at the first public showing was a professional magician, Georges Méliès, who within a year or two would start making a series of fantasy films of unique style and individual charm that would earn him a firm place in early cinema history. Méliès, in his excitement at the Lumière invention, rushed up to Auguste and offered to buy it for everything he possessed. "Young man," said Auguste Lumière, declining the offer, "you should be grateful, since, although my invention is not for sale, it would undoubtedly ruin you. It can be exploited for a certain time as a scientific curiosity but, apart from that, it has no commercial future whatsoever."

Despite their pioneering role, including the making of the first newsreel and documentary, the Lumière brothers virtually withdrew from

Above: one of the first movie advertisement posters, depicting the Lumière *cinématographe*.

active motion-picture making after about 1898 to concentrate on photographic research and equipment. They did, on the other hand, send a team of professional cameramen out world-wide to gather documentary material and demonstrate their invention. Within five years of Lumières' original public display, motion-picture-makers were at work in every developed country laying the foundations of the main entertainment industry of the 20th century.

Charles Martin Hall

1863-1914

commercial exploitation. The cost and unwieldiness of the process meant that pure aluminum cost about $100 a pound, and consequently it was regarded a rare and valuable metal. The French emperor Napoleon III ordered a set of cutlery made from it for his dinner table.

Charles Martin Hall, born at Thompson, Ohio, became a science student at Oberlin College. His imagination was fired by a statement

Left: Charles Martin Hall

Right: Paul-Louis-Toussaint Héroult, who independently discovered a process identical to Hall's for extracting aluminum.

Opposite page, above: view of the electrolytic cell in a modern aluminum smelter.

Opposite page, below: Héroult's furnace for producing aluminum by electrolysis. The components of the cell were similar to Hall's, with carbon rods acting as the anode, and the carbon-lined steel crucible as the cathode. The molten aluminum sunk to the bottom of the furnace and could be tapped off.

Below: the electrolytic cell in Pittsburgh that made the world's first commercially produced aluminum in 1888. The tank contained molten cryolite in which alumina (aluminum oxide) had first been dissolved. An electric current was then passed through the molten mass.

made by one of his professors to the effect that anyone who could come up with a cheap way of refining aluminum would make their fortune. Hall started to work on the problem, basing his researches on the earlier discovery by the British chemist Humphry Davy that purified metals

The light and versatile metal, aluminum, remained unexploited until the late 19th century. The American chemist Charles Martin Hall invented the electrolytic extraction process which transformed aluminum from a semi-precious metal into one readily available for a vast number of technical and industrial uses.

Aluminum is the third most common element in the earth's crust. It does not, however, occur freely in nature, and consequently its extraction has always presented a problem. Aluminum was first isolated from its base, alumina (aluminum oxide), in 1825 by the Danish chemist Hans Christian Øersted. He was able to produce only a minute amount of the impure metal.

Twenty years later, in 1845, the German physicist Friedrich Wöhler succeeded in producing purified aluminum, though still only in very small quantities. Then, basing his work on Wöhler's methods, a French chemist Henri Sainte-Clair Deville managed in 1854 to perfect a process that brought the minute fragments of aluminum together into larger lumps. For the first time aluminum was available for some

could be deposited on cathode plates by passing an electric current through their molten bases. This formed the basis of Hall's process. The pure metal sank to the bottom of the cell where it could be easily recovered. Hall needed a substance that was capable of dissolving the alumina and quite by chance discovered that molten cryolite (sodium aluminum fluoride) was ideal for the purpose.

The year after he graduated, in 1886, Hall made his first practical experiment and succeeded in producing a deposit of pure aluminum globules. He continued the electrolytic process until he had enough to make several ingots. The processing of aluminum by industrial methods was at last made practicable.

By a strange coincidence, a young chemist in France, Paul-Louis-Touissant Héroult, who was born in the same year and would die in the same year as Hall, discovered virtually the same process at about the same time. Both men took out patents, but Hall was quicker to pursue the commercial possibilities. There was a period of

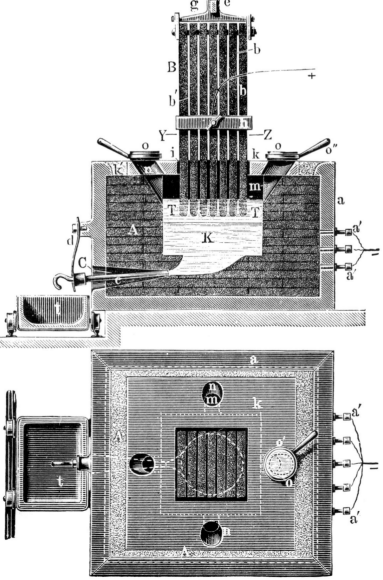

litigation in an attempt to establish a precedence of patent, but in the end it was mutually agreed that the process should be known as the Hall-Héroult process. Héroult also invented an electric smelting furnace which is still widely used.

In the United States, Hall entered into a consortium of businessmen in 1888 to found the Pittsburgh Reduction Company, which was to maintain its monopoly of aluminum production in the United States for over half a century. It became the first major industry to take advantage of the availability of the cheap hydroelectric power produced at the Niagara Falls in 1895, and the applications of and demands for aluminum increased steadily. At the beginning of World War I the price of aluminum had dropped to 18 cents a pound. The company was renamed the Aluminum Company of America (Alcoa) in 1907, and among its valued relics are the first aluminum ingots which Hall refined in 1886.

Héroult set up his aluminum plant at Neuhausen, Switzerland, where water power was available from the Rhine falls. The applications of the new metal were slower to gain ground in Europe than in the United States. Its initial use was in transportation and during World War I, a new strong alloy of aluminum was used in the Zeppelin airships. Thereafter its use spread rapidly into all kinds of operations where a light but very strong metal was required. In addition its high ductility and resistance to corrosion proved very valuable. Alloyed with other metals, aluminum became widely used for cooking utensils, building, and transport components. Its compounds have found a wide variety of medicinal applications. The world's known natural deposits of bauxite (hydrated alumina), from which aluminum is nowadays obtained, are calculated as being capable of keeping the industry supplied for several centuries to come.

Leo Hendrik Baekeland

1863-1944

The synthetic plastic Bakelite was the first thermosetting plastic and the direct forerunner of today's plastics technology. It was invented in the United States by the Belgian-born chemist Leo Baekeland.

The development of organic chemistry during the 19th century created many important off-shoots, including the introduction of many synthetic products with their potential for industrial exploitation. Among the earliest attempts to make an artificial plastic material was the development of "Parkesine," devised by a British chemist, Alexander Parkes, who also discovered a cold method of vulcanizing rubber. He adapted the process used in making the explosive gun-cotton (nitrocellulose) from cotton waste, and

found that by mixing in castor oil and camphor he was left with a malleable substance that could be shaped and hardened. The technique did not adapt to an industrial process, as Parkes discovered when the company he set up to market Parkesine went bankrupt within two years.

An American inventor, John Wesley Hyatt, turned to Parkes's method when he set out to find a way of winning a prize of $10,000, offered to the first person who could invent a substitute for ivory in the production of billiard balls. He

Right: John Wesley Hyatt, inventor of Celluloid and also of roller bearings.

Below left: Leo Baekeland, at work in his laboratory.

Below right: a shirt collar of celluloid, one of the many uses of this versatile thermoplastic.

tested out variations in the quantities of the ingredients, and applied greater heat and pressure. Before long he was able to make a billiard ball which claimed the prize. He named this material, the first ever plastic, "Celluloid."

Celluloid turned out to be remarkably versatile. It was easily shaped at 212°F (the boiling point of water). It could be drilled or cut to shape when cool, while still retaining its strength. It could also be drawn out into thin and flexible strips, which led to its use in shirt collars and the first flexible photographic film, invented by George Eastman. Its only drawback was its extremely high flammability, based, as it was, on

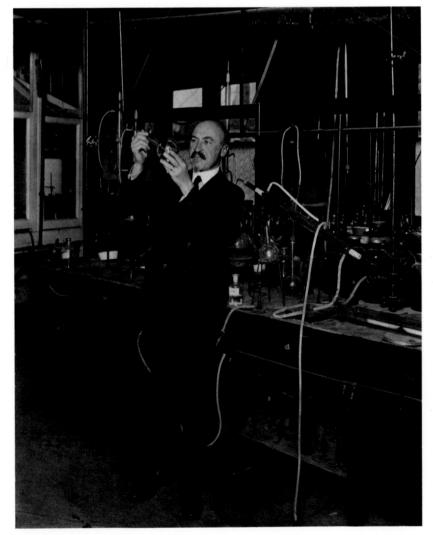

others tried to find a practical use for what was, in effect, a synthetic resin. No one succeeded until Leo Baekeland began his researches in the United States.

Baekeland, who came from Ghent, Belgium, was a lecturer at the University of Ghent until he decided to emigrate to the United States in 1889. There he became involved in photographic research and invented Velox, a photographic paper that could be developed in artificial light and which quickly became a commercial success. He eventually sold out his patent and factory to George Eastman in 1899 for what was reputed to be a million dollars.

Baekeland returned to research and began investigations into a substitute for the varnish shellac. In the course of his investigations he examined the resins produced from phenol and formaldehyde. He discovered that heating them under pressure yielded a soft solid which could be molded and hardened. Alternatively, it could be powdered and set under pressure, and heated into a hard solid shape. It was nonconductive, and consequently could be used for electrical equipment and plugs. It was also resistant to heat and corrosion. Baekeland christened the substance "Bakelite."

nitrocellulose. There were some horrifying accidents, and attempts were made to produce a safer type of Celluloid, some of which were partially successful.

Celluloid was a thermoplastic; in other words it softened when heated, and this restricted its uses. Attempts were then made to develop a thermosetting plastic which, once cooled, would not soften. The first experiments were carried out in 1872 by the German chemist, Adolph von Baeyer. While studying the reactions between phenol (carbolic acid) and various aldehydes, he found that he was left with a thick, sticky deposit. This he regarded primarily as a nuisance, though

Above: Bush radio, in Bakelite case, with a Bakelite insulated plug.

Right: car body bonded with Bakelite polyester resin.

Below left: electric iron with heat-resistant Bakelite handle.

Below right: Velox being developed in artificial light. The nature of the silver chloride emulsion in Velox enabled the washing process to be dispensed with, improving the tone of the photograph and speeding up the printing.

Bakelite proved to be a very versatile material, and it was used in the manufacture of many household objects, from radios and ashtrays to molded furniture. It was also the starting point of the plastics industry, whose products have become a hallmark of the 20th century.

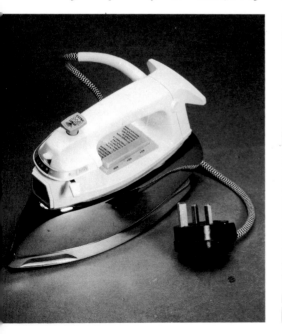

Henry Ford

1863-1947

The innovations in assembly-line methods which the American industrialist Henry Ford introduced into his Detroit automobile factory had two far-reaching social consequences. They revolutionized the whole basis of automobile production, and brought the motorcar within the financial reach of the average person.

Henry Ford did not invent the principles of mass production. That was done by a long line of industrialists, starting with Eli Whitney and his standardized gun components at the beginning of the 19th century. George Eastman was another who applied assembly-line methods in his photographic-film processing factories. Ford's achievement was instead to take the process to its logical conclusion in a large-scale plant manufacturing automobiles.

Ford was the son of a farming family, his parents arriving in the United States as immigrants from Ireland in the 1840s, and settling down in Wayne County, Michigan. In the tradition of so many American pioneer industrialists and inventors, he received only the limited schooling of a rural community, but from an early age showed a talent for coping with machinery. He progressed from being a machine-shop

Right: picnicking out in the country with the Model T, a family activity made possible through the introduction of the cheap motorcar.

Below right: the Model T.

Below: Henry Ford at the wheel of his first motorcar, 1896.

apprentice in Detroit to chief engineer in the Detroit Edison Company. Then, in 1899, he left to help run the Detroit Automobile Company. Ford had built an automobile himself in 1892.

At that time the motorcar was still very much a luxury item. The early automobile companies for the most part continued to produce each vehicle as an individual, custom-built machine. Ford was anxious to introduce other ideas which involved the cutting of costs by standardizing

the production of each automobile component, and its complete assembly. He believed that as the price was brought down the market would expand and profits would increase, enabling the price of the motorcar to be reduced again. This cycle would produce cheap motorcars and generate a huge profit.

His contemporaries, by contrast, regarded such notions as folly. Ford left Detroit Automobiles to create his own racing cars. These

were so successful that they attracted the attention of potential backers and partners, and in 1903 he was able to set up the Ford Motor Company. He was still some way from his objective as he found himself facing the opposition of his shareholders and fellow directors to his ideas of an automobile for the average working man. In the end he had his way, and the inexpensive Ford Model T went into production in 1908.

Above: an early Ford Model T assembly line. Here it was possible to cut costs by using relatively unskilled labor to assemble various simple components, and to save time by delegating a specific task to each worker. In time, the workers' specialization led to greater speed and accuracy which could be reflected in a lowering of the unit selling price. Every component was deliberately utilitarian in design for cheapness, ease of operation, and simplicity of maintenance, the gearbox being the supreme example of this. The epicyclic system was used to cut the high cost of gear-wheel making.

There was one main assembly line for the Model T chassis and engine unit. The body unit was assembled separately and, once the engine and chassis were tested, was brought down a chute to be lowered onto the chassis and bolted into place. Once this was done, the car could be driven away. Ford's concept paid off handsomely and a cheap car was made available to a potentially huge and growing market of people in the moderate-income bracket.

He increased the salaries of his workers while reducing the working hours, and introduced a profit-sharing scheme. He also believed that the profits should be used to enable the company to expand. This was an unusual idea at the time and the other stockholders wanted to divide the profits among themselves. Ford disliked the opposition and eventually bought all his stockholders out.

By 1913 any American who could afford to spend $500 could buy himself a car, and 1000 cars were coming off the assembly line each day. Between 1908 and 1927, a total of 15-million Model T Fords emerged from the factory in Detroit, and by the time this classic car ceased production its price was down to $290.

Ford thus demonstrated the advantages of mass production to the customer. The Model T only ceased production because the demands of the market were changing. The customer wanted extra comforts and the latest model designed in the current fashion to advertise his social standing. Never again would there be automobiles so cheap, so durable, and so available across a wide social spectrum. The market dictated the ethos of built-in obsolescence, and even Ford was forced to adapt.

During the years which followed, Henry Ford remained in complete financial control of the vast industrial empire that was his creation. He introduced other cars and new types of engine, despite the distrust of new ideas which is often a characteristic of a veteran innovator. Even so, the Ford company gradually lost its lead in automobile manufacturing.

Much of Ford's personal wealth went to establish the Ford Foundation, a leading philanthropic organization with a remit to assist a whole range of social needs, from patronage of the arts to famine relief. He also dabbled in politics, standing for Senator, but without success. It is for his work in the organization of technical and industrial processes that his fame is established.

Below: the Ford works at Dagenham, Britain, 1937.

Wright Brothers
Wilbur and Orville

1867-1912 1871-1948

The Wright brothers then turned their ingenuity to designing from scratch both a far lighter gasoline engine than any then in existence and an effective propeller. By the end of the following year, 1903, they were ready to make an attempt at the first sustained airplane flight. An aircraft which they called *Flyer I*, but which has since then been rechristened the *Kitty Hawk*, was taken to a carefully chosen piece of flat ground in the Kill Devil Hills near Kitty Hawk,

The first practical powered airplane capable of controlled flight was built and flown in the United States by Orville and Wilbur Wright, two brothers who were self-taught mechanics and bicycle manufacturers.

The Wright brothers, Orville and Wilbur, were born respectively at Dayton, Ohio, and Millville, Indiana, the sons of an Evangelical bishop. Both showed an early interest in machinery and in discovering for themselves how things worked. As young men they went into partnership, first to build and sell printing equipment, and then to make bicycles. The success of their business ventures brought them enough income to enable them to start developing a personal enthusiasm: the idea of building a heavier-than-air, self-powered flying machine.

Their approach to the problem was careful, practical, and methodical, starting with observations of the hanging flights of buzzards in air thermals as well as of the birds' controlled dives. They realized that it was not just stability that was important but control as well. The problems to overcome before the aircraft could be under complete control concerned its three axes of movement: pitching up and down, rolling from side to side, and yaw – the tendency of the plane to move either to the left or right.

In 1899 they built a biplane kite to test out their ideas and this was followed by three biplane gliders of progressive sophistication, taking into account the experience of other gliding pioneers, including that of the German Otto Lilienthal who died in a crash after making many flights in gliders he had built himself. By the time they had built their third glider in 1902 they had mastered most of the problems concerned with steering and stability, including three-axis control.

Above: the Wright brothers' first flight at Kitty Hawk, North Carolina.

Right: Otto Lilienthal flying one of his hanging gliders at around 1892. He built his gliders from cotton fabric stretched across willow ribs. Lilienthal controlled his machines by shifting the weight of his body against the wind, and his successes paved the way for fixed-wing powered flight. He crashed to his death in 1896 when the wind dropped suddenly.

Below: Orville (left) and Wilbur (right) Wright.

North Carolina, on December 14. Wilbur was to pilot, but at take-off he made an error of judgement and the attempt failed. Three days later they tried again, this time with Orville at the controls. History was made on December 17, 1903, when Orville Wright, lying flat at the controls, piloted the *Flyer* on a flight lasting 12 seconds. They made three other flights that day, the best being one of 59 seconds with Wilbur as pilot.

The local and national press paid almost no attention to this event. The Wright brothers, on the other hand, gained the assurance of knowing that their work was proceeding along the right lines. "Faith in our calculations and . . . confidence in our system of control developed by three years of actual experience in balancing gliders in the air," wrote Orville Wright some years later, "had convinced us that the machine was capable of lifting and maintaining itself in the air, and that, with a little practice, it could be safely flown." During 1904 they built and flew *Flyer 2*, and the next year the plane which was the culmination to their first series of pioneering

250

flights, *Flyer* 3. This sealed the conquest of the air by a heavier-than-air machine. In a series of test flights it demonstrated banking and turning, returning to its starting point and flying in figures-of-eight.

Still the world paid little attention to what it obstinately regarded as dubious or exaggerated antics: "Flyers or Liars?" asked one skeptical newspaper headline. The brothers therefore concentrated on consolidating their practical know-

Below: plan view of a Wright aeroplane.

to hold their world lead in airplane design, but then new patents and determined competitors managed to seize the initiative, while new aviation techniques outstripped the Wright's original concept. Nevertheless they achieved what many thought to be impossible: a powered, controlled flight in an aerodynamically designed heavier-than-air machine. All subsequent developments in aeronautics have their legitimate ancestry in the Wrights' initial series of airplanes.

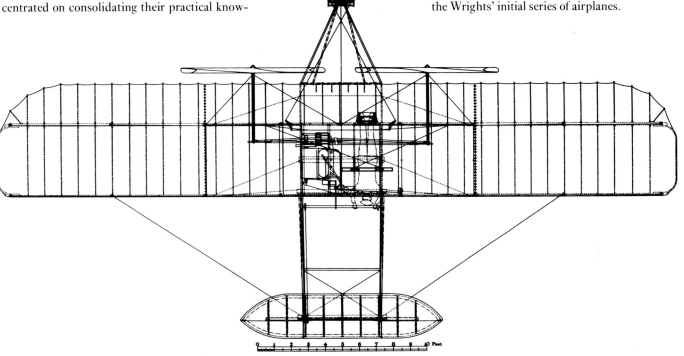

ledge of aerodynamics. It was not until 1908 when Wilbur went to Europe with a demonstration model of a new machine that their achievement made its full impact on the public imagination. In the United States in the same year they suffered their first major setback when Orville crashed while conducting flight trials to win an army contract. His passenger, Lieutenant Thomas E Selfridge, was killed, and Orville suffered serious injuries.

Demonstrations continued, however, and license agreements were concluded for aircraft production in Europe. The US Army confirmed its order for a military model in 1909. For about another two years the Wright brothers were able

Below left: the Wright brothers' pioneering flights captured the public's imagination and created a great deal of speculation on the future of air travel. This French illustration, entitled *Le Monde en l'an 2000*, depicts an airliner.

Right: Wilbur Wright demonstrating fixed-wing flight at Les Hunaudières, France, 1908.

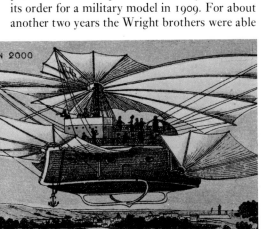

Marie Curie

1867-1934

Marie Curie, the Polish-born chemist, was a woman of tremendous courage and determination. Together with her husband, Pierre, she created the most famous husband and wife partnership in the history of science. They discovered the radioactive element polonium, and later another new element, radium. Their work confirmed the existence of the phenomenon Marie termed "radioactivity" and so helped to usher in the era of atomic power.

Marie left her home in Warsaw in 1891 to pursue her consuming interest in science. Unable to obtain a university place in Poland she saved enough money to travel to Paris and attend the Sorbonne. Living in terrible poverty and often on the verge of starvation, she still managed to come top in her year. In 1894, shortly after graduation, she met the talented young French chemist, Pierre Curie, and a year later they were married.

The Curies were excited by news of Henri

Becquerel's discovery of a new kind of radiation emitted, apparently spontaneously, by compounds containing uranium. When they started their own research they found that certain compounds were emitting far more radioactivity than could be accounted for by the quantity of uranium in them. In particular, the Curies were puzzled by the extremely high degree of radiation emitted by the mineral ore pitchblende. They set about refining the ore and in 1898 were re-

Above: part of the purification process in the Curies' laboratory, using sodium carbonate. After many years of labor, it yielded a tenth of a gram of radium.

Right: Pierre Curie.

warded by the discovery of a totally new element which they named "polonium," in honor of Marie's homeland. Polonium, although a hundred times more radioactive than uranium, could still not account for all the radiation emitted from pitchblende. The Curies were convinced that an even more intensely radioactive element must be present, although in minute quantities. They named this mystery element "radium." So determined were they to confirm its existence that they spent the next four years trying to extract a sample from tons of pitchblende, in what has proved to be one of the great epics of scientific research. The Curies first needed a plentiful supply of the ore. Fortunately, huge quantities of it were available from the waste heaps of Czechoslovakian ore mines, and the mine owners were delighted to be able to sell the useless material. Marie and Pierre spent their life savings buying every ounce they could. They then managed to find a leaky wooden shed near their lodgings where they could work on refining the ore. For four exhausting years they purified and repurified tons of pitchblende into smaller and smaller quantities of increasingly radioactive material. The work was not only delicate and technical but extremely grueling. The heavy pitchblende had to be dug and carried by hand, and with little money to buy food to keep up their strength, only a remarkable determination kept them going. Finally, in 1902, the tons of pitchblende yielded a tenth of a gram of the new element.

In 1903 Marie and Pierre were awarded the Nobel Prize for Physics but were too ill and

Left: Marie Curie in her laboratory.

Right: autunite, a radioactive uranium ore, fluorescing under ultraviolet light.

Center: the penetrating qualities of the radiation from pitchblende causes objects such as this key to form a radiostat when placed between a photographic plate wrapped in opaque material and a lump of the ore.

Below: the Radium Institute at the Charity Hospital, Berlin. Patients were placed in a sealed room where they breathed in the radioactive emission from radium. Until its dangers were realized radium was used indiscriminately in medicine.

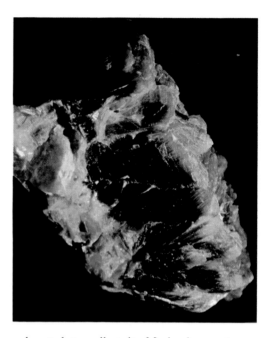

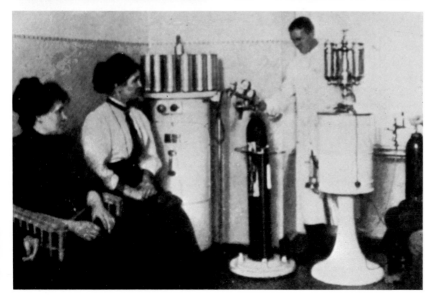

exhausted to collect it. Marie, however, was fascinated by the vast energies pouring out of the radium atoms and could hardly wait to start new lines of research. But in 1906 tragedy struck when Pierre was killed in a road accident. With characteristic courage, however, Marie took over her husband's professorship at the Sorbonne, the first woman to hold that post, continuing her research and teaching at the same time. In 1911 she was awarded a further Nobel Prize, this time for chemistry, and so became the first person ever to win two science laureates.

The last years of her life were spent administering the Paris Institute of Radium which soon became a major research center for nuclear physics and chemistry. She pioneered some of the earliest medical applications of X-rays and radium. In the treatment of cancer, radium therapy quickly became a technique of major importance and remains so to the present day. With tragic irony, however, Marie had paid more dearly than she realized for the years of hardship in the search for radium. The constant exposure to radioactivity had affected her blood and she died in 1934 of leukemia.

Marie Curie is remembered today not just for the discovery of radium and her contribution to our modern understanding of the atom. Her name symbolizes a spirit of dedication and commitment rarely equalled in the history of science.

Wallace Clement Sabine

1868-1919

young physicist, Wallace C Sabine, originally from Richwood, Ohio. Sabine was at the time an assistant professor of physics at Harvard.

Sabine adopted an empirical approach. Using an organ pipe he measured the length of time each note persisted in the lecture hall and found it to be 5.62 seconds (incidentally coining the use of the word "reverberation" in this context). With the help of a small team of assistants, he then borrowed for his experiment the entire

The American physicist Wallace C Sabine formulated the rules by which acoustical reverberation can be calculated and utilized in the building of an auditorium. He thus turned architectural acoustics from a matter of trial and error into a science.

Contrary to what is often supposed, Greek and Roman amphitheaters were not particularly efficient in their acoustical design. The semicircular arrangement of seats focused the sound back into the center stage and there was severe distortion. From post-classical times until the end of the 19th century the acoustics of auditoriums and theaters depended largely on good luck and were often based on mistaken theories. Until a concert hall was built it was impossible to predict quite how the sound would project. An outstanding acoustical disaster was the Royal Albert Hall, London, whose very grandeur created reverberations and a notorious echo well known to generations of musicians and concertgoers which has only recently been corrected by new techniques.

There was a need for a scientifically-based theory of acoustics as Harvard University was embarrassed to discover when in 1895 it opened the Fogg Art Museum. The reverberation in the lecture hall was so bad that in many parts of the auditorium the lecturer's voice was totally inaudible. The problem was handed over to a

Above: London's Albert Hall, long infamous for its echo and reverberation. In 1969 over 100 fiber-glass saucers suspended from the dome and a 20-meter reflector over the orchestra banished the worst of the hall's echoes.

Below right: the lecture hall at the former Fogg Art Museum (now Hunt Hall), Harvard University.

stock of seat cushions from a nearby theater. As more cushions were brought into the hall and placed on the seats the duration of the sound decreased. When every seat was covered, the reverberation time was reduced to 2.03 seconds. Sabine went further and packed cushions into the aisles and over the platform, even piling them against the back wall up to the height of the ceiling. The reverberation of a single note was ultimately reduced to 1.14 seconds.

Sabine plotted a graph to show the relation-

Opposite page, above: relationship between duration of sound and length of cushions (top) and the same curve extended algebraically. The solid part of the graph was plotted from experimental results, and the broken part to the right measures the theoretical absorbing power of the actual walls of the room.

Acoustics

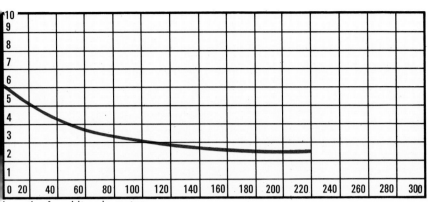

Length of cushions in meters

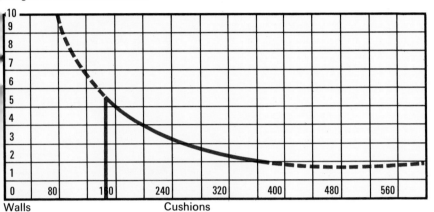

Walls   Cushions

Left: a Helmholtz resonator in a chipboard panel which absorbs the reverberation.

Below right: the seats in London's Royal Festival Hall were designed so that when tipped up they absorb as much sound as a seated person. The reverberation time is about the same whether the auditorium is full or empty.

ship between length of reverberation and the total length of cushions measured in meters. From this he formulated what subsequently became known as Sabine's law. This states that the room's total absorption multiplied by the length of reverberation is a constant which varies with the volume of the room. As cushion length is a rather cumbersome unit, Sabine chose as his unit the absorbitivity of an open window, and the absorption coefficient of each material is measured in relation to this.

Sabine's law has influenced the design of every auditorium built since. The first to be built according to Sabine's specifications was the Symphony Hall in Boston, Massachusetts, which was opened for public concerts in 1900. It is still regarded as one of the best concert halls in the world for symphonic music.

Concert halls can now be built to provide the optimum length of reverberation. This depends to a great extent on what the hall will be used for. Choral music, for example, requires a much longer reverberation than symphonic music. Sabine pointed out that there are two other factors to be taken into account. Interference, when a direct sound wave meets a reflected one, occurs when there are large smooth sound-reflecting surfaces, as in the Royal Albert Hall. This can be overcome by using sound-absorbent materials such as awnings, and breaking up the continuity of the reflecting surface. The other problem is resonance, which can be damped down by using less resonant building materials.

Sabine was an outstanding teacher of practical science, and he helped found the Harvard Graduate School of Applied Science (later merged with the Massachusetts Institute of Technology) in 1908. His work on acoustics, *Collected Papers on Acoustics* was published posthumously in 1922, and the *sabin*, a unit of acoustic frequency, commemorates his name.

Karl Landsteiner

1868-1943

The safety and effectiveness of blood transfusions depends on the use of compatible blood. This was made possible in 1900 when the Austrian-born physician Karl Landsteiner discovered the ABO blood-group system.

The recorded use of blood transfusions dates back to the mid-17th century. The British physician Richard Lower introduced the operation of transfusing blood from the veins of one dog to another, an operation made feasible by William Harvey's discovery, published in 1628, that blood circulates around the body. The first successful transfusions on humans were performed by the French physician Jean-Baptiste Denis, consultant to King Louis IV. Denis used lambs as donors. Unfortunately, in 1668 one of his patients died after a transfusion. Denis was

arrested and the practice was outlawed, although it was later proved that the patient had been poisoned by his wife. Blood transfusion fell into disuse until the early 19th century when it was revived. However, the technique as it stood then was dangerous, mainly because the transfused blood frequently clotted.

It was this problem which Karl Landsteiner, an Austrian-born physician, chose to study when he joined the Institute of Hygiene in Vienna as a research assistant. Landsteiner was puzzled by the fact that blood from different subjects was mixed, sometimes there was coagulation and at other times not. Working on the assumption that there were intrinsic dissimilarities and similarities in the blood of individuals, he collected samples of blood from his laboratory colleagues and mixed them with one another. Some pairings clotted while others did not.

In 1900 Landsteiner published the analysis of

Right: an 18th century blood transfusion, using a lamb as a donor. The use of animals as donors was abandoned after several fatalities.

Below right: photomicrograph of human blood. The blood-group antigens reside in the walls of the red blood cells (olive green staining). The large nucleated body is a white blood cell.

Below: like other physical characteristics, blood groups are inherited according to a Mendelian pattern. The compatibility of two people's blood, especially taking into account the various subgroups, is greater the closer they are related. An inbred family such as the Hapsburgs (illustrated below by Charles V of Spain) would possess not only the same physical characteristics, in this case the prominent nose and underslung jaw, but also virtually identical blood groups.

his results. He had found that there were distinct blood groups which he named A, B, and O. A fourth group, AB, was discovered the following year. These groups are in fact proteins in the blood cells called antigens. Subjects with blood-group A also had a protein in the serum, called an antibody, which clotted and destroyed group-B cells. Likewise blood-group B people had an anti-A antibody. AB subjects had no antibodies and O subjects, with no antigens, had both

anti-A and anti-B antibodies.

This established the pattern for safe blood transfusions. Group A subjects could receive blood from A and O donors, group-B subjects from B and O donors, AB from all donors, and O only from O donors. Incompatible transfusions not only result in the donor's blood being destroyed but can produce severe kidney failure.

Landsteiner's discovery enabled blood banks to be established and at last many operations,

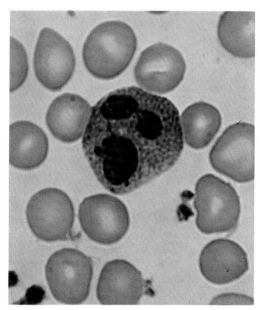

Medicine

previously inconceivable, could be performed. Complete transfusions on, for example, newborn infants with jaundice, were also possible.

Because blood groups are inherited they have been used in cases of disputed paternity to prove that a subject is *not* the father, if the child concerned has a blood antigen not present in either parent. As yet it is not possible to provide positive proof of paternity. As more groups were discovered, it became possible to use blood stains as forensic evidence in a similar way to fingerprints.

Landsteiner's achievement was recognized by his appointment as Professor of Pathology at the University of Vienna. However, he was dissatisfied with working conditions there, and moved first to The Hague, Netherlands, and then to the Rockerfeller Institute for Medical Research, New York. It was there that he made several more important contributions to medicine, including the discovery of blood groups M and N, and, in 1940, the Rh or Rhesus factor.

The Rhesus factor was so called because it was discovered in the Rhesus monkey. It was one of Landsteiner's co-workers, Philip Levine, who in fact saw the connection between this group and a condition of severe jaundice which can occur in newborns. During a pregnancy a

Right: the tests used to identify a blood sample according to the ABO classification.

Center: ABO-compatible blood shows no reaction on mixing (top sample), but agglutination is clearly visible in the mixture of ABO-incompatible bloods (bottom sample).

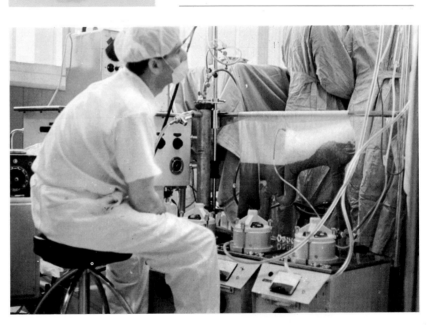

taken. After the first pregnancy the mother can receive a complete transfusion which removes any fetal cells that would otherwise provoke an immune response.

Landsteiner's work, in addition to saving countless lives, was one of the cornerstones of immunochemistry. A timid man with a dislike of publicity, he devoted most of his working life to the study of blood. In 1930 he received the Nobel Prize for Medicine.

Red cells in saline solution	Anti-B serum containing β agglutinins	Anti-A serum containing α agglutinins
A	−	+
B	+	−
AB	+	+
O	−	−

+ = Agglutination   − = No agglutination

Left: mechanized blood grouping.

Above: in Western hospitals heart-lung operations, impossible before the introduction of safe blood transfusion techniques, now account for the greatest use of donated blood.

Rhesus-positive fetus in a Rhesus-negative mother stimulates the mother to produce anti-Rhesus antibodies. In subsequent pregnancies these antibodies act against the blood of the fetus, causing severe jaundice, brain damage, or even a miscarriage. The discovery of the Rhesus factor enabled preventative measures to be

Right: British blood donor badge.

257

Fritz Haber

1868-1934

The chemical synthesis of ammonia was a discovery of fundamental importance to both chemistry and industry, as it enabled scientists for the first time to fix atmospheric nitrogen. This process was invented by, and named after, the German chemist, Fritz Haber. Still in use today, it laid the foundations of the fertilizer industry which has since revolutionized agricultural production.

Nitrogen, a colorless, inert gas, makes up over 78 percent of the earth's atmosphere. It is a vital component in the chain of life and passes through a complicated cycle. Animals obtain their nitrogen, directly or indirectly, through plants, which in turn absorb it from the soil in the form of salts such as nitrates. These salts form the basis of fertilizers which man uses to increase his crop yields.

By the beginning of the 20th century supplies of naturally occurring nitrogen, in the form of minerals such as the sodium nitrate (saltpetre) deposits of Chile, or organic nitrates such as

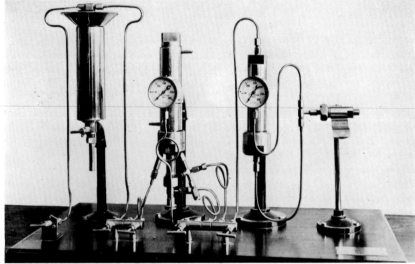

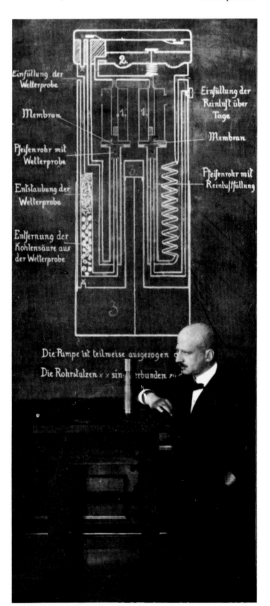

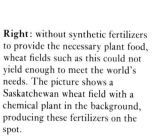

Above: Haber's test apparatus for the continuous synthesis of ammonia, 1908.

Right: the chemical reactions used by industry to produce nitrates. Top: Haber-Bosch process – one molecule of nitrogen reacts with three molecules of hydrogen to form two molecules of ammonia. Bottom: in the Ostwald process one molecule of ammonia reacts with two of oxygen to form nitric acid and water. The ammonia gas has to be passed over heated platinum gauze which acts as a catalyst. The bulk of the ammonia produced goes toward making nitric acid – itself the starting point for making other nitrogen compounds.

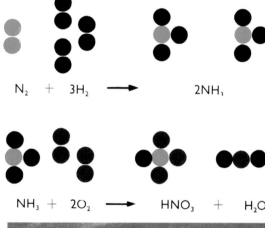

$$N_2 + 3H_2 \longrightarrow 2NH_3$$

$$NH_3 + 2O_2 \longrightarrow HNO_3 + H_2O$$

Right: without synthetic fertilizers to provide the necessary plant food, wheat fields such as this could not yield enough to meet the world's needs. The picture shows a Saskatchewan wheat field with a chemical plant in the background, producing these fertilizers on the spot.

compost or manure, were beginning to be out-stripped by industrial and agricultural demand. A new source of nitrogen was needed, and Fritz Haber considered the possibility of chemically fixing the large amount of nitrogen present in the atmosphere.

Haber was born at Breslau in Lower Silesia (now Wroclaw in Poland). His education was classically orientated and Haber decided to teach himself science. He was so successful that eventually he obtained a teaching post in physical chemistry at the Polytechnic of Karlsruhe. He also began a program of research in thermo-dynamics and electrochemistry, for which he was awarded a professorship.

It was as a result of his studies in thermo-dynamics that Haber got the idea for chemically fixing atmospheric nitrogen. Haber saw that one way to fix gaseous nitrogen was to combine it chemically with hydrogen to form ammonia. Thermodynamically the problem was that although the process needed a high temperature to make the gases reactive, this high temperature would then inhibit the production of ammonia. Haber overcame this by heating a mixture of nitrogen and hydrogen and passing it under a very high pressure over a catalyst (a substance which affects the speed of a chemical reaction while itself remaining unchanged). The ammonia

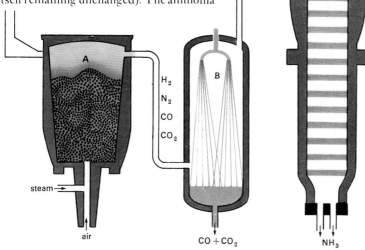

could then be used directly on the soil or converted into other nitrogen-containing chemicals.

Haber's achievement of synthesizing ammonia established in the laboratory the basic principles for a large-scale industrial process. The establishment of such a process was all the more urgent as World War I had broken out and Germany was cut off from outside supplies of nitrates. The task of putting Haber's process onto an industrial basis was undertaken by another research chemist, Carl Bosch. He added improvements and refinements, and researched into suitable catalysts. In due course the method became officially known as the Haber-Bosch process.

In the meantime, Haber, an ardent German patriot, placed his skills at the service of his country and its war efforts. He was involved in the development of gas as a military weapon, and after World War I ended was instrumental in an unsuccessful scheme to extract traces of gold from seawater in an attempt to meet the sum required of Germany as reparation payments. In 1918 he received the Nobel Prize for Chemistry for his process of synthesizing ammonia. His colleague Carl Bosch was to receive one in 1931 for developing techniques in high-pressure chemical processes.

During the 1920s Haber built up his laboratory into what was probably the world's foremost unit for the study of physical chemistry and its industrial applications. He enjoyed an international reputation in this field and was anxious to establish a tradition of cooperation between scientists of all countries. However, when the Nazis came to power in Germany in 1933, Haber found himself one of the first targets of anti-semitic policy. In the same year he left Germany to work in England at the University of Cambridge, but his health was failing and he died in Switzerland while on his way south to avoid the northern European winter.

Above: caliche (sodium nitrate) being blasted from the huge natural deposits in Chile. Until Haber's process caliche beds were the world's chief source of nitrate.

Center: Haber-Bosch process. Steam and air are alternately blown through hot coke in tower (A), forming a mixture of gases (hydrogen, nitrogen, carbon monoxide, and carbon dioxide). The carbon oxides are washed out in tower (B), leaving nitrogen and hydrogen. These are compressed and pumped into reaction tower (C) where they combine to form ammonia.

Sir Ernest Rutherford

1871-1937

Christchurch. He graduated with honors in 1882 and three years later won another scholarship, this time to Cambridge University in England.

It was a turning point in Rutherford's life. At Cambridge he met the distinguished physicist J J Thomson who encouraged him to begin research on X-rays, then only recently discovered in Germany by Wilhelm Röntgen. For Rutherford it was the beginning of a lifelong interest in radioactivity and atomic structure.

Right: Rutherford's first notes on the structure of the atom.

Center right: the simplest atom, hydrogen, according to Rutherford's model. He suggested the mass of an atom was concentrated in a positively-charge nucleus, with electrons spinning around it like planets orbiting the sun.

Below: Rutherford's room at the Cavendish Laboratory, Cambridge University.

Although he dealt with some of the most complex scientific concepts, Ernest Rutherford had the gift of simplifying explanations with graphic illustrations. His great contribution to modern science was to show what happens to an element during radioactive decay, which enabled him to construct the first nuclear model of the atom. A cornerstone of present-day physics, his work is an example of the remarkable power of an original mind to work out commonsense answers to scientific problems.

A few years before he was born, Rutherford's parents had left England to settle in Nelson, New Zealand. His father was a tough, practical man, a wheelwright by trade, who successfully turned to farming in his new homeland. Ernest shared his father's pleasure of hard work in the open and often helped with the running of the farm, but he also showed great promise as a student and won a scholarship to Canterbury College in

Physics

Röntgen's work on X-rays led directly to the discovery of radioactivity, a phenomenon that intrigued Rutherford. He began a series of experiments analyzing the radiation emitted by elements such as uranium, and discovered that such radiation consisted of three components. Two of these were made up of beams of tiny particles that he called alpha and beta rays. The third component was a high-frequency electromagnetic radiation that he named gamma rays. In later experiments carried out with English chemist Frederick Soddy, Rutherford showed that elements such as uranium and thorium are spontaneously transmuted into other intermediate elements during radioactive decay. Further, each intermediate element itself breaks down at a fixed rate so that half of a given quantity of it decays within a certain period of time. Rutherford called this period the "half-life" of the element.

Rutherford's findings caused a sensation, and scientists derided his ideas of elements being transmuted as no better than medieval alchemy. It was not until 1904 with the publication of his classic book *Radioactivity* that Rutherford's outstanding achievements won him deserved worldwide recognition.

Retaining his youthful delight in hard work, Rutherford maintained a high level of activity. In one seven-year period he published over 80 scientific papers. Most important of these were investigations of alpha and beta radiation, work that led him directly to his greatest contribution to science, the nuclear model of the atom.

Rutherford wanted to find some means of exploring the atom and decided to try shooting a projectile at it to see what happened. But first he had to find a suitable projectile, something as small as the target itself. He decided to use a beam of alpha particles and chose the element radium as a convenient source. In 1909 he began a historic series of experiments in which he fired narrow beams of alpha particles at a gold foil target less than 1/3000 of an inch thick. Most of the particles passed straight through the foil but sometimes one was deflected as though it had struck something solid. By examining the pattern

Above right: carbon-14 dating of bone. Rutherford's discovery of the half-life of radioactive elements has since been utilized to date archaeological and geological specimens. The ratio of radioactive carbon-14 to the total carbon content is related to the age of the specimen.

Above left: alpha-particle scattering apparatus used by Rutherford to disintegrate the nuclei of nitrogen, 1919. This was the first artificial disintegration of an element.

Center: Rutherford holding his original alpha-scattering apparatus.

Below right: the uranium ore autunite.

of the particles scattered in the impact with atoms in the foil, Rutherford found that he could build up a detailed picture of the internal structure of the atoms themselves. He deduced that all the atom's positive charge and most of its mass are concentrated in a tiny central nucleus about 10,000 times smaller in diameter than the atom as a whole. Electrons, with negative charges, orbit the nucleus, much as the planets of the solar system orbit the sun.

Rutherford's model of an atom as a tiny solar system became the basis of most future developments in atomic physics. Although modified in the years that followed by complicated mathematical theories, it still remains one of the simplest and most valuable ways of visualizing the internal workings of the atom.

Throughout his life, Rutherford's warm and humorous nature won him many admirers. He was violently opposed to the rise of the Nazi party in Germany and in the 1930s, the last years of his life, he helped Jewish refugees to flee from Nazi persecution. In 1931 he was honored with the title of Baron Rutherford of Nelson.

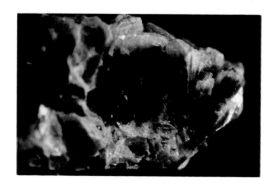

Guglielmo Marconi

1874-1937

Many scientists have made decisive contributions to the theoretical and practical aspects of wireless or radio broadcasting. It was the Italian physicist Guglielmo Marconi who synthesized all the ideas, including his own, into the first working radio telegraph.

In the 1860s the British scientist James Clerk Maxwell, having shown the electromagnetic nature of heat and light rays, predicted the possibility of generating electromagnetic radiations through the so-called ether. Twenty years later the German physicist Heinrich Hertz demonstrated the existence of such rays, subsequently called "Hertzian waves." He found that when he generated sparks between two metal balls they could be detected by a metal loop with a gap in it. Smaller sparks were seen jumping across this gap. Later experimenters managed to widen the distance across which Hertzian waves could be transmitted, and in 1894 a British scientist, Sir Oliver Lodge, sent Morse-code signals over a distance of half a mile.

Yet where Hertz and Lodge considered the phenomenon a scientific curiosity, others were aware of its practical implications. The Russian physicist, Aleksandr Stepanovich Popov, regarded in his home country as the true founder of radio, saw Hertzian waves as a possible way of communicating between ships over long distances. In 1895 he built a receiver to detect electromagnetism in the atmosphere and pre-

Right: replica of radio transmitting apparatus used by Marconi in 1895 in some of his earliest radio experiments.

Below: Marconi at Signal Hill, Newfoundland, 1901, with the instruments used to receive the first wireless signal across the Atlantic, from Polhu, Cornwall.

dicted that it might be used to pick up generated signals. The next year he arranged a demonstration in the University of St Petersburg (now Leningrad) where messages were sent and received between different points.

Meanwhile, work was being carried out independently in Italy in 1894, by a young scientist Guglielmo Marconi. Marconi was the son of a wealthy Italian landowner and an Irish mother. He completed his education at the Leghorn technical school where he developed an interest in physics. Marconi began his experiments at his family's estate near Bologna.

He found that he could boost the range of a signal if he attached one end of the transmitter to a long wire running to a metal plate at the top of a pole, while the other end was run to earth. A similar arrangement of what was, in fact, a prototype aerial was connected to the receiver. In September 1895 he succeeded in transmitting a signal beyond the line of vision, with a hill in-between. He also found that by using metal sheets around the antenna the radio waves could be reflected into narrow beams. The Italian government was uninterested in Marconi's work, so he left for London in 1896. With the help of an Irish cousin he took out his first patent and, encouraged by the interest of the British Post Office, improved his system to the point where he was able to send a signal nine miles across the Bristol Channel. With his cousin he set up the

Communication

Wireless Telegraph and Signal Company to demonstrate the potentials of radiotelegraphy. In 1899 Marconi successfully set up a wireless station to communicate with a French station 31 miles across the English Channel.

It was thought that the curve of the earth's surface would limit radio transmission to 200 miles at the most. When, on December 11, 1901, Marconi transmitted a signal from Poldhu, Cornwall, to St John's, Newfoundland, 2000 miles away, he created a major sensation. For this Marconi replaced the wire receiver with a coherer, a glass tube filled with iron filings, which could conduct radio waves. At the time there was no scientific explanation for this phenomenon of long-distance transmission, and it was postulated that there was a layer in the upper atmosphere – the ionosphere – which reflected back electromagnetic waves.

Marconi certainly did more than any other inventor to establish radio communication. He

Right: the home wireless set became the major source of entertainment in the early 20th century.

Below left: experimental mobile station, 1901. When the vehicle was moving, the aerial was hinged back to lie horizontally. Marconi and Professor John Ambrose Fleming can be seen at the rear of the vehicle. Fleming made a major contribution to radio development by inventing the diode, a vacuum tube with two electrodes, one hot and the other cold. The diode acted as a rectifier, keeping the current flowing in one direction only.

No 1 'All about Wireless' – A New Paper for ALL

POPULAR WIRELESS weekly 3d

THE WORLD'S LATEST HOBBY FULLY EXPLAINED

PUBLISHED EVERY FRIDAY ORDER IN ADVANCE

PACKED WITH PICTURES AND EXPERT ADVICE

continued to make many discoveries, particularly in the use of reflectors to produce much shorter wavelengths. These could produce much stronger signals and were less easy to intercept. The Marconi Wireless Telegraph Company, which he founded in Britain, still exists as one of the world's leading electronics manufacturers. In 1909 Marconi received the Nobel Prize for Physics jointly with Karl Ferdinand Braun, who made important modifications which considerably increased the range of the first Marconi transmitters.

Above: Marconiphone broadcaster receiver, 1922, designed to be used with headphones. It was the earliest of commercially manufactured radios.

Below left: a Marconi Syntonic Receiver for receiving several messages simultaneously.

Right: triode or audion. It was invented in 1906 by the American Lee de Forest who discovered that a grid of fine wires placed between the filament and plate of a diode could control the flow of electrons. A small negative potential on the grid repels the electrons and prevents them from reaching the plate, while a small positive voltage accelerates them. The triode could thus amplify very weak signals to enormous power levels.

Albert
Einstein
1879-1955

Recognized in his own lifetime as one of the most powerful and creative intellects in human history, the German-born American physicist Albert Einstein is today best known for his Theories of Relativity. In formulating these theories, Einstein reexamined some of the most fundamental ideas in science and created a completely new outlook on the nature of space and time.

Born in Ulm, Germany, Einstein showed little intellectual promise in his early school days. During his spare time he learned to play the violin, demonstrating a fine talent and developing a deep love of music that remained with him throughout his life. In the 1890s his family left Germany for Switzerland where Einstein completed his education. Except for mathematics, in which he excelled, his record was poor and his efforts to find an academic post were unsuccessful. Eventually he settled for a job as a junior clerk in the Patents Office in Berne.

Einstein found the work so undemanding that he had plenty of time for his own research. The only equipment he needed was a pencil and

Right: solar eclipse, with the moon's disk all but hiding the sun. Using his General Theory of Relativity, Einstein predicted that light rays passing near the sun would be bent out of their path by twice the amount that classical Newtonian physics accounted for, due to the intense gravitational field. Detailed study of eclipses showed that this prediction was in fact correct.

supposed ether and its strangely negative result. By simply manipulating ideas and following where the mathematics led him, Einstein produced a remarkable new picture of the universe. Published in 1905, the Special Theory of Relativity, as Einstein called it, challenged the views of time and space that had been accepted since Newton's day. For over two centuries scientists had unquestionably believed that the basic quantities of measurement – mass, length, and time – were absolute and unvarying. Einstein showed that in fact they depended very much on the relative motion between the observer and whatever he was observing.

In 1915 the General Theory of Relativity gave a mathematical description of the structure of space. He maintained that the universe consisted of a continuum of space and time in the form of a complicated four-dimensional curve. The implication of this difficult idea was that the force of gravity, first identified by Newton, was actually created by localized bending in the fabric of space, caused by the presence of large

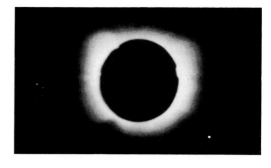

accumulations of mass such as stars and planets.

The new theory created a violent controversy. Most scientists found Einstein's work incomprehensible, and even those who could follow the mathematics were unable to accept conclusions that seemed so contrary to common sense. But although Einstein had conceived the theory entirely in his own mind he knew that certain simple experiments could prove it. If publication of Einstein's ideas created a controversy, the proof of its predictions published in 1919 caused a sensation. As scientists finally began to take his work seriously, the full measure of his achievement became clear. The young physicist had caused the greatest revolution in scientific thinking since Isaac Newton.

Einstein was embarrassed by the sudden glare of publicity surrounding him, but like it or not, he had become a worldwide celebrity. The public regarded him as an unparalleled genius, and his name quickly became a synonym for someone with great intellectual ability.

About nine years after his first work was published, Einstein was invited to join the University of Berlin as Professor of Physics. He remained there for about 20 years. During that time he traveled widely in Europe and the United States on lecture tours, speaking not only on his work but also on social and political

RELATIVITY
THE SPECIAL & THE GENERAL THEORY
A POPULAR EXPOSITION
BY
ALBERT EINSTEIN, Ph.D.
PROFESSOR OF PHYSICS IN THE UNIVERSITY OF BERLIN

AUTHORISED TRANSLATION BY
ROBERT W. LAWSON, D.Sc.
UNIVERSITY OF SHEFFIELD

WITH FIVE DIAGRAMS
AND A PORTRAIT OF THE AUTHOR

METHUEN & CO. LTD.
36 ESSEX STREET W.C.
LONDON

paper, the only laboratory, his own mind. Working completely on his own, Einstein took the first steps toward the formulation of a theory that shook the very foundation of science. He started by looking again at the Michelson-Morley experiment on the speed of light in the

Above: frontispiece of the first English edition (1920) of Einstein's *Relativity: the Special and the General Theory.*

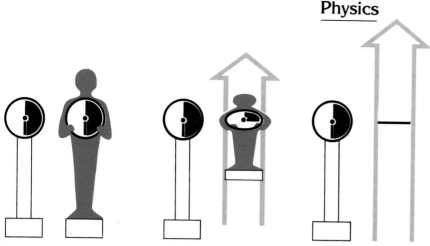

"Einstein is not difficult, only unbelievable."
A consequence of relativity theory is that moving objects should show increase in mass, shrinkage in length and slowing down of time. At the speed of light any object would have infinite mass, zero length and time would stand still – predictions confirmed in the study of high speed (relativistic) particles.

The explanation of gravity as space curvature required that light, like material bodies, should also be affected. Observations during the 1918 solar eclipse showed that starlight passing close by the sun does indeed follow a curved path.

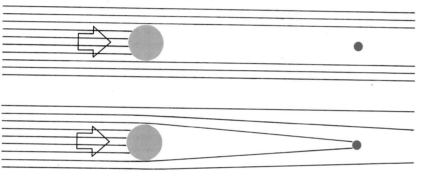

questions. Although he disliked public appearances, he used his name and fame to fight the rise of the Nazis in Germany and to support the establishment of Palestine as a homeland for the Jews. He also backed the pacifist movement and other humanitarian causes.

When the Nazis came to power in 1933, they confiscated his property and took away his German citizenship while he was on a trip abroad. Rejected by his homeland, Einstein was warmly welcomed by the United States. That same year he joined the Institute for Advanced Studies in Princeton, New Jersey, and remained there for the rest of his life.

After he settled in the United States, Einstein came under attack from Hitler himself who said that no Jew could have formulated the Theory of Relativity. The Nazi dictator even suggested that Einstein had stolen the concept from papers carried by a German army officer who had been killed in World War I.

By 1939 American scientists were becoming alarmed that the Relativity Theory could be applied by German scientists to build a devastating new weapon. They based this fear on the aspect of the theory showing that mass could be converted directly to energy, and that a minute piece of mass could release a vast amount of energy. This opened the possibility of an im-

Above center: the estimated passage of starlight before (top) and according to (bottom) the General Theory of Relativity.

Above right: this photograph of Einstein was taken shortly before his death. It was shown at the first *Family of Man* exhibition (1955), at the Museum of Modern Art, New York.

Below right: Voyager space probe to Mars. Planetary space probes, traveling millions of miles, have their journeys programed according to Einstein's equations.

Below: Einstein's equation which states that the energy contained in any particle of matter is equal to the mass of the matter multiplied by the square of the speed of light (186,000 miles per second). As this equation implies, even a tiny amount of a matter would release huge amounts of energy, and it is on this basis that nuclear scientists built the atomic bomb.

mensely powerful new kind of bomb. Under the threat of another world war, American scientists persuaded Einstein to write to President Roosevelt to suggest that the United States develop a counterweapon. Torn between his pacifist beliefs and his deep opposition to Nazi brutality, Einstein agreed – partly because he never expected such weapons to be used except as a deterent. However, his letter led directly to the building of the first atomic bombs and to their use against Japan in 1945, despite Einstein's desperate last-minute appeal that such a devastating weapon should not be dropped.

Einstein spent his last years in semiretirement in Princeton where he continued to work and teach. Respected for his mind and beloved for his gentle humanitarianism, he remained the world's most widely admired scientist until his death.

$$E=mc^2$$

Max von Laue

1879-1960

theoretical physics. By 1903 he had gained a doctorate and was ready to begin a successful academic career.

In 1909, shortly after joining the staff of the University of Munich, von Laue began the research which was to make him internationally famous. Since their discovery in 1895, X-rays had baffled the scientific world. Some researchers argued that the radiation consisted of streams of particles while others held that it was a

German physicist Max von Laue founded the modern science of X-ray crystallography. By demonstrating how a crystal's regular internal structure could be used to bend beams of X-rays to form characteristic diffraction patterns, he not only proved that X-rays were waves much like light but also discovered a means for exploring the make-up of a wide range of crystals and crystalline substances.

The son of an army official, von Laue was born in Pfaffendorf, near Coblenz. His father's work meant that the family rarely lived in one place for more than a few months at a time and Max was educated at a wide range of schools and colleges. But it was in Strasbourg that his interest in science was kindled and in 1899 he entered Strasbourg University to specialize in

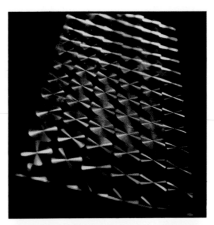

Right: a conventional diffraction grating has a series of fine lines etched onto it. The distance between the lines is comparable to the wavelength of visible light.

Center right: the colored components of white light are reflected by a diffraction grating at different angles, and the rays fan out in a spectrum.

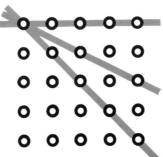

Above: the much shorter wavelength of X-rays compares with the regular distance between atoms in a crystal lattice. At different angles an X-ray beam will encounter the atoms at regular spacings, diffracting in a predictable fashion. Crystal structure can therefore be determined, and almost any science uses X-ray diffraction as a necessary tool.

Right: von Laue (left) with some of his colleagues from the physics department at the University of Munich.

kind of wave, similar to light. Von Laue subscribed to the view that they were waves, like light but of much smaller wavelength, and began to devise an experiment to prove the idea. It had been known for many years that the wavelength of ordinary visible light could be calculated by the way in which it was broken up into patterns of light and dark, called diffraction patterns, using glass gratings in which the etched rules were separated by known distances. The shorter the wavelength of the light, the narrower the spacing between rules had to be to produce this pattern. Von Laue knew that if X-rays were a form of radiation similar to light but of very short wavelength, the grating capable of producing a diffraction pattern would need to be etched with microscopically fine rules. Although at that time no techniques could produce such a grating, it occurred to von Laue that perhaps nature itself could supply one. A crystal consists of layers of atoms spaced as regularly but far more closely than the lines on a man-made grating. Von Laue reasoned that if X-rays were similar in nature to light a beam directed at a crystal target should form a diffraction pattern. Because the "rulings" on the crystal grating were actually lines of atoms in three dimensions, the pattern would be extremely complex, but recorded on a photographic plate it would confirm the nature of X-rays beyond all doubt.

In 1912 von Laue tested his idea using a crystal target of zinc sulfide. The results were a spectacular success. A photographic plate registered a complicated pattern of bright dots – an unmistakable diffraction pattern.

In the years following von Laue's experiment, other scientists seized upon his technique. For the first time the wavelengths of X-rays could be calculated by using target crystals of a known structure and measuring the amount of diffrac-

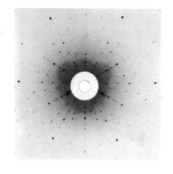

Above: an X-ray diffraction pattern of a single crystal of silicon.
Right: one of the X-ray ionization spectrometers used by William Henry Bragg, and his son William Lawrence Bragg for early crystallographic measurements. The Braggs were pioneers in the study of crystal structure using X-ray diffraction.

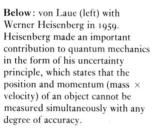

Below: von Laue (left) with Werner Heisenberg in 1959. Heisenberg made an important contribution to quantum mechanics in the form of his uncertainty principle, which states that the position and momentum (mass × velocity) of an object cannot be measured simultaneously with any degree of accuracy.

tion they caused. More important still was the possibility of evaluating the structure of an unknown crystal by analyzing the diffraction pattern formed by X-rays of a known wavelength. This application of von Laue's work made possible major advances in the chemistry of crystals and in recent years has even provided insights into the structure of vital biological molecules such as the nucleic acids.

Von Laue received the Nobel Prize for his work in 1914. Shortly after, he became Professor of Theoretical Physics at Berlin University. He remained there until the early years of World War II when he resigned in protest against the Nazi regime. Not until Hitler's overthrow did he return to academic life, becoming the first postwar director of the Max Planck Institute.

Otto Hahn

1879-1968

The German chemist and physicist Otto Hahn made the vital discovery which led to the development of the first nuclear reactor. Working with his lifelong friend and associate Lise Meitner, he uncovered the process of nuclear fission by which nuclei of atoms of heavy elements can break up into smaller nuclei, in the process releasing large quantities of energy.

Hahn was born in Frankfurt-am-Main and studied science at the University of Marburg. He was a brilliant theoretician but was dogged by a sense of modesty which in later years would lead him to understate or even withhold his most important discoveries. After graduating with a doctorate in science in 1901, Hahn spent a few years working with some of the most distinguished scientists in London and Cambridge, Britain. In 1906, soon after his return to Ger-

A relatively stable uranium 235 nucleus receives an extra neutron, the atom transmuting momentarily into the highly unstable uranium 236.

The nucleus divides explosively ejecting more neutrons which in turn can split other uranium nuclei in the vicinity.

Right: nuclear fission chain reaction. A relatively stable nucleus of a uranium-235 atom accepts an extra neutron which transmutes it for a fraction of a second into the highly unstable isotope uranium-256. The unstable nucleus divides explosively, ejecting more neutrons which can then bombard other uranium atoms in the vicinity.

Center left: Lise Meitner in 1949.

Below: apparatus used by Hahn to demonstrate nuclear fission.

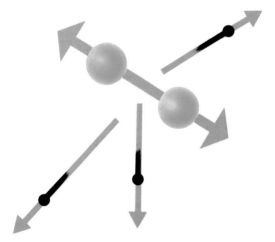

many, he was given the position of director of the prestigious Kaiser Wilhelm Institute for Chemistry.

The early years of his research established Hahn's lifetime interest in atomic structure, especially in the behavior of atomic nuclei. Soon after his appointment at the Kaiser Wilhelm Institute he met the Austrian-born physicist Lise Meitner and they quickly formed a remarkable research partnership which was to last more than 30 years. Meitner's personality was more forceful and she complemented Hahn perfectly. Throughout their joint researches Meitner, full of confidence, would urge on the diffident Hahn and together they made important contributions to our knowledge of atomic nuclei.

Hahn made his most important discovery in 1938 soon after Meitner had been forced to leave Germany and make a new home in Sweden. For

some years he had been studying the way atoms of uranium behaved when bombarded by subatomic particles known as neutrons. He suspected that they were being transmuted into atoms of some other element. Hahn conducted a series of painstaking experiments which finally revealed that a new element was indeed being created, a radioactive form of the metal barium. Hahn realized that something very strange must be taking place. Uranium atoms are extremely heavy, having large nuclei made up of numerous protons and neutrons. These nuclei were evidently being changed by neutron bombardment into atoms of a much lighter element. The only mechanism Hahn could think of to explain this phenomenon was a process by which nuclei of uranium atoms actually broke up to form nuclei of much lighter atoms, at the same time emitting neutrons and a large amount of energy. He called the process "nuclear fission."

If Hahn had been collaborating with Meitner throughout his historic experiments he might have had the confidence to publish his ideas immediately. But the rise to power of the Nazi

Above: the contrasting peaceful and military uses of nuclear power. Right: the Hunterston "A" nuclear power station, in operation since 1964. It has two magnox reactors, each with a generating capacity of three million watts. Left: Hiroshima after the explosion of the "A" bomb, 1945.

Party in Germany had placed Meitner, an Austrian Jew, in a dangerous position. To escape persecution she had left Germany to take refuge in Sweden. Alone, Hahn wavered, unsure of his interpretation of the results and fearing ridicule if he published such a revolutionary theory. Lise Meitner, once more, took the decision for him and from her new home in Stockholm clarified the results and published Hahn's work on fission in a leading scientific journal. It was Meitner who also realized that during the fission process some of the uranium was converted into a vast amount of energy.

Immediately the process of nuclear fission was seized upon as the working principle for a nuclear reactor and the first successful prototype was built in Chicago in 1942 by the Italian-born physicist Enrico Fermi. Hahn was delighted by this first peaceful application of his work, one which held the promise of enormous future benefits for mankind. However, his satisfaction was shattered by the news that the United States was also developing the first fission bombs. In 1945, when atomic bombs were dropped on Japanese cities, Hahn felt a deep sense of responsibility. For a time he could barely live with his guilt and even contemplated suicide. Gradually, however, his feelings hardened into a determination to oppose the further development of nuclear weapons and during the years following World War II until his death in 1968, Hahn was a vociferous opponent of the military use of nuclear technology.

Right: Otto Hahn and Lise Meitner in 1959.

Sir Alexander Fleming

1881-1955

The discovery of penicillin was the result of a laboratory accident, the significance of which was quickly appreciated by Alexander Fleming, a Scottish bacteriologist. As a result he produced the first in a series of antibiotic drugs which revolutionized the treatment of bacterial disease.

Fleming was born in Lochfield, Scotland, the son of a farmer. Medicine was not his first choice of a career, and for four years he worked for a shipping company. He then enrolled at St Mary's Hospital, London, as a medical student, graduating in 1906. He remained at the hospital, though, and specialized in bacteriological research.

During World War I he spent a period as a medical officer in military hospitals. Suppurating wounds were a major problem and Fleming realized that there was a serious need for a bactericidal agent which would deal with the infection without damaging the tissues.

After the war he returned to St Mary's and devoted himself to the problem. In 1928 Fleming was researching into staphylococci, a group of bacteria responsible for, amongst other things, septicemia and abcesses. Returning from a short holiday he found that the glass plate covering one of the cultures had slipped off and the culture had become infected with mold from the atmosphere.

Fleming was about to throw the culture away but decided to give it a quick inspection. He noticed that in the region where the mold was growing the bacterial cells had dissolved. He was particularly struck by the resemblance of the clear regions in the culture to the effect produced by the chemical lysozyme. This agent, discovered by Fleming himself six years earlier in tears and nasal secretions, had mild bactericidal properties.

Above: many fatalities during World War I were due to gangrene and septicemia. Fleming's experiences as a medical officer at that time prompted him to search for an agent to combat the bacteria responsible for infecting wounds.

Opposite: photomicrograph of *Penicillium notatum*, showing the end of a developing sporangium. The antibiotic penicillin is produced from the rounded spores. It diffuses out into the culture medium from which it can then be extracted.

Fleming realized the significance of this would-be accident. The mold, a strain of the fungus *Penicillium*, was secreting a substance which destroyed bacteria. In fact mold had, for centuries, a place in medical folklore, with moldy bread and cobwebs being used for the treatment of festering wounds. However, it had not occurred to any researcher to investigate the scientific basis of this treatment.

Fleming's next step was to try and isolate sufficient quantities of the bactericidal substance, which he called "penicillin." In this he was unsuccessful as penicillin proved to be very unstable and Fleming lacked the chemical resources to overcome this.

Ten years passed and World War II broke out. Once again scientists began to search for germ-killing agents to deal with infected wounds.

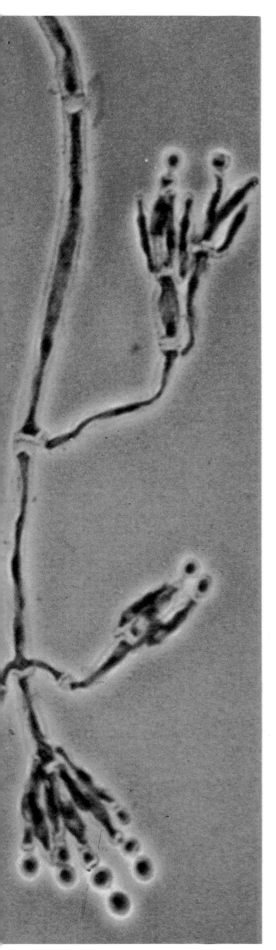

Fleming's original paper on penicillin was rediscovered by Howard Florey, an Australian-born pathologist, and Ernst Chain, a German biochemist. At the time both were working at Oxford University, where there happened to be some samples of penicillin available. They researched further into the drug and succeeded in stabilizing its structure. The also found that it was completely harmless to the tissues and that it needed to be administered over a period of several days to have any effect because it was rapidly excreted by the body. In 1940, a policeman suffering from acute blood poisoning was

Above: an antibiotic at work. Cells of *Staphylococcus aureus*, the bacterium responsible for many inflammatory and septic infections, are shown before and 20 minutes after treatment with cloaxillin, a penicillin derivative.

Above right: a mock-up of Fleming's original culture.

Below: antibiotics are medicine's most potent tool against infectious disease. This picture shows an Indian girl before and after treatment with the antibiotic aureomycin for trachoma – an eye disease that affects some 400 million people.

the first patient to be treated with the drug. His rapid recovery was the go-ahead for mass production of penicillin, in which the United States led the way.

Other fungi were also found to produce anti-bacterial substances, and the word "antibiotic" was coined to describe penicillin and penicillin-like drugs. Penicillin and its derivatives proved to be one of the most useful drugs known to man. For their work in this field, Fleming, Florey, and Chain received, in 1945, the Nobel Prize for Medicine.

Shortly before his death from a heart attack, Fleming said "Everywhere I go people want to thank me for saving their lives. I really don't know why they do that. Nature created penicillin. I only found it."

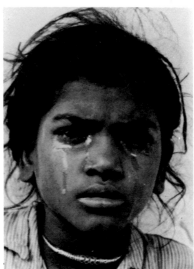

Robert Hutchings Goddard

1882-1945

Robert Goddard was one of the pioneers of the space age. His invention of the first liquid-fueled rocket led directly to the huge boosters that have in recent years blasted astronauts, space stations, and satellites into orbit around the earth.

Goddard's childhood was spent in Boston, Massachusetts. Frequent illnesses and a weak constitution left him plenty of time for thought and in those early years Goddard's unique imagination returned repeatedly to the concept of manned flight into space. He was convinced that the technology could be created to enable man to travel to the stars. But Goddard was not merely an idle dreamer. He studied engineering and physics, and was awarded a doctorate in 1911. Armed with a deep knowledge of physics

he returned to his childhood ideas of space flight, determined to make them reality. He studied all the available writings on the subject and in 1919 published a short textbook called *A Method of Reaching Extreme Altitudes* which was to become a classic. In it he argued that the way into space was through the use of rocket boosters.

Goddard's breakthrough came in the early 1920s. Rockets powered by gunpowder had been used for centuries. On the whole, they were unreliable and inefficient, certainly quite impractical for launching heavy payloads into space. Goddard decided to try a new fuel source and hit upon the idea of using a liquid. His idea was to build two fuel tanks, one containing gasoline, the other liquid oxygen. If the contents of the two were combined and ignited in a specially reinforced chamber, a tremendous rocket thrust would be produced by the expanding gases generated by the burning mixture.

In 1926, in an open field on his aunt's farm in Auburn, Massachusetts, Goddard tested the first liquid-propellant rocket. The launcher was a simple frame made from water pipes. The rocket itself was about four feet high and six inches in diameter. To ignite it, Goddard used a blow torch on the end of a long pipe. The first test was an unqualified success and in 1929, after securing a small grant from the Smithsonian Institution, Goddard launched a larger rocket

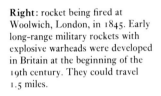

Right: rocket being fired at Woolwich, London, in 1845. Early long-range military rockets with explosive warheads were developed in Britain at the beginning of the 19th century. They could travel 1.5 miles.

Below: Goddard posing beside the world's first liquid propellant rocket, which he designed and built in 1926. His launch assembly was a remarkably simple structure made from lengths of medium-bore water piping. The launch site was an open space on his aunt's farm in Massachusetts.

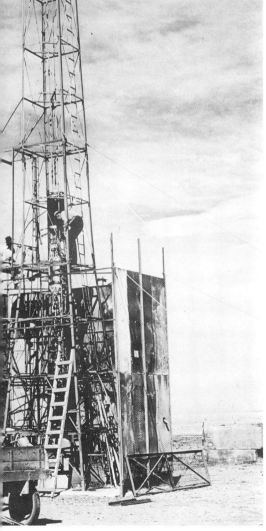

Above: Goddard (left) with three of his assistants at work on a rocket with the casing removed, in their workshop at Roswell, New Mexico.

Left: much of Goddard's later work was done privately in New Mexico, where he launched a rocket that reached a record height of 7500 feet.

containing a barometer, thermometer, and a small camera.

But Goddard's pioneering work was not appreciated by more than a handful of admirers. Most people regarded him as a crank and were alarmed by his noisy experiments. His second successful launch led to a public outcry and the state police ordered him to stop his experiments. For a few years it seemed to Goddard that his research would have to be abandoned.

Fortunately the flying ace Charles Lindbergh was interested in Goddard's ideas and managed to obtain funds for Goddard to continue his research. From a lonely site in the New Mexico desert Goddard spent years of patient research, testing and refining designs for new combustion systems and sophisticated guidance devices to control the course of the rocket. In the course of his experiments his rockets reached altitudes of 8000 feet; by 1935 he was shooting rockets faster than the speed of sound. Working alone and in complete isolation, Goddard perfected many of the techniques that are now a fundamental part of modern rocketing.

Sadly for Goddard, the American government ignored his work. While German rocket scientists in the 1940s were financed on a vast scale to develop the V-2 rocket bomb, Goddard was enlisted to design small boosters to help navy planes lift off the decks of aircraft carriers. Only in 1945, when victorious American troops entered the German rocket base at Peenemünde did the American government's interest in rockets stir. But by then, his work unrecognized, America's greatest rocket expert was dying of throat cancer in a Baltimore hospital.

Niels Bohr

1885-1962

The early 1900s were years of rapid progress in research on the inner structure of the atom. The Danish physicist Niels Bohr made one of the most important breakthroughs of the time by proposing the first model of the atom to incorporate the ideas of quantum physics. Bohr's work explained many natural phenomena, in particular the way in which atoms emit light in a characteristic spectrum of wavelengths. Even today much of the understanding of the atom is based upon Bohr's picture of its structure.

The son of a physiology professor, Bohr grew up in Copenhagen in an atmosphere of learning where scholarly interests were a natural part of home life. But although determined to follow his father in an academic career, Bohr still found time for less serious pursuits. As a young man he was an excellent soccer player and retained a lively interest in sport throughout his life. Bohr obtained his doctorate in theoretical physics

from the University of Copenhagen in 1911 and spent the following five years on a research scholarship at Cambridge University. There he met Ernest Rutherford and under the great man's influence became deeply interested in the structure of the atom. By 1913 he had devised a radical new theory which was to make him internationally famous.

Bohr was impressed by Rutherford's idea of the atom as a kind of miniature solar system with a positively charged nucleus around which orbited negatively charged electrons. A major flaw, however, was that by the known laws of physics, electrically charged particles moving in circles should emit electromagnetic radiation, lose energy, and spiral inward to the center. If Rutherford's solar system model was to be tenable, a new mechanism for the way electrons emitted energy had to be worked out.

Opposite page, above left: the atom of uranium as pictured by modern physicists. The nucleus contains 92 protons with 143 neutrons (uranium-235) or 146 neutrons (uranium-238). There are 92 electrons circling the nucleus in orbits which may be regarded as seven shells containing (from the nucleus) 2, 8, 18, 32, 21, 9, and 2 electrons.

Right: Bohr's view of the atom improved upon Rutherford's version in that the electrons circling the nucleus had defined orbits.

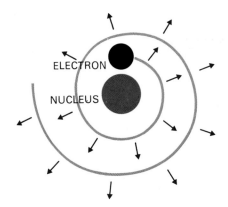

Like balls set circling in a cone, electrons in Rutherford's atom would spiral inwards losing energy continuously.

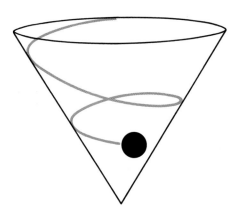

ELECTRON

NUCLEUS

Bohr took hydrogen as his example. It was the simplest atom known, with a single positive charge on its nucleus and a solitary electron orbiting it. Bohr then asserted that so long as the atom was in its lowest energy state – Bohr called it the "ground state" – the electron would not emit energy and could therefore continue orbiting the nucleus indefinitely. However, the electron could occupy any of the several possible orbits, each representing a different energy level in the atom. If energy was fed into the atom, the

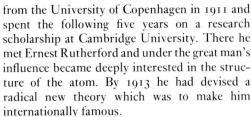

electron could "jump up" to an orbit of higher energy than the ground state. If then left to itself the electron would jump back down the energy levels until it reached its ground state again. As it did this it would shed energy, mainly as light in packets, or quanta, just as Max Planck had predicted in his quantum theory. The size of the quanta – and consequently the

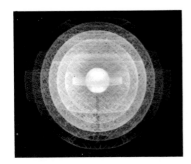

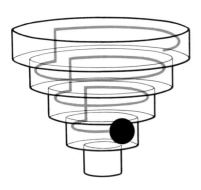

In Bohr's fixed orbits atom, electrons behave like balls in a "stepped" cone, following a series of circular tracks separated by jumps; atoms losing energy do so in fixed units, called "quanta."

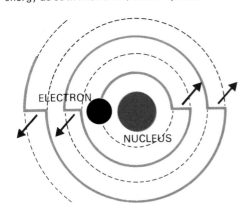

Above right: the annual gathering at the Institute of Theoretical Physics, of which Bohr became director in 1920. In the front row, reading from left to right, are Wolfgang Pauli, Pascual Jordan, Werner Heisenberg, Max Born, Lise Meitner, Otto Stern, and James Franck.

Center right: Bohr (second from right) receiving the Honorary Diploma of Lomonossow University, Moscow.

wavelength of the light – would depend on the differences in the levels of energy through which the electron had jumped down on its way back to its ground state.

Bohr's concept of specific energy levels within the atom is today a cornerstone of atomic theory. In 1913 it was a revolutionary new idea to which many scientists were openly skeptical. The justification of his work, however, lay in the accurate explanation it provided for the spectrum of light emitted by hydrogen. In 1922 he was awarded the Nobel Prize for Physics and although his work was refined and modified in later years, Bohr has continued to be regarded as one of the founders of modern atomic theory.

In 1940 Bohr's fame became a deadly threat to his freedom. When the Nazis invaded Denmark, Bohr was seen as a potentially valuable addition to the atomic research efforts of Hitler's Third Reich. Like most of his countrymen Bohr loathed everything the Nazis stood for and repeatedly risked arrest and imprisonment by defying them. By 1943, he knew he could avoid arrest no longer, and decided to flee to Sweden. His Nobel medal was to precious to risk on his escape attempt, so before setting out he dissolved it in a bottle of acid and hid the bottle securely in his apartment. Years later he returned to his homeland, reclaimed the gold from the acid, and had the medal recast.

John Logie Baird
1888-1946

The television of today was the result of many inventors, both amateur and professional. It was the Scots inventor, John Logie Baird, however, who achieved the first live television transmission in his attic workshop in 1925. The following year he demonstrated the world's first working television system to a meeting of the Royal Institution in London.

Once Guglielmo Marconi had demonstrated, in the late 1890s, that sound could be conveyed by radio waves, it was only a question of time

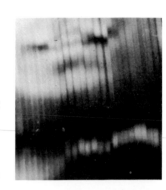

rudimentary apparatus which was constructed from an old tea chest, a cake tin, pieces of electrical equipment rescued from scrap, some knitting needles, a bicycle lamp, wires, string, and sealing wax. The vital component was a cardboard Nipkow disk.

On October 2, 1925, in his attic, Baird succeeded in transmitting a recognizable image of the head of a discarded ventriloquist's dummy called "Bill." He at once ran down to the office on the ground floor and persuaded a startled office boy to come upstairs with him. The boy, sitting under the bright lamps, became the first

before an equivalent system would be found to transmit a visual image. John Logie Baird, born at Helensburgh in Scotland and educated at Larchfield Academy in Glasgow, was an amateur scientist and an enthusiast with single-minded determination. He was convinced that the basis of a working broadcasting television system lay in the scanning disk invented in 1884 by the German scientist Paul Nikow.

After leaving Glasgow University, Baird earned a living as a shoe-polish and razor-blade salesman, while trying to attract commercial backing for his ideas. Unfortunately the new electrical companies could see little point to or profit in such a novelty. Baird therefore used his own meagre earnings to continue his research, and often found himself in extreme poverty. In 1924 he realized that he was on the right track when he successfully transmitted the silhouette of a Maltese cross over a distance of more than 10 feet. He continued to experiment with his

Above center: 30-line scan of the human face.

Above left: Baird with his transmitting equipment.

Above right: Baird at his transmitting station, using a disk based on Paul Nipkow's design to send an image of a face.

living image to be transmitted by television. Overnight Baird became famous, and the money which he desperately needed to continue his research was at last made available. In 1927 he made a transmission from London to Glasgow, and in 1928 one from London to New York.

As it turned out, the Baird "mechanical" system remained simply a stage, if a vital one, in the development of television technology. Its significance was that it stimulated the next phase of technical design. Beyond a certain point, the flickering images produced by the Nipkow disk could not be appreciably improved upon. The aged Nipkow, brought out of obscurity to see the German version of Baird's invention, remarked himself that the television, as it stood then, needed technological rethinking. This was to come with the development of the electronic scanner, which in principle existed already.

The cathode-ray oscilloscope, in which a beam of electrons passes through a tube filled with

Communication

fluorescent gas and forms an image where it strikes the screen at the far end, was invented in 1897 by the German physicist Karl Ferdinand Braun to aid his study of electric impulses. This, in turn, had been developed from the Crookes tube designed by British physicist William Crookes. The cathode-ray oscilloscope became the basis of the first television scanner or camera, the iconoscope, for which the Russian-born inventor, Vladimir Zworykin took out patent specifications in 1923, four years after he arrived as an immigrant in the United States. The next year he patented the kinescope, which

Below: Zworykin's inconoscope. Light from the scene (red) is focused onto photosensitive elements which become charged in direct proportion to the light they receive. They are then scanned with the electron beam (blue). This converts the brightness of each element into an electric signal.

acted as the receiver for the iconoscope. So in fact the first electronic television system already existed on paper at the time of Baird's breakthrough. Despite a lack of commercial interest Zworykin continued to improve his design, and in 1929 had built a working demonstration model.

The visual definition of the electronic television was far superior to the mechanical system, and Zworykin's work laid the foundation on which all modern television systems are

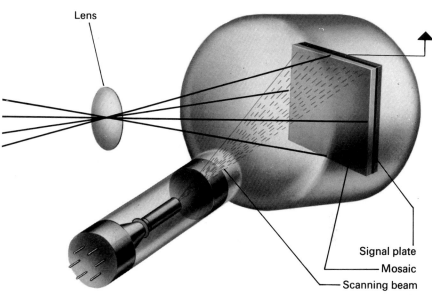

Lens

Signal plate
Mosaic
Scanning beam

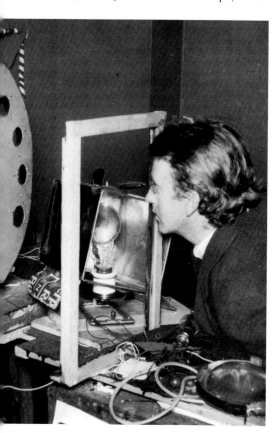

Below left: Baird's 30-line electromechanical televisor, completed about 1928. It was the first television receiver commercially available to the public, and was used briefly by the British Broadcasting Corporation in their experimental broadcasts.

Below right: Baird demonstrating his latest advance in color television. He successfully produced color-television pictures in 1929.

constructed. He also made important early developments in color television, as well as the electron microscope and various infrared devices for seeing in the dark. Baird, the restless genius, saw his own television system come into use in Britain and Germany and then lose out to the electronic version. Undeterred, he continued experimenting, and his last years were spent exploring the possibilities of color and stereoscopic television and the projection of television images onto cinema screens.

Igor Ivanovich Sikorsky

1889-1972

The Russian-born American aeronautical engineer Igor Sikorsky was one of the most important pioneers in aviation. He built the world's first four-engined aircraft and in the 1930s played a leading role in developing amphibious aircraft. He is best known, however, as the foremost contributor to the development of the helicopter.

Sikorsky was born at Kiev, Soviet Union, the son of a psychology professor at Kiev University. He became a naval officer cadet in 1903, but resigned three years later to pursue his true vocation – engineering. In the course of his

studies he traveled to Europe where he first learnt about the European developments in aviation which were following in the wake of the Wright brothers' pioneering flights of 1903.

Sikorsky had a firm belief that the future development of aircraft lay in vertical flight. On his return to his homeland he set about designing a helicopter. This was not his first attempt. At the age of 12 he had built a working toy helicopter with a rubber drive, taking as his source of inspiration a drawing of Leonardo da Vinci's helicopter model. He built two experimental helicopters with twin rotary blades, but they lacked sufficient lifting power to raise any weight additional to their own.

Realizing that the technology and materials did not as yet exist, Sikorsky postponed the idea of a working helicopter, and turned his energies toward building and improving conventional fixed-wing aircraft. In 1912 he was appointed chief designer to the new aircraft design division of the Baltic Railway Car Factory, Leningrad, and a year later he built the *Le Grande*, one of

the most extraordinary of early airplanes. This giant aircraft had a 92-foot wingspan and four engines, and was 10 years ahead of its time in incorporating an enclosed cabin area for crew and passengers. It was the predecessor of modern commercial aircraft and bombers.

With Russia's involvement in World War I, Sikorsky built a series of similar planes for military use. For a time he was the only man in Russia capable of flying his own invention, so

Below: Sikorsky at the controls of one of his earlier helicopters.

found himself also acting as test pilot and chief instructor. In all, 75 of these huge machines were built, and they flew according to Sikorsky himself like "something out of Jules Verne."

With the general disruption of the October Revolution of 1917 and the collapse of Germany, Sikorsky saw little future for aircraft development in Europe and left for the United States, arriving in New York in 1919 with a minimal amount of capital.

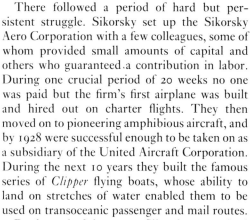

There followed a period of hard but persistent struggle. Sikorsky set up the Sikorsky Aero Corporation with a few colleagues, some of whom provided small amounts of capital and others who guaranteed a contribution in labor. During one crucial period of 20 weeks no one was paid but the firm's first airplane was built and hired out on charter flights. They then moved on to pioneering amphibious aircraft, and by 1928 were successful enough to be taken on as a subsidiary of the United Aircraft Corporation. During the next 10 years they built the famous series of *Clipper* flying boats, whose ability to land on stretches of water enabled them to be used on transoceanic passenger and mail routes.

By the end of the 1930s, Sikorsky recognized that, with the advent of larger airports with longer runways and a new generation of long-range aircraft, the era of the flying boat was ending. He returned to the helicopter, three decades after his initial experiments. By this time research into aerodynamics and new materials had made the idea of a working heli-

copter feasible. One of the major innovations in this period had been the autogiro, invented in 1928 by the Spanish aeronautical engineer, Juan de la Cierva. The autogiro received an initial forward thrust from a conventional propeller in the nose of the engine, and was then lifted upward by rotating rotor blades. However, it could not hover.

A helicopter was developed by the Focke-Achgelis Company in Germany in 1937, so the prototype which Sikorsky built and flew in 1939 was not the world's first. In addition to being able to hover, ascend and land vertically, and fly backwards and sideways, the Sikorsky VS-300 was, however, the first successful single-rotor helicopter, from which all further developments in this field of aviation have grown. He built an improved version in 1941, but during World War II all plans were placed on one side. In 1945 he began work again, and in fact spent the rest of his life on helicopter design and the advantages which followed from the principles of vertical lift and hovering.

In the years following World War II the helicopter proved to be indispensible in many types of rescue and relief operations. With its ability to hover it also added a new dimension to the military technology and played a leading role in the Vietnam war. Its inventor will always remain one of the outstanding innovators in the history of aeronautics.

Left: Sikorsky's first four-engined aircraft, *Le Grande*, showing the balcony, pilot's cabin, and inboard engines.

Below right: a Sikorsky helicopter airlifts a fully loaded truck as part of a New York Civil Defense exercise.

Sir James Chadwick

1891-1974

The British physicist James Chadwick is best known for his discovery of the neutron. One of the fundamental particles making up the nucleus of atoms, the neutron differed from all other particles then known by having no electrical charge. In later years this property enabled it to be used as a subatomic "bullet" to probe into the interior of atoms. Unaffected by the positive and negative electrical charges of the atom, the neutron not only revealed important new insights into nuclear structure but also provided scientists with a valuable tool for further research into the atom.

Born and brought up in Manchester, Chadwick studied physics at his local university. After graduating in 1911 he went to Cambridge where he worked under the distinguished New Zealand-born physicist Ernest Rutherford. Encouraged by Rutherford, Chadwick began the research into atomic structure which was to become a lifelong interest and which would eventually make him internationally famous. A scholarship enabled him to travel in Europe and while he was in Germany World War I was declared. Chadwick was refused permission to leave Germany and was eventually interned as an enemy alien until the end of the war. Despite this setback, Chadwick was determined to continue his research and by 1919 he was back in Cambridge working with Rutherford.

Despite intensive work by scientists throughout the 1920s, the theory explaining the atom's structure was still unsatisfactory. Following Rutherford's solar system model, attention had been concentrated on the structure of the nucleus around which the electrons were thought to orbit. It was believed to consist of positively charged protons held together by a kind of "glue" of negatively charged electrons. According to this theory, the helium nucleus for example, with a mass of four and a charge of two, consisted of four protons and two electrons. The negative charge of the electrons supposedly neutralized two of the positive charges on the protons giving the correct mass and charge characteristics. But there were major theoretical objections to the theory and Chadwick helped to lead the search for an electrically neutral particle which would provide a simpler and more elegant theory.

In 1932 Chadwick was investigating the intense radiation given off when the metal beryllium was bombarded by alpha particles (helium nuclei). He showed that the beryllium

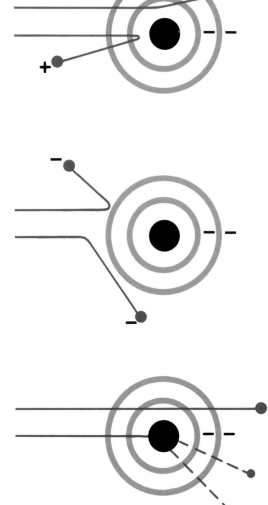

Opposite page, above: the seventh Solvay Physics Conference, 1933. Chadwick is in the seated row, on the extreme right. Other participants included Frédéric and Irène Joliot-Curie, Marie Curie, Lord Rutherford, Niels Bohr, John Douglas Cockcroft, Ernest Walton, Enrico Fermi, Louis de Broglie, Werner Heisenberg, Lise Meitner, and Erwin Shrödinger.

Right: the suitability of the neutron as a projectile in exploring the atom's core. Like charges repel each other, unlike charges attract. If a particle with a positive charge such as an alpha particle is used it tends to be deflected by the nucleus (top). If a negatively charged particle is used it will be deflected by the outer electron shell (center). The chargeless neutron pierces the electromagnetic defenses of the atom (bottom) and ejects particles out of the nucleus, enabling scientists to make deductions about its composition.

emitted secondary particles which, in turn, displaced protons from a nearby target of hydrocarbon wax. Chadwick performed complicated calculations which showed that this behavior could be explained by assuming that the alpha particles were ejecting neutral particles, of a similar mass to protons, from the nuclei of the beryllium atoms. Had the particles been charged, they would have been absorbed by the protons in the hydrocarbon wax. He called this new particle the "neutron."

Chadwick's discovery was a major breakthrough and the neutron soon proved to be a valuable tool in research. Because it carries no electrical charge, it is undeflected by electrical fields and as it has slightly more mass a proton (therefore, by subatomic particle standards it is massive) it is a particularly effective means of probing deep inside atoms. Physicists bombarding target atoms with beams of neutrons can penetrate their interiors far more deeply than ever before. The study of the neutron soon lead to the discovery of nuclear fission and the first nuclear reactor. Moreover, the discovery of the neutron provided a straightforward explanation of the structure of atomic nuclei. The helium nucleus, for example, could now be regarded as being made up of two protons and two neutrons.

Chadwick received the Nobel Prize for Physics in 1935. Although he continued his academic career, becoming Professor of Physics at Liver-

Below left: the helium atom's nucleus is composed of two protons and two neutrons, with its net positive charge balanced by a pair of electrons.

Below right: the use of neutrons in atomic fission led to the production of the atomic bomb.

pool University and receiving a knighthood in 1945, he made few other major contributions to science. His single discovery was sufficient to win him worldwide reknown providing as it did a remarkable new insight into the structure of the atomic nucleus and an important tool for tapping its vast energies.

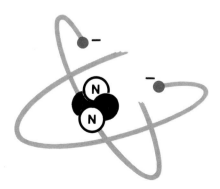

Louis-Victor de Broglie

born 1892

in Paris to study history and it was not until his graduation that he began to concentrate on science. During World War I he served as a radio engineer and later grew increasingly more interested in theoretical physics. He then broke with family tradition and chose to do his doctorate in theoretical physics. His thesis, published in 1924, was a work of brilliant insight which had resounding effects on fundamental scientific thinking.

The French physicist Louis de Broglie was the first to suggest that matter, usually thought of as solid and well-defined, could also show the characteristics of a wave, much like light. His idea of "matter waves" anticipated some of the most important advances in modern physics, especially in atomic and nuclear structure. In particular, it led directly to a new understanding of subatomic particles such as electrons, protons, and neutrons, which in certain circumstances behave in ways apparently contrary to common sense. By attributing a dual nature to them so that sometimes they act as waves and at other times as solid particles, scientists could at last begin to explain their strange behavior.

De Broglie was born in Dieppe, Seine-Marne, of affluent and aristocratic parents. For generations the de Broglie family had served French kings in the military and diplomatic services. The French revolution had been a dangerous time for them and at least one de Broglie died at the guillotine. In the late 1800s, however, they were still regarded as one of the most important French families. Louis enjoyed a sophisticated and scholarly home life and cultivated a wide range of interests. He enrolled at the Sorbonne

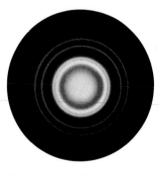

Above center: diffraction rings formed by electrons passing through a film of gold, demonstrating their wavelike nature.

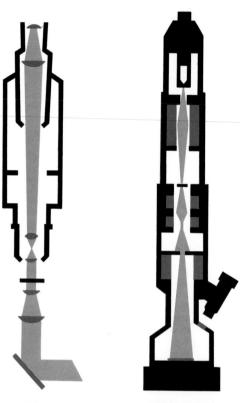

Below center: Clinton Davisson. In 1927 he accidentally discovered that electron beams could produce diffraction patterns and thus confirmed de Broglie's hypothesis.

Above right: comparative optics of light (left) and electron (right) microscopes. The difference in resolving power of light and electron microscopes is analogous to the difference in clarity of photographs printed with coarse and fine dots, as in the two portraits of de Broglie shown here.

Like most young theoreticians, de Broglie was fascinated by Albert Einstein's theory of relativity and the quantum theory worked out by Max Planck. These two major theories had revolutionized physics, though in the early 1920s their full implications were only dimly realized. In particular Einstein had shown that light could sometimes behave like a hail of tiny particles. De Broglie considered the possibility that if waves could behave like particles then perhaps particles could behave like waves. By a series of complex

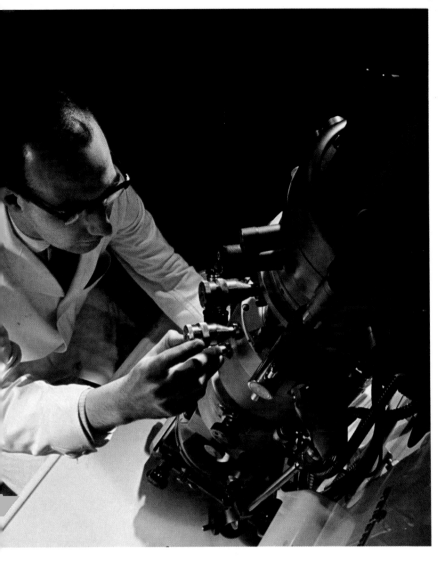

considered as tiny solid particles were somehow behaving as "matter waves."

The verification of de Broglie's strange-sounding ideas brought him international acclaim and a well-deserved Nobel Prize for Physics. But while de Broglie had provided the initial insight, it was left to other scientists to develop the implications of his work more fully. The Austrian physicist Erwin Schrödinger founded the science of wave mechanics and developed a series of equations which described the behavior of a wave. His wave equations became widely used to provide extremely accurate descriptions of electron movement and energy. Soon atomic structure was being described in terms of matter waves and far more precise theories of how matter is constructed were possible. Sweeping advances in science, however, still left an unsolved philosophical problem. If an electron behaves like a particle when we examine it in one way, and a wave when we look at it in another, what is it when we are not studying it at all? It is a mystery as yet unsolved.

The new concept of matter waves made several major practical advances possible. One of its earliest applications was in microscopy. Ordinary optical microscopes are limited by the size of objects that light can define sharply. The resolving power of a beam depends on its wavelength, and the shorter the wavelength, the smaller the distance that can be resolved. Once scientists realized that electrons have a wavelength much shorter than visible light, they immediately began investigating the possibility of building a microscope using an electron beam focused by magnetic fields which acted as lenses. In 1937, in Canada, James Hillier and Albert Prebus built

mathematical deductions he found that it was indeed possible to describe the momentum of a solid particle in terms of a wavelength, a quantity normally associated with waves like light or sound. The wavelike nature of the electron also accounted for the hitherto unexplained restrictions on its movements as it orbited the nucleus of the atom.

Studying the mathematics more deeply, de Broglie saw that the wavelength associated with any sizeable body such as a football would be undetectably small. But for tiny particles such as electrons, the wavelengths would be comparable to the wavelength of X-rays and should therefore be detectable by such phenomena as interference and diffraction patterns.

In 1927 de Broglie's hypothesis was vindicated. Quite by chance, while working on electron beams, American physicists Clinton Davisson and Lester Germer noticed that under certain conditions the beams would produce complicated patterns on photographic plates. To their astonishment, further examination showed the patterns were due to electron-beam diffraction, a phenomenon exclusively associated with waves. There was no doubt that the electrons, usually

Above: an electron microscope. The electrons are emitted from heated metal and accelerated by a high voltage in a vacuum. They are focused by powerful magnets.

Right: electron micrograph of silicone rubber cast from Apollo astronaut's helmet. The blunt spikes are casts of cosmic ray tracks.

the first practical instrument. While the best optical microscope of their day could magnify 2000 times, their prototype had a magnification of 7000. Today the most powerful electron microscopes can magnify up to 2,000,000 times, revealing the surface structure of particles as tiny viruses and even giving glimpses of the patterns of molecules.

Sir Robert Watson-Watt
1892-1973

Although the principles of radar have been developed by a long series of scientists, it was the Scotsman Robert Watson-Watt who made it practicable. The need to detect enemy aircraft during World War II provided the actual impetus for research into radar, especially its ability to detect the location, height, and speed of a target. Radar played an important role in the Allied victory over Germany in 1945 and it has subsequently found many nonmilitary applications.

Watson-Watt was born in Brechin, Scotland. He was educated locally and took an engineering degree at University College, Dundee. As a student he developed an interest in radio telegraphy, and in 1915 became a research scientist at the London Meteorological Office. With the increasing use of aircraft, approaching thunderstorms had become a matter of concern, and Watson-Watt was given a project to locate developing storms by radio. In 1921 he supervized two government radio research stations, and then headed the National Physical Laboratory's radio section, where he worked on radio beacons and navigational equipment – aspects of radio technology in which the Air Ministry was taking an increasing interest during these years.

The word "radar" is an acronym of RAdio Detection And Ranging. It works on the principle of radio waves being bounced back as echoes when they hit an obstacle. The distance of the obstacle, usually termed the target, determines the time the echo takes to reach the receiver. In nature bats use a similar system for navigating. The target is scanned by an antenna, and the echoes are usually displayed on a cathode-ray tube. Radar research can be traced to the discovery of electromagnetic waves. Even so, it was not until the 1930s, when the military potential of radar was realized, that practical work was intensified in the United States, France, Germany, and Britain.

Initially the signals were transmitted in a continuous wave. The disadvantage of continuous-wave radar was that it could detect the presence of an object but not its location. One of the most important developments was the introduction of pulsed radar, in operation by 1936. The changes in time between the echoes indicated the direction and speed of the target. Pulsed radar also had the advantage of being able to dispense with separate signalling and receiver components. A device called a duplexer automatically switched the antenna from transmission to reception as required.

Britain's obvious vulnerability to air attack made the development of radar a priority and Watson-Watt's research attracted generous government funds. In due course he was appointed scientific adviser to the Air Ministry and the Ministry of Aircraft Production. By 1935 he had developed a long-range radar system which could detect advancing aircraft over a range of

Right: painting of a coastal fighter direction radar station (Type 16) during World War II.

Below: a picture of London Airport recorded on a radar screen. Radar provided an electronic eye which sees independently of visible light. Its use is invaluable in aircraft at night or during fog.

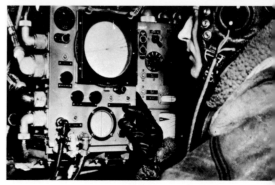

Right: cathode-ray tube and controls of the H28 radar system in operation in an aircraft during World War II.

40 miles. By 1938 a whole network of defensive radar stations had been established.

The next decisive advance in radar came in 1939 with the introduction of the first practical high-power microwave transmitter, the multi-cavity magnetron. It was this top-secret invention which gave Britain a lead in radar research at a critical stage. The very short radio wave, the microwave, can be focused into a narrow beam with highly accurate sighting, and can operate efficiently in both cloud and fog. Microwave radar also had the advantage that it could be transmitted and picked up by much smaller antennae, thus opening up the possibility of portable radar. During the Battle of Britain ground-control intercept radar enabled the British Royal Air Force to deploy its outnumbered force of fighter planes to maximum effect. Before long the German air force was confined to night-time bombing, at which point microwave aircraft-intercept radar was installed in the British

Above: the conspicuous bulge on the underside of this Lancaster bomber contains the scanner for the H25 radar system.

After the war, radar continued to find applications, in addition to its uses in military technology. It plays an invaluable role in marine, aircraft, satellite, and rocket navigation. Tornadoes, hurricanes, and storms can be spotted at a distance of over 200 miles. Traffic policemen equipped with radar can gauge the speed of passing vehicles. Radar has also been used to explore the surfaces of other planets and to provide accurate measurements of distances between planets. Watson-Watt has been called "the father of radar," and it was certainly his pioneering achievements which have made radar such a versatile tool.

Below: the giant radio telescope at the Mullard Radio Observatory, Cambridge, Britain. The dish aerials are used to pick up signals from, and measure the distances of, other bodies in the solar system.

fighter planes themselves, enabling them to engage targets in the dark. Radar came into its own again later on in 1944 as part of the counter-strategy to Germany's launching of the V-1 and V-2 rockets. It enabled some V-1s to be intercepted, and the trajectory of the flights of the V-2s to be plotted back to their launching sites. Radar was used during the D-Day landings in Normandy in 1944 to direct attacks against German defence installations, and in the Allied bombing raids over Germany in the war's closing stages.

Wallace Hume Carothers

1896-1937

The du Pont research chemist, Wallace Hume Carothers, invented nylon, the first true man-made fiber. Its manufacture was the starting point of the synthetic textile industry which grew up after World War II, revolutionizing fashion and industrial fabrics.

The first artificial fiber was made from nitro-cellulose by the British chemist Sir Joseph Swan as a byproduct of his research to develop a filament for the electric-light bulb. Swan's technique was reproduced by a French chemist, Hilaire Bernigaud de Chardonnet. The cellulose solution was squeezed through minute holes, and it formed fibers which could be twisted into threads. These were then treated chemically to make them less flammable. The resulting fabric was initially named artificial or Chardonnet silk. It was later renamed rayon because of its shine.

Various types of rayon were developed, but it was never a fully satisfactory substitute for silk. It was still relatively expensive to produce and inflammable. It was after World War I that a serious search began for a product that would retain or improve upon the qualities of silk while being cheap to manufacture. For the United States it became an especially important objec-

tive as trade and political relations with Japan, the world's leading supplier of natural silk, began to deteriorate.

The search focused on polymers. These substances were formed by combining two or more molecules, called monomers, into long chains of much larger molecules. The polymerization process was being widely developed at the time

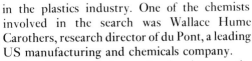

Above: the nylon molecule is built up from repeating units of carbon, hydrogen, and oxygen atoms. Individual molecules consist of 100 or more units similar to the one shown here. Filaments of nylon contain a million or more molecules, each taking some of the strain when the filament is pulled.

Above right: the birth of a completely synthetic fiber. Chemist Julian Hill of E I du Pont de Nemours and Co Inc shows how molten material was pulled from a test tube at Wilmington, Delaware, in the early 1930s. The molasses-like material stuck to the glass rod and was drawn into a thin fiber – the forerunner of nylon.

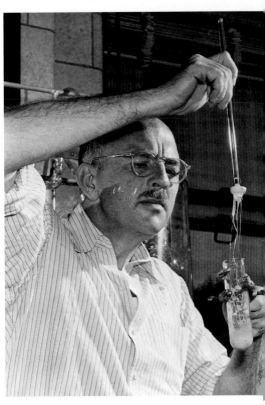

in the plastics industry. One of the chemists involved in the search was Wallace Hume Carothers, research director of du Pont, a leading US manufacturing and chemicals company.

Carothers studied organic chemistry at the universities of Illinois and Harvard before being appointed to his research directorship at the age of 32. His speciality was polymerization – a chemical process which he first came across while researching into the molecular structure of perfumes. During the early 1930s he developed a polymer called "nylon" by combining adipic acid with an amine, hexamethylene diamine. The first fibers he produced, however, turned out to be weak. The polymer was formed by what is known as a condensation reaction in which the individual molecules joined together with the elimination of water. Carothers discovered that the water droplets, falling back into the reacting solution, inhibited the polymerization process. He changed the arrangement of his equipment so that vaporized water could be distilled onto cold glass and removed. Having perfected the technique in 1935 he produced the first nylon threads by melting the polymer and forcing it through spinnerets in a similar way to the manufacture of rayon fibers.

Unlike rayon, which was made from a chemically-treated natural product, nylon was derived entirely from chemicals. It was thus the first man-made fiber. Highly elastic and very strong it had industrial as well as clothing potential. Nylon fabric was found to be resistant to grease, dirt, and many detergents.

Initially Carother's invention was kept an industrial secret. He himself suffered from a

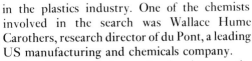

Right: the extrusion process was also used to produce this 18-inch-diameter pipe being laid by these workmen. The solid resin was pushed through a heating chamber and the molten material forced through openings of the required diameter.

improving upon natural fabrics. They do not shrink and are resistant to moth and mildew. In general they are hard-wearing and can be mixed with natural fibers to improve the latter's wearing qualities and crease-resistance. On the other hand, when required, permanent creases can be heat-impressed in man-made fabrics for pleating and the like. In addition to clothing and furnishing, they have found a wide application as industrial materials.

Below: rolls of nylon yarn at Imperial Chemical Industries.

severe depressive illness and committed suicide two years after completing his research. The next year du Pont publicly announced their plans to put the new fiber into commercial production, just at the beginning of World War II in 1939. Practically all the nylon produced was used by the US armed forces, where it found limitless applications with its combination of fineness, elasticity, and great strength. In particular, its qualities made it ideal for the manufacture of parachutes.

The first nylon stockings were made in 1938. Thereafter it quickly overtook silk as the main fabric of underwear and hosiery. In addition it became used for making fishing lines, brushes, sheeting, and surgical threads. Nylon could also be powdered and heat-molded in a similar way to plastics.

Du Pont continued to hold the patent rights, which led to an intensification of effort by other research laboratories to produce other polymer textiles. "Terylene" ("dacron" in the United States) was developed in Britain in 1941, "orlon" in the United States in the 1950s.

Man-made fibers have shown themselves to be highly versatile by mimicking and sometimes

Sir John Douglas Cockcroft

1897-1967

Sir John Douglas Cockcroft, one of the leading scientists of his generation, is counted among the father figures of modern nuclear physics. With his colleague Ernest T S Walton he developed the Cockcroft-Walton particle accelerator, a highly important research tool in nuclear physics. With this equipment he and Walton demonstrated in 1932 that it was possible to split the nuclei of atoms of lithium. This was the first artificially induced nuclear disintegration, and it brought the two men the Nobel Prize for Physics in 1951.

Cockcroft was born at Todmorden, Yorkshire, where his family ran a small business. In 1914 he entered Manchester University to read mathematics; one of his lecturers was the New Zealand-born physicist Ernest Rutherford. Cockcroft spent only one year at Manchester. World War I was declared and Cockcroft became a signaler in the Royal Field Artillery. After the war was over he took up a college apprenticeship in electrical engineering, but displayed such a remarkable ability in science that he was eventually persuaded to study mathematics at Cambridge University.

On graduating he joined the staff of the Cavendish Laboratory in 1922, "towards," as he said, "the end of what might be uncharitably described as the Old Stone Age of nuclear physics." He thus joined the illustrious team of researchers brought together to work under Rutherford. To this group of physicists and scientists, mainly trained in pure scientific

Above: the men who split the atom. From left to right: Ernest Walton, Lord Rutherford, John Douglas Cockcroft.

Below right: the discharge tube used by Cockcroft and Walton to bombard lithium with protons accelerated to a high velocity.

theory, he brought valuable practical abilities from his engineering and mathematics backgrounds. He and Walton started work on their proton accelerator in 1929.

The purpose of a particle accelerator is to speed up atomic particles to very high velocities in order to increase their energy. This is achieved by passing the particles across very high voltages. The electric field created across the particles' path causes an increase in their velocity. As research into atomic structure increased, so physicists required adequate sources of high-energy particles to bombard atoms, and this stimulated many researches in the 1920s to attempt to devise practicable accelerators.

Robert Jemison van de Graaff, an atomic physicist in the United States, built his first particle accelerator, an electrostatic generator, in

Physics

PROTON

LITHIUM NUCLEUS

NUCLEUS UNSTABLE WITH ADDITIONAL PROTON

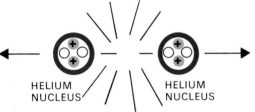

HELIUM NUCLEUS

HELIUM NUCLEUS

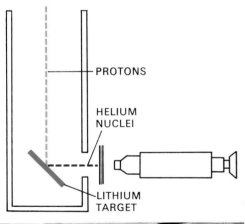

PROTONS

HELIUM NUCLEI

LITHIUM TARGET

Center: a later Cockcroft-Walton positive ion accelerator with a close-up detail (right) of the accelerator spiral.

Above left: Cockcroft and Walton accelerated hydrogen nuclei (protons) to very high energies and concentrated them in a very fine beam onto a lithium target. Those lithium nuclei receiving direct hits flew apart. The fragments proved to be helium nuclei, whose impact upon a fluorescent screen could be observed by a microscope (lower diagram). The energy emitted came from the disintegration of a small quantity of matter.

Left: the intersecting storage rings of the giant CERN accelerator, Geneva.

1931. By the following year, Cockcroft and Walton were ready to test their own proton accelerator. It consisted of a vacuum tube through which flowed a stream of hydrogen ions (protons). A series of rectifiers kept the current flowing in one direction only and, to keep the current steady, a series of condensers maintained the voltage between peaks in the current cycle. This system of rectifiers and condensers acted as a voltage multipher. Cockcroft and

Walton managed to boost the speed of protons up to the point where the voltage was high enough to energize each atom of lithium, their target metal, to form two atoms of helium. This was the first example of man-made nuclear transformation.

The Cockcroft-Walton accelerator became a widely used piece of equipment in research laboratories around the world for many years. Besides its use in atomic research accelerators also have many direct applications in industry, such as detecting flaws in metal casing, and in medicine, for the treatment of cancer. Today's descendants of the original machines are often enormous constructions, producing particles with energies of several million electron volts.

Shortly before World War II, Cockcroft became closely involved with setting up the radar defence system which followed on the developments in radar research by Robert Watson-Watt. During the war, in 1941, he became chief superintendent of the Air Defence Research and Development Establishment, and in 1944 he left for Canada to take over the Atomic Energy Commission, National Research Council of Canada. This set the pattern for the next phase of his career, in which he showed himself to be an outstanding scientific administrator. Between 1946 and 1958 he was director of the Atomic Energy Research Establishment at Harwell, Britain, during its formative years. In 1959 he returned to the academic world, however, accepting the post as the first Master of Churchill College at Cambridge. Here he built up this new foundation into an institution of academic distinction, and he was still Master at the time of his sudden death at the age of 70.

Frédéric and Irène Joliot-Curie

1900-1958 1897-1956

The French physicist Frédéric Joliot-Curie was born Jean Frédéric Joliot. He changed his name when he married Irène Curie, daughter of the famous husband and wife team who discovered radium, Pierre and Marie Curie. Frédéric and Irène themselves formed a remarkable scientific partnership, jointly discovering a means of creating artificial radioactivity. Their work led directly to the manufacture of a range of artificially radioactive elements known as radioisotopes, which today have a multitude of important applications in medicine, industry, and scientific research.

Frédéric studied engineering and chemistry in Paris and in 1925, soon after graduating, found a post working for Marie Curie as one of her research assistants. Although fascinated by the research in which he was involved, Frédéric found himself more interested by one of Madam Curie's other assistants, her daughter Irène. Within a few months of their meeting they were engaged, and in 1926 they married and set up a working partnership.

In 1934, they made their historic discovery, creating almost by chance, the first man-made radioactive element. They were studying the effect of firing beams of tiny positively-charged particles called alpha particles at targets of light metal such as aluminum. They were startled to

Above: the Joliot-Curies at work in their laboratory.

find that after an intense bombardment by alpha particles, their tiny aluminum target appeared to have become radioactive. But an even greater surprise was in store for them. When they examined the target more carefully they found that it no longer consisted entirely of aluminum. Some of the original metal had been transmuted into phosphorus. In addition, the phosphorus was of a special kind. The nucleus of its atoms contained many more neutrons than natural,

making it much heavier, unstable, and consequently radioactive. Likewise, the bombarding of boron produced radioactive nitrogen, and that of magnesium yielded radioactive silicon. They had produced the first example of man-made radioactivity. Their discovery, which in 1935 gained them the Nobel Prize for Chemistry, was conclusive evidence that not only heavy elements such as uranium were radioactive but that virtually any element could be made so by converting it into a radioisotope.

In the late 1930s, as World War threatened, Frédéric and Irène began work on nuclear fission in uranium. This process, in the course of which uranium nuclei split up releasing large quantities of energy, is the working principle on which nuclear reactors are based. The Joliot-Curies were making rapid progress toward a design for the first practical reactor when the German invasion of France cut short their efforts.

Violently opposed to the Nazis, the Joliot-Curies were determined not to allow any information on nuclear research to fall into enemy hands. One of the vital keys both to the building of a nuclear reactor and the first atomic bomb was the preparation of a substance called "heavy water" – water in which the hydrogen atom is replaced by its heavier isotope, deuterium.

Physics

Heavy water acted as a moderator in the nuclear reactor, slowing down fast neutrons. These retarded neutrons were then far more likely to cause fission. The only plant which was capable, at that time, of producing sufficient heavy water was the Norsk Hydro in Norway, and it was imperative that the Nazis did not get their hands on the stock. Frédéric persuaded the French Minister of Armaments to buy up the entire stock of heavy water. This precious consignment was then smuggled out to Paris – a month before Norway was invaded. When France herself was invaded, Frédéric ensured that the cans of heavy water were again removed out of Hitler's reach, this time to Britain.

During the war the Joliot-Curies remained in France, taking an active part in the Resistance, and frustrating German efforts to utilize French facilities for and expertise in nuclear research.

After the war, the Joliot-Curies found their research hampered by authorities suspicious of their political sympathies. Always left-wing in outlook, their views had become more extreme under the pressure of Nazi occupation. Both were now members of the French Communist Party, and although they were permitted to make major contributions to the building of Europe's

Above: a miniature nuclear battery. One of its uses is in implanted heart pacemakers.

Above right: detectors placed in the kidneys and heart to monitor rate of flow of injected radio-isotopes.

Center right: a colored picture of the brain constructed by a tomoscanner. The picture is based on the radiation patterns from the tissues after injection of a radio-active substance into the blood. Red indicates maximum radio-activity, black total absence.

Below left: repacking a radioactive piece of debris in a garbage can.

Below right: "Fat Man," (background), the bomb dropped on Nagasaki, used the radioisotope plutonium-239.

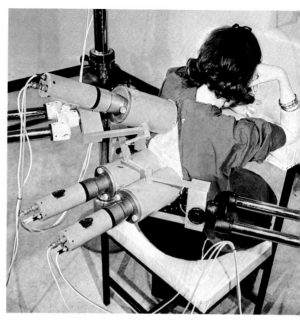

first nuclear reactor in 1948, they were soon removed, without explanation, from their positions. Thereafter, despite their past achievements and heroic war efforts, they were largely ignored by the scientific establishment.

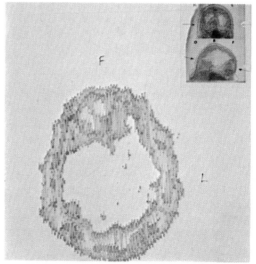

Enrico Fermi

1901-1954

Italian-born physicist Enrico Fermi helped to found the age of atomic power by designing and building the first nuclear reactor. The main problem Fermi solved was how to keep a nuclear chain reaction under control. By doing so he discovered a safe means of tapping the huge potential energy of the atom.

Born in Rome, Fermi studied physics at the University of Pisa, obtaining a doctorate in 1922. Although dedicated to his research on the behavior of the neutron, he could not ignore the fast-developing political situation in Italy. Benito Mussolini had seized power and fascism had the country in its grip. Fermi found himself in direct confrontation with the government when, in 1938, his work in neutron physics was acknowledged by the award of the Nobel Prize. Mussolini expected Fermi to attend the ceremony in Stockholm in a fascist uniform. Fermi, who loathed fascism, refused. Already unpopular among Italian fascists because of his Jewish wife, Fermi's refusal was regarded by them as traitorous. Vicious attacks on him in the Italian press followed and Fermi, with his wife, left Stockholm for the United States where they settled permanently.

Fermi's new home was Chicago and it was here that he began the research which culminated in the building of the first nuclear reactor. Scientists knew that the radioactive element uranium was potentially the key to the vast

supply of cheap energy. The problem was how to tap it without causing a nuclear explosion. The source of the energy was the fission of the uranium atoms. Fission, the breaking up of single atoms of an element into two new atoms of a different element, was accompanied by the release of neutrons, and energy in the form of heat and light. These neutrons could themselves cause other atoms to undergo fission, so creating a self-sustaining chain reaction which could theoretically provide a constant flow of fission energy. The major problem to be overcome was that the chain reaction could easily become too rapid, leading to overheating and an eventual atomic explosion.

Above: sketch of the first self-sustaining nuclear chain reactor operated at Chicago on December 2, 1942. It was the first atomic pile.

Below right: refined uranium billet, approximately 24 inches in diameter.

Several eminent scientists, including Fermi and Albert Einstein, realized that the fission process could be used to build a devastating weapon – the atom bomb. They wrote a letter to Franklin D Roosevelt, alerting the President of the implications if Hitler's scientists developed such a weapon. The American government responded immediately and appointed Fermi as the head of the research team brought together to design a practical nuclear reactor. Fermi's knowledge of neutron physics soon enabled him to design a means of keeping the chain reaction

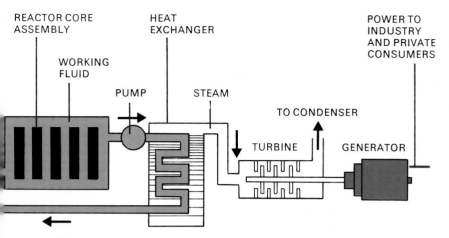

REACTOR CORE
ASSEMBLY

WORKING
FLUID

PUMP

HEAT
EXCHANGER

STEAM

POWER TO
INDUSTRY
AND PRIVATE
CONSUMERS

TO CONDENSER

TURBINE

GENERATOR

Above: nuclear power generation sequence.

Right: the fuel storage "pond" of the steam-generating heavy-water reactor at Winfrith, Britain, showing cerenkow radiation from the irradiated fuel.

Left: fuel assembly element assembly of an advanced gas-cooled reactor.

under control. He decided to use cadmium rods which could be inserted or withdrawn from the reactor to act as neutron absorbers. Fermi's plan was to damp down the chain reaction if it became too fast by inserting the rods and reducing the number of neutrons available for further fission. The rate of reaction could then be raised simply by withdrawing some of the rods.

Fermi and his team set to work to build the reactor and by the end of 1942 they were ready for the first test. It was an extremely tense moment for Fermi. If his design was faulty the reactor could quickly change to a bomb capable of devastating most of Chicago. On December 2, on one of the squash courts in Chicago University, some of the reactor's cadmium rods were withdrawn and fission began. As more rods were removed the chain reaction became self-sustaining. By adjusting the rods it soon became clear that Fermi's idea had worked. The reactor was under control. Using a prearranged code, news of the success was cabled to the government with the words "The Italian navigator has entered the New World." It was an appropriate message. Fermi's achievement was indeed the herald of a new world for man – one in which the promise of a limitless source of energy is overshadowed by its potential dangers.

Since Fermi's historic experiment, the scale and sophistication of nuclear reactors have increased immeasurably. Today a complex new

Below right: the US submarine *Nautilus*, the world's first nuclear-powered naval vessel (1955).

technology has evolved to monitor and control nuclear power output. But the danger of even a single nuclear accident capable of devastating whole cities, together with the problems of disposing of the lethal waste products from reactors, has led to a public debate inconceivable in Fermi's time. For the first time people are seriously questioning whether nuclear power should be encouraged, limited, or even abandoned.

Felix Wankel

born 1902

It had occurred to many engineers that a considerable saving in energy and space could be achieved if the combustion of gasoline could be used to produce rotary motion directly, instead of via the linear motion of pistons. Several engines were built, but none exploited the principle so efficiently as the rotary-piston engine designed by Felix Wankel.

Felix Wankel was born in Germany at Lahr, a town close to the French border. During the late 1930s and throughout World War II he worked at the German Aeronautical Research Establishment, researching into the use of rotary valves and valve-sealing techniques. In 1951 he joined a motor corporation at Neckarsulm and began to design a rotary car engine. By 1957 he had built a working prototype, and applied for a complete range of patents including the special tools which were needed to make his engine.

The Wankel rotary engine differed from the conventional four-stroke internal-combustion engine of Nikolaus Otto in that the pistons did not move inside the cylinder in an up-and-down sequence. Instead, the triangular shaped piston was itself the rotor. This rotated within a casing the shape of an epitrochoid (and oval shape slightly constricted in the middle). The apexes of the triangular rotary piston moved in precise contact with the walls of the casing, so forming

Right: a Wankel engine, showing the rotor, the main shaft, and the gearing inside the combustion chamber, as well as the cooling area.

Right: the internal structure of the Wankel engine. As the rotor rotates about the central gear (the output gear), its three apexes remain in constant contact with the inner walls of the casing. A mixture of air and fuel drawn in through the inlet port is compressed as the rotor rotates. It is then ignited by the spark plug and the gases provide the power stroke. As the exhaust outlet is uncovered, the exhaust gases escape and the sequence restarts.

three crescent-shaped chambers, each of which was sealed off from the other two. As the rotor turned, a mixture of fuel and air was fed in turn into each segment by a carburettor. The fuel-air mixture was compressed and then ignited by a sparking plug; the gases expanded and were ejected through the exhaust valves. Both the inlet and outlet valves were opened and closed automatically by the movement of the piston. Thus the rotary engine produced three power

cycles for each rotation, as opposed to one cycle per four strokes created in the conventional Otto engine. A central shaft coupled to the rotor made it rotate. The rotor itself was connected to an output shaft by a system of gears. The internal gearing of the rotor had three times as many teeth as the gear wheel of the output shaft, so that the latter turned at three times the speed of the rotor itself.

The resulting engine was exceptionally

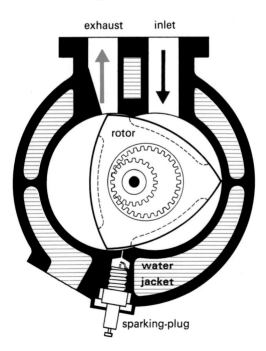

exhaust   inlet

rotor

water jacket

sparking-plug

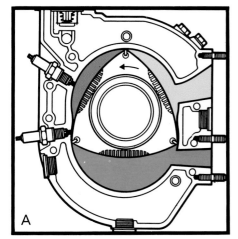

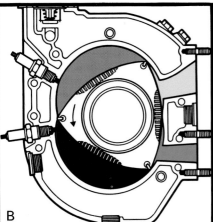

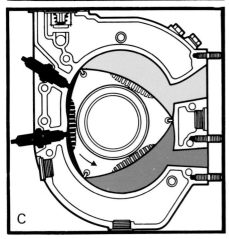

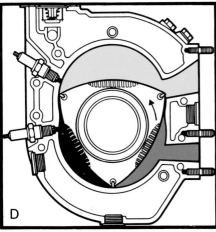

Left: stages in the four-cycle system of the NSU-Wankel rotary engine. Fuel (yellow) enters and is compressed (green) by the flank of the triangular rotating piston. Two spark plugs simultaneously ignite the fuel (now red), and finally the exhaust of burnt gases (blue) is effected by the rotating piston.

Center right: the Wankel engine used in the NSU RO80 car.

Below right: the NSU RO80 motorcar.

smooth-running. It was also much smaller than the conventional Otto engine providing equivalent power. The Wankel engine had two other advantages over the Otto engine which has made it the engine of the future. It used less fuel, and with fewer parts, it was much cheaper to manufacture.

The major problem in its design is the need to maintain absolute sealing between the apexes of the rotor and the casing. Any intercommunication between the chambers results in a loss of pressure and a consequent decreasing of power and efficiency. Wankel himself designed a system of sprung sealing plates to overcome this.

The first car powered by a Wankel engine was produced in Germany in 1968. Its superiority over the Otto engine encouraged major motor companies in other countries to acquire licenses for the manufacture of Wankel cars, including General Motors in the United States, Rolls-Royce in Britain, Alfa-Romeo in Italy, Citröen in France, and Toyota in Japan. It has been estimated by one major automobile company that by the 1980s eight out of ten cars produced by them will be powered by a Wankel engine. Felix Wankel himself now heads his own research establishment at Lindau in Germany devoted to further development of the rotary-piston engine.

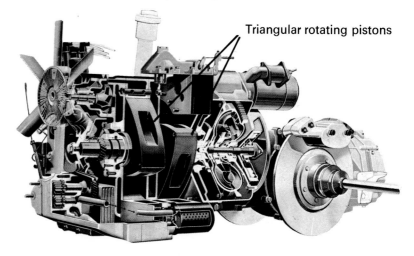

Triangular rotating pistons

J Robert Oppenheimer

1904-1967

J Robert Oppenheimer distinguished himself as an administrator, physicist, mathematician, researcher, and teacher. He is best known for his role as director of the Manhattan project which created the first atomic bomb in the closing years of World War II.

Oppenheimer was regarded as having one of the best scientific minds of his generation. Born in New York City, the son of a German-born businessman, he graduated from Harvard in 1925 with unusually broad cultural interests, having studied classics and oriental philosophy as well as science. He came to Britain to spend some time working under Ernest Rutherford in Cambridge at the Cavendish Laboratory, at that time the world's leading center of atomic research. Oppenheimer spent four years in all in Europe. He developed a strong interest in the quantum theory and wave mechanics, and soon established himself as a theoretical physicist of unparalleled intellect. He published several papers and was invited by many prominent scientists to participate in research.

He returned to the United States in 1929 to take up an appointment at the University of California, Berkeley and at the California Institute of Technology. During the subsequent 18 years he was at the peak of his career as a theoretical physicist, and his analyses anticipated

Below: *Enola Gay*, the aircraft used to drop the first atomic bomb on Japan. It was named after the pilot's wife.

Below: the Los Alamos scientific complex. It encompassed 30 square miles of laboratories and technical centers, as well as administration, housing, and shopping facilities.

the discovery of several subatomic particles including the neutron, positron, and meson. Oppenheimer was also a brilliant teacher with a vivid, memorable style, and he trained many of the United States' top physicists.

By the mid-1930s, Oppenheimer developed strong political convictions and took an uncompromisingly antifascist stand after the National Socialist rise to power in Germany in 1933, and the outbreak of the Spanish Civil War in 1936. During these years he also continued a specific research program, examining the implications which Max Plank's quantum theory held for atomic physics.

During the 1930s, studies in nuclear physics had reached the point where it was considered possible to set off a chain reaction from the release of energy involved in certain types of nuclear disintegration. By 1939, in the months leading up to World War II, the implications of nuclear fission, in which the nucleus of an atom is split by the impact of a neutron, with the release of large quantities of energy, were clearly understood. Uranium was known to be a suitable material, and it was estimated that the fission of only 1 ounce of uranium could yield an explosion equivalent in effect to 600 tons of TNT. The fear that Germany might be the first country to develop such a weapon of terror prompted Albert Einstein to send a warning letter to President Roosevelt on the eve of Germany's invasion of Poland.

The US government took the warning seriously, but a long program of research was needed before such a weapon could be produced. There were immense problems not only in purifying uranium from its ores but also in separating out and concentrating its unstable isotope, uranium-235, which was ideal for fission. Later, plutonium-239 was discovered to be a suitable

Physics

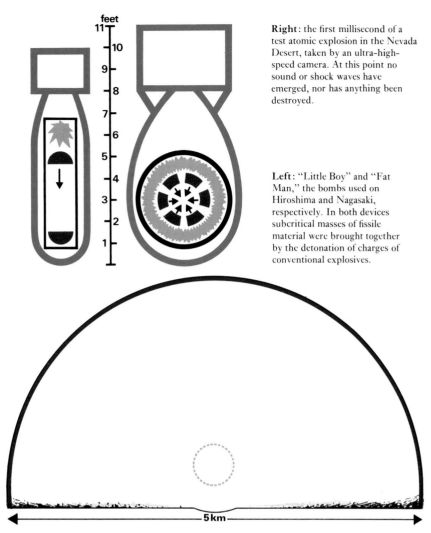

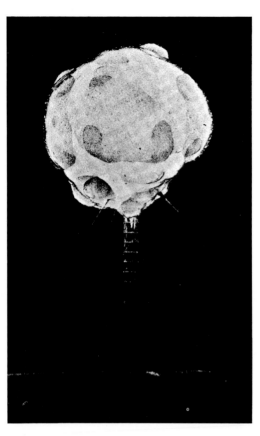

Above: the blast effect of "Little Boy" on Hiroshima spanned a radius of about 3 miles. The bomb exploded not by impact but by detonation before it hit the ground.

alternative. On December 6, 1941, the day before the Japanese attack on Pearl Harbor and the United States' entry into the war, President Franklin D Roosevelt took the decision to set up euphemistically named "Manhattan Engineering District," later officially called "Project Y." This was in fact a project to develop an atomic bomb. It included leading American and British physicists, and such exiles from fascism in Europe as the Italian physicist Enrico Fermi. From June 1942 its director was J Robert Oppenheimer.

The preliminary research continued at a variety of locations while, under Oppenheimer's directions, plans were made to house a whole scientific community at Los Alamos, New Mexico. The difficulties remained immense, and the solving of one problem as often as not presented the scientists with a fresh series of challenges. There were still difficulties in getting together sufficient quantities of uranium-235 and plutonium-239. When Roosevelt died in April 1945, to be succeeded by Truman, victory in Europe was less than a month away. The target therefore became Japan.

On July 16, 1945 a plutonium bomb was exploded in the New Mexico desert. Its power, equivalent to 20,000 tons of TNT, vastly exceeded all expectations. On August 6, the first uranium bomb was exploded over Hiroshima; three days later a plutonium bomb was dropped on Nagasaki. The unprecedented devastation inflicted on these two cities was instrumental in Japan surrendering on August 10 of that year.

After the war, Oppenheimer became chairman of the advisory committee to the US Atomic Energy Commission, where he aligned himself with those who opposed developing the infinitely more appalling weapon, the hydrogen bomb. It was an issue that raised fundamental questions about the role of science in service to the state.

Partly because of his opposition to the bomb in 1953 Oppenheimer had his security clearance taken away. This was at the height of the Cold War and the purges of the McCarthyist era, and because of his association with antifascist, left-wing radicals in the 1930s, Oppenheimer also found himself accused of having Communist sympathies.

This effectively finished his career as an influential scientist, though he continued to hold a distinguished academic post as director of the Institute for Advanced Study at Princeton University. He became a symbol of the scientist faced with the dilemma of making a compromise of conscience for state reasons, and he devoted some time during his last years to trying to define the problems of man's intellectual and moral integrity. In 1963 Oppenheimer was presented with the Fermi Award of the Atomic Energy Commission by President Lyndon B Johnson. This has been seen as a muted apology for his treatment 10 years earlier.

Chester F Carlson

1906-1968

Chester F Carlson, an American technician, invented the xerographic copier. Easy to use and very speedy, it was the first duplicating process which dispensed with the need for stencils, the services of specially trained operators, and the use of wet chemicals.

The demands of both modern business routines and academic research have prompted the invention of various ingenious systems of copying documentary material for reference or distribution. Some are based on the diffusion-

transfer process, where a stencil or master copy of the document must first be made on a sheet of special material before it can be reproduced. Others are based on the application of heat or infrared rays to which the special copying paper used is sensitized. This method is called thermography, and it involves bringing the document to be copied into direct contact with the copying paper. They are then passed through the machine together and the heat or infrared rays are absorbed by any dark areas or marks on the original, and transferred as clear impressions onto the copy.

Xerography, on the other hand, exploits an entirely different principle, and it was first investigated by Chester F Carlson when he was looking for a practical solution to a specific problem. Carlson had studied for a degree from the California Institute of Technology while at the same time working to support his invalid

Right: the first xerographic print, made by Carlson and Otto Kornei on October 22, 1938. The process, known then as electrophotography, used dyed lycopodium powder. The characters were fixed onto waxed paper.

Below: an early xerographic print (1948) being stripped from the selenium plate. The print was then heated to fuse the developer powder to the paper.

parents. He had worked briefly at the Bell Telephone Company, and then found a post in the patents department of a large electronics corporation in New York. Obtaining copies of blueprints and the texts of patent descriptions was a continual problem and a hindrance to efficient working. He became determined to find a quick, clear, and inexpensive method of duplication.

For four years Carlson explored the possibility of devising a system which would operate electro-

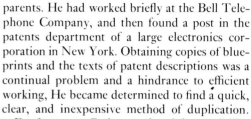

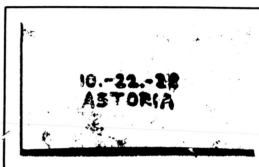

statically, and in 1938 he produced his first xerographic copy of an original document. The term xerography is derived from the Greek meaning "dry writing." The transfer technique uses the semiconductor selenium, which conducts electricity in light but not in darkness. In Carlson's system the document or page to be copied was scanned by a mirror. The image of the document was then reflected by the mirror onto a drum which was coated with electrically charged selenium. Where the dark sections of the image were reflected, the selenium retained its electrostatic charge. In the light areas it became photoconductive and the charge was dispersed.

The drum was then dusted with a negatively charged powder which adhered only to the positively charged (dark) areas. The copying paper, also positively charged, then came into contact with the drum, and because it also carried a positive charge it, in its turn, attracted

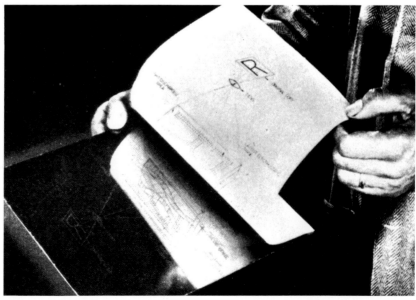

Communication

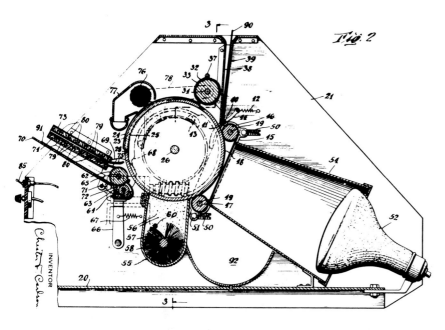

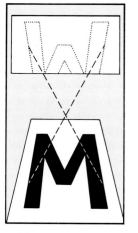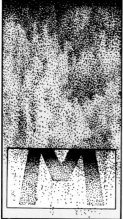

1) An image of the document to be copied is projected through a lens onto a light-sensitive surface, such as a selenium coated electrostatically charged drum. The charge disappears from the exposed areas which were white on the original, and is retained where the original is black.

2) Powder is then dusted over the drum and clings to the charged portion of the drum. The image can now be seen on the drum.

Above left: Carlson's patent drawing for his electrophotographic apparatus.

Above right: Carlson's original device; the patent was filed in 1940.

Left: stages in the operation of a modern dry copier. The process is essentially similar to Carlson's original device.

the powder. Finally the powder image was fused onto the paper by infrared heat to form a permanent impression. The result was a clear copy of the original document.

For six years after he first succeeded in making his photocopier work, Carlson strove in vain to attract commercial backing. It was not until 1947, after a last brief period of research, that the Haloid Company, a small firm in New York, agreed to take on the manufacturing and marketing rights. In due course this enterprise developed into the giant Xerox Corporation and Carlson became an extremely wealthy man on the strength of his royalties and dividends.

Xerox and other plain paper copiers are today standard office equipment, capable of producing clear copies of virtually any type of writing or line drawing. They have also been developed to copy colored images, and to produce enlargements and reductions of the original.

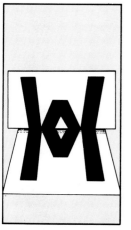

Right: the Rank Xerox 3600 copier, so-called because of its hourly output. More up-to-date copies exist which can double this output, automatically sort documents, reduce, and copy photographs.

3) Bond paper is brought into contact with the drum and an electrical charge (opposite to that of the powder) beneath the paper attracts the powder from drum to paper.

4) The powder image is then softened and fused onto the paper, usually by heat.

Sir Frank Whittle

born 1907

The development of the turbojet engine by a young British test pilot and aeronautics engineer, Frank Whittle, revolutionized every aspect of the aeronautics industry, from the military aircraft and guided missiles to passenger airlines and helicopters. By dispensing with the piston-crankshaft-propeller system, the jet aircraft could be driven by a much smaller, lighter engine. Its tremendous power also paved the way for travel at supersonic speed.

The principle on which a jet engine operates was first stated by the British physicist Sir Isaac Newton in 1687: to every action there is an equal and opposite reaction. In the case of the jet, as the fuel is burnt, so hot gases are expelled. The reaction to this is a thrust which drives the engine forward.

In 1921 A A Griffith, an engineer at the Royal Aircraft Establishment in Britain, tested out the first gas-turbine aircraft engine, in which a rotor, powered by the force of hot gases on a system of blades, drove a propeller. This gave Frank Whittle, then a young flight lieutenant at the Royal Air Force College, the idea for designing a turbojet. In 1930 he took out his first patent specifications for a jet engine in which incoming air was compressed and heated by a series of vaned wheels, (the compressor). The compressed air was forced into a combustion chamber where it ignited. The exhausted of the burning gas

Above: the British Meteor Mark III twin-engined jet aircraft. It was used during the later stages of World War II.

Below: Whittle (right) explaining an early jet engine to an industrial correspondent.

turned a turbine, which was itself connected to the compressor, thus keeping it turning.

Unfortunately, Whittle could not initially interest the British Air Ministry or obtain government finance. He also had difficulties in finding metal alloys that were hard enough to withstand the high temperatures generated by such an engine. It was not until 1935, when Whittle was seconded from the Royal Air Force to a newly founded company, Research Jets Ltd, that there seemed to be much hope of further progress.

Meanwhile in Germany a young aeronautics designer, Hans von Ohain, was employed in 1936 by the aircraft manufacturer, Ernst Heinkel, to develop a jet engine. Von Ohain's work was completely independent of Whittle's research but based on the same principles of adapting a gas-turbine engine. With generous resources available, Ohain was able to develop his ideas rapidly, and on August 27, 1939, a Heinkel aircraft made the first historic jet-powered flight.

Von Ohain's turbojet engine was a considerable success, and he continued to improve its performance. However, with World War II in progress the German authorities decided to concentrate research resources on rocketry instead. Von Ohain did develop the first jet fighter, the Messerschmitt-262, in 1942, but it came too late to save the war for Germany.

Whittle in the meantime, having tested his first engine in 1937, saw the first plane to carry it make its maiden flight in May 1941. The next month a prototype engine was flown to the United States and served as a blueprint for the engines of the first American experimental jet plane, the XP-59A, which made its maiden flight in October 1942. Although extensive work was now begun in order to exploit the principle of Whittle's jet engine, and some jet aircraft were put into service during the closing stages of

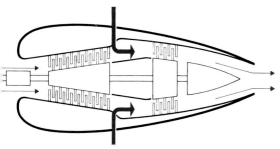

Above: turboprop engine or "prop jet." It is a turbojet with an external propeller which is driven by the turbine shaft. A system of gears reduces the high speed of the turbine to a useful propeller speed. Although the engine has some jet thrust, which assists the forward propulsion of the propeller, most of its power comes from the propeller itself. Turboprops are economical in fuel usage and power low-speed aircraft.

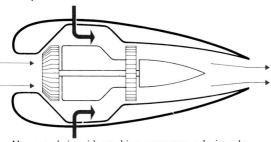

Above: turbojet with a turbine compressor and a jet only. As air enters the engine, a turbine compresses it and pushes it into the combustion chamber, where it is mixed with fuel. The mixture is ignited and the hot expanding gases rush out of the exhaust, thrusting the engine forward. As the expanding gases exit, they drive another set of turbine blades connected to the compressor shaft. Most modern high-speed aircraft are powered by turbojets.

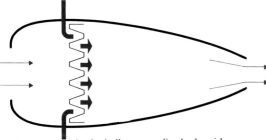

Above: the ramjet, basically a streamlined tube with no moving parts. At speeds over 300 miles an hour air is rammed into the engine with such force that it is compressed within a specially designed air intake. The air mixes with the fuel and explodes in the combustion engine. Because a ramjet cannot start from rest it needs another engine such as a turbojet to start it. It operates poorly at low speeds, but at high velocity is the most efficient of the jet engines and is used in guided missiles.

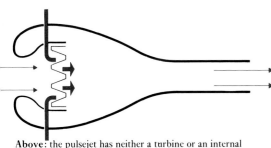

Above: the pulsejet has neither a turbine or an internal mechanism to compress the air-fuel mixture. Instead it requires a build-up of air pressure to start its combustion. At that point a valve shuts off the air flow and the exhaust gases can only leave the combustion chamber through the tail-pipe. This causes the pressure in the combustion chamber to decrease and more air is drawn in and ignited. Pulsejets were used in V-1 flying bombs.

Right: the German Heinkel 162. It was the 178 version of this aircraft that made the first historic jet-powered flight.

Right: the prototype of the Messerschmidt, the first jet fighter plane. It was developed by the Germans from the Heinkel and saw limited action during World War II.

Below right: the de Havilland Comet 4C, the first commercial jet airplane. It was developed by the British, who in 1952 began the world's first jet passenger airline flights, between London and Johannesburg.

World War II, their advent was too late to have any great influence on the outcome of the war.

In the postwar years, however, the development of Whittle's turbojet was extensive. During the Korean War, jet fighters made their first major military contribution. Meanwhile jet engines were introduced into civilian airlines, and nowadays power all commercial aircraft.

Whittle, who retired from the Royal Air Force and received a knighthood in 1948, set down his own account of the role he played in *Jet: The Story of a Pioneer* (1953).

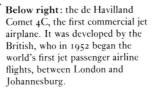

Edwin Land

born 1909

Edwin Land invented the Polaroid process, in which a positive photographic image is produced immediately after exposure. The process dispenses with the need to take out and develop the negative, and it is regarded as the single most important advance in photographic technology since the invention of flexible roll film by George Eastman.

Edwin Land is a physicist who, while still a student at Harvard University, became interested in the properties of polarized light. A ray of ordinary, unpolarized light vibrates in all directions. Certain substances have the property of absorbing all but one plane of vibration, a phenomenon known as "polarization". The transmitted light is said to be polarized. In nature, the light from a rainbow is polarized, as is to some extent the reflection of sunlight from the still surface of a stretch of water.

Although polarized light had many potential uses, the polarizers then available were made with small, perfect crystals and they were very expensive. On leave from Harvard, Land set out to make a large, continuous sheet of polarizing material by embedding submicroscopic crystals within a plastic sheet, and by 1932 had produced the first synthetic sheet polarizer. So absorbed did Land become in this work that he never graduated but continued his research on polarized light and its applications. In 1937 he established the Polaroid Corporation in Cam-

bridge, Massachusetts, to develop further inventions and to increase the range of his products. Polarizing filters found a wide variety of uses in scientific and optical equipment, including camera filters, which absorbed the glare reflected from shiny surfaces to produce clearer pictures, and Polaroid sunglass lenses. Because they absorb much of the glare which otherwise would reach the wearer's eyes, Polaroid sunglasses became very popular.

Opposite page, above left: optical stress analysis of acrylic molding, the left part being covered with a polarizing filter. The light passing through the filter is polarized and shows up the stress marks as a pattern.

Right: the Model 95 roll-film camera, the first of the Polaroid Land cameras, introduced in 1948 along with Type 40 film.

By 1941 Land had developed additional types of polarizers, had demonstrated polarizing systems for automobile headlights, and had worked out ways of making three-dimensional films for projection in the cinema. Then, during World War II, he concentrated on adaptations of light polarizers for military uses, such as rangefinders

Below right: how light is polarized. Light from a lamp vibrates in all directions, like the spokes of a wheel. The polarizing material cuts out all the vibrations that do not lie in a particular plane. The light emerges vibrating in one plane only, as shown in this diagram.

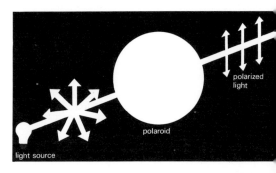

and gunsights, and the production of other optical devices, such as infrared viewers to assist in night vision.

In 1947 Land produced what is perhaps the best-known of all his inventions: the Polaroid Land camera. This camera, so to speak, incorporates its own processing laboratory, and is capable of producing a finished positive print within less than a minute of exposure. The film unit includes a photosensitive negative sheet, a

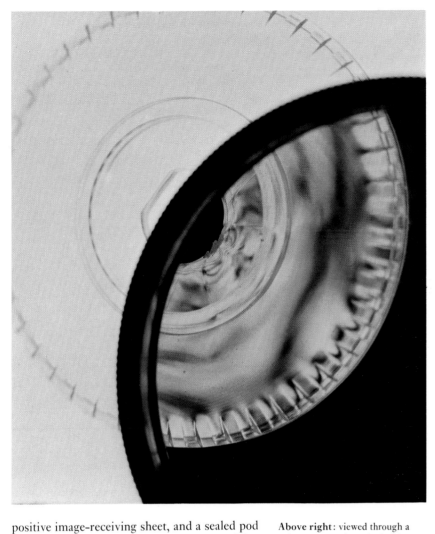

and professionals. Film could be obtained in rolls, packs, or individual sheets.

In 1963 the Polacolor process was introduced. This multilayer instant color film incorporates color-sensitive emulsions and dye developers, substances that are both image-forming dyes and photographic developing agents. This film can produce a stable full-color print within 60 seconds.

Further innovations in chemistry, electronics, and optics led to the SX-70 system, introduced by Land in 1972. The SX-70 camera automatically ejects the integral SX-70 color film unit between processing rollers, and processing reaches completion within the film unit without timing and without peeling apart. Land introduced Polavision, the first system for instant motion pictures, in 1977. The film can be exposed, processed, and viewed without being removed from a sealed cassette. In investigating color phenomena, Land was prompted to reassess the theoretical basis for perception of

positive image-receiving sheet, and a sealed pod containing a viscous processing reagent. After the negative sheet is exposed, the unit passes between a pair of rollers inside the camera, which break open the pod so that the reagent spreads evenly under pressure between the two sheets, which are now held together by the reagent layer. In forming a black and white image, the reagent both develops the exposed silver halide grains and dissolves the unexposed silver halide grains. The dissolved silver halide is transferred to the receiving sheet, where it is developed to form the positive print. Finally, as soon as the development process is complete, the two component films can be peeled apart. The Polaroid photographic process was subsequently adapted to fulfill a variety of needs in science and industry, as well as in photography for amateurs

Above right: viewed through a polaroscope, a photoelastic fringe pattern can be seen along the lines of constant stress in a ball-bearing under running loads.

Below right: the revolutionary Polaroid Land SX-70 camera.

Below left: the picture area of an exposed SX-70 film unit automatically ejected from the camera first appears turquoise. Within moments the picture color image begins to emerge even in the brightest light. It continues to develop for several minutes until clear.

color, and the experimental work that followed led to his "retinex" theory of color vision.

Land has continued research in each of the fields described, and he remains an example of a researcher whose outstanding scientific intellect has constantly sought expression in practical applications.

Jacques-Yves Cousteau

born 1910

The French underwater explorer Jacques-Yves Cousteau is best known for his films of underwater life. The revelation of this previously unexplored world was made possible through his own invention – the aqualung.

Man has always been fascinated by the depths of the sea. Limited by his need to breath air he made his first attempts to explore the oceans in submarine vessels containing air. Glass diving bells have been recorded as early as 500 BC by the Greek scholar Herodotus. Legend has it that Alexander the Great descended to the bottom of the sea in a glass barrel in about 300 BC.

Whether he wanted to observe marine life or swim, unrestricted, like a fish, man had an additional problem to overcome. However he obtained his air, it had to be supplied at the

correct pressure, increasing as he went further down into the water, otherwise the air would simply not enter the lungs. It was a factor which the Rennaisance artist and engineer, Leonardo da Vinci, did not consider when he designed the first set of diving equipment. This included flippers, goggles, and a stout headpiece which was connected to the surface by an airtube. Fortunately the apparatus was never used.

Over the centuries submersible containers and diving suits were developed. But, to be able to swim freely underwater for any length of time man needed a portable supply of air which he could carry on his back. As the technology to pressurize gases developed, so primitive lungs of compressed oxygen were constructed, but these were highly dangerous.

It was a problem which greatly concerned Jacques-Yves Cousteau, a French naval officer. Cousteau was a highly experienced diver who in

1941 had made the first documentary film of underwater fishing. At that time France was occupied by German forces, and Cousteau, working for Naval Intelligence against the Nazis, realized that a self-contained breathing system would be of great use to Resistance fighters in sabotaging enemy ships. He knew that the answer lay in a device which could supply air at the correct pressure and on demand.

In 1942 Cousteau met Emile Gagnan, a

Above: modern aqualung.

French engineer who specialized in gas-control valves. Gagnan showed him a demand valve that he had developed to pump cooking gas into motorcars. They adapted the valve to a pressurized-air cylinder so that it regulated the supply of air to the pressure appropriate at the local depth. When the diver breathed in the external pressure closed an outlet valve and pushed a diaphragm, the regulator valve, in. This opened up the air supply from the cylinder. On breathing out the outlet valve was pushed open, simultaneously shutting the inlet valve and cutting off the air supply. The inlet and outlet valves were placed next to one another to minimize air-pressure differences which would otherwise block air coming in.

Cousteau experimented with this aqualung, as he called it, in a test tank in Paris. The tests were done in secret to prevent the German authorities from getting hold of the idea. Then,

Oceanography

one June morning in 1943, in a remote part of the French Riviera, Cousteau tested the equipment undersea. He waded in while his diving colleagues and wife waited on the shore in case of an emergency. Breathing freely, Cousteau was the first man to experience the exhilaration of swimming like a fish. The first dive reached a depth of 60 feet, and Cousteau made subsequent dives, each of which took him further down.

For Cousteau the aqualung opened up hitherto unforeseen horizons. Freed from a cumbersome airline he started underwater filming, initially of sunken ships. It was for this purpose that he took command of the vessel *Calypso*, originally a British mine sweeper. Cousteau adapted the *Calypso* for oceanographic research and he still uses it today for whichever project and location he chooses to film.

Although lacking any formal biological training, Cousteau then turned to studying marine

Below: Cousteau's diving saucer. This free-swimming submersible is equipped with outside mechanical arms and is propelled by water jets. It can carry two men underwater to a depth of 1000 feet.

Below: *Conshell II* on the remote Sh'ab Rumi Reef in the Red Sea. Cousteau's second underwater habitat consisted of a starfish-like complex of cylinders that looked more like a village than a house. In 1963, five men stayed in the habitat for a month. They were chosen not for their diving abilities or physical condition, but their individual skills, either as mechanics, cooks, or scientists. Cousteau was not so much interested in breaking depth records – *Conshell II* was only 36 feet below the surface – as in setting up the forerunner of a possible future underwater society.

life. In 1953 he pioneered underwater television and revealed to the rest of the world what he had been privileged to observe. His films have since gained him worldwide popularity.

Another of his innovations has been the *Conshelf*, the first of which was built in 1962. This was a series of underwater habitats which could house divers during long explorations.

Today Cousteau continues to devote himself to undersea research. In particular he has turned to the problem of the pollution of the sea and the pillaging of its resources. For this purpose he has founded the Cousteau Society in the United States. His films, as informative as they are entertaining, have educated people about the oceans. His aqualung has freed man to swim like a fish.

Sir Christopher Cockerell

born 1910

The hovercraft was a new concept in vehicle design and function. Traveling on a cushion of air, it spread its weight across the whole area. Consequently it could maneuver on any type of surface, including water, without the need for specially built tracks. The world's first practicable machine in this new line of vehicles was built in 1959 by the British engineer Sir Christopher Cockerell.

"Hovercraft" is a popular term for an air-cushion vehicle or ACV. The first man to design a vessel that would ride over water on a cushion of air was Sir John Thornycroft, a marine engineer and designer of the British Royal Navy's first torpedo boat. In 1877 he took out a patent for a vessel with a hollow bottom into which air was pumped; the purpose of this idea was to reduce drag on the hull. The main difficulty was to find a way of containing the air so as to maintain the pressure and resulting cushioning effect. Little progress was made until the early 1950s when a few engineers decided to tackle the problem again.

One of these was Christopher Cockerell, an electronics engineer who changed his career to

sides of the air cushion while maintaining the pressure and keeping the craft above the surface of the terrain.

Cockerell first tested his idea using an industrial fan drier, a set of kitchen scales, and some tin cans. When he placed one can inside the other and blew air in with the drier, the weight lifted by the resulting thrust was far greater than when he used a single can. The results bore out Cockerell's theories and he submitted his designs

Right: Cockerell's first working demonstration of the peripheral-jet principle used tin cans, an industrial drier, and kitchen scales. By pumping air into two tins of different diameter, one inside the other, a much greater pressure was achieved than by using only one tin.

Center: four types of air-cushion arrangement. In the plenum chamber (A) air is pumped in and simply escapes under the surrounding wall. In the early peripheral jet (B) air pumped down the inward-sloping slit keeps the cushion pressure above atmospheric. The flexible skirt (C) increased hoverheight. In seagoing craft (D) air escapes only at the bow and stern, providing improved buoyancy and stability but at the cost of greater drag.

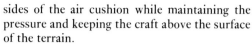

A   B

C   D

Right: testing a working model of the hovercraft on a pond. Cockerell can be seen on the right.

boat-building. He realized that a boat's performance could be greatly improved if the friction between the water and hull surface was reduced by interposing a layer of air. He turned to Thornycroft's original notion of pumping air into an upturned chamber. However, instead of pumping the air directly into the chamber, he conceived of a design where the air was pumped down through a narrow, inward-sloping slit which ran around the periphery and fed into the chamber. The effect would be a "curtain" or jet of air which could escape in a jet from the open

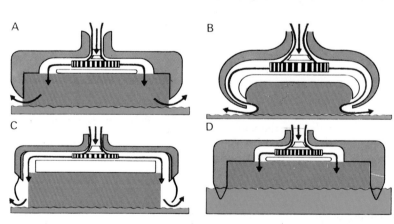

both land and water, though its above-surface clearance was still only about 9 inches. Consequently it could not have negotiated little more than an obstacle-free surface.

The triumphant demonstration in fact obscured several difficulties which remained to be solved. The craft was strictly limited in the kind of terrain it could cross or the type of sea it could tackle. Scientists calculated that a craft of this design would need to be several hundred yards

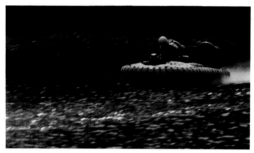

wide if it was to be able to clear an obstacle 8 feet high. Once again Cockerell provided a solution. He suggested using a flexible skirt that would extend below the rigid part of the structure. When tested out on the SR.N1, a 4-foot skirt enabled the craft to ride smoothly over waves 4 foot high and on land clear an obstacle 3.5 feet high.

The hovercraft has proved its value on terrain previously impossible to maneuver. It can travel through dense grass, on soft land such as snow and mud, and abrasive surfaces like desert sand. In addition it is amphibious, though in practice the design specifications for a type in-

to the British Government for financial support. The implications Cockerell's air-cushion craft held for developing a completely new type of amphibious vehicle with a high load-carrying capacity were clear. In 1956 his plans for an ACV were declared "secret" by the government, and it was not till 1958 that he obtained official and financial support from the National Research Development Corporation, who placed a development contract with the Saunders-Roe engineering company.

In June 1959, the first working hovercraft, the SR.N1, was unveiled and demonstrated to a great fanfare of publicity. It traveled well over

Above left: first full-scale demonstration of air-cushion principle – the SR.N1 – 1959.

Above right: small two-seater hovercraft, 1978.

Below left: the air-cushion principle can also be used to move heavy containers, as in this 530-ton storage tank.

Right: *Princess Anne*, the largest hovercraft in existence. It weighs 300 tons and can carry 416 passengers.

tended to operate primarily on water have turned out to be rather different to those for a terrestrial AVC.

Although it is unlikely to replace wheeled vehicles in the forseeable future, the hovercraft has carved out a useful role for itself. It has several advantages over wheeled vehicles, including the ability to carry considerable loads, and can achieve very high speeds on water. Whatever future forms it takes, the hovercraft seems certain to become a major feature of travel and freight carriage in the 21st century.

Wernher von Braun
1912-1974

Pioneer rocket engineer and architect of the United States space program, Wernher von Braun designed many of America's modern space boosters and conceived the flight strategy which made possible man's first landing on the moon. Combining a deep knowledge of engineering with a unique vision of man's future in space, von Braun provided the technical expertise and inspiration that maintained America's enthusiasm during the slow and costly development of space-flight technology.

The son of a German baron, von Braun was educated in Zurich, Switzerland, returning to Germany in 1930 to study engineering at the University of Berlin. Even as a child he dreamed of the possibilities of space-flight and read every book he could find on the subject. When he entered Berlin University he became a founder member of the German Society for Space Travel, a group of enthusiastic amateurs who shared an obsession for rocket engineering. In the two years of its existence the group made over 80 successful launches, their rockets reaching altitudes of up to a mile. By 1932 the German army

had become interested in the amateur rocket builders and when, a year later, Hitler came to power, the army recommended the building of a rocket research center. Hoping that rocket-powered bombs might someday help him to dominate Europe, Hitler ordered the establishment of such a center at Peenemünde on the Baltic Coast. Meanwhile, rocket tests and research for purposes other than military use were outlawed. Von Braun was one of the first

Above: a V-2 being launched at Peenemünde, destined for London.

Left: Wernher von Braun (second right). Seated, in the foreground, is Hermann Oberth, who reawakened Germany's scientific interest in space travel with his book *The Rocket into Interplanetary Space* (1923). Oberth maintained that there was already at that time sufficient technical expertise available for constructing rockets that could escape the earth's atmosphere, and predicted interplanetary and manned space flights.

engineers to be recruited and throughout the late 1930s and the war years he helped to direct the development of powerful rocket engines.

His most important achievement was the first true missile, the V-2. This devastating new weapon could deliver a 1600-pound explosive warhead to targets over 200 miles away and as it traveled at a supersonic speed of one mile per second there was no advanced warning of its approach. Fortunately the V-2 was perfected too late to save the war for Hitler and when Germany fell, von Braun left Peenemünde and surrendered to the advancing American troops. Despite his former work and his membership of the Nazi Party, he was warmly welcomed in the United States where he soon became a key member of the American missile research team.

During the 1950s von Braun played an important role in developing American rocket technology. His designs were initially based on the V-2, but his new boosters soon outstripped the comparatively modest capabilities of their forerunner. By 1958 von Braun had designed and built the four-stage booster known as Jupiter which was used to launch America's first satellite into orbit. Despite his background in military rockets, von Braun's true interests lay in the possibility of manned space-flight, which he believed would one day take man to the stars. The opportunity to realize his dreams came soon after the Jupiter success. The United States congress established American's first civilian space agency, the National Aeronautics and Space Administration (NASA) and charged it with the job of investigating manned space-flight. One of its first appointments was America's top rocket expert, von Braun.

In the years that followed, von Braun helped

Above: a night launch for the Juno 1 booster that carried the United States' first satellite, Explorer 1, into orbit. The Juno was a modification of the Redstone ballistic missile, the United States' equivalent of the V-2.

Right: the huge Saturn V rocket during construction in the purpose-built Vehicle Assembly Building. The rocket could put a total of 120 tons of payload into orbit or 45 tons on a lunar trajectory.

40-ton moonship into the earth's orbit. Von Braun's answer was the most powerful booster ever built, the giant Saturn V. Its three stages towered over 360 feet and weighed around 3000 tons. At lift-off its engines delivered an incredible 7,500,000-pound thrust, burning more than 10 tons of fuel each second. Saturn was the ultimate in booster technology and despite its complexity proved to be a completely reliable mainstay for the lunar landing program.

While the Apollo flights to the Moon were making headlines throughout the world, von Braun was already drafting plans for the first flights to Mars. But despite his enthusiasm and exciting design proposals, NASA had to defer all plans for interplanetary flights. Americans were beginning to count the cost of the space program and NASA was soon hit by financial cutbacks leading to canceled plans and redundancies. Von Braun knew that he would have to leave interplanetary missions to another generation of space engineers. Bitterly disappointed and frustrated he resigned from NASA and spent his last years working in private industry.

to mastermind the three major manned space-flight programs: Mercury, Germini, and the lunar landing missions of Apollo. His greatest achievements were to conceive the scenario for a moon landing and to design the giant booster to launch the moonship on its epic journey.

Von Braun's idea for a moon landing was bold and complex. It required a sophisticated new spaceship built in three sections: a service module containing fuel, power, and life support systems, a command module and a lunar landing vehicle. Von Braun's plan was to place the ship in lunar orbit and then separate the lunar lander from command and service modules. Piloted by two of the three-man Apollo crew, the lander would swoop down to the surface. The astronaut's return would then entail a tricky lift-off from the moon and a rendezvous and docking maneuver with the "mother ship." The lander could then be jettisoned while service and command modules blasted out of orbit on course for earth. Before plunging into the earth's atmosphere the crew would discard the service module and reenter in the cone-shaped command module, splashing down in a designated area of the Pacific Ocean.

The novel concept was a brilliant success. But it demanded a rocket capable of boosting the

Jonas Salk

born 1914

The American virologist Jonas Salk developed the first vaccine effective against poliomyelitis. He discovered it at a time when this paralyzing disease was reaching epidemic proportions in many parts of the world.

Jonas Salk was born in New York City, the son of a garment worker. A brilliant student, he studied medicine at New York University School of Medicine, graduating in 1939.

From the start of his career Salk was interested in viruses, tiny parasitic organisms visible only under an electron microscope. In 1942 he went on a research fellowship to the University of

Right: Egyptian carving showing a priest's limb atrophied by poliomyelitics.

Below: Salk reading the results of a new polio color test developed in his University of Pittsburg laboratory under a March of Dimes grant. The test determines the presence of the virus and the level of antibodies against it in human blood.

Michigan to continue his studies in the virus responsible for influenza, and eventually rose to become Assistant Professor of Epidemology.

In 1947 Salk moved to Pennsylvania to be Research Professor of Bacteriology at the University of Pittsburg School of Medicine. He also directed the Virus Research Laboratory. At that point Salk's interest turned to poliomyelitis, against which there was no known method of protection.

The disease was common and world-wide, and by the early 1950s several epidemics had broken out in Europe and the United States. The virus enters the body through the throat and attacks the spinal cord. In most cases the patient recovers, but where the attack is severe it can destroy the nerves. As a result the patient can become severely paralyzed.

Paradoxically, although improved sanitation reduces the chances of infection, it also increases the possibilities of an epidemic. In under-developed countries infants come into contact with the disease and develop immunity to it. Where the standard of hygiene is high natural immunity is rare and the disease, once introduced, can become an epidemic. Also the chance of the disease becoming severe and causing paralysis is much higher in older, more active children than it is in infants.

Salk studied all the works available on viruses and vaccination, from Edward Jenner's discovery of the smallpox vaccine onward. He

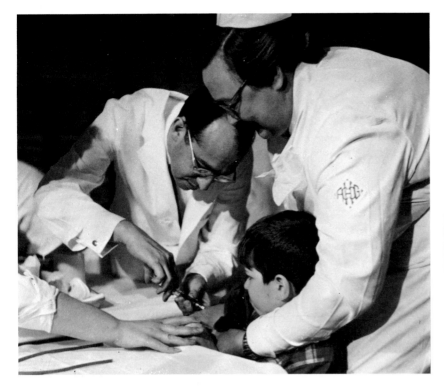

In addition to the injected Salk vaccine, an oral one has been produced which is now widely used. It was first introduced in 1961 and was developed by Albert Sabin, an American virologist born in Russia. The Sabin vaccine uses an attenuated virus, one which has been grown in artificial conditions until it loses its virulence but not its ability to confer immunity. Polio vaccination is now part of a child's routine inoculation program and the disease is virtually under control. Salk has since devoted himself to cancer research and heads the Salk Institute for Biological Studies, La Jolla, in California.

decided to develop a vaccine using a dead virus. The problem was to kill the vaccine in such a way that it still had the ability to induce an immune response.

In 1953 Salk announced that he had developed his trial vaccine. It consisted of the three then-known types of polio virus killed with a formaldehyde solution. The vaccine also contained some penicillin. Salk, with his wife and three children, were among the first to receive the vaccination. It proved to be safe and effective, and the next year a mass trial, sponsored by the National Foundation for Infantile Paralysis, was launched. Nearly two million schoolchildren were inoculated.

Above: Salk administering an injection during the mass vaccination trials of 1954.

Right: electron micrograph of poliomyelitis virus, Type II.

Below left: Salk inspecting chromatographic fractions of serum, March of Dimes.

Below right: polio often causes paralysis of breathing and the victims have to be kept alive in an iron lung.

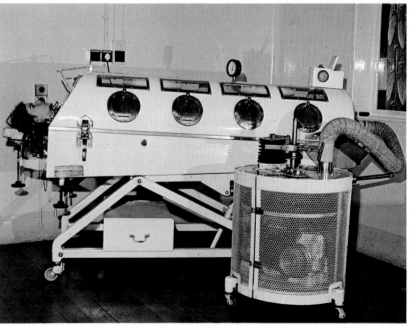

Charles Hard Townes

born 1915

American physicist and engineer Charles Townes invented a way of powerfully amplifying electromagnetic radiation. By triggering an energy cascade in the molecules of certain substances he produced the first maser, a device emitting intense, undeviating beams of microwaves, a form of heat radiation. Townes then extended the technique to amplify visible light and so paved the way for the invention of the laser.

Townes was born in Greenville, South Carolina. As a young man he had few ambitions other than to be a scientist and he entered Greenville's own university to study physics. He graduated in 1935 and spent the next four years on postgraduate research which culminated in a doctorate in science from the prestigious California Institute of Technology. In the war years that followed, Townes worked for the Bell Telephones Laboratories developing new kinds of military radar.

His years with Bell Telephones provided him with a deep knowledge of microwave physics. Microwaves, a form of electromagnetic radiation

much like light but of far longer wavelength, share some of the properties of both radio and infrared waves. Although extremely useful in radar and communications sytems, they were difficult to generate artificially and many physicists had been investigating ways of overcoming this problem. Soon after leaving Bell Telephones for the science faculty of Columbia University, Townes joined the search for a new microwave generator.

In 1951 Townes struck upon a brilliant and

original idea. While many of his contemporaries had been trying to develop a new kind of electronic circuit, Townes realized that the molecules of certain substances might themselves be turned into excellent microwave generators. He knew that if molecules were excited to a higher state and then allowed to drop to their original energy state, radiation would be emitted. If the radiation could be stored in some way it could be used to stimulate other molecules to emit radia-

Above: an experiment in microwave communication across the English Channel in 1931. This contemporary photograph shows the French terminal at Calais. The high frequency of the microwave part of the spectrum means that a wide band of modulation frequency can be carried. Consequently many thousands of telephone channels can be carried on a single microwave carrier, and black-and-white and color television can use the same carrier. Another advantage of microwaves in communications systems is that their wavelength is short enough to allow relatively small reflectors to focus the signal. The need for a microwave generator which would amplify the signals without distorting them provided the impetus for the invention of the laser.

tion of the same wavelength. The result of this cascade reaction would be a series of waves, in step with, and superimposed on one another – overall a highly amplified beam of radiation.

By 1953 Townes had built his prototype microwave generator. It consisted of a cylindrical cage of metal rods, through which passed a stream of ammonia molecules, heated up to vibrate more rapidly. The metal rods were electrically charged, with alternate rods having opposite charges, and this created an electrical field which separated unexcited molecules from excited ones. The latter were focused into a metal resonator which made the molecules emit radiation of the same frequency and stimulate incoming ones to do likewise.

Townes' generator produced a highly amplified and consistent microwave, and was rapidly acclaimed as a huge success. It became known as the "maser," the name being an acronym for Microwave Amplification by Stimulated Emission of Radiation.

Masers were soon utilized in long-distance communications where the powerful and undeviating maser beam could be accurately directed on a distant receiver. They also became important as amplifiers of minute radio signals, in particular as ultrasensitive detectors in space research.

In 1957 Townes began speculating about an exciting new possibility. If his technique amplified microwaves successfully, would it also work for waves in the visible-light spectrum. Three years later, following Townes' suggestions, the American physicist Theodore Maiman built the first optical maser, or laser as it is now known. The letters stand for Light Amplification by Stimulated Emission of Radiation.

Maiman used a cylinder of synthetic ruby around which was wound a helical glass flashtube. On firing the flashtube, Maiman triggered the molecules of the ruby crystal to emit light, which was reflected back and forth into the crystal by a pair of mirrors, and amplified into an intense pencil beam of red light. Not only was the beam the most intense ever produced by artificial means, it was also almost perfectly parallel. Even over huge distances the laser beam spread and diffused only by the merest fraction. As with the maser, it was therefore possible to direct a laser beam with remarkable accuracy over thousands of miles. When a laser beam was directed onto the moon, in 1962, the light spread out across only two miles and the reflection was bright enough to be seen on earth.

Since Maiman's first prototype, lasers have developed into versatile, almost commonplace instruments. In scientific research they have provided new insights into our understanding of the nature of light while in industry they have become important in communications systems, precision welding, drilling of previously heat-resistant materials, and highly accurate measure-

Above: holography, a three-dimensional reproduction of an image produced by a laser beam. One half of the beam (the reference beam) is reflected by a plane mirror directly onto a photographic plate. The other half (the signal beam) is reflected by the illuminated object onto the same plate. The result is an interference pattern known as a hologram. To reconstruct the image a laser beam is shone through the plate in the same direction as the reference beam and an image of the object can be seen from the other side of the plate. The image is genuinely three-dimensional in that if the observer moves his head around he will see around and behind the object.

ment. Lasers are also used to create three-dimensional images known as holographs. Military applications include new navigation and weapon targeting systems. Meanwhile, in medicine lasers have the potential to revolutionize the treatment of cancer and are already used for delicate operations on the eye.

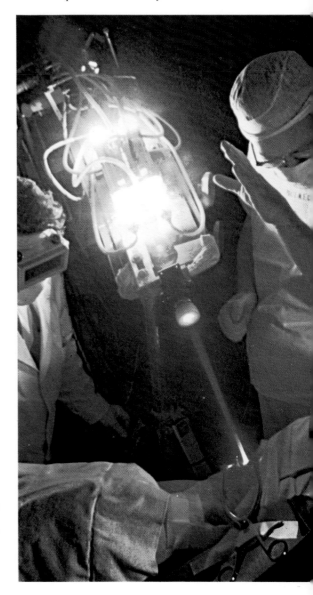

Left: in 1962 a beam from a laser (in the lighted area at lower right) was flashed to the moon. It lit up an area of the moon's surface only two miles across. The reflected light was bright enough to be detected back on earth.

Right: a laser beam replaces the surgeon's knife in a cancer operation in the United States. The laser beam provides a more precise method of destroying diseased cells and has been employed for many delicate operations. Detatched retinas have been welded using the intense energy of the beam.

Francis Crick
born 1916
James Watson
born 1928

The most important biological discovery of the 20th century was that of the structure of DNA. Although several groups of scientists were working on the problem, it was the British biophysicist Francis Crick, and James Watson, an American biologist, who found the answer. Their double-helix model showed at once how a cell divides to form two identical copies of itself, and how genetic information can be stored.

Deoxyribonucleic acid (DNA) is found in the nucleus of every cell. Its role in heredity had long been suspected and it was generally accepted that it formed the basis of genes, the units of heredity. Little was known about its structure except that it was made up of the purine bases adenine and guanine, the smaller pyrimidine bases thymine and cytosine, a sugar called deoxyribose, and phosphates. These chemicals were linked together somehow to form an extremely large molecule – a macromolecule.

James Watson had initially become interested in DNA when Maurice Wilkins, a British physicist engaged in crystallographic research, showed him an X-ray diffraction picture of the molecule. It strongly suggested that DNA was a helix. In 1951 Watson arrived at the Cavendish Laboratory at Cambridge University to work on the three-dimensional structure of proteins. He met and struck up a friendship with Francis

Right: the historic X-ray diffraction pattern of a deoxyribonucleic acid (DNA) molecule, taken in 1952. This photograph, taken with its clear black cross of reflections, strongly suggested a helical structure and confirmed the discovery of the double-helix structure of DNA.

Below left: James Watson (left) and Francis Crick (right), standing by their model the DNA molecule at the Cavendish Laboratory, Cambridge University, Britain.

Crick, also engaged in research at the Cavendish. Watson infected Crick with his enthusiasm for the mysteries of DNA. The aims of the physicist and the biologist became fused into a mutual passion to discover the secret of life.

Although DNA research was not taken very seriously by many, there were some scientists making progress, notably Maurice Wilkins in London and the American chemist Linus Pauling at the California Institute of Technology.

Crick and Watson entered the race at the point when Linus Pauling had announced that he thought DNA to be a single-stranded helical structure. Crick and Watson were convinced that the helix was made of two strands. They obtained structural scale models of all the components and tried to fit these together. Initially they failed. Either the model fell apart or it did not conform to the chemical and crystallographic evidence already available.

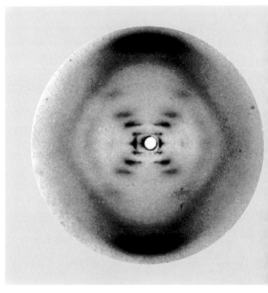

A vital clue to the solution was the fact that in any species of DNA the amounts of adenine and thymine are always equal, as are those of cytosine and guanine. Wilkins' crystallographic evidence also pointed to the sugar-phosphate component being on the outside of the molecule.

Then one day, in early spring 1953, all the clues fell into place. Watson saw that the shape of the structure formed by the bonding of adenine to thymine was identical to that of the cytosine-guanine pair. If in nature adenine always bonded to thymine, and guanine to cytosine, then this would explain why equal amounts of each member of a pair were always found. The identically-shaped pairs could also be packed neatly inside the helix without any distortion. It also meant that the strands were complementary to one another and one could form a template for the synthesis of the other.

Crick and Watson were thus able to build their now-famous model, intrinsically simple and to them very beautiful. It satisfied both the crystallographic data and stereochemical laws. Basically

Biochemistry

it consisted of a double backbone of sugar and phosphate in repeating units. Between these, like rungs in a ladder, were the flat pairs of bases. On April 2, 1953, they sent a paper to the British journal *Nature* announcing their discovery.

Many considered the elucidation of DNA's structure the most exciting discovery of the 20th century. Not only did the double helix explain how a cell could divide, but it showed how genetic information could be stored. Each group or unit of three bases on a strand could code for an amino acid, the basic constituent of proteins. A series of the units, read in sequence, would produce a string of amino acids linked in a defined order to form a particular protein. This series of base units is the gene.

In 1962 Crick and Watson received the Nobel Prize for Medicine. They shared it with Maurice Wilkins, whose crystallographic evidence had made their discovery possible.

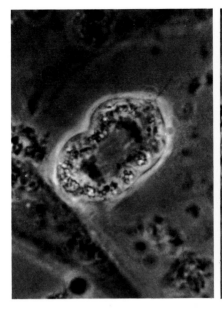

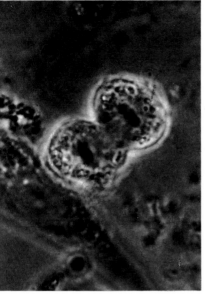

Above: a cancer cell divides. The chromosomes, which have already doubled in number, can be seen as dark masses at either end of the pole.

Far left: at cell division two chromosome threads unravel; each then makes a new thread. Because bases (yellow) can pair only one way, the sequence of bases on the new threads is predetermined. The result is two chromosomes, each identical with the original.

Center left: each amino acid is programed by a group of three bases on the DNA molecule. Reading from one end, a definite sequence of amino acids is obtained, and this determines the type of protein synthesized. A group of base triplets, coding for a protein, is a gene.

Right: the nucleotide (top left) from which chromosomes are built, consisting of a sugar (deoxyribose), a phosphate, and a base. The sugar-phosphate backbone never varies but there are four different possible bases. Many nucleotides join to form a polynucleotide thread (bottom left). Two such threads coiled around each other form the DNA molecule. The bases of the two threads are joined together by hydrogen bonds (dotted). Guanine always pairs with cytosine and adenine with thymine.

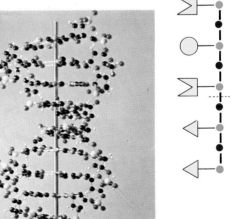

Below left: model of DNA. The colored spheres represent different atoms.

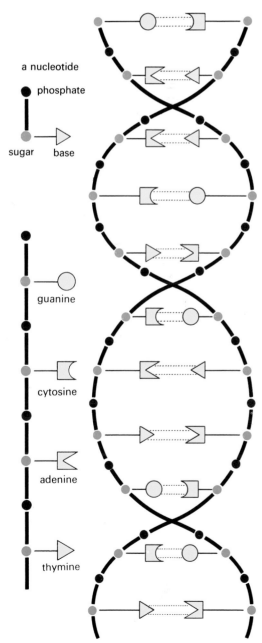

a nucleotide

phosphate

sugar   base

guanine

cytosine

adenine

thymine

315

Christiaan Barnard

born 1922

In December 1967 Dr Christiaan Barnard, a South African physician, performed the first successful heart transplant on a human being. Although the patient survived only 18 days, this complex operation pioneered the way for many more successful ones by Barnard and other surgeons, and extended medical understanding of the body's immunity responses.

The transplanting of tissue from one human being to another is not a recent practice. Though

perhaps not as old as Adam's rib, Egyptian manuscripts, dating back to 2000 BC, record the use of skin grafts. Hindu surgeons were performing grafts of noses at around 600 BC, and the technique was in use in Europe by the 15th century, having been imported from the East.

There are two problems inherent in transplant operations. The first is a surgical one; the technique must be sufficiently well advanced and performed with such skill as to enable the transplanted tissue's blood vessels to join up (anastomose) with those of the patient. This process has to occur quickly otherwise the grated tissue will die.

The second problem, rejection, is more complicated and serious. The body's defense mechanism has evolved to destroy organisms such as viruses and bacteria. It recognizes these organisms as undesirable not by their pathogenic

Below: transplanting a living kidney. The picture on the right shows the kidney just before its transfer into a human recipient. Tapes are used to minimize handling of the organ. When the kidney is removed from the donor or cadaver it is immediately perfused with a sterile liquid that is isotonic (of the same concentration) with the blood (left). This picture shows the perfusion cannula being inserted into the artery of the transplant. The perfused parts of the graft have become pale. The perfusion helps to exclude air from the graft and increases its viability. Restoration of color after the operation is an instant indication that the kidney's circulation is still intact.

intentions but because they have foreign or "not-self" proteins called antigens.

A tissue or organ graft contains many such antigens. These are inherited and the more distant the relation between donor and recipient, the less chance there is of a graft being compatible – not rejected. The early skin grafts took because in general the tissue came from the patient himself. Identical twins have identical antigens and the problem does not occur. Nor does it with fraternal twins whose blood has mingled in the womb. These "blood chimeras," as they are known, have developed tolerance to each others antigens.

Transplant rejection also depends on the type of tissue being transplanted. Grafts of the cornea always take because the cornea has no blood supply. It is the white blood cells called lymphocytes that produce antibodies against foreign antigens and are responsible for the ultimate rejection. As lymphocytes do not come into contact with the cornea, rejection is unlikely. In the case of blood transfusions, the most common tissue transplant, the antigens are located in the red blood cell and there are fewer of them. Consequently it is much easier to find donors with compatible blood.

Compatible donors for complex organs such as the kidney, liver, and heart are less easy to find. With the exception of identical twins and blood chimeras, the chances of finding a donor and recipient with identical antigens is, for practical purposes, nonexistent. Surgeons tend to concentrate on certain groups of antigens, those which provoke the strongest reaction, and search for compatibility in that area. Patients about to receive organs are also given drugs such as steroids, and radioactive therapy to depress their immunity response.

The kidney was the first organ to be transplanted successfully. In the early 1960s transplant operations were made on the liver, lung, and pancreas. In December 1967, accompanied by a blaze of publicity, the first successful heart

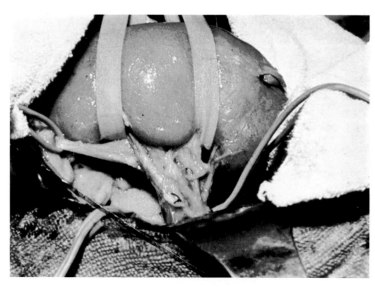

Medicine

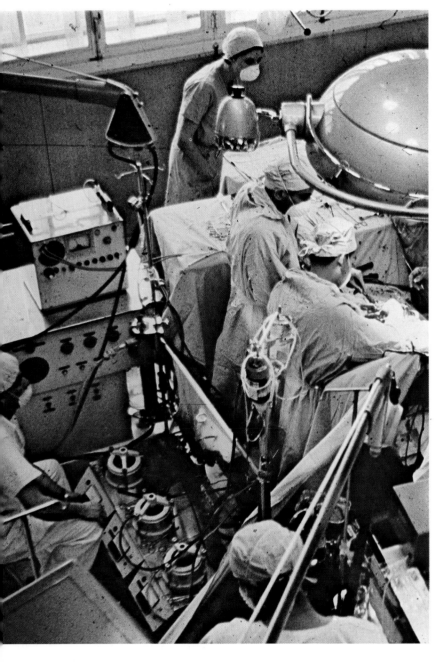

transplant was performed. The physician leading the five-hour operation was Christiaan Barnard, senior cardiac surgeon at Groote Schuur Hospital in Cape Town, South Africa.

Barnard was a leading South African surgeon, educated at the Universities of Cape Town and Minneapolis. As senior cardiothoracic (heart–lung) surgeon at Groote Schuur Hospital, he pioneered many surgical innovations, including the introduction of open-heart surgery in South Africa. He also provided a new artificial valve for the heart.

Barnard's triumphant achievement was the culmination of many years' research and experimentation, initially on transplanting the hearts of dogs. His patient, a diabetic with an incurable heart disease, was a South African grocer called Louis Washkansky. The donor, a 24-year-old woman, had been fatally injured in a car traffic accident. The donor and recipient were of the same blood group and their tissue compatibility was considered high.

For three hours before the operation the heart was kept in cooled, oxygenated blood. Because it was about half the size of Washkansky's own, there were difficulties in getting it to take on the workload of pumping blood around a much larger body. The patient was kept alive, in the meantime, on a heart-lung machine. Barnard knew that the operation was a success from a surgical viewpoint when he applied electrodes to the newly-installed heart and it started beating.

Washkansky in fact died 18 days later, ironically as a result of the drugs and radioactive therapy which he had received to suppress his immunity. He caught double pneumonia, a common postoperative illness, against which his body was defenseless.

Many transplant operations have since been performed by Barnard himself and leading surgeons in the United States, Europe, and Japan. Although the chances of survival are still low, some recipients lived for several years.

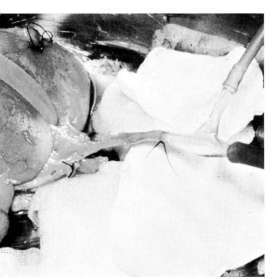

Above: open-heart surgery. While the surgeons (upper right) are working on the opened heart of the patient, the heart-lung machine (lower left) takes over the heart's circulatory load and also oxygenates the blood. Before the advent of the heart-lung machine, surgeons could not open a heart for more than 10 minutes. Even then the patient's body had to be cooled so as to lower his metabolism. Barnard pioneered open-heart surgery in South Africa.

Right: Barnard operating.

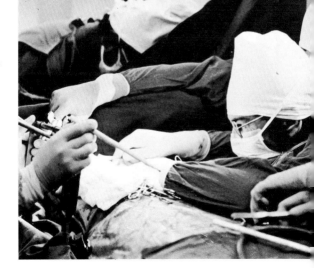

Scientists and Inventors

INDEX

Opposite: the laboratory at Zurich, where, during the early 1900s, Albert Einstein formulated his revolutionary theories of relativity. Einstein's theories marked a drastic departure of scientific thought from the rigid framework of Newtonian physics. With the publication of his relativity theories, a new examination of space and time was opened up.

Bacon, Roger, 28
bacteriology
    application to food preservation, 80
    Fleming's work, 270
    Jenner's work, 79
    Koch's work, 198–9
    Leeuwenhoek's work, 44, 45
    Pasteur's work, 162–3
Baekeland, Leo Hendrik, 246–7, *246*
Baeyer, Adolf von, 247
Baird, John Logie, 276–7, *276*, *277*
bakelite, 246, 247, *247*
ballooning
    Montgolfier brothers, 70–1, *70*
    see also airships
Baltic Railway Car Factory, 278
Barbier, Charles, 140
"barber-surgeons," *172*
barium, 269
Barnard, Christiaan, 316–17, *316*, *317*
barographs, 39
barometers, 38, *39*
batteries, *235*
    electric, 74, *74*; *see also* Leyden jars
    nuclear, *291*
Battle of Britain, 285
Bauer, Andreas, 104
Bauer, Georg, *see* Agricola, Georgius
bauxite, 245
    see also aluminum
Beagle, 142, *142*
Beau de Rochas, Alphonse-Eugène,
    181
Becquerel, Antoine Henri, 210–11,
    211, 252
    Curies' interest in work, 252
    link with work of Arrhenius, 235
Beemster Lake, 34
Behaim, Martin, *27*
Behring, Emil von, 218
Bell, Alexander Graham, 204–5, *204*
Bell, Henry, 91
Bell Telephones Laboratories, 312
bellows, *25*
Benz, Carl, 184, 200–1, *200*
    exploitation of Otto's engine, 181
    merger with Daimler, 185
benzaldehyde, 131
benzene, molecular structure, 176, *176*,
    177, *177*
Bergeron, Tor, *240*
Berlin Academy of Science, 228
Berlin University, 264, 308
Bertillon, Alphonse, 214–15
Bertillonage, *see* anthropometry
beryllium, 280
Berzelius, Jöns Jacob, 130
Bessemer, Sir Henry, 148–9
Bessemer process, 148, *148*
beta rays, 261
Bible, printed by Gutenberg, 16, *17*
bicycles, 196, 197
Bienvenu, — , *278*
"big bang" theory, 133
binomial nomenclature system, 54
biochemists
    Crick and Watson, 314–15
biology
    Aristotle's influence, 13
    Darwin, 98, 142–3, 161

    see also biochemists; botany;
        genetics; marine biology;
        zoologists
Bjerknes, Jacob, 240, *240*, 241
Bjerknes, Vilhelm, 240–1
Blanchard, Jean-Pierre-François, *71*
blind people, use of Braille, 140–1,
    140, *141*
blood circulation, 36–7, *36*, *37*
blood groups, 256–7, *257*
blood transfusions, 256–7, *256*, *257*,
    316
Blücher, 110
Bohr, Niels, 233, 274–5, *275*, *280*
bombast, derivation of word, 22
bombs, *see* weapons
Borgia, Cesare, 19
boring machines, 66
Born, Max, *275*
boron, 290
Bosch, Carl, 259
botanists
    Linnaeus, 54–5, *54*
    see also biology
Boulton, Matthew, 66, 86, 87
Bovedere, Jacques, 28
Boyle, Robert, 40–1
Boyle-Hooke vacuum pump, *40*
Boyle lectures, 41
Boyle's Law, 41, 188–9
Brady, Matthew, 129, *129*
Bragg, William Henry, 267
Bragg, William Lawrence, 267
Brahe, Tycho, 32
Braille, Louis, 140–1
Braille alphabet, *141*
brain, *291*
    areas of higher nervous activity, *209*
Bramah, Joseph, 76–7
Branca, Giovanni, *220*
Braun, Karl Ferdinand, 263, 276–7
Braun, Werner von, 308–9, *308*
bridges
    Abraham Darby's iron bridge, 51, *51*
    Clifton Suspension Bridge, 137, *137*
Bristol Iron Company, 50
British Association for the Advance-
    ment of Science, 124
    Joule elected president, 153
Brno, 160
broadcasting, *see* radio broadcasting;
    television
Broglie, Louis-Victor de, *280*, 282–3
bromide paper, 175
Brown, Samuel, 164
Brunel, Isambard Kingdom, 77, 136–7
Brunel, Sir Marc, 136, 138
Bullock, William, 105
Bunsen, Robert, 168, *169*
Bunsen burners, 168
buoyancy, 14
burning glasses, *60*, *64*, *72*
Burton, Sir Richard, 28
Bushnell, David, 90
Byrne, Charles, 58

C

cable-laying, submarine, 170, *170*

caesium, 169
calculus
    differential, 15
    infinitesimal, 47
    integral, 39
caliche, *259*
California Institute of Technology, 296,
    298, 312
Calley, John, 48
caloric, 84
calorimeters, *72*
calotype, 119, 128–9, *129*
Calypso, 305
camera obscura, 94, *94*, 128
cameras
    box, 222, *222*, 223, *223*
    Polaroid, 302–3, *302*, *303*
    see also cinematography; photo-
        graphy
canal rays, 227
canals, 90
cancer
    cell division, *315*
    chemotherapy, *219*
    radium therapy, 253
    treatment by lasers, 313, *313*
canning, 80–1, *80*, *81*
carbon dioxide, discovered by Priestley,
    64
carbon-14 dating technique, *261*
carbon microphones, *205*
carbon-resistance transmitters, 206
carbon tissue, *175*
carburettors, 184
Carey, George, 238
Carlson, Chester F, 298–9
Carnot, Sadi, 165
Carothers, Wallace Hume, 286–7, *286*
cartographers
    Gerardus Mercator, 26–7
Cassegrain telescope, 139
catapults, 15
catastrophism, theory of, 98
cathode-ray oscilloscope, 276–7
cathode rays, 202, 226, *226*
    Crookes' research, 183
cauterization, *172*
Cavendish, Henry, 60–1, *60*
    discovery of hydrogen, 70
Cavendish Laboratory, Cambridge, 179,
    226, 288, 296, 314
Caxton, William, 17, *17*
Cellarius, Andreas, *21*
Celluloid, 246, *246*
Celsus, 11
    see also Paracelsus
Chadwick, Sir James, 280–1, *280*
Chain, Ernst, 271
Chalcis, 12
Chardonnet, Hilaire Bernigaud de, 286
Charité Hospital, Berlin, 218
Charles, Jacques-Alexandre-César, 71,
    170–1
Charlotte Dundas, 91
chemical compounds
    behavior in solution, 234
    organic, 130
    proportions of constituent elements,
        97
    valency theory, 177

Researches on Fossil Bones, 98
resistance, *see* electrical resistance
resonance, 255
resonator, *255*
respiration, *73*
"resurrection men," 58
retrograding, 32
reverberation, 254-5, *254*
rheostat, toroidal, *115*
Rhesus factor, 257
"right-hand grip rule," 106
rinderpest, 199
roads, macadamized, 88-9, *88, 89*
Rochester University, 223
Rockefeller Institute for Medical
　　Research, 257
Rocket, 111, *111*
rockets, *272*
　　Goddard's work, 272-3, *272*
　　liquid propellant, 272, *272*
　　V1s and V2s, 285
　　von Braun's work, 308-9
Röntgen, Wilhelm, 183, 202-3, 210,
　　260
rotary engines, 220-1, 294-5, *294, 295*
rotary steam engines, 66, *66*
Royal Aircraft Establishment, 300
Royal Albert Hall, *254*
Royal College of Chemistry, 182, 190
Royal Festival Hall, London, *255*
Royal Institute for Experimental
　　Therapy, Frankfurt, 218
Royal Institution, 84, *85*
Royal Society, 40, *40*
　　Babbage's attack, 124
　　correspondence with Leeuwenhoek,
　　　45
　　Isaac Newton, President (1703-27),
　　　47
　　Joule elected, 153
　　Ohm admitted to membership, 115
　　Watt and Boulton elected Fellows,
　　　67
rubber, 196
rubidium, 169
Rumford, Count, *see* Sir Benjamin
　　Thompson
Rumford stove, *85*
　　Rutherford, Sir Ernest, *227, 233,*
　　　260-1, *261, 280, 288*
　　influence on Bohr, 274
　　influence on Chadwick, 280
　　influence on Oppenheim, 296
　　lectured to Cockroft, 288
　　solar-system model of the atom, 227
　　use of Crookes' spinthariscope, 183

S

sabin, 255
Sabin, Albert, 311
Sabine, Sir Edward, 116-17
Sabine, Wallace Clement, 254-5, *254*
Sabine's law, 255
safety lamps, 108, 109, *109*
safety matches, *153*
Saint-Cloud, 194
St John's, Newfoundland, 263

St Mary's Hospital, London, 270
Salk, Jonas, 310-11, *310, 311*
saltpetre, 258
"Salvarsan," 219
sanitary engineering, 76
Santos-Dumont, Alberto, 194
Saturn (planet), *21, 42, 43, 69*
Saturn (rocket), 309, *309*
Savery, Thomas, 48, 49
scanning devices, *238, 239*
　　see also television
schlieren photography, *133, 193*
Schöffer, Peter, 17
Schott, Otto, 151, *151*
Schrödinger, Erwin, *280,* 283
Schwabe, Samuel Heinrich, 117
scientific method, 31
scientific positivism, 192
screw threads, 134, *135*
screws, *see* propellers
sea currents, 52
Seddon, George Baldwin, 201
Seebeck, Thomas Johann, 100-1
Seebeck effect, 100, *101*
selenium, 238, 298
self-inductance, 127
Selfridge, Thomas E, 251
Semmelweis, Ignaz, 172-3
Senefelder, Aloys, 94, 102-3
sewing machines, 154-5, *154, 155*
Shelton, Thomas, 146
's-Hertogenbosch, 35
shipbuilding, *see* marine engineering
shock waves, *192, 193*
Shoenberg, Isaac, *239*
Sholes, Christopher Latham, 158-9
shorthand writing
　　Gregg's system, 147
　　Pitman's system, 146-7, *147*
Siemens, Werner, 166
Siemens, Sir William, 166-7
Siemens-Martin method of steelmaking,
　　166-7, *166*
Sikorsky, Igor Ivanovich, 278-9, *278*
Sikorsky Aero Corporation, 279
silicon
　　chips, 125
　　radioactive, 290
silk
　　substitutes, 286
　　weaving, 82-3
silvering of glass, 157
Singer, Isaac Merrit, 154-5, *155*
siphon recorder, *171*
sleeping sickness, 199, *199*
smallpox, 78-9
smelting, *24,* 50, *51,* 245
Smith, Sir J E, 55
Smithsonian Institute, 127
Socrates, 12
　　criticism of Democritus, 9
soda water, 64
Soddy, Frederick, 261
sodium chloride, 235
　　ions, *234*
sodium nitrate, 258
solar eclipse, *264*
solar spectrum map, *113*
solar system, 20
solutions

behavior of compounds in, 234
Solvay Physics Conference (1911),
　　233 (1933), *280*
sonic booms, *193*
Sorbonne, 252, 282
Soulé, Samuel W, 158
sound
　　nontransmission in a vacuum, 41
　　radiation from static source, *193*
　　see also acoustics
sound recording, 205
space applications
　　of Einstein's mathematics, *265*
　　of thermoelectric effects, 101
space engineering
　　Goddard, 272-3, *272*
　　importance of cryogenics, *189*
　　von Braun's work, 308-9
Species Plantarum, 54
spectra, 46, 47
　　Fraunhofer's work, 112-13, *113*
　　Maxwell's work, 179
　　see also colors
spectral signatures, 168, 169
spectrometer
　　X-ray ionization, *267*
spectrophotometer, *113*
spectroscopes, *113,* 168, *168, 169*
spectroscopy
　　Crookes' work, 182
　　Fraunhofer, 112-13
　　Kirchhoff's work, 168-9
　　use in astronomy, 169
speculum, 69
speech communication, 204-5
speed limits, 164
speedometers, 124
spinning, 56, *57*
　　see also water frame
spinning jenny, 56-7, *56,* 62
spinning mule, *56,* 57
spinning wheels, *19*
spinthariscope, 183
Spithead naval review (1887), 221
spontaneous generation, theory of, 44
SR.N1 (hovercraft), 307, *307*
Stagira, 12
Standard Elocutionist, 204
Staphylococcus aureus, *271*
star gauging, 69
steam-blast engines, 110
steam carriages, 87
steam engines
　　double-action piston, 66-7
　　first practical type, 48
　　locomotives, 110-11, *110, 111*
　　rotary, 66, *66,* 87
　　use of atmospheric pressure, 49
　　used in automobiles, 164
steam gun, 87
steam hammer, 138-9, *138, 139*
steam turbines, 220, *220, 221*
steamships, 136-7
　　early designs, 90-1, *91*
steel
　　Bessemer process, 148, *148*
　　open-hearth method, 149, 166, *166,*
　　　167
　　Siemens-Martin method, 166-7, *166*
Stenographic Sound Hand, 146

W

Picture credits

334

227(BR) The Cavendish Laboratory, Cambridge
228(T) Bildarchiv Preussischer Kulturbesitz
(BL)
228(BR) Walter Greaves and Michael Mellish © Aldus Books
229(T) The Mansell Collection, London
229(BL) Photo Paul Brierley
229(BR) Nuffield Radio Astronomy Laboratories, University of Manchester
230(L) British Crown Copyright. Science Museum, London
230–231 Bildarchiv Preussischer Kulturbesitz
(C)
231(TR) I.B.A.
231(BR) Robert Harding Associates
232(L) Max Planck Institute
232(TR) © Aldus Books
233(T) U.S. Naval Observatory
233(B) The Cavendish Laboratory, Cambridge
234(T) © Aldus Books
234(B) Universitetsbibliotet Uppsala
235(T) Photo Paul Brierley
235(B) © Aldus Books
236–237 Ann Ronan Picture Library
(T)
236(BL) Museum Boerhaave
236(BR) The Mansell Collection, London
237(C) © Aldus Books
(BL)
237(BR) Photo Donald B. Longmore
238–239 Reproduced from *Design and Work* and *Journal of the Röntgen Society*
(T)
238(BL) Bilderdienst Suddeutscher Verlag
238(CR) © Aldus Books
(BR)
239(CR) Photo Ray Dean © Aldus Books
239(BL) Alistair Hay © Aldus Books
239(CB) EMI photo
239(BR) John Cura
240(T) Aldus Archives
240(B) Universitetsbiblioteket I Bergen
241(L) Sidney W. Woods © Aldus Books after S. Petterssen, *Introduction to Meteorology,* © McGraw-Hill Book Company, New York, 1958
241(R) Meteorological Office, Bracknell
242(T) Mary Evans Picture Library
242(BL) Historical Pictures Service Inc.
242(BR) Cooper-Bridgeman Library
243(TL) British Crown Copyright. Science Museum, London
243(TR) Roger-Viollet
243(B) Photo J.-L. Charmet
244(T) Ullstein Bilderdienst
244(B) Courtesy Aluminum Company of America
245(T) Photo Paul Brierley
245(B) Ann Ronan Picture Library
246 Brosn Brothers
247(T) Picturepoint, London
247(CR) *Radio Times* Hulton Picture Library
247(BL) Photo © Aldus Books, courtesy of Sunbeam Electric Ltd.
247(BR) Lee Davies © Aldus Books
248(BL) Brown Brothers
(TR)
248(BR) Bildarchiv Preussischer Kulturbesitz
249(TR) Brown Brothers
249(B) Bodleian Library, Oxford (Filmstrip 252.4)
250(T) British Crown Copyright. Science Museum, London
(B)
250(C) Mary Evans Picture Library
251(T) British Crown Copyright. Science Museum, London
251(B) Mary Evans Picture Library
252(T) Ann Ronan Picture Library
252(BL) Archiv Gerstenberg
252(BR) The Mansell Collection, London
253(TL) Archiv Gerstenberg
253(TR) Photo Paul Brierley
253(CL) G. Motley, London/Photo Jarmain © Aldus Books
253(CR) Aldus Archives
253(B) Archiv für Kunst und Geschichte
254(T) Spectrum Colour Library
254(BL) Aldus Archives
255(T) W. C. Sabine, *Collected Papers on Acoustics,* Dover Publishing Inc., New York. Reproduced by permission of the publisher
255(C) Photo Paul Brierley
255(BL) Fogg Art Museum, Harvard University
255(BR) Michael Holford Library photo
256(TL) Photo J.-L. Charmet
256(TR) Wellcome Historical Medical Museum
256(BL) Kunsthistorisches Museum, Wien/Photo Meyer © Aldus Books
256(BR) Photo Archee, x 4,000
257(T) Ken Moreman, Chester Beatty Research Institute
257(BL) National Blood Transfusion Service
257(BR) Photo Donald B. Longmore
258(T) Deutsches Museum, Munich
258(BL) Ullstein Bilderdienst

258(CR) Brian Lee © Aldus Books
258–259 Photo Saskatchewan Government
(B)
259(T) By courtesy of The Anglo Chilean Society
259(C) Shirley Parfitt © Aldus Books
260(TL) Cooper-Bridgeman Library
260(TR) United Kingdom Atomic Energy Authority
260(CR) © Aldus Books
260(B) The Cavendish Laboratory, Cambridge
261(T) United Kingdom Atomic Energy Authority
261(CL) The Cavendish Laboratory, Cambridge/Photo John Webb © Aldus Books
261(CR) The Cavendish Laboratory, Cambridge
261(B) Photo Paul Brierley
262 The Marconi Company Ltd.
263(T) Bodleian Library, Oxford (Filmstrip 252.7)
263(CL) Mary Evans Picture Library
(BL)
263(CR) By courtesy of the Director, Science Museum, London (lent by Thomas A. Edison)
263(BR) Photo Paul Brierley
264(L) Courtesy Methuen & Co. Ltd., London
264(R) Courtesy McDonnell Aircraft Corporation
265(L) © Aldus Books
265(BR) Ernst Hass/Magnum
265(BR) Space Frontiers
266(TR) Photos Paul Brierley
(CR)
266(BL) Bildarchiv Preussischer Kulturbesitz
266(C) © Aldus Books
266–267 Bildarchiv Preussischer Kulturbesitz
(CB)
267(TL) Casa Editrice G. C. Sansoni, Firenze
267(TR) British Crown Copyright. Science Museum, London
267(CL) X-ray diffraction pattern by R. Franklin and R. C. Gosling, *Nature*, 1953
267(BR) Bildarchiv Preussischer Kulturbesitz
268(TL) Roger-Viollet
268(CL) Bildarchiv Preussischer Kulturbesitz
268(TR) © Aldus Books
268(B) Ullstein Bilderdienst
269(T) United Kingdom Atomic Energy Authority
269(C) Courtesy Office of the Assistant Secretary of Defense, Washington
269(B) Bildarchiv Preussischer Kulturbesitz
270 *Radio Times* Hulton Picture Library
271(L) Photomicrograph Dr. Gordon F. Leedale, x1800
271(TC) By courtesy of Beecham Research Laboratories
(TR)
271(BR) WHO photos
272(L) National Air & Space Museum, Smithsonian Institution, Washington, D.C.
272(CB) Photo Mrs. H. Goddard
272(TR) Royal Artillery Institute Museum, Woolwich/ Photo Michael Holford © Aldus Books
272–273 Courtesy Mrs. H. Goddard
(CB)
273(T) Courtesy Mrs. H. Goddard; photo by B. Anthony Stewart, © National Geographical Society
274(L) Bilderdienst Süddeutscher Verlag
274–275 © Aldus Books
(CB)
275(TL) Union Carbide Corporation
275(R) Bildarchiv Preussischer Kulturbesitz
276(TL) Photo Paul Brierley
276(BL) *Radio Times* Hulton Picture Library
(R)
277(TR) © Aldus Books
277(BL) British Crown Copyright. Science Museum, London
277(BR) *Radio Times* Hulton Picture Library
278(TL) Historical Pictures Service
278(TR) The Bettmann Archive
278(B) Internationale Bilderagentur
279(B) Sikorsky Aircraft
280(L) Camera Press
280(R) © Aldus Books
281(T) The Cavendish Laboratory, Cambridge
281(BL) © Aldus Books
281(BR) United Kingdom Atomic Energy Authority
282(TL) British Crown Copyright. Science Museum, London
282(TR) © Aldus Books
282(BL) Bildarchiv Preussischer Kulturbesitz
282(CB) Brown Brothers
282(BR) Roger-Viollet
283(T) Leeds University/Photo Christopher Ridley © Aldus Books
283(B) General Electric Co.
284(L) Imperial War Museum, London
284(C) Decca Radar Ltd.
284–285 Imperial War Museum, London
(C), 284
(BR)
285(T) Imperial War Museum, London
285(BR) © BICC Ltd.
286(TL) Brian Lee © Aldus Books
286(TR) Courtesy Du Pont Company
286(B) E. I. Du Pont de Nemours & Co.

287(TL) Courtaulds Ltd.
287(TR) Plastics Division, Imperial Chemicals Limited
287(B) Courtaulds Ltd.
288(BL) Camera Press
288(R) Photos United Kingdom Atomic Energy Authority
289(TL) © Aldus Books
289(TC) Photos Paul Brierley
(TR)(B)
290(T) Roger-Viollet
(BR)
290(BL) Internationale Bilderagentur
291(T) United Kingdom Atomic Energy Authority
291(BL) UPI Inc. (Compix)
291(CR) Central Office of Information
291(BR) Los Alamos Scientific Laboratory
292(T) United Kingdom Atomic Energy Authority
292(BL) Brown Brothers
292(BR) Photo Paul Brierley
293(TL) © Aldus Books
293(CL) Photo Paul Brierley
293(TR) United Kingdom Atomic Energy Authority
293(B) U.S. Navy photo
294(T) NSU Motornwerke Aktiengesellschaft
294(BL) Bilderdienst Süddeutscher Verlag
294(BR) after Donald H. Marter, *Engines,* Thames and Hudson Ltd., London, 1965
295(L) © Aldus Books
295(TR) NSU (Great Britain) Ltd.
295(BR) Lee Davies © Aldus Books
296(T) Keystone
296(BL) The Bettmann Archive
296(BR) U.S. Atomic Energy Commission/William H. Regan, Los Alamos Scientific Laboratory
297(L) © Aldus Books
297(R) Harold E. Edgerton
298, 299 Courtesy Rank Xerox Ltd., London
(T)(BL)
299(BL) © Aldus Books
300(T) Imperial War Museum, London
300(B) *Radio Times* Hulton Picture Library
301(TL) Walter Greaves and Michael Mellish © Aldus Books, after G. Geoffrey Smith, *Gas Turbines and Jet Propulsion,* Iliffe & Sons Ltd.
301(TR) Cooper-Bridgeman Library
(CR)
301(BR) British Aerospace
302(T) Polaroid Corporation
(BL)
302(BR) Harold King © Aldus Books
303(TL) Photo Paul Brierley
303(TR) Photo by courtesy of Rolls-Royce Limited
303(B) Polaroid (U.K.) Ltd.
304(L) Brown Brothers
304(R) Flip Schulke/Black Star, New York
305(TR) © Les Requins Associés, Neuilly
(B)
306(T) National Research Development Corporation/ Photo Ken Coton © Aldus Books
306(BL) Hovercraft Development Ltd
(BR)
306(CR) © Aldus Books
307(TL) British Crown Copyright reserved
307(TR) Neil MacDonald
307(BL) Mears Construction Ltd.
307(BR) British Hovercraft Corporation
308(T) Stern Archiv, Hamburg
308(B) NASA
309(T) U.S. Army photo
309(BR) NASA
310(L) The National Foundation-March of Dimes
310(R) Ny Carlsberg Glyptotek, Copenhagen
311(TL) The National Foundation-March of Dimes
(BL)
311(TR) Courtesy of Dr. R. C. Williams
311(BR) Ken Moreman
312(T) Reproduced with permission from International Telephone and Telegraph Corporation
312(B) Internationales Bilderagentur
313(T) Photos Paul Brierley
313(BL) Massachusetts Institute of Technology
313(BR) *World Medicine*
314(T) X-ray diffraction pattern by R. Franklin and R. G. Gosling, *Nature*, 1953
315(T) Institute of Cancer Research: Royal Cancer Hospital and Royal Marsden Hospital
315(CL) Sidney W. Woods © Aldus Books
(BR)
315(BL) Courtesy The Bio-Chemistry Department of University of London/Photo Michael Holford © Aldus Books
316(L) Karsh of Ottawa/Camera Press
316(B) Photo Dr. G. Alexandre, Transplantation Unit, Department of Surgery, Hospital St. Pierre Louvain, Belgium
317(T) Photo Donald B. Longmore
317(BL) Photo Dr. G. Alexandre, Transplantation Unit, Department of Surgery, Hospital St. Pierre Louvain, Belgium
317(BR) Camera Press